# We All Choke The Same Herring

## Vince Cameron

CAMERON PRESS

CAMERON PUBLISHING
PO BOX 2125
FERNDALE, WA 98248

ISBN-13: 978-0-9785745-0-5
ISBN-10: 0-9785745-0-8

Library of Congress Control Number: AVAILABLE UPON REQUEST

www.weallchokethesameherring.com

*This book is dedicated
to the three women in my life
Mom,
My wife Trish,
and our daughter, Deann*

# Acknowledgments

I started writing this book in Happy Cove, a small mudhole in Tebenkof Bay, Alaska. The year was 1965. Several days of very poor weather and some dismal reading material got it started, with no inkling of a book in mind. Out of boredom, I thought I'd see if I could write something better than the shoot-em ups I'd been reading. The result was "Rickie's fish," a story about fishing steelhead in the Dungeness River. I decided my abilities in selecting reading material, and writing, were about the same, but it survived and is now chapter 6.

Twenty five years later we ran a load of frozen albacore tuna up the Columbia River, to sell off the dock in Scappoose Bay. On the way in, this guy came alongside in his skiff, said he'd be in at dark and that he wanted to visit for a bit. This was Tom McAllister, the outdoor sports writer for the Oregonian. We talked for several hours, and in between fish stories I mentioned that I was wondering about writing a book, but was worried about being able to do it. Tom said, "Look, just write down what you've got to say, exactly as you've been talking to me. No one else is going to write about the things you've been telling me about." So that's what I've been doing. I know—it's been fifteen more years.

In acknowledging help along the way, the teachers from the Sequim School District would be among the first. I wasn't much of a student, but they knew I'd be better off in school, than not. Their help and encouragement kept me in school, and several years after graduating I used a tidbit learned in a National School Assembly Program that kept me alive. I don't know if I'd have made it as a fisherman without the help of Ernie Erickson, Lee Harbaugh, Bill and Nada Small, Bill Wilcox, and Kenny Chace. You have to survive getting started and these people got me there.

There's a wonderful bunch of people in the fleet and help in various forms is a constantly flowing thing. I was especially lucky to have fished with Steve Prader, Lloyd Gowdy, and Sid Ward in Alaska, and again with Steve, Lloyd, and his brother Joe, in a larger group off the Washington coast. All this acknowledging might not have much to do with writing a book, but they all helped me get from there, to the book you're holding.

My home team has been Trish, Deann and Abu Cameron, Toni Kreiger, Roger and Helen Granger, Al and Karla Richardson, Marilyn George, Gail Stromme, and also Burt Orchard and Hal Olstead, who have both passed on. Being computer illiterate to an extreme, their support, technical and otherwise, has been great. Over a few short years, Keith and Chris grew from a couple kids who could barely see over the stern, into two good, hard working deck hands, and their help in the family business was tremendous. I also want to thank Tony Bozanic for sharing his story with us.

The following librarians were a great help. In Canada—Louise Archibald —Library / Bibliotheque Fisheries and Oceans Canada—Gordon Miller—Library & Scientific Archives—Pacific Biological Station—Fisheries and Oceans Canada—Helen Gillespie—Library and Archives Canada, and Christian Boudreault Crown Materials PWGSC Canada.

In the U.S.—Charlotte Gaston at the Ferndale Wa. Library—and Margaret Fast at the Western Washington University library.

And the Brannons. My hopes for the future of salmon lies in people like the two Ernie Brannons I've known. I'm very grateful to them, the others mentioned here, and thousands of others that have given me a nudge or allowed me to help them along the way. What a wonderful bunch of people.

# Contents

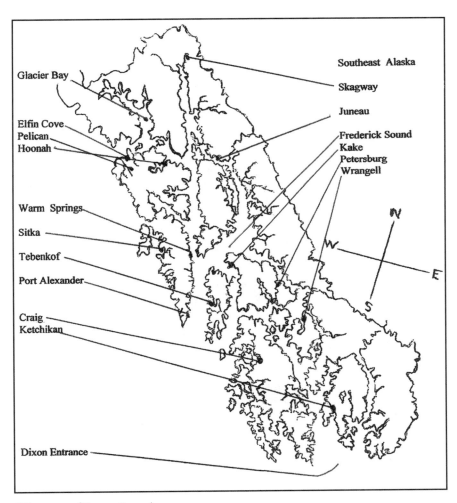

Southeast Alaska
Skagway
Glacier Bay
Juneau
Elfin Cove
Pelican
Hoonah
Frederick Sound
Kake
Petersburg
Wrangell
Warm Springs
N
Sitka
W
Tebenkof
E
Port Alexander
S
Craig
Ketchikan

Dixon Entrance

*(Courtesy of Laura Lucas)*

*When you look at a picture often, or long enough, you'll start seeing things you missed earlier. Maybe you're seeing it from a different angle, or in a different frame of mind. Look at it long enough, from enough angles, and your point of view might be altered. The faint smile of the woman in the picture has almost become a sneer.*

*I'm not the budding young artist that has been messing with the picture, only one of millions who love the subject matter. She has turned into a river, salmon and steelhead, and a young kid trying to catch a trout. There's trees and a frustrated biologist in the background, and all those other people. It's a picture of a coastwide fishing industry, the lives of the people in it, and the fish it involves. The picture keeps changing and so do our points of view. Here's mine.*

# Chapter 1
# October

I always liked fall the best. The southeast storms would come sweeping down over the foothills behind Blyn, across the valley, and then on across the Straits of Juan De Fuca towards Victoria, B.C. Then more cool, crisp days, sometimes picking apples, or digging potatoes, or burning piles of brush we'd cut during the summer. And then it would blow again. More wind and rain and a million leaves blowing out of the trees in flurries, and when I was a kid, our wire haired terrier, Mick, and I would be running full speed through them, heading for the river. I didn't care about football or who was in the World Series, but in the fall, just as everything else was ready for a good rest, the river came to life.

The first good rains in October would send thousands of silver salmon up the river, most of them ocean bright, with a few already showing the rose pink sides that, in less than a month, would be turning to a deep red. They couldn't travel as fast in the Dungeness as in some of the bigger, slower moving rivers, but a good shot of water could easily see them the six miles up towards our house, on the second or third day. Then the weather would turn off cool and clear again, and they'd stack up in the holes and log jams. Before long, the next freshet would move them on upstream to another good holding spot, or maybe as far up as the salmon hatchery, a few miles above our house.

This was the first good fall storm, and I had gone down to the mouth of the river to watch them start upstream. I had a favorite spot where I could see into a deep hole, bordered on one side by the log jam I was on. There were 600 or so silvers here, and almost that many in a spot just downstream. Another few hundred feet below that, the river went into the outer portion of Dungeness

1

Bay. At high tide the river would back up almost to these two holes, and a few hours after the tide started in, salmon would be moving into the river. Today I was pretty sure they'd start moving on upstream. The tide would be high in a couple more hours.

It seemed that there would always be a few fish that came in early, only going upstream a few holes above the estuary, and depending on the year, they might be there several weeks before the first good rainfall. Some of these had been here that long, and quite a few thousand more were in the inner bay, or out around the lighthouse. Like these, they were waiting for that first smell of higher water the rains would bring. The inner bay was alive with jumping silvers. I remember one fall that it seemed like it never would rain, and many of the silvers had started turning that deep red color, before they were able to move upstream.

I had fished down from the school house, and after trying a few spots for sea- run cutthroats, had managed to get completely soaked, but not much else. Not many cutthroats around yet, but they'd move in with the silvers. The rain was coming down hard now, and the wind was blowing a steady stream of alder, maple and cottonwood leaves into the water. It had been blowing when I got up that morning, but the rain had only started three or four hours ago. I wondered how long it would take to start showing in the river. They might not start moving until after dark, but I hoped not.

Most of these were 7 to 10 pound fish, with some bigger and smaller ones thrown in, but the one that kept catching my eye was a little male around six pounds. He was his own one fish parade and seemed to be making a tour of the hole, every few minutes. The rest of them were pretty much staying in place, as they will if they're not disturbed, but he'd move up to the front of the hole, and before long he'd come drifting back down with the current, or sometimes he'd turn around and swim down so he could hurry up and do it again. I think he was winking at the lady silvers as he went by, and I'd told myself that he'd be one of the first to move up over the riffle.

The wind eased up for a bit, and the rain started really pounding down, and I couldn't see into the water as well because of the raindrops on the surface, and I thought, hopefully, just a bit of color in the water. I had been soaked now for over three hours, and was cold, cramped, and miserable, and I was thinking quite a bit about dry clothes I had in the pickup. On the other hand, I had the best seat to the best show in town. Might as well stick it out a bit longer. I had positioned myself so I could easily watch the riffle upstream, and still keep an eye on the main part of the hole where the fish were. By watching close I'd be able to see the first fish start up the riffle, but I wouldn't be in a good enough position to see if the little male would be the one to lead the charge. Too much turbulence at the front of the hole for that.

When it finally let up for a few minutes, I noticed that things appeared a little more active, with fish moving past me all the time. Where several hundred of the fish had been below my spot, now everything seemed to be more at the upper portion of the hole. My attention was diverted by a small wave, moving up into the hole from downstream. Fish had come up the lower riffle, and into the bottom of this hole without me noticing, probably because of the noise of the rain and still some occasional hard gusts of wind. Soon it was constant, one or two fish looking like a small torpedo moving up through the shallower water, and bunches of 20 or more fish, pushing a decent little wave along with them. I could see fish in five or six spots, coming up the riffle below the hole. Now when I looked upstream, I saw fish already on the riffle, above this spot I'd been watching.

For some reason, I'd convinced myself it would be a big deal to see the first fish leave this first hole, and I'd been looking the other way and missed it. On the other hand, I might have missed the first moment of the great stampede, but I was pretty sure which way they went. So much for that. I climbed out of the log jam, and headed upstream towards the pickup and some dry clothes. In a few days our new smoke house would be full of cohos, one of the reasons that I loved October best.

# Chapter 2
# My River

When the east end of the Olympic Peninsula was settled, several things pretty much dictated the main areas of population. Access to salt water as shipping points were a must, so Port Angeles, having a fine deep water harbor was, and still is, the most populated area on the peninsula. Ediz Hook, a long natural sand spit, extends out and down the Straits of Juan De Fuca several miles, protecting the harbor from any wind chop or ocean surge that might be coming down the straits from the west. The straits runs pretty much east-west, about 45 miles from the ocean entrance, in to Port Angeles. The Olympic Mountains provide a good lee from all but the worst southeast weather. It's one of the better winter harbors around, and is pretty much across the straits from Victoria, B.C.

Further down the straits to the east, is an even longer sand spit. The one at Dungeness is about five miles long, from the beach bank to the end of the spit, and encloses a large inner bay that is too shallow to accommodate anything but smaller boats. Two more sand spits protect the inner bay, one extending out from the main beach bank, and the other extending towards the beach from the end of the spit, barely overlapping the first. The outer bay is wide open to the east, and any southeast weather.

The first settlers in the Dungeness area kept mostly to the west of the river, to what is now known as "Oldtown," and to the northern portion of the Dungeness valley. A small town known as Dungeness, gradually developed on the east side of the river, and this soon became home to many more settlers. They could grow most anything in either area, and were straddling a river full of salmon. They built a long dock that extended almost a quarter mile out into the shallow outer bay, and it was used for years to load, and off load, products from and for the community. Now only a few rotten piling remain.

At about this same time, there were people settling in the lower foothills, because there was generally a good amount of ground water available. Like their counterparts at Dungeness, these early homesteaders were able to raise, grow, hunt, or fish for most of what they needed. There were small schools and churches in each area, and a trip out to Dungeness or Port Angeles, usually by horse and wagon, wasn't an every day thing.

The Sequim prairie, or valley, is between these two areas. Farming in much of the valley was very limited, due to a general lack of water, mostly because of a 13 to 15 inch annual rainfall. Before you take up your tent, this doesn't mean 340 days of sunshine; just a lot of days that it looks like rain, but doesn't quite get around to it.

The water situation began to change in the late 1800s, when a group of these early settlers put in the first irrigation ditch. Other ditches soon followed, and gradually the lower foothills and valley on each side of the river would realize the availability of year around water. Now the entire area is covered by a massive network of ditches, extending miles to the east and west, finding their way through woods and farms across the valley. The Sequim Prairie wasn't a prairie anymore.

As has been the case a million other times, it all gets down to water, in this case, both fresh and salt. Over the years the Sequim prairie/valley developed into a small dairying community. The town itself wasn't that big, but there were hundreds of dairy farms, most of them in the twenty to sixty cow range, with a few larger herds. There was also a lot of beef and berries and hundreds of small places that had a few head of stock, gardens and orchards. Most of this would have been impossible without the ditch system, not to mention the hundreds of wells that wouldn't have existed. When some of the major ditch systems were shut down for repairs, lots of wells went dry.

You can see that the Dungeness River had a major importance, besides being a very productive salmon stream. For quite a few years, the community existed and developed without a real obvious impact on the river and its fish stocks. As long as there's enough of anything, declines are usually slow to be recognized. One flaw appeared soon after the first ditches were flowing. Salmon fry migrating downstream, wound up in the fields by the thousands. Fish screens were installed near the outlet to each system, preventing outbound salmon fry from getting past them, and a diversionary channel would funnel them back into the river.

When I arrived on the scene, not that many of the farms had sprinkler systems. Each farm would be fed from the main ditch, or a spur leading from it, and on some of the less flat areas the high spots went without. These spurs would follow along any higher ground on the property, with other smaller spurs moving the water to where it was needed. Depending on the piece of property, there was a lot of ingenuity involved in keeping these fields green. The sprinkling systems usually involved a small pond, a large pump, and a lot or three or four inch pipe, with sometimes a section of larger mainline going down the middle. This allowed an even flow of water over a large area at one time. Moving the pipe several times a day, you could soak up quite an area.

When we moved to the Sequim area in 1950, I was ten years old. After we got settled in, I thought the river, only about 400 yards away, needed some investigating, but mom used some pretty good judgment in making it off limits. I'd have to settle for the ditches, so I'd get home from school, do my chores, and Mick and I would run for the headgates. Just up the road from where we lived, two of the main ditches left the river, and when they reached the property just north of ours they split into five separate ditches, three big ones and two smaller spurs. From here, they started their trip down through the valley. These small streams ran through man made channels, through woods, meadows and fields, culverts and flumes, over small falls, and now and then they went underground, through a pipeline. Each was a beautiful stream with fast water, slow water, and ideal conditions for trout. And there was lots of trout, but at first I couldn't seem to catch that many. I had picked out a nice willow for a pole, with the line tied to its end, and even with this great outfit, the catchin' didn't come close to the wishin'. I couldn't seem to tell when they were biting, and when I figured that out, I wasn't very good at hooking them. A little practice started making a difference though, and we started coming home with a few. Mick would even spend part time watching, but not for long. Then he'd be back in the brush looking for more important stuff. One thing for sure, when we caught any, mom was really impressed. She'd never seen such big trout, and, "boy are they good eating."

By the next year, the neighbor kid and I were cleared to approach the river. He lived on the place where all the ditches split up. "Stay off the log jams! Don't get in the river" You bet. Rich had some kind of a spaniel named Bruce, and if the fishing wasn't too hot, we'd throw the dogs in the river. That was always neat but before long they'd developed poor hearing and followed along nicely behind us. They didn't mind following us across somewhere, but they'd get in by themselves. We got lots of little rainbow trout, six or seven inches long, and along towards late summer, these would start moving downstream towards the straits, to spend a year or more in the ocean. Dolly varden were a big deal, because they were bigger than the little rainbows, and we'd take them home for the cats to eat, since they weren't very good eating. Sea run cutthroat were a real prize, for size, and eating, but you didn't get many that far upstream in the Dungeness. We saw and hooked a few salmon and summer run steelhead, but those battles never lasted long with our light trout outfits. My "outfit" was now a three joint, steel, telescoping pole, with a $1.00 fly reel, out of Sears and Roebuck catalog. The pole cost $3.79 so, I went fishing for not much over $5.00 after getting some hooks. Rich had the same sort of an outfit, but with a better reel. The limit was 15 trout over six inches long, and there were signs all over, stating that - It shall be illegal to gaff, snag, net, spear, stone, or otherwise molest salmon in this stream. Maybe not the exact wording, but as close as I can remember it.

About this time, some guy from the government showed up, and told a dozen or so families that lived down in the valley, that they would have to sell their property to the government. They needed a thousand or so acres to put up a Voice of America radio tower. They probably wanted to tell the guys over on Vancouver Island what a corrupt government they had. They could move their possessions, homes, whatever, but they had no choice, they would definitely have to move. One of the refugees was my cousin, Coleen. Her family brought property across the road, extending all the way to the river. She was a few years older than I was, a mediocre football player, a little better at baseball, and loved to fish, so I had another fishing partner.

Before long, to prove that good things occasionally come in bunches, government officials changed their mind and offered to sell the Voice of America property back to the owners at a much reduced price. This, after people had moved homes, and taken apart farms that had been in some families for a good many years. They had all re-established, and in the meantime the government had hired local loggers to clear cut woods that had been major windbreaks, brought in bulldozers to trash beautiful farm land that wasn't quite flat, and even hired local labor to build a nice fence around the place.

In the early part of the summer we'd pick strawberries in the mornings, and head for the river in the afternoon, most of our attention being in the trout department. It was one of the best times to be on the Dungeness. The river would have the slightly milky look from melting snow and glaciers, and would still be

7

carrying quite a bit of water. The spring kings were in and moving upstream, and most of them would be ocean bright, with only a few starting to change color. It was a thrill seeing them move upstream, but you wouldn't see them for long before they'd move into a little deeper water, and be out of sight.

One day on my way to the river, I was just starting across a little trickle, too small to even be considered a side stream, when a fish splashed by on his way upstream. I'd scared him so he really poured it on, and I had to run along pretty fast, just to keep up with him. I hoped that if he got close enough to the edge, I might be able to kick him out. It was only about a hundred yards from where the stream left the river, to where it re-entered it, downstream. It was almost all riffle and not much bigger than one of the smaller irrigation ditches. He was getting close to going back into the river, but he didn't know that, and with me chasing him, he got excited and turned around, heading back downstream. It's hard to run over the river rock, as it can be slippery, but I managed to stay close and he finally got a bit off course and ran himself out on the bank. It was a male humpie (pink salmon), weighed four or five pounds, and being one of the first in the river, he was nice and bright. This was the first salmon I ever caught. Or captured. The humpies mainly run on the odd numbered years in Washington rivers, and this year there would be lots of them.

It didn't take too long for us to figure out how to snag them, which was quite easy considering their numbers. I would use a weight at the end of the line, and a single hook up the line a bit, so the hook would be the first thing that hit the fish. Then the fight would be on, and what a lot of power in a little package. Sometimes Coleen and I would go, or Richie or the Jones kids, or all of us. We even took Ethel, the lady that owned the strawberry patch. She had a really good time, and the next day she canned salmon.

Ethel thought that each year a kid ought to be able to eat all the strawberry shortcake they could hold, and each year she made sure her whole berry patch crew, did just that. She had ten acres, about half of it in strawberries, and if you wanted to work, she would always find something for you to do. You never thought about it as a kid, but looking back, she was one of those who gave a lot to the community, generally in ways that not too many noticed. Ethel's, and a few other local berry farms, provided work experience, and a few bucks for quite a few kids. My goal, like most of the other kids, was to make a dollar in the morning. Some of the local moms really worked at it, and probably made fair money.

With the humpies in the river, our abilities to catch a fish expanded quite a bit in one short summer. It's hard to explain how many there were, but if you try to visualize a river of a size that you can barely cross over the riffles in hip boots, being full of salmon, every hole, riffle, and side stream, from the mouth of the river in Dungeness Bay, up the 13 miles to Two Forks, and up each branch a few more miles, that's the way it was. They aren't a big salmon, 4 or 5 lbs in early July, but fish still coming in the river in late August or September could occasionally go 8 pounds or more. As the males matured, they would get a big hump on their backs, and a pronounced face with big teeth. Their coloration gradually became a sort of olive, pink, and purple with a white belly. It made them a whole lot less to look at, than when they had first entered the river, ocean bright. The female would realize the same color change, but true to nature, would keep the more streamlined feminine look, her belly bulging with around 2500 eggs. When they first entered the river they were strong, and pound for pound they'd put up as good a fight on hook and line, as any other salmon specie. Not a lot of the fancy jumping that a few of the others will do, but a good strong fight.

Eating wise, the only way we ever had them was filleted, chunked, and pan fried, or being quite oily, they were pretty good smoked. This, only when they were still bright. Like any of the other salmon species, their quality went downhill fast, as soon as they started showing any color. Once the humpies had matured to a point that they weren't too desirable, we went back to the trout department, but it wasn't too good with that many salmon in the river.

I remember one day, that one of us had caught a bullhead. Mr. Schade, the high school football coach, had just come down past us, stopped and BS'ed for a few minutes, and mentioned that Pavalunas was just upstream. Then he'd gone on downstream. We decided to go up to where Pavalunas, the baseball, basketball coach, was fishing, and we'd stand on each side of him, Rich would get his attention, and I'd drop the bullhead in his fish basket. I forget what kind of a big tale Rich was telling him, but as soon as I deposited the bullhead it got awfully funny, and Pavalunas was laughing right along with us. He didn't catch anything, or if he did, hadn't kept it, so when he got home he'd hung the basket on a nail in the garage, and forgot about it until his wife mentioned this "odor."

"Nope, couldn't be the basket." He hadn't kept anything. A day or so later he couldn't ignore the basket any longer, and zoned in on the punch line to Rich's story. He looked us up when school started.

The first heavy storms in October brought the river up, and the cohos (silver salmon) started moving into the river. When the river was still up and flowing the silvers would keep moving upstream, but as soon as the rain stopped, and it cleared up, they would stack up in the deep holes and log jams. The silvers were bigger than the humpies, depending on the year, averaging 7 to 10 lbs. Their flesh wasn't as oily as the humpies, but was deep red in color, and had its own excellent flavor. Each fall would see a few batches of them go into the smokehouse, or freezer, and mom would fill a shelf, or two with jars of canned cohos. After a few weeks in the river they'd start coloring up, and the ocean bright appearance would give way to a pinkish, rose color, and then gradually go to a very deep red. You'd look into a hole that held a bunch of them, and that spot of river would appear almost black, or purple.

The fall months were my favorite time, on the river and otherwise. The river bed, and the woods on each side had nearly every kind of tree common to the area, and the cottonwood, maple, vine maple, alder, and wild cherry, mixed in with all the evergreens, put on a gorgeous show. The air had a fuller feel to it, and it was great to be on the river! The run of silvers and the winter steelhead virtually overlapped, and along in November you'd start seeing a few, almost invisible, grayish streaks mingled in with the silvers. These would be the first of the winter run steelhead. In early December the season would open, and the limit being three fish, I can remember a couple guys who took their wives, and they would come out with a dozen nice steelhead. Most of them were first year, 6 to 8 pound fish, but there were a lot of bigger fish in the river, too. Each year, right after the opening, I'd go uptown, and the display case at Sody's Hardware would hold a nice fish, usually 15 pounds or more. Some guys named Charlie, Clyde, or Leroy always caught them. One afternoon I caught three with the gaff hook, next to the bank in a small log jam. I can remember stopping half a dozen times on the way home, laying them in the maple leaves to admire them. I didn't get into the hook and line mode on steelhead, until later in the winter.

I got up early and peddled my bike the six or so miles down to McDonald Creek, which ran along the west edge of what would have been the "Voice of America" property. The creek was up slightly, with the reddish tinge to the water that so many of the smaller Olympic Peninsula streams have. It was of a size that you could cross in hip boots on every riffle, but being up a bit now, a lot of the spots were borderline for crossing. They said that years earlier, it carried more water, but between all the clear cutting in the foothills, and the use of the creek to carry one of the ditches for aways, its volume wasn't as much or as stable as it used to be. During the summers a lot more was taken out than went in, and the flow during the winter is a lot more erratic than in years past.

I had my three joint, steel telescoping pole with the fly reel, and had cut the red top off a wool sock for some lures. It had started snowing before I got there, and it was really beautiful down in the creek bottom. It's nicely wooded with mostly alder, lots of big maple and a mix of cedar, fir, and spruce. Now with the snow falling, it was beautiful.

After cutting the sock up in little squares, and sticking a hunk of it on the hook, I was fishing. With the creek being as high and murky as it was, the fish could be moving during the day, so I had lots of possible spots to fish. It was in one of the better holes, though, when one picked up the yarn and the fight was on. There was a bit of brush and logs on one side, so I had to lean on him for all my old trout pole would allow, but in a few minutes I could see it was getting tired, and began to think I had a chance.

It had splashed around a lot when I had first hooked it, and although it wasn't a big one, it was right out of salt water, and ocean bright. I couldn't get around to the bottom of the hole very easy, so when it was so tired that I thought I was pretty much in control, I eased it up to the head of the pool to a little sand beach, and boosted it up the bank with the side of my boot. It was a perfect silvery bright fish, about six pounds, and it was a female, so now I would have fresh eggs for bait. I fished on through, all the way down to where the creek dumped into a big lagoon, before pouring out into the straits, but didn't get anything else. I had stayed too long, fishing just one more spot and then another, and now I had a long ride home with four inches of snow on the road.

A few days later I was behind Coleen's house, fishing one of the nicest spots I can remember on the river. The river separated upstream, and the two branches of the river came together behind their property, and made a deep hole with a long drift for another hundred feet below it. It was fishable from both sides, and some guy already had two steelhead when I got there. He yelled across that they were here, and to give it a try. He started fishing again, and before long, had another one on. After playing it around for awhile he was just getting ready to beach it when my line stopped, and I felt that subtle pressure that might be a steelhead bite—or maybe I'd hung up on a snag. No snag this time, and I could tell it was a lot bigger than my McDonald Creek fish. The guy across the river kept offering some encouragement while he cleaned his three fish, and had just offered to come over and help me land it, when Coleen's dad came out from the trail, through their woods. It still took awhile, with my flimsy outfit and flimsier experience, but Norris talked me through it, and he finally boosted out a beautifully speckled, ten pound male.

11

After getting this big one, it was no trick to handle them up to that size and although I didn't get that many, I did start coming home with a fish or two most of the time. Pretty soon I was fishing as far down as the railroad bridge, and up to the narrows, above the fish hatchery. When I first started going upstream, quite a bit above Coleen's, I used some big cottonwoods on the west bank, as markers for an easy walk up a fence line, and then down an old logging road until I came out on the main road. Years later, we would own the land those trees live on.

During the winter the river flooded, and when the water dropped, a few people who lived too close to the river didn't live there anymore, and there was a bit of bridge and road repair to be done. Below where we lived there were five bridges including the railroad bridge, and it seemed like the only one that didn't occasionally get some kind of damage was the highway 101 bridge. When I went over the bridge on the school bus, I noticed there was what seemed to be a lot more water than up behind Coleen's house. That evening I went back and looked, and there was no doubt about it, a lot of water was missing at that point. Before seeing the river from the bridge I'd thought, boy, it sure went down quick.

When it cleared, to a point of being almost fishable, I crossed the river behind Coleen's house and went up the east branch, hoping to find where all the water had gone. It didn't take long. A short way upstream, I found what amounted to about half of the river. The high water had washed out an area that I could see across now, and about two hundred feet to the east, a major volume of water was leisurely running down through the woods. When I got over to it I could see that it was next to a meadow behind Clarence Iverson's place. Judging from the size of trees along the bank, it had been awhile since this much water had been through here. I picked my way upstream, finding one nice hole after another, some small log jams, and pretty easy riffles, although there was generally too much water to get across with hip boots. It ran through fairly thick, but not too old, woods, and is still one of the nicest stretches of water that I can remember on the Dungeness. This branch left the main river a hundred yards above where it had split, prior to the flood, making this portion of the river unique, with three good sized branches, although the middle branch was only about a quarter mile long. The uppermost portion of this new branch took me up through what is now known as Dungeness Meadows.

I took Coleen over and she agreed with me, that the area where you walked out on the new branch, looked like the Suwanee River. Not that we'd ever seen the Suwanee, but this stretch was slow for the Dungeness, moving down through some big maple and alder, and fit our image of the deep south. In a few days I checked the downstream portion of my new channel and found it quite a bit faster than upstream, but still a great stretch of river.

Aside from these three separate branches, the mile and a half of river above Highway 101 had at least one good side stream nearly all the way, on one side or the other or both, as well as another major ditch outlet. The new channel joined the side stream that held furthest to the east, and fed the lowest ditch outlet on the east side of the river. Another 200 yards below the ditch outlet, this east branch would join the other half of the river, and the Dungeness would be one stream for the short distance down to Highway 101. With these smaller main channels and all the side streams, this section of the river was where most of the coho spawning in the Dungeness took place.

You'd think, as excited as I was about this new spot, that I would spend full time over there, but at first it didn't work out that way. The weather turned off clear and cold, the river dropped, and the fishing in any of the branches wasn't as good as it was down below the spot where they all came together, and it was just one river for a ways. I did go back, but only occasionally caught anything, the main reason being inexperience. When the water is low and clear you can't fish like some cave man, and expect good results. I'd walk up to each hole from the side or front, and the fish would know I was there well before I was even fishing. With a little more experience I would have approached each spot from downstream, carefully, and saw many of the fish before they saw me. Later, I learned to fish many spots in such a way that I wasn't exposed when I fished them. But for now, fishing downstream in the larger volume of water, with the fish less diluted, seemed to be my best bet.

I was walking up the road one evening, real proud, as I had another of those chunky ten pound males, and a car stopped and this guy says, "Ya wanta sell that fish?" I hesitated and he said "How about two bucks for it?" Two dollars was a lot of strawberries, and there wasn't much work for me at that time of year, so I sold my first fish. Not long after that, a friend approached me at school, and said that his mom would like to buy all the fish I could catch at 25 cents a pound, dressed out. She would be buying for their family and also for her parents, and I was one happy buffalo. Before long I had more customers, even to the point of having to fish a little harder, but that was solved February 28th, when they closed the river to steelhead fishing. This would mean staying off the road, and out of sight of the bridges, but it would also mean that I would have the entire run of spring (late winter) steelhead to myself.

13

The steelhead after mid March were kind of a mixed bag. You would catch one that put up quite a struggle for half a minute, and then just quit. These would invariably be a return, a fish that had already spawned and was heading downstream to salt water. If it was a female, it would have lost the pink stripe on its side, and appear ocean bright except for its gill plates, which would still show the rose coloration of a fish ready to spawn. It would be very thin, its body weight depleted by spawning and not eating all that much while in the river. The males wouldn't lose the coloration they had, but would be in similarly poor condition. They would go on out of the river, into the salt water, and some of them might live to return and spawn in other years. This would account for some of the larger fish, and there were likely others that had just spent an extra year or so in the ocean, before their first return to the river. Some of these "returns" would be in pretty tough shape, and I imagine the seals and sea lions did well at the estuaries. The healing powers of salt water, plus the diet it affords, puts them back in better shape before long. About ten percent of the fish I caught were these returns, and I released all of them, as they would have been really poor eating. This still left the whole spring run to fish on. I'd get home from school, run through my chores, and run for the river. If the river had a little color, or sometimes as it was getting dark, you would catch one after another.

In early May of that year, I was looking around upstream from Highway 101. I had found quite a big king salmon, and had spent awhile trying to figure out some way of catching it. This was one of those rare instances where the river was running over higher ground than the channel that ran alongside it, and water from the edge of the river overflowed all along a narrow bar that separated the two streams. So the further you went downstream, the larger the small channel became, as the main channel gradually lost about half its volume into it.

The fish was in the side stream, laying under a bunch of willows that were still rooted in the bank, across from me. They laid along the bank, extending out about ten feet into the pool, and the fish was at the bottom end of these. Ten feet below him, it started shallowing up for the riffle, and twenty feet above him, the pool would start getting nearly over my head. I had put the gaff hook on a pole, and had sized up my options if I was lucky enough to hook him, but I couldn't see any good choices. There was too much water running over the bar to be able to handle him on it, and it was too far up, or downstream, over the bar, to consider taking him either way. Too much brush upstream, and against the bank on the west side, so that it would have been impossible to try to pull him up into it. My

14

only chance, that I could see, was to take him over the bar, across the river, and up a bank that ran down into the river. First I had to get the hook in him.

I waded out carefully and waited forever, but he kept up under the brush, and I rarely saw more than a foot above his tail. Then he drifted down those extra few inches below the brush, and I went for it, and found myself being pulled into the river. I had visualized reaching out and hooking him, leaning back while he thrashed around, and gradually moving out of the water, and up onto the bar, with him splashing along behind me. Instead, I reached out as far as I could, hooked him not too far ahead of the tail, and he lunged upstream with me following along behind him, being pulled forward off my feet, and at one point, nearly being pulled under.

I finally got both feet, and one hand under me, before he got up into the deeper water. Now I could get him stopped, and then going in what seemed to be the right direction. I was completely soaked and my hip boots were full, so there wasn't much reason to hold back now. Back over the bar, and across the river to the bottom of this bank, which was the only spot halfway clear of trees and brush along this side. As I pull him over the top of the bank, the hook is ready to pull through, but it holds and I've got my first king salmon, and what a beauty. It was early in May, so he was one of the first in the river that year. He was ocean bright, and was forty two inches long. Our little scale wouldn't weigh him, but this one wasn't for sale anyway! Some neighbors ate king salmon, and quite a bit of him went in the freezer.

Aside from the river, I had another major pastime. We lived on 13 plus acres, and most of it had been logged within the last two years, prior to our moving there. Tree tops, limbs, and hard tack. Hard hack? I never did learn it's real name, but it loved logged off, or grassy meadow like, areas. If you didn't get ahead of it, it took over, as it had here. Mom and I would go out, armed with a big hatchet and a small round of wood, and when she'd pull the leads over the block I'd grind them off with the hatchet. Twenty or so leads and off to the next clump, which was never more than ten feet away. In the fall, or winter, we'd build a fire, and in the summer we'd just stack up decent piles and burn later, when things weren't too dry. This gave the grass a chance, and opened up the property to grazing. The new shoots from the hard tack-hack? were fine chewing, and once chopped close to the ground, the cows kept them chewed down.

Before long, the Jones kids, and Rich, and I were getting to an age that we could do a little heavier summer work. None of the big outfits wanted kids that

15

young, but we did pick up a lot of work on the smaller farms. They were doing some baling then, but a lot of the places we worked for were still shocking hay. You'd rake the hay with a side delivery or dump rake into windrows, and then go around with a pitch fork and stack it in round piles called shocks, each about four feet high. After it was all shocked you'd load it on a wagon, haul it into the barn, and unload. We enjoyed the work, and most of the people we worked for, and got to where we were all in darned good shape by mid summer. The farm wives could really cook! In the following years, good haying crews were in demand, and when there was a choice, these smaller farms that had given us a chance, came first. Several would turn into milking jobs, later on.

Rich asked me one day, if I wanted to go with him and his dad up to Three Forks. This was my first trip into the mountains, beyond what you could drive to. To save time, we hiked in after Charlie got off work. We used a Coleman lantern, and the four mile hike in from Deer Park went well. I can still hear Charlie singing in his deep, rich, baritone. "Oh, that royal puddin, it's so goodin, and it's good, good, for you. Good, good for you. Good, for you." He had a good time. We all did. It was steep with lots of switch backs, and my legs would be sore tomorrow, but being on the river first thing in the morning was worth it. The Graywolf joins the upper two branches about half a mile below their junction, and eight miles downstream, the Graywolf and East Dungeness join to make the Dungeness.

The upper river, down to about the fish hatchery, is a fast piece of water. It's about nine miles, from the hatchery to the mouth of the river, and that stretch is still considered fast, but its placid compared to the upper river. We caught lots of trout, and some of the rainbows were really nice. Downstream from where the Graywolf comes in, I got one nineteen incher, which was the nicest rainbow I ever got in the Dungeness system. I would get a few that size and even larger, later on, but in early June, this one was a perfect fish. The hike back out of Three Forks tests your legs. They say its four miles down, and sixteen back out. Years later, I went straight up the ridge, and cut well over half off my best time on the trip out.

This was another odd numbered year, and once again the humpies poured into the river. While they were still bright, I ran a couple batches through the smoke house, and before long they had colored to a point that I tried not to get one. One day I was over on my new channel, not doing too much, as there were so many humpies you could hardly get a trout to bite. Now and then I'd get a few on some riffle, or some dollys out of a log jam, or maybe at the bottom end of a hole. No matter what, I enjoyed being there, as you couldn't have found a spot where salmon were thicker. When people talked about "salmon being so thick you could walk across on their backs," this was what they were describing. It looked like if you jumped flat out, into any of the deeper holes, it would be awhile before you sank.

Half a mile downstream, where this branch re-joined the other side, there was a big hole with both sides of the river coming into it, the west side over an open, long, riffle, not very deep, and not a very appealing side for the fish to go up. The east side was another story, with a shaded, slow, deeper entrance into the hole, and this was the side that most of the humpies had taken going upstream, to where I was now.

They were to the point of maturity that they had stopped moving quite as fast, and where there were many on the riffles, there were several thousand stacked up in many of the bigger holes. I was in that portion of the branch that I liked so well, and had about two hundred yards to go upstream, to where this east branch separated from the river. It took me by surprise when the river suddenly turned muddy. It had been nearly clear. In another few seconds, the volume of water had dropped by half. Another minute, and it was cut in half again. Soon there was less water coming down this side than in a small irrigation ditch. The humpies were going crazy, mostly trying to get downstream, as there suddenly wasn't enough water for them in the holes. When hundreds, or a thousand fish at a time hit a riffle, now becoming just a trickle, most of them didn't make it. Soon their dying bodies formed stops that would gradually become salmon dams, making pools in spots that had been riffle, before. When it first happened, I ran around trying to get some of them back in the water, but it was no use. I headed upstream, and it was the same in every hole, so many fish in so little water that they were forcing themselves out on the banks, and down riffles that were soon plugged.

It finally dawned on me, what must have happened, and I started running up towards the junction, but they were long gone when I got there. The east branch had been bulldozed closed. Apparently the woods had muted the sound of the dozer, that and all the commotion the fish were making on the riffles. The trickle of water, still running down that side, was what managed to seep through the bulldozed river rock. The ditch company had closed off that side, completely, to put more water down to the head gates, which were a ways downstream on the west side.

I told Coleen about it, and we went over and looked, a few days later. Already it was a poor place to be, and we left. In a week the smell was so bad you could chew it. Half a mile of rotting salmon, in many places several feet deep, but strangely a few still lived in some of the bigger holes, towards the top end. I went back after that, cutting through the washed out stretch where I'd first found the spot, and everything was dead. Probably the water had become so putrid that they couldn't exist in it. When I got up to the top end, just below the closure, there were maybe a dozen fish still alive, and several of these had started to spawn. These few had tried to get upstream instead of down, and they were above the polluted water.

I was upset about it for a long time. When you're that age everything is black and white, and you aren't inclined to try and see things in any different light. I talked to a few people about it, and most of them seemed like they didn't want to hear it. I don't know if the ditch people ever knew what they'd done.

I've often wondered since, if the best thing wouldn't be to have a river walker, or some kind of a river authority, whose job would be to oversee everything on his river, or maybe his portion of a bigger river system. As I just mentioned, I don't think the ditch people were ever aware of what they'd done that day, but if they'd had to inform such a (river authority) of their intentions, he would have known, and perhaps that channel wouldn't have been completely closed off. The way things are nowadays, there needs to be someone who can say no, at least until a situation can be looked at, and a sensible solution worked out.

There were years when most of the rivers water was going down these seven ditches, and their tributaries, usually along in late August or September, when the river was low. This wasn't as big a threat to the fish population, before the log jams were taken out, since they did provide shade and some protection, besides nurturing a lot of the stuff that the fingerlings like to eat. The summer months would see quite a downstream migration of small steelhead, and it would have been a lot better, in terms of survival, if the river had run fuller at these times. I can remember crossing rock to rock on a long riffle, at a point in the river where there were no sidestreams, and the water never getting above my work shoes. This was above the highway, below where the last ditch was taken out. At that same time, all of the ditches were as full as they ever ran them. We ought to be able to do better than that.

These are some of my memories from those first few years on the river. The river had become a friend, and had provided the beginning of a livelihood, that I would spend most of my life at. This was during a time when scarcity of salmon, steelhead, and other fish, just wasn't something people thought about, much. Yet.

# Chapter 3
# Milking Cows

When I was fourteen, I got my first milking job. There were around three hundred dairies in the east end of Clallam County at that time, most of them the smaller twenty to fifty cow herds, now virtually extinct. A good portion of these were owned by couples getting along in years, their families raised, but still needing the income from the farm to get by on. Many of them would hire a young school kid to help milk and do chores, paying them a few bucks a month, plus room and board. Then, there were younger people who had a job, or something else going on the farm, besides the dairy herd, so a little too much on their plates to get it done by themselves. This would be the situation in my first milking job.

It didn't start off all that well. He talked me through it the first two milkings, and the third milking I was on my own and #16 kicked my front teeth out. Dr. Wilcox dug out what was left and later on would make me a bridge. There was a school bus to catch each morning and to be on it I had to move things right along. Set up the milk house, feed calves, and put out the silage. We fed in the stanchions, so the silage was there waiting for them when I opened the door. Once inside the barn, they all headed for their own niche in this long row of stanchions, and I'd move amongst them snapping the stanchions down. Then I'd start milking. This was the old string system, prior to milking parlors, so you'd have a row of cows down one full side of the barn, and sometimes on two or more sides. The milk machines ran off a vacuum line, which ran along the wall above the cows, and you'd plug the hose onto a valve, turn it on, and put the four inflations on the spigots. The milk would be squeezed gently out of the cow, through tubes and into the milking machine.

With her cooperation. She had to be pretty much relaxed for the operation to work well, and a lot of this was in the washing, prior to putting the machine on. The water would be quite hot and they liked it. Maximum flow was less than two minutes after you washed them, so I tried to have the machine on not much more than a minute after washing. A few squirts from each spigot, prior to putting on the machine, helped get things going nicely and also improved the quality of the milk. The highest bacteria is in the first few squirts, and the highest butterfat content came at the last. Putting the machine on five minutes after you'd washed a cow was right next to bucking the tide. You'd eventually get there, but a lot more wear and tear on the boat. Harder on the cow too. Depending on the cow and how much she was producing, they'd milk out in 3 to 5 minutes. A few took longer. I eventually figured out my formula for a good job of milking. "Get all the cows milk in the least possible amount of time, with the least possible amount of trouble to yourself or the cow." A good job of washing was time well spent.

When she was done, you'd do a little machine stripping by holding down for a few seconds on the inflations, then pour the milk into a ten gallon can, rinse the inflations, and on to the next pre washed cow. When the can was full, or almost, I'd roll it into the milk house and dump the milk through a strainer that emptied into a refrigerated stainless steel milk tank. This particular tank held 250 gallons, and some of the bigger farms tanks were four times that big. Prior to the milk tanks they ran the milk through the strainer, and over a cooler into a ten gallon can. The cans were kept in a cool vat of water in the milk house until the milk truck came along. Once a day for the cans, and every other day for the refrigerated milk tanks. At first I could barely hold the can up to pour it in the strainer, but I was at an age when strength comes on fast. Before long, pouring milk in the strainer, or handling the silage cart, was no problem.

So the cows would all be in the barn except one. Almost every morning and evening I went to the very farthest corner of his place, at best, or onto the neighbors place too frequently, to get #16. If there had been a tall tree she'd have been well up in it. Whatever was in her history, she didn't like the barn or milking or something. Couldn't have been me, because she had already figured this out before I got there. He'd warned me about her, and showed me how to block a kick by reaching across and grabbing the other leg. She was so fast that this was often too late, and the only defense was to get in as close as possible, so that she wouldn't get the shot that I'd given her the third milking. I'd been afraid and was back too far, and out in the open. With my head against her leg I could feel her thinking about it.

20

A couple of the other kids that had milked there had whispered in my ear, and they were right, this turned out to be the milking job in hell. One major problem was the mud in the barnyard. The ground in that area has a lot of clay in it, and once wet, it gets gooey. After a bit it was just soupy. When the cows would come up out of it, onto the slab, some of the older ones would be up to their bellies, and the udders on all but a few heifers would be covered with mud. This was before milking parlors with unlimited water from a spray hose to wash them down with, so you'd wash them quick and get the machine on. If they moved before you got the machine on, you washed them again. I packed lots of buckets of water.

So set up the milk house, feed calves, put out the silage, get em in the barn and milk them which should have taken about 2 hours with two machines, but with the mud conditions you never knew. Give everybody a shot of grain, wash up the machines and milk house, turn the cows out, clean the barn, and shoot for the house on the run—something to eat—and the school bus. I was always thinking about some way to get things done faster, but after the first six weeks, I was streamlined about as good as I would get. As it got more into the winter the mud conditions got worse, so I pared another half hour off the sleep department, and 3:30 to 7:30 got the job done nicely. I'd be in bed by 8:30, so that was plenty of sleep.

The guy I worked for had around 3000 chickens, plus I don't know how many young ones that were running loose outside. I suppose a 1000, but sometimes it seemed like 50,000. When I'd go to give the cows grain the chickens would be there, and a cow would have to fight the chickens for the grain. When you cleaned the barn, there was a long ramp just outside the barn, that you ran the wheelbarrow up, and dumped the loads of manure from. The ramp gradually went up until you were about seven feet above the ground, and then went out for another 30 feet, making it around 70 feet long overall. Over the winter there got to be quite an accumulation that would spread out from the ramp thirty to forty feet, taking up a good sized piece of the barnyard. The chickens would get out on the edge, which was crusted over, and get bugs and flies. At some point things became less crusty, and you could always see twenty or more chickens in varying stages of unhappiness, out in that thick lake.

I made up my mind that no matter what, I wouldn't fall off the ramp. I could always fish for the wheelbarrow if it got away from me. It worried me, as I wasn't too strong yet, and sometimes getting to the top was all I could do. It all depended on how much of a run you got, coming out of the barn. He didn't want you washing the barn floor down, because all the water wound up in the barnyard, so you scraped it, and then put lime on the floor, when you were done. In certain conditions it got slick, and one morning it caught up with me. I started slipping and losing momentum before I was out of the barn, and by the time I got to the bottom of the ramp I'd pretty much lost it. I was only about four feet up the ramp when my foot slipped behind me, and I went down on my knees behind the wheelbarrow. A good portion of the contents came back over my head and shoulders.

Evenings were pretty much the same except, for washing the milk tank every other day, and loading silage out of an upright silo, next to the barn. I'd load two loads, one for that evening and another for the morning, and offset that by scraping down the floor after milking but not cleaning out the gutter till after milking in the morning. Cleaning the slab and calf pens was something I could do on the weekends, plus any fudging in the silo I could do, to get ahead for the next week. All the weekend silage came from the longest throw across the silo.

Saturday between milkings was whatever he wanted done, which involved a lot of fence building, probably with #16 in mind. His neighbor told me later, that he wouldn't have minded feeding her if he'd been milking her. I told him, "that's what you think." Anyway, I got pretty good at fences and gates. Also, weekends involved a lot of candling eggs and other work in the chicken house. I remember reaching around into the next nest without looking, and a rat ran up my arm and jumped off my shoulder. I've never quite got over that. But generally I liked the work. Candling eggs was enjoyable, and I liked listening to the radio while we worked. His oldest boy would usually be helping, and we'd tell each other rat stories. And fish stories.

They only lived a few hundred yards from the river, and he was pretty impressed with a nice steelhead I brought back one Sunday. A few Sundays later, I was going over to McDonald Creek, and he came along. This was before the road cut through by what is now the golf course, so it was a little longer pedal than it would be now, but well worth it. Every spot had a few steelhead, and quite a few of them saw us before we saw them, but we finally got to a deeper hole that held quite a few. I forget how many we caught, but the first one stands out in my mind. He had it about half played out, and was standing back from a foot high bank at the edge of the water. "Here he comes!" I couldn't believe it, as the fish came splashing across the water, against the bank, up and over, and away from the creek in a matter of seconds. I couldn't believe the leader, or even the pole hadn't broke. I must have had a pretty good outfit. After I explained to him that playing them out would get the majority of them that might not be hooked so well, he took it a little easier on them, and we went home with a nice bunch of steelhead on the handlebars, with my outfit intact. After that, most Sundays he'd get out to the barn not long after I did, and help me get done so we could go over to the river. I can remember when it was so cold our noses about broke off, but he'd still be out there Sunday morning, ready to go.

I got to where I really enjoyed being up early and out in the barn. From where this dairy was located, I could see the barn lights from five other dairies nearby. With the exception of Gustafsons (now Mil Key) each of the other farms had kids like myself, who milked out, or were owned by people who had kids around my age in school. As the long strings of barn lights came on around the neighborhood you knew who was a few minutes late or, not. A thousand times in the years to come, I would think of these strings of barn lights when I passed another boat at night, their lights always a sort of greeting.

I played the barn radio, and listened to a classical music station from Victoria, and another station that played country western, or what turned out to be some of the fifties music. I can still hear Slim Whitman singing "Oh Rose Marieeee, I love you." Country western version. There was quite a shot of cold weather which froze the mud in the barnyard, and the cows stayed nice and clean, being able to walk up on the surface. You never know what you'll be thankful for tomorrow.

The old guy that lived across the road would be up early, and would walk over about 6:00 most mornings. We'd have a mug of extra fortified cocoa, and visit as I milked my way down the line. Not much going on at that time of morning, and he'd usually be over unless the weather was something he didn't want to deal with. They'd apparently had cows at one time, since he knew a lot about them, and if one of the ladies was having udder trouble or anything else was going on, he'd take a look, and was quite a big help. Another big help was that on my day off, #16 kicked the boss, and when I came back he said that was enough, he was going to get rid of her. I milked her for another month, and just before my next day off, she was on her way.

Spring meant fresh grass, and with the cows out on pasture, no feeding of silage or hay. Also, less barn cleaning and the milk production came up quite a bit with the new grass, and the cows seemed to milk a lot easier. Now, getting up at 3:30 got me done by 6:45, and with my bike parked at the barn I could be at the river by 7:00, in position - casting. My shadow couldn't get permission to go on these quickie runs, and runs they were. Pedal as hard as you could to get there, run up to the first hole, fish till the Carlsborg mill whistle gave its 7:25 warning blast, and then repeat the operation to catch the bus on time. I had a good spot, and time after time I'd get the first fish within the first two or three casts. If the next one didn't come in another few minutes, I'd dress the first one out, and head back.

I would work for room and board- plus, on four more farms, three of them while I was still going to school, and enjoyed all of them. On these other jobs I'd be working with the owner, and although I'd generally do the milking, or most of it, two people in the barn was just better than one.

Here's a worst-case example. While I was milking at my second job I had bought a pair of the striped overalls with the straps over the shoulders, that so many of the farmers wore then. Probably I wanted to at least look the part. I was crouched down, getting ready to take the machine off this cow, and the cow behind me raises her foot and suddenly I'm sitting against her leg, pinned to the floor. When you were crouched down, the overalls would pooch out in back between the straps, and she brought her foot down perfectly, and there I was, with no slack at all. I don't know what she thought she was doing with that foot, as she was one of those that never kicked. Maybe the pants brushed against her leg or something. This was one of those rare times when Joe brought the buckets back on schedule, and after he looked the situation over he tells me, "Now what in the hell are we gonna do?" We finally unbuckled the straps, and got everything as close to flat on the floor as we could, and when he gave her a quick shove, I rolled away. Cutting the overalls down from the back might have been better, but we didn't think of it. If it had been #16 she'd still be shaking me back and forth.

I milked and cleaned the barn; he did the washing up, and also packed the milk into the tank, using a couple three gallon buckets. Everything else was pretty much joint effort. He was quite a piano player, and would play with all the local bands at the Grange dances, Friday and Saturday nights. He'd play several hours every day, and if his wife went somewhere, as soon as the car was out of sight, no matter what we were doing outside of milking, he'd head for the piano. When he'd head for the milk house with full buckets, it depended on what was playing on the radio when he went by, as to how soon I got the buckets back. I'd be over on the other side of the barn, full machines, and when I went over to the other side to get them, he'd be leaning against the wall, tapping his foot and concentrating on the song.

He had one cow that was extra tame, and she'd follow you around outside, hoping for a handout or maybe getting her head scratched. They'd bought a box of peaches, and while I was eating one she comes up and thinking it was an apple which, she always got part of, she starts drooling gallons. I gave her half and had a friend for life, sort of. The next day I got home from school, changed clothes, grabbed a peach, and as soon as the screen door closed I can hear this cow trying to call in her hero, and her share of a peach. The cows are already in, and when I open the big side doors in front of the stanchions, I've got a barn full of eyes on me, the owner of one pair drooling up a storm. So she wound up eating half of quite a few peaches.

Milk wise she wasn't doing all that well though, and after hearing a suggestion that she might not be around too long, I started sneaking her an extra scoop or two of grain. Then more. It started showing up in the bucket, and she did well enough that she made it until I left, which was about all I could hope for. Maybe she wound up on a cloud with a peach orchard.

Then I was down on a place in Oldtown, which was the closest I came to milking in a parlor while I was in school. Actually it was just five stanchions on each side, and I would run the two machines, "Surge", which was my favorite, and the boss would let out five, bring in five more, and so on through around 50, mostly Jerseys. Also my favorite.

He had one Guernsey though, that was probably the best cow I ever milked. Kelly had freshened (calved) in November, and had three bang up months in the milk poundage, and butterfat department. Then this, and nearly every other dairy in the area, was out of silage and hay. I forget what the weather conditions were the previous summer, but this was the only time I can remember any major shortage of feed in the valley. Almost everyone was in the same situation, and apparently no hay in eastern Washington, so the government had some kind of an emergency grain subsidy thing, so that everyone could afford a larger volume of grain than they'd normally feed, and try to get the cows through until pasture time in March.

He ordered a very low protein content grain, allowing them an even bigger portion of it, and he was able to find some pea straw, which he got quite a bit of. Then we'd heat hot water in a drum, add molasses, and pour it from a sprinkler can onto the straw. The cows loved it and it filled the belly, so unlike most herds in the valley, this one was pretty quiet. Straw didn't do too well for milk production, so Kelly sagged a bit for three months, but when she went out on grass she went back up to over 100 pounds of butterfat in the 7th month of her lactation.

25

Considering the winter and the fact Guernseys tend to sag after the 5th or 6th month, she was quite a gal. One of the other farmers had what appeared to be an identical twin named Crickett, also one of the best. Probably somewhere down the line, theirs crossed.

Couldn't tell you about this place without mentioning Kelly. The farm was only a few hundred yards up from the beach bank, above the inner part of Dungeness Bay. My little room was outside the house, and had good ventilation where you could see through in a couple places, but the roof didn't leak. I had an electric blanket, and the nights were a little shorter, so getting to sleep wasn't any problem. It was neat listening to the thrumm, thrumm, of the freighters going down the Straits, or their fog horns when it was foggy. Better yet was the fog horn at the lighthouse at Dungeness. At night, the light would come through my window, since the only thing between us was a row of medium sized firs along the bluffs edge. Half a dozen revolutions, and I'd be out like a light.

On some of the jobs you'd work between milkings on Saturdays and school vacations, but this one had a little different twist. No days off during the month, but once I'd finished washing up the milk house, I was off till the evening milking. If you wanted to work he'd find something he wanted done—$1.00 an hour, and if he needed help with anything he'd let me know ahead of time. So I had between milkings off during spring vacation.

The river had been low and clear almost the whole winter, and not many steelhead except for the few who could be on the lower river first thing in the morning. A day or so before spring vacation it rained pretty hard, and the river shot up to un-fishable, then right back down to a nice volume of water with good color. Two school buddies, Frank Jones and Dick Taylor, dropped me at the hatchery, and then drove downstream a mile or so. I'd fish down to them. We knew there would be fish somewhere along this stretch, just a matter of finding where they were at. I lost one at the hatchery, and then fished a mile of river without another bite.

Clarence Iverson, and some other fellow had been working on the outlet to the ditch that runs down through what is now Dungeness Meadows. They were sitting on the river bank, taking a break, when I got there. We gabbed a minute, and I threw out, and had a bite the first cast, but missed him. Then I got my three, and one for each of them, and headed out to the car. Frank and Dick had done even better downstream, so we were definitely looking forward to tomorrow.

We had a week of steelhead fishing about as good as it gets, and the second day, had three separate times with the three of us playing fish in the same drift, at the same time. What I got were mostly 8 to 12 pounds, but they each had a few bigger ones and we kept out only the nicest ones to keep. We saw Charlie Knapman out by his car when we drove by, and stopped to see how he'd done that morning.

"Not a damn thing." He'd been on the lower river and said that no one else had anything either. Apparently, what fish were at the mouth, waiting for some water, had shot on upstream. We offered to show him the one we got that morning, and opened the lid to a trunk pretty well full of nice steelhead. To Charlie, we may as well have opened the trunk to a hundred bars of gold. We tried to tell him they were from the Dungeness, but he said they weren't Dungeness fish. He said they weren't Elwha fish either, but he sort of believed it when we said we'd gone down to the creek, and chased them out of the lagoon at low tide, then kicked them out as they went down the beach, trying to get to salt water. Frank and Dick were model citizens, but Charlie knew me fairly well. We never saw him through the next week on the upper river, so I guess he really figured they weren't Dungeness fish. It was tough, being semi legal, and he wouldn't believe it, but it was still great to crank up old Charlie.

There was quite a friendly competition between him, and two other of the local fishermen, Clyde Towne and Leroy Lotzgesell. They were good friends, but Charlie would do anything to get the best of Clyde and Leroy, who usually fished together. Of course that worked in reverse. One year, before I started the milking jobs and was still in the fish selling mode, I started getting calls from all of them, a week or so before the opening of the lowland lake trout season. "You get any eggs (steelhead roe) a couple days before it opens, give me a call." No one was boraxing eggs yet, and everyone thought fresh eggs were much better than salted or frozen eggs.

This generally wouldn't have been a problem, except back then the steelhead season closed February 28, and none of these guys felt like taking a chance. So, they'd give me a call. My problem was that I didn't really like to take steelhead that were getting kind of rangy, and by early April there were lots of these, the eggs still tight, but belly walls you could almost see through. Anyway, I went down, and caught a bunch of steelhead, but aside from some nice bucks, I hadn't caught a female that I felt like taking back. Another nice buck, and a few more paper bellies and I was ready to bunch it, but then I got a nice bright female about 12 pounds, a beautiful fish and not very long in the river, but she was already about half eggs.

I called Charlie and in record time he was in the driveway, all smiles. I brought out the steelhead, and a coffee can with both skeins of eggs, and when I went to put the steelhead in his trunk—"wait a minute, I don't want that damned thing!"

"You want the eggs, you take the fish, two bucks for the fish, 50 cents for the eggs."

"You little bastard!"

"That's all right, Leroy and Clyde will take them." It made my day, and I suppose it made his. He likely gave the fish to somebody and they'd have been glad to get it. Charlie made sure lots of people had fish.

My next job was one where the boss had a job besides the farm. When I had milked for the piano player, who lived down the road, one of my best friends milked here, so I was well acquainted with these people, between visiting while Jerry worked there, and then haying in the summers. They had three kids, two and a half when I got there, and Gary arrived a few months later. Christie was just starting first grade that year.

Rickie, or as the little neighbor girl called him, Icky, was already enthused about the fishing operation. He'd ride on his dads, or my shoulders most of the way to the river, as it was still quite a hike for a little guy, and he'd held the pole for awhile on quite a few steelhead or silvers that we hooked. It was hard for him to hold the pole, and turn the reel handle at the same time, so most of the time he'd just back up, away from the river. If the fish felt like arguing, sometimes he would move back towards the river pretty fast. I can remember several times when we'd be looking in the water at the fish, or the line, and hear a commotion

*Gary Quinn and "Christie"*

28

behind us. You'd look back, and there would be a pair of feet, and the pole sticking out from whatever he'd backed over.

Alfred and Nellie lived across the road, and Alf was also an avid steelhead fisherman. He had put up a nice smokehouse, with the fire pit back aways, and then piped the smoke into the house. Some fine batches of silvers and steelhead found their way through his house that fall and winter. Some of the time Alf would go to the river with us, or it might just be him, and me, but whoever went, they generally had a little shadow.

I remember a few years later Alf and I were trying to get enough silvers to smoke and, being along in mid November, it was kind of picky. We had been looking in the log jams, and there was no shortage of fish, but most of them were already looking like fire engines. We had hoped for a little better than that. A few big hooknose that had barely started to change color would be fine, but we finally accepted that we were two or three weeks late. I had just finished my two years active duty in the army, November 13th, or we'd have been earlier.

We were walking upstream, next to a deep riffle, and Alf was carrying the pole with a gaff hook on the end. Out of habit I was staring into the river as we moved upstream. I saw a flash of movement, and realized it was the tail of a nice bright fish. It apparently sensed we were there, as it took off at a good clip up into the current. I grabbed the hook from Alf, and ran up to the top of the riffle, hoping to get a swipe at it, as it went by. There was a good sized rock in mid current, and I figured this would be the path, as it offered a little protection and it also caused enough turbulence to make me a little obscure. I hoped.

The river was clear, but I couldn't see a thing. I thought I had got past him, as I had watched the top of the riffle, and hadn't seen him go up into the next hole. Alf had moved down aways from where I'd first seen it, and now started moving upstream, throwing a few small rocks ahead of him. I still didn't see a thing. Then the turbulence around the rock cleared for just a moment, and I could just see what I thought was a head showing above the rock, the rest of the body hidden by the rock and turbulence. A few seconds later he was on the bank, an extra nice 14 pound male steelhead. We ditched it in an area of thick alder and willow, then on upstream to look at one more spot. If we saw nothing there, we'd bunch it. We were pretty happy with what we had, but it's a lot of effort to smoke a batch of fish, and one more would make it a bit more worthwhile.

When we weren't watching the water, we watched everything else. At that time there were no seasons on salmon, so our presence on the river would have been suspicious, but not illegal. Our gear would have been hard to explain. It would be nice to see a game warden before he saw us, and he had the edge, because he would have had less going on than someone trying to catch a fish. There he was, several hundred yards upstream, standing on a log jam, and looking straight at us through the binocs. He's the guy that's supposed to stay hidden.

I kept my head down and told Alf, "don't look up, keep looking down or ahead." Then I told him where our company was, and watching out of the corners of my eyes, I could see him bailing off the log jam. We kept walking ahead, as if we hadn't seen him. The side stream left the river just ahead of us, and we moved into some brush along its edge. We watched him pounding downstream, and it looked like he could go right along. A few years earlier they'd had another fellow that could really fly, and I was glad this wasn't him. If he didn't catch you it wasn't because you out ran him. I'd seen him run once when I'd gotten behind him, thanks to a maze of logging roads, and some big stumps. He was way out of my league.

So now we had about a hundred yards on this guy, with the river between us. We got in the side stream, crouching low enough that he couldn't see us over the gravel bar, and in a few feet we had the brush patch between him and us. Then downstream to where I thought our steelhead was, and I started through the brush for it. Alf crossed the side stream, and headed for a logging road that ran along, not too far from the river bank. I'd told him to keep going for home.

When I got to the edge of the brush, I about died. He was almost to the middle of the river, directly across from me, head down, watching what he was doing in the wading department. Being even with me made it better, because if he happened to glance up, I would be more on the edge of his vision. When you wade a fairly fast river like the Dungeness, you angle downstream, and if you aren't watching the bottom directly ahead of you, you'll soon wish you had been. Luckily, he had the right idea, and luckily, I had gone through the brush at the perfect spot, and hit the steelhead dead center. This was just plain luck, and it held, because he didn't look up all the time the fish and I were backing out of sight into the brush.

Alf had waited on the logging road and that worried me, as I wanted to put some distance behind us now. He wouldn't be able to move like I had in mind. Three or four hundred yards later, we left the logging road, and went down a fence line through the woods, that butted into the property next to Alf's place. He kept up pretty well. Probably in his early seventies by then, he was a husky little guy about 5-4 and the old legs were churning. Ahead of us some brushy swales ran through small fields, and we followed one of them almost over to his house. Lots of good memories. I went over to visit him towards the end, and it was one of the things we laughed about.

Another part of my life was showing up more frequently now. I had always had lots of headaches, but occasionally there would be one that about tore me apart. These were few and far between, earlier on, and weren't as big a factor in my life if I could find a dark spot and wait it out, but that's not possible with a milking job. A few of the milkings seemed like they lasted a year. I had decided I wasn't going to be a dairy farmer.

I think a lot now, about these jobs on the farms. From strawberries, to haying and silage in the summers, and all the milking jobs for me and a bunch of other young kids. Where would we have been without these jobs? For that matter, many of the people we worked for would have been up against it, without this help. We didn't make a lot of money but money isn't always the object. There's so many restrictions now, on kids working, and granted, in today's world there needs to be, but its costing certain kids a lot. I see so many young people, now, who have no idea, whatsoever, how to do a job. Where to start, sequence or order, a good fast job, and some pride in accomplishment at the end. And the work? If there's this pride in accomplishment, and you've enjoyed doing it, is it really work? Anyway, a good work ethic is a wonderful thing and I'm proud to see it in our three kids. I think this is one area where our country has slipped, but I'm not sure how to correct it. Things aren't as simple as they used to be.

# Chapter 4
# Boats

I can remember way back, pestering mom to buy me a P.T. boat. Whether it was the dime store, or the library, "where's the P.T. boats, mom? Can you buy me a P.T. boat?" Considering where we lived at the time, I had to be four years old. The war was still on, mom built bombers for our side, and we were the good guys. Before the war ended I had three or four of these boats and would sit in the bathtub while they rolled in a light chop, and when it got really rough they rode it out. They were plastic, about four inches long, brightly colored, and were the beginning of a long friendship with the boat department.

Before long I was taking a board with the front corners cut off to make a V shaped bow, nailing blocks on it for a cabin, and a stick going straight up, for a mast. Sometimes the mast would fall down, and the soldiers and cowboys I had stationed on deck fell off, but they always got back on. A string tied to a nail in the bow let me pull the boat along, and when you pulled it through soft sand, you could see the sand fall away from the bow, like water.

We'd go over to the Olympic Peninsula pretty often on weekends, and I'd be the first one to get up on the top deck to watch over the stern as the ferry, often the Klickitat or Nisqually, pulled away from the dock. The first and last five minutes were the best parts of the ferry ride. On the trip across we'd eat the picnic dinner mom had packed, always hot tea and sandwiches, and something good for desert. We always went the Edmonds way, and then, before the Hood Canal bridge, there were two ferries, and you usually just missed one or the other. Sometimes you had to wait in line for hours and it always took forever to get to Sequim.

We moved to the peninsula in 1950, and for years after that, my trips on the salt water were few and far between. I didn't go back to Seattle till I got out of high school, so there was only the occasional trip sport fishing when someone might take me along. The most memorable of these trips was when our neighbor, Charlie Roberts, took Richie and I out to Sekiu.

It was midsummer and the fishing for king salmon had been good. Charlie rented one of the little boats, and while he was putting their motor on it, I watched a boat come in with several of these beautiful fish. I couldn't believe I was actually going. I'd never caught a salmon in salt water before, but I would today.

Before long, we were out with the rest of the boats, and you could see an occasional fish being caught. Charlie had rigged up two poles, each with a flasher and herring held down by a sport lead, and we were trolling fairly close to shore. He had told us what to do if we hooked one, mostly hang on, and had set the star drags on our reels so the line wouldn't run out while we were fishing. Once a fish was hooked, the strain of it fighting would allow the line to go out with no danger of breaking the leader. We could see several boats playing fish now, and suddenly I had one. The line was screaming off the reel, and Charlie was telling me, "let him run, you're doing fine." Rich had pulled his line into the boat, and my fish was still going out. About half the line was gone from the big Pakron reel, and I tightened up on the drag just a bit to slow him down. Apparently a bit too much and he broke the leader.

So I was pretty down in the lips. Charlie rigged me up again, along with a little consoling, and some advice on…if I hooked another one. Rich wanted to run the outboard, so Charlie took the other pole, and pretty soon we were fishing again. "Look at that." We watched some guy playing a really big fish that jumped several times and eventually he got it. Charlie said "maybe a 40 pounder." Lots of other fish being caught.

We turned around and Charlie mentioned to Rich that he was going just a touch too fast. "No he's not! He's going just right." I had another one on. This one really took off, and I couldn't do a thing but sit there and watch the line disappear. It was fairly melting off the reel, and showed no sign of stopping. He had already run out more line than I'd allowed the other to do, and if he didn't stop soon he'd be at the end of the line. Charlie told Rich to turn the boat around, and head after him, but before he got it around I tightened the drag, just a bit, to conserve those last few feet of line. Those were the only two bites we had and the lump in my throat was like a football. We put the two lines back

33

in, and were just getting in the hopeful mood when Charlie told us, "well, it's all over for today." Coming down the straits from the ocean were what I remember as hundreds of groups of blackfish, (Orcas) (killer whales), from the beach, to as far out as you could see. They went by, moving on down the straits, for what seemed like forever, and before long there was a parade of sport boats running for the docks, giving it up for the day. We went home empty handed, but I knew that someday I was going to catch some of these big kings!

The sport fishing trip that probably affected my life the most, was during my senior year in high school. The fellow that milked up the road from where I was working at the time, suggested that we both take our day off at the same time, and go out to Sekiu. He had heard they had been doing pretty good on Blackmouth. We didn't catch any that day either, but during the day he suggested that anyone who liked the water and fishing as much as I did, ought to get a boat and go commercial fishing. He knew of someone who did, and after he had told me the bits and pieces of what he knew, I was convinced that this would be my future.

One of my steelhead fishing buddies introduced me to a friend of his who fished part time out of La Push. Ray suggested that if I wanted to come out with him over a weekend and see what it was all about, I'd be more than welcome. One of his friends went along the first day, and then he and Ray's wife both went on Sunday. The fishing wasn't what you'd call hot, but it was good enough. What fish he got were nice ones, and the weather was beautiful. I must have uncovered the first fish he got ten times, just to look at it, and before we were through he'd added enough more that he was satisfied with the day. Sunday was another good day, and I was hooked.

From then until school got out, I would spend the time between milkings on Sundays on the docks in Port Angeles. I talked to anyone who would answer questions, and gradually I began to form some ideas as to what it would take to get me out there.

My best bet was to start as a kelper. They fished small boats, usually in the 16 to 24 foot range, and usually fished with one or two hand gurdies, sport poles, or a combination of both. There were a few boats of this type for sale in the boat haven, but nothing that took my eye. I'd be living aboard, so I needed a bunk and a place to keep a coleman stove, but most of what I looked at was more than I could afford. I had been saving most of what I made since I was six, but however proud I was of this, it wouldn't afford anything very fancy. Finally

I came up with something that might do, complete with gear. I had pretty well memorized all the good points the owner had told me about it.

I had done quite a little haying for a friend named Hal Olstead. He had fished tuna when he was younger, and after hearing about some of these good points, he decided he'd like to take a look at the boat before I bought it. When we walked down the dock and I pointed it out, he suggested we go up around Seattle and look around. I knew he was well versed in the boat department, so I didn't mind that he wasn't too impressed with my first choice.

We spent several days looking in Seattle, Port Townsend, and Poulsbo, but never did see anything that took Hal's eye. When we got home he called an old friend of his from Shelton, and asked him if he knew of anything in that area. He did. He and a friend had built a 19 foot plywood boat with an inboard engine, and a trunk cabin. They had intended fishing either La Push or Neah Bay, but now they weren't going to get time to do this, and he would give me a good price on it. Hal told me that this would be a good rig. John worked on the tug boats out of Shelton, knew boats, and he said that any boat John built would be a dandy. It was nineteen feet long, seven wide, with a semi vee bottom, and the engine was a 12 horse Universal. There was a trunk cabin with a full sized bunk on each side, and the steering and a small fuel tank had been installed. The price was $850.

I had rented a trailer to bring the "Judy" up from Shelton and had spent a few days on poles, gurdies, lights, and a big fish box. Now it seemed like the best thing was to get the trailer again to take it on out to La Push, rather than dumping it in at Port Angeles and running it out to Tatoosh and down the beach. Ernie Jones, one of my neighborhood buddies, was going to go out with me for a few days, "to see that you get off to a good start." I was happy for his company and before long, we were in La Push, geared up, fueled up, licensed up and ready to go.

The money I'd been saving for years was almost gone, so we'd have to catch something right away, just to keep going. We left La Push that first morning in what was probably pretty good weather, but there was a big swell running, and a little chop to go with it. Not too many boats out either. We got the five spreads out on each line, but it didn't look like it had on Rays' boat. Nothing looked right. By the time we had fished out to the Whistler Buoy, I was so sick that dying sounded good, and we decided that fishing back with the swell, and calling it a day might be a good idea. Maybe tomorrow the weather would be better, and the fuel would be better spent if I was more able to fish. We had nothing but sandwich makings to eat, so that afternoon we borrowed a skiff, and rowed up the Quilleute to where the Dickey comes in, going a short way upstream to fish for trout. Hal had given me a little one burner primus stove, and I had a frying pan. A nice mess of trout would take up a little slack in the belly.

Not much doing in the trout department either, so the next morning saw us on the ocean at daylight. Getting hungry is a pretty good incentive program. Armed with the remainder of our sandwich makings, and a tip as to where a few salmon might be, we were in good spirits. The ocean being a lot nicer than the day before, accounted for most of this good mood.

The little universal didn't move us along too fast, so I decided to put out the gear in close, and fish on out. There was a little group of boats up ahead of us, and we could have the gear out, and be ready for action when we got up to them. This was roughly in the area where we had been told about at the dock, so our hopes were up.

The first thing was to get the poles down, so that our lines could be hung from them. They were short, and even with the boat separating them, they didn't space the lines very far apart. Even fishing as shallow as we were, a 32 foot separation at the poles would make some interesting tangles 90 feet down the lines.

A hand gurdie is a big spool with a handle for cranking the line in, and some kind of a braking system to keep the line from running out while you were working with a fish, or maybe just working on the line. They were usually attached to the side of the boat, and the stainless trolling wire went through a block attached to a davit and over the side. A round 15 to 25 pound lead was hung on the bottom of the line and leaders were snapped on between markers spaced at intervals on the mainline. Once the line was out, you attached the clamp on the end of the "tag line" to the wire, and when you let out more line, the tag line, which went to the tip of the pole, came tight, putting your line the length of the pole away from the boat. This helped to avoid tangling the two lines and you could see when a fish got on the line, and started jerking on the end of the pole.

I used a 15 pound lead on each line, which was a seven strand stainless wire of about 600 pound breaking strength. As I dropped it down, I attached five leaders, three fathoms apart. Each leader had a line snap on one end to attach the leader to the line, and a variety of lures could be tied on the business end of the leaders. There were dozens of kinds of spoons and plugs, or you could use flashers with a herring or some other kind of lure behind them. My gear department wasn't too great, so I used two flashers and herring, and three spoons on each line.

We moved into the area where these other boats were, seeing a few fish being caught, but nothing for us yet. When we were nearly past the last of the boats, there it was. The spring on the tip of the pole was bouncing up and down, and the line was pulling back much further in the water, than it had been previously. We had one on. A big one. Anything yanking like that had to go thirty pounds at least. Ernie said he'd steer the boat, so we wouldn't tangle the lines, like we had when we tried to run the gear, the day before. I grabbed the crank on the hand gurdie, and started cranking. First I took off the clamp on the tagline, and just below it, the first leader. Nothing. Several more leaders and nothing and I was getting pretty excited. Now the line was acting different as I brought it up, first pulled back more, then not quite so much, and it was sort of shaking or chattering. I could see him shining down in the water, and what a thrill. Just a few feet more. Soon I had hold of the leader and could see him shaking and then pulling down in the water. When he got a bit to the side the flasher would chatter more, so when he was deeper I'd been seeing the flasher shaking, instead of the fish.

"Don't lose him."

"Yeah, I know." If I could get him, we could buy dinner and fuel to fish tomorrow.

"Be careful."

"I am."

"How big is he?"

"Take a look. You can see him good now. 18 Pounds?"

"Yeah, maybe."

I had him within six feet of the boat now, and he wasn't really going wild, but then he wouldn't hold still either. The club gaffs are designed for driving straight down through a fishes cheek, or the top of his head, but they have to be holding still for you to do this. I probably missed some good chances, but finally he held still long enough, and he was in the boat. We had done it! We were fishermen! I suppose everyone within half a mile was wondering what all the yelling was about, but we didn't care.

I was a lot more confident when I put the line back out. Nothing like the first taste of success to boost the confidence. Then it was time to admire our fine king salmon. He wasn't as big as he'd looked to be in the water, but I thought he'd still be big enough to make the 12 pound dressed break that it took to be graded as a large. That was the size they paid the most for, and this one should be worth about five dollars.

Now we fished inshore, back towards the boats we had gone by, and before long, there it was again, the strong, insistent jerking on the line, like someone trying to tear the pole off the boat. Gradually it quieted down, with just occasional movement on the line to show he was still there. I started bringing him up. This one was a lot nicer about it, and before long I had him in the boat. It was about the same size as the other one, and I was excited. These would bring enough to keep going for several days, and I was bound to get more in the meantime. The fish seemed to have stopped biting that day though, and although we fished on through till evening, we only got one more fish, a 5 pound silver.

Ernie figured I had everything under control, so he went back home that night and would be back in a few days to see how I was doing. I had met a few of the guys who tied to the dock I was on, and there was lots of help, tips on gear, fishing the current in the ocean, boat handling, and if any particular area had been good that day, it was shared with the other boats. None of us had radios then, so comparing notes on the dock was about the best you could do.

After several incidents brought on by my own stupidity, I took the time to think my situation over. I had virtually no knowledge of running a boat, practically no gear, and the "Judy" wasn't exactly a lot of boat for anything but pretty good weather. I'd lay in the bunk and listen to the "Skunk" buoy, which was a mile or so offshore. It moaned, and groaned, and bellered when the ocean wasn't quite happy, and I'd think that tomorrow probably was another day I wouldn't get out. Then, more often than not, in good weather it would be foggy. I'd lay in the bunk listening to the fog horn blow, and be thinking that I would go, but would hate being out there in the fog. For now the program would be to get in what time I could in better weather, learn what I could in the meantime, and gather up what I could dollar-wise to approach next season in a little better shape. I knew I was going to do this, but also knew I had started out with one foot in the bucket.

Ray Balch would come out Friday night, and go back after fishing on Sunday. We would compare notes on what had been going on, and he would always have a few good tips on how I might improve on things. "We're both gonna have to get bigger rigs, Vince." He was right—beyond either of our dreams.

Another kelper had worked on the freighters going to and from Alaska, and he suggested that would be the place for me to fish. He said it was mostly inside waters, and flat calm all the way through British Columbia to Alaska. "It's so calm that if you want to, you can just tie off on a tree limb at night." I talked to Ray about it, and he thought it would be a good idea. He'd fished there, and was able to give me a little better idea of what to expect. He couldn't remember a limb anywhere that he'd felt like tying to, but he was enthusiastic about the country.

So now I spent a good deal of time thinking about what it would take to get to Alaska. I would either have to get a bigger boat, or do quite a little work on the Judy. Either way would take some money, and the few dollars I'd managed to save up from fishing wouldn't get me far. The fishing right around La Push hadn't been good, along with my not being much of a fisherman. My catch usually fell in with the average of the other kelpers, but all too often the better fishing was way up or down the beach, or way out, and the little 12 horse Universal just didn't get you there and back fast enough to make the long runs worthwhile. Along in early September I decided to bunch it, and took the boat home. In a few days I headed for eastern Washington to pick apples.

Mom had picked fruit years before, and said that if you worked at it you could do all right. I headed for the Wenatchee area, but got there about a week too early. The orchard owner showed me a little shack to move into and said they would start color picking in a few days, and that he would work with us to show us how he wanted his fruit picked.

I had a few days to look the country over and one of my first stops was the Rock Island Dam, downstream from Wenatchee. A bag of apples later, I was fast friends with the man who counted the fish, and he invited me to spend a couple hours with him in the fish counting station. We went down into a small room equipped with controls to open the gate which let the fish move through. They moved over a white panel that gave him a clear definition of the fish he was looking at. Other controls let him raise or lower this panel for better visibility, depending on water clarity. He had a board with a bunch of clickers on it, which he could make sound like a runaway typewriter when the volume warranted it. The amount of summer run steelhead amazed me, but I was really surprised at the lack of king salmon. Where I had expected to see thousands, there were only a few hundred, and considering that he alternated this ladder with at least one more, not too many kings were going by. He told me that I'd missed the parade, that a few weeks or a month earlier would have given me a completely different impression. He suggested that I go up the Wenatchee and Entiat rivers, if I wanted to see kings.

I spent most of the next day on the Wenatchee River, and I had never seen anything to compare with it on any of the Olympic Peninsula streams. From where the road coming from Stevens Pass first meets the river, most of the way through to where the Wenatchee dumps into the Columbia, the river was full of king salmon. Thousands of them already dead in the river, and every drift and tail-out alive with more spawning fish.

Years later the Assistant Director of Fisheries told me that the Columbia, prior to any dams being built on it, produced more king salmon than all of the rivers combined, above it. "You mean up to the straits?"

"No, I mean above it! He said above it meant from the Columbia—north. I told him I didn't believe it and he said he didn't believe it either, when it was first told to him. "When you learn enough about it you'll know it's so."

It took me about two years. The Columbia system had had most of the best rivers, with thousands of miles of the best spawning grounds in the world. They hadn't found a good way of getting the smolts downstream, around the dams and the tremendous runs of kings that spawned in the upper river didn't exist anymore. No salmon got above Grand Coulee Dam because it was too tall for fish ladders. Now there are thousands of miles of river, with tributaries that could be excellent salmon producers, without any salmon in them. And they were building more dams.

Once the apples had colored enough to start picking it was a week or so of color picking, and then full bore on through the season. I picked in three different orchards that fall, and met some neat people, and some who weren't exactly neat, but mighty interesting. I never did get to be a fast picker, but tried to pick good fruit, and worked steady at it. I'd start early, finish late, and pick till around 3:00 Saturday afternoon, and knock off for the weekend. Then I'd be up the Entiat or Wenatchee rivers trout fishing, and watching the salmon. The Entiat was always the best trout fishing, and the scenery on either river is spectacular at that time of the year.

The last orchard I picked in, had an interesting situation that I still occasionally think of. Earlier that fall they had color picked a block or two of common delicious, south side only, and not every tree. I didn't get there until later when they were picking winesaps. I spent all of the next season there, and got to pick some of these big common delicious trees which is something I'm still happy I got to do. At the end of that season they hired me, and a few other pickers to help clean up the orchard. After a week or so of hauling out props, the boss asked if I'd ever ran a chain saw. He wanted me and another worker to take turns with the saw, and reduce these trees to a point that they could be hauled out and put through the buzz saw for firewood.

These were about as big as apple trees get, to the point that you went to the

40

top of a 14 foot ladder, and started as high as you could reach or the top fruit would be beyond your reach if you took any weight off the limbs first. A few of the better trees produced over 120 boxes of apples. They were the best delicious apples I ever ate, and the other big difference in them, compared to today's delicious apples, was the color. Instead of the deep red of todays apple, these were more of a buckskin, with a lot of yellow in with the red. Mrs. American housewife wanted the nice, deep red color. She got it.

Now everybody complains about the red delicious being ultra bland and they like the flavorful Fuji, Gala, and Braeburn, which look a lot like the old common delicious did. Chuck, and a good many other fruit growers, went to a great expense to satisfy another fickle trend. Now many of the orchards have smaller trees, closer together. Easier to care for, pick, take out, and replant the next star apple.

I got a milking job when I got back to Sequim and that, along with the fishing and apple money, gave me enough to make some big changes in the Judy. Hal suggested I do the work in his machine shed where there was plenty of room, a table saw, and lots of technical advice. Sometimes (advice) was a lot like getting elbowed aside.

Someone had suggested I fiberglass the bottom of the boat, and I had quite a list of other improvements I wanted to make. At the top of the list was more power. We went up to Seattle, and struck gold when a person from the Gray-marine dealership, told us that New England fish company had just shipped a bunch of engines down from Alaska, with the intention of selling them, and putting more power in their fleet of Bristol Bay gillnetters. He said they hadn't been used, and the price would be right.

$400.00 later a 42 hp Gray Lugger, still in the crate, was sitting in the back of Hal's pickup. Pete, at Doc Freemans, agreed to take the little Universal as a trade in on a new prop, and a bunch of other equipment, plus enough material to fiberglass the bottom of the boat. Now I had my work cut out for me.

We turned the boat over, and I sanded the bottom down and soon we were fiberglassers, adding considerable strength and toughness to the boat. Whenever I needed an extra pair of hands, Hal, or Ernie Jones would be there, or both of them. It's occurred to me more than once, that when people like myself happen to make a success of something, a few others might have had quite a hand in it. Accordingly, over the years I've spent considerable time being one of the "few others." What goes around ought to come around.

We installed the new engine, and rebuilt the little trunk cabin. A sliding hatch in the roof of the cabin let me stand up when I was running or fishing, with the steering wheel and controls within easy reach. The roof came to just under my armpits so it was quite comfortable, and I would spend most of my time in good weather running the boat from this position.

The engine was right behind the cabin and was enclosed with a plywood cover. The exhaust went up just behind the cabin so the panel in front of the engine box kept your back comfortably warm. I didn't change the two bunks, which were toe to toe in the bow, and used one for sleeping, and one for storage. Between the bunk and back wall, opposite the door, I put in a storage cabinet with a Coleman stove bolted to the top.

A self draining fish box went across the stern and set above the rudder quadrant. Then I attached a tiller to the quadrant, so I could sit back against, or on the box and steer with one foot. I added another fuel tank and found two big lengths of bamboo that would make dandy, lightweight trolling poles. For hand gurdies I used two line spools with a V- belt pulley, and a handle screwed to each one. A piece of V- belt went up over the pulley, and was solid to the boat on one end, with a piece of rubber snubber tied to the other end, the snubber also solid to the boat. You lifted the snubber to let the line run out, and easing the belt into the pulley acted as a brake.

I realized how little I knew about Alaska and nothing about British Columbia, so I asked the dad of one of my steelhead fishing friends, if I could come down and look at his charts, make up a chart list, and get some pointers as to where a rig the size of the "Judy" might fish. After several hours of going over charts with Ernie Erickson, and listening to his ideas, I began to get an inkling of how big a thing I was taking on. After looking at the charts of British Columbia, I wondered how I'd ever find Alaska. I stewed and fussed about it for a few days, and called Ernie and asked him if they would mind my following them up to Ketchikan. I could go it on my own once there. He said he'd talk it over with his father in law, and let me know. The next day he called, and said "it was fine with them." This would be one of the best things to happen to me in a lifetime of fishing.

We had put the boat in the water at Port Angeles, and I ran it around to Sequim Bay the day before we left. I had dinner that night with the Ericksons, and met Lee Harbaugh, Ernie's father in law. He was in his seventies, and had a bum hip, leftovers from a fall while hunting moose.

Ernie had fished on the Nira with him for years, and when Lee had the Eel built, the Nira was Ernie's. The Eel was 34 feet long and although it was quite

*In Port Angeles—ready to go.*

beamy, it was very shallow. Like one of Lee's friends said, "he can run around on a wet blanket." He'd had the boat built with several things in mind, mainly hunting moose up the Stikine River. To be able to do that he needed something that could operate in skinny water. It was built heavier than the plans called for, so wasn't the fastest thing around, but there's a slough up the Stikine river that fits the Eel perfectly, and when you back up into it at high tide, till you can't go any further, the Eel made the perfect fall hunting camp. The Eel would be wedged comfortably between both banks of the slough, and you could easily step from the boat to the bank, on either side. He told of one time when the tides had got quite a bit smaller than on the day they went in, and when they went to leave for town, the Eel wouldn't budge. He ran the machine in gear for awhile, until he'd pushed a bunch of water further up the slough behind him, and when he kicked it out of gear and this false ebb came rushing out, back in gear and away went the Eel.

The Nira was 37 feet long, beamy, and much deeper than the Eel. Both boats had their living quarters "down below" in the focsle, which was typical of most small commercial fishing boats built in the early 1900s through the 1940s. They had a trunk cabin, which allowed head room in the focsle, and the engine was just forward of the focsle-fish hold bulkhead, still pretty much in the focsle. The floor for the wheelhouse was above the engine, and a hinged hatch opened to three or four steps alongside the engine, going down into the focsle.

43

There wasn't much in the way of electronics then, so if you had a radio, fathometer, auto pilot, and a direction finder, you pretty much had it all. Some of the boats that fished offshore had the old surplus lorans that had been used in the World War II bombers. The Nira had a fathometer and a direction finder. Unlike most boats it tended to not run off, one way or the other, and Ernie could leave the wheel without having the boat turn around on him. It was horrible in the trough, poor bucking into it, but one of the finest boats around in a following sea. The EEL was somewhat better equipped, with an auto pilot, radio, and fathometer, and considering its size and some of Lee's ideas when building it, it wasn't too bad of an all around sea boat. Then again, like the Judy, even 34 footers have their limitations.

Ernie's place was right on the water, and the Nira and EEL were both moored fore and aft between piling in the bay below his house. I had tied the Judy alongside the Nira, and at barely daylight the next morning I awoke to the sound of them pulling his skiff on deck. Cliff Heath was with him, and would spend the whole season aboard, cooking and helping with whatever needed to be done, outside of the actual fishing. Bud Stewart would ride up with Lee and look for work in the Petersburg area.

It was a beautiful morning, the sun not up yet, but with the first twinge of orange just starting to show. Ernie blew a farewell blast on his horn, and we were on our way to Alaska. I couldn't believe this was happening to me. The first two days were flat calm, perfect weather, beautiful scenery, and I figured I'd gone to heaven. We anchored in Departure Bay at Nanaimo the first night, and tied up at Stewart Island the second evening. The next morning the tide was right, and we shot down through the channels north of Stewart Isl. There are four separate areas in this stretch, where the tidal currents are a major consideration. You try to hit the summit at Stewart Isl. (the Yucultaws) at, or just after, high water so you can go up to that point with the current, and then take the ebb out, whichever direction you happen to be going. The tide floods from both ends of Vancouver Island, through the Strait Of Juan De Fuca from the south, and through Queen Charlotte and Johnstone Straits from the north. They meet at Stewart Isl. The other route would have been over by Campbell River, and up through Seymour Narrows.

Before we got out into Johnstone Straits, it was pretty obvious that the wind was blowing. Each exposed bay or channel was showing quite a little white, and when we finally broke out into Johnstone Straits things became a lot less comfortable in my little boat. I had a hand pump, and was kept busy pumping the

*Judy and the Nira crossing the Straits of Juan De Fuca*

spray that came into the boat, and I tried to keep in behind Lee so that he could break it down. I could just barely reach the pump with one hand, while steering with the other, and it was hard to keep the boat in position behind the EEL. For the next few hours, the only time I quit pumping was when I happened to be adjusting the throttle, which was also a near constant thing. Eventually my arm felt puffy and numb.

The little 12 volt pumps weren't out yet, or if they were I hadn't heard about them. A little pump on a belt tightener off the engine would have been nice, or a tarp over the back, to fend off the spray. These ideas come with experience, and at that point I didn't have much, but I could tell I was getting some. Finally Lee and Ernie had enough, and pulled over into Forward Bay, where we would wait the rest of that day, and the next, for it to lay down. I was certain that I'd pumped all the water in Johnstone Straits through the little pump. The next day I ran ahead, and went into God's Pocket and filled my tanks with gas. This was the first of many visits with Pete, and in the future a lot of days would be cut short, or run long, to get to God's Pocket and B.S. half the night away. He sold fuel, groceries, and bought fish, and would always have some good stories on his summer or winter, depending on which way I was going.

We waited two more days in Cascade Harbor for Queen Charlotte Sound to get decent, but I'm certain that some of this was due to the fact that I was along. This was sunny, westerly weather and since that trip I would always prefer going north earlier in the year, when the prevailing wind would be from the southeast. We had nice weather for the next two days, until we got up to Chatham Sound, above Prince Rupert, where it was blowing out of Portland Canal. This was big enough of a slop that I could bob around on top while the other boats rolled, and rolled, and rolled. In years to come I would have more miserable rides through this stretch than any other area on the way north.

For those who love beautiful scenery, the trip through British Columbia, and on through Southeast Alaska is hard to beat. My uncle rode north with me a few seasons later, and on a clear, sunny morning as we entered Finlayson Channel, he expressed it pretty well. "If I'd known this existed fifty years ago, I'd have spent my life here."

We stopped in Ketchikan, and got our licenses, fueled up, and I bought some hooks for choking herring. Things were falling into a familar pattern because, at this point, I had one dollar and some change left. My fuel tanks would allow about a week of fishing, and I had what gear I needed to get going. I wouldn't starve, either, as I had a couple boxes of canned stuff aboard, and I liked to eat fish.

We tried Steamer Pt. and the Big Bend, and I caught my first Alaska king salmon, a seven pound white—not much of a start. That afternoon we went through Wrangell Narrows to Petersburg, and Ernie put out his herring net along the dock. We got enough herring to last at least three or four days. He suggested I fish along with him for a while, and learn the area. He and Lee each showed me their system of choking herring, which is a system using whole herring without a flasher. You take the herring needle, and split out the tail, leaving two flaps of side, about an inch long, at the tail end of the fish. Then run the needle through one side, about an inch above the flaps, out through the eye on the other side, and a hook with a gangeon, swivel, and short wire is pulled up through, with the hook sticking out the side of the herring, and the gangeon and wire sticking out the eye. Then the gangeon goes under the jaw, through the other eye. and back through the first eye, locking the herrings mouth closed. The small swivel should lay alongside the herrings head and being pulled from the side of its head, plus a slight twist accomplished by inserting a small cedar stick down through the eye, and along the backbone, gives the herring it's movement. Trolled slowly, they should just barely roll over, fall off fast, and just barely get over again. Splitting out the tail allows a little bleeding into the water.

Of course, this takes a little practice. At first my herring neither rose or fell off, and spun so fast that if a salmon had approached one head on, the herring would likely have killed it. Quite a few buckets of herring later, I began to get a little better at it, but not until Frank Gordon gave me some lessons, did I start to get good at it. Frank was one of the natives from Kake, and along with being an expert at teaching a herring how to swim, he played a mean clarinet. He was Alaska's version of Pete Fountain.

Petersburg's fishing fleet was typical of most towns in southeast Alaska at that time. There were quite a few bigger boats that longlined halibut and blackcod, or seined for salmon during the summer and fall. Some did both. A few other boats fished shrimp or crab, and then there were a bunch of smaller, 30 to 45 foot boats, that either trolled or gillnetted for salmon. Petersburg's longline fleet was an exceptionally well maintained and operated bunch of boats. It still is.

I'll always remember that first day out of Petersburg. The scenery is fantastic; snow covered mountains of the mainland across Frederick Sound, and Kupreanof Island's Lindenberg Peninsula on the side we would be fishing. Mountains and foothills ran right down to the water, and what wasn't covered with snow was either granite cliffs, heavy timber, or areas of muskeg, a sort of boggy wasteland with stunted trees that covers quite a bit of Alaska. Fishing right next to the beach, you were glad you were there. We are fortunate there was a William Henry Seward!

Ernie had told me to follow him along the beach, and he'd show me the reefs to turn out for and some of the hot spots worth knowing about. We ran out from town for about an hour and when he slowed down to throw out the gear I fell in behind him and put out my five herring per line. Before long I got one, another small feeder about seven pounds. So far I wasn't too impressed with the size of these Alaskan kings, but he was still worth enough fuel for me to fish for a full day.

I decided to turn around to see if I could catch another, and didn't, along with getting way behind Ernie. I fished along a little faster to catch him, but soon noticed birds working on a spot just inside me. Heading in towards them, both poles started going crazy before I quite got there, and I knew I was on bottom. I was still determined to put my herring through this patch of birds so I sped up, and then sped up some more. The turn was kind of a high speed quickie, and then full bore, straight out. Then I slowed down and one pole started bouncing again, so more high speed. The next time I slowed down, and it bounced, I was a little suspicious. It was a nice salmon and definitely not a seven pounder. After being towed along at high speed he wasn't too ambitious and before long he was in the boat. Over twenty pounds, and a red, so he'd be worth around eight dollars, and combined with the other two I'd already caught, would allow for nearly another weeks worth of fuel. Things were looking up.

I caught up to Ernie and showed them my two fish and while we were yelling back and forth, I noticed another good fish on my gear. They cheered me on as I captured him, and then Ernie said, "It doesn't look like there's too much here, leave em in the boat and we'll go over to Bay Point." I would have liked to stay, and maybe add a bit to my fuel pad, but Ernie was right. We weren't getting enough that we couldn't afford to look the country over, and it was less than an hour back across Frederick Sound.

The Pegge was the only other boat when we got over there, and Ernie pulled in close while they exchanged greetings, family news, fish news, and introductions across the water to Fred and Willie McGilton, and myself. Fred had already caught a nice amount of fish that morning and I assumed, correctly, that he must be some kind of a killer-diller. I fished up and down the beach with Ernie and Fred for hours without a bite. Then along in the late afternoon, I noticed a few birds working way up the beach from the spot where we had been turning around. I kept going, got up to them without crashing into a high spot and was rewarded with a nice fish yanking on my gear. Before I got him in I noticed the boat pulling around more than usual and looked over to see the other line pulled way back, and jerking with yanks that I was sure couldn't be a salmon. Maybe I was on bottom again.

I turned the boat out into deeper water, and by the time I had the first fish aboard I was pretty sure that I had a really big salmon on the other line. Without putting the line back out I started cranking this big one up. It was a dandy and after a few minutes of every kind of maneuver a fish might do, he wasn't on the hook anymore. He hadn't held still long enough for me to even think I might get him, and I was remembering Lee saying that it was a good idea to give the big fish a minute or two on the line, letting them cool down a little before starting them up.

I put the lines back out and was sitting there feeling sorry for myself, when I noticed another large fish on the same line. This one was almost as mean and miserable as the one I'd lost, but after awhile he got close enough and I used Lee and Ernie's trick of stunning him with a light tap, using the back of the gaff hook. A good rap across the nose and they laid still so you could gaff them in the cheek, and lift them aboard. Also, stunning them in the water eliminated any commotion on deck, and the bruising and scale loss that went with it.

When I cleaned him he was white. This was common in the fish that went up the Stikine, and the 30 to 40 percent white ratio that Lee had told me of, would prove to be about right. They didn't pay as much for the white kings, but the weight was there and in the next hour I caught three more nice fish, although none like this big white. What I had caught would be the cushion that I had hoped for, and I was very happy with the day.

The meat of the white king is as white as a halibut, and has a completely different flavor than the red kings. They are especially good when baked, barbecued, or boiled. There was a good ratio of them in the Taku, and in the rivers on up in Lynn Canal, as well as in the Stikine. There's also white cohos in some of the Lynn Canal rivers, but not all that many.

That evening I tied alongside Ernie and Fred and iced my fish on the Nira. This would allow me to stay out as long as he did, which was a blessing, as I had no facilities to ice fish for any extended period of time. Before I put the big fish into the hold we weighed him with a little deck scale Ernie had, and it dressed out at 44 pounds. The next day would be slower fishing for me, although Ernie and Fred did fine, and the following day we went back across the Sound, where a thirty pounder broke one of my dandy bamboo poles. I thought I heard a little creaking on one of the bigger fish, and this one, being a real athlete, finished it off. Ernie suggested I go into town and borrow an ax from someone, and go cut a pair of good spruce poles. Lee was there when I got in, and told me about "Pop Frantz" who lived across the narrows from Petersburg. He'd have an ax I could borrow, and could probably point me towards some small spruce up behind his place.

The next morning I went over, and like Lee said, "holler till he comes down to the beach, and he'll row out and get you." He did, and I anchored the boat, and rode in with him. He knew right where we could get some good poles and he'd go along and show me, but first we'd go get a cup of coffee. A couple hours later we headed for the pole patch. Pop's place was one of three or four across the narrows at that time, and he didn't get all that much company, and he liked to gab. He was typical of so many elderly Alaskans I would meet over the years. Always something going on, some new idea or big deal. They only sat in the rocking chair to catch their breath or BS, then up and at em again.

We cut two nice spruce poles, and I took advantage of having an ax handy and peeled them before dragging them out of the woods. Ernie would be along that evening, and anchor in Scow Bay to fish herring. I'd tie along side and rig the poles

49

across his deck. At that time Pop made most of the gaff hooks used in Alaska, and he'd been looking for a skookum young feller to provide the horsepower behind an elaborate bolt cutter he'd rigged up. He fed the long metal rods while I nipped off enough pieces to keep him making gaff hooks all summer. Then back to the coffee pot until I saw Ernie coming down the narrows. A very enjoyable day.

We stayed on the Stikine fish until along in June, and then moved out further into Frederick Sound. The Sound is one of my favorite pieces of water, extending to the Stikine River on the east end, and about eighty miles out to junction with Chatham Straits. Stephens Passage joins it at its northernmost point, it and Chatham Straits being two of the access routes to Juneau. At high water you can run across Dry Strait over to the Wrangell side, but I don't recommend it unless you have some local knowledge, and a boat that doesn't draw much water. In a few years I'd follow Lee across, and once was enough! Wrangell Narrows and Keku Straits join the sound to Sumner Straits, so it's a pretty impressive piece of water. At that time quite a few boats were able to make their seasons there, fishing salmon or halibut. That's not the case anymore.

Ernie told me we were through choking herring for the summer, and from now on it would be spoons and plugs. With a little coaching from Ernie and Lee, I had bought gear in Petersburg, and felt I was pretty well equipped for these feeder kings. Ernie called the spring fish that would go up the mainland Alaskan rivers, spawners. He considered everything else to be a feeder, even the kings that would spawn that fall in the Washington, Oregon, and British Columbia rivers. Most of the kings spawn as four and five year olds, but some live longer, so the term feeder, or blackmouth means different things to different people. Different names or nicknames in different areas and fisheries, but chinook, king, spring, tyee, and blackmouth are all the same salmon. It's interesting that you could catch two kings that wouldn't spawn till the next year, and one might weigh seven pounds and the other might go fifty or more. I always considered anything that would spawn that same year to be a spawner.

We tried several spots without much luck, and finally wound up at one of the bays on the Admiralty Island shore. He didn't like to work around small fish, and if there were very many at all, he'd move from them. Where we were now, suited him just fine. Ernie's thing was catching big kings. Like Lee said, "Ernest would rather catch one fifty pounder than three twentys." He was the best I ever saw at handling big fish.

He had shown me on my chart where to fish and several shallow spots, where not to fish. He taught me to take line ups, using trees, rocks, snags, prominent points of land, anything that I could use to go around shallow spots and fish more effectively. In a few years a fathometer would solve this problem, but it amazed me later, when I tried my old line ups on a few spots, and found that I had fished certain spots closer than I would with the sounder.

Generally I fished shallow, 8 to 12 fathoms, and my favorite spot was in this little channel between two islands. You'd go up into the current holding to one side, and when you turned there was barely enough room to turn around to go back out. On our first day there, I caught four king salmon, the largest two dressing out at fifty and fifty one pounds. One of them was on an eight superior behind a flasher, a combination I probably wouldn't use now. Landing those fish around the Islands and reefs, and up in the channel, took a little planning and sometimes you'd have to turn the boat slowly out, or even around, before you started a fish up. You didn't want to be dragging your gear over a reef while you were concentrating on getting a fish, so it was better to move into a little deeper water to give yourself room.

Ernie had it figured out which tides "fished" in this spot, and we would make it a point to get the slack tide on each end, and when it worked out tide-wise we might work a tide in the morning and again in the evening. That's not to say you couldn't get anything on the off tide but the way the current washed through the channel and around the islands made this particular spot "catch" on the flood. When the tide was ebbing we'd try another couple spots in the bay, or sometimes go ashore, or maybe get a couple hours sleep.

A day that especially sticks in my mind was when Ernie had six fish that dressed over fifty pounds. The two largest ones were 66 and 64. He weighed these two biggest ones before he cleaned them and they weighed 74 and 72 pounds - round. I don't remember what I caught that day, so it must not have been remarkable. He usually wound up with two to four times what I would, and his ability to handle these big fish so successfully, resulted in a larger average.

He pointed out that I needed a running line, instead of snapping the fish onto a long piece of rubber snubber. Already it had cost me a few big fish, and a big welt across a forearm, where I had blocked it from hitting my face, when a leader broke. He used a free running spool that he could lightly brake, allowing a fish to run out as far as it needed, instead of breaking the leader. Then he'd pull it back to the boat, hand over hand. A large fish on deck was a lot better than a broken leader or a hook that had pulled out. Most of the fish we caught there were between 20 and 35 pounds but it was a thrill to get the occasional big one, and being in such a small area, I was able to watch him catch most of what he got. We stayed there that complete trip and most of the next one, before the herring left and we moved on to other spots. In a lifetime of fishing, it's one of the times I think of most.

The next spot we fished was near Security Bay, at the junction of Frederick Sound and Chatham Straits. Same thing here, some really big fish with Ernie catching about 3 to my 1, which didn't bother me at all. In my mind, every day was another perfect one. They had one of the fish traps there, and I did fairly well fishing below it. What usually saved the day was a couple nice big ones to get a little poundage. We weren't getting that many fish, but I do remember him getting 13, one day, that dressed out 505 pounds, all red. That's some pretty nice fish, even if a 20 pounder messed up his average. I won't give my score for that day because I didn't get one. Skunked!

One evening we had anchored in the little harbor on the right side of the bay, and were on the Nira, having dinner. Someone was tapping on the hull, pretty urgent sounding. I was sitting closest to the steps and shot up out of the focsle and looked out the back door. No one there, but the whole harbor was jumping about six inches high, like it would if you could really rev up a tiderip, only lots more activity, or frequency. What we'd heard was the water cavitating against the hull. Ernie said there had to be quite an earthquake to have caused this, but other than the jumpy water in the harbor, there wasn't any big tidal surge, or other indication. The little spot he had anchored in, was so shallow that any quick ebb, prior to a tidal wave, would have sucked the place dry, but nothing of the sort happened. The next morning he listened to the Juneau radio station on his direction finder, and got the story.

The earthquake was either centered at Lituya Bay, or near there, which is about 150 miles from where we were, at Security Bay. Lituya is on the outside coast, across a few mountains and glaciers from Glacier bay. The quake caused a landslide near the back of the bay, on the south side, and when everything but bed rock slid into deep water, it caused a wave that went almost 1700 feet up the hillside across the bay, the largest wave in modern history. When all the trees, topsoil, and loose rock on that hillside washed back down into the bay, it caused an enormous wave to start outward towards the ocean entrance. It didn't go straight out and this is evident by looking at the hillsides where the new growth replaced woods that the wave had stripped away.

Now, years later, we take fresh water at a spot on the south side of the bay, and on the hillside above this place, the area of new growth reaches two to three times higher than in other areas at the edge of the bay. This extends along quite a large area and must have been where the first echo, coming back from the north side, would have hit. Years later I met Sonny, who fished with his dad on the "Edrie." He was eight years old when it happened, and remembers being pretty impressed while the Edrie went up the wave, carried quite aways on it, and then eventually was deposited back in the bay when it receded. He had briefly looked down on trees that had always been way up the hillside. When it was over, most all of the trees that had been on the lower hillsides, were in the bay. As soon as they could, they got out of the bay, and the last I saw of the Edrie it was still fishing.

After spending quite a little time there in later years, and seeing the results of what happened, I can say this is the most fascinating place I've ever seen. Several other boats had been anchored in the outer part of the bay that day. No other boat survived. Some of the people made it. Some didn't. I've often thought of them while laying in the bay, amongst a large fleet of boats.

Lee stopped on his way to town one day and told us the cohos had set in, down at Malmesbury. We ran into town and unloaded that afternoon, got our fuel, ice, groceries and gear and we were headed back out through the sound that evening. We ran till about midnight and were charging again early in the morning, down Chatham Straits. Over the years this became one of my favorite places and I would get to know the area from Petersburg to Cape Decision like the back of my hand.

We didn't throw out the gear till we got down to Harris Cove. Not too much going on, but they'd had a good bite that morning. We called it a day early, intending to be back out at first light. I sold to the packer in Malmesbury that evening, as the plans were for me to stay down in Chatham with the cohos most of the rest of the season. There would always be at least one packer around and they'd have fuel, groceries, and gear and would bring out orders from town, as well as buy your fish. Quite a few of the boats would sell to the packers all season and each packer usually had his following of boats. A lot of these were mom and pop operations, or boats with whole families aboard, but also quite a few people fishing alone, many of them winding up lifetimes of fishing that went back 40, and even over 50 years. Nobody got rich, but each year a good number of people made a major portion of their livelihoods from this one, relatively small, area. I think that's what a natural resource should be about. The incidence of fiddlers (small ones you had to throw back) was close to none and when the silvers hit, usually around the first week in July, they'd average 5 to 6 lbs. dressed, and 8 to almost 10 by September. Alaska has many spots like this, that are a tremendous source of income to people fishing there, not to mention the many jobs the fisheries created in various ports.

I happened to be unloading at the same time as the "Wingfoot" one evening, and met Cal Olds. We would fish together a lot after that, as he usually spent the summer in lower Chatham. It was through him that I met Jack and Ruth, who fished a small double ender called the Elmira B. We would usually all tie together at night, and it was fascinating, listening to Jack tell about the halibut trips in the Gulf of Alaska, and getting into tuna off Vancouver Island. This was when he owned the "Vansee." He was in his sixties when I met him and was the best boat man I ever knew, all hundred or so pounds of him. He had fished all his life, most of it when the electronics, hydraulics and all the other technology we take for granted now, didn't exist. The things I learned from him and some of the other old timers would be constantly used, even after I had acquired some of the modern stuff. Everyone running a boat should be able to do it without all the fancy electronics we take for granted now. It's a way of thinking you need in your background.

We went across to Port Alexander, and fished there at the mouth of the Straits, and around Cape Ommaney, into the ocean. Port Alexander had been one of the best king salmon producing ports in the pre-Columbia River dam days, and it was interesting now, to fish the same grounds where this production had occurred. We did get good silver production, but the first couple times on that side, we didn't do much in the king department.

The herring fleet was laying in Larch Bay, and every so often you'd see one of the boats loaded down, heading into Washington Bay or Little Port Walter. Those first few years I fished Alaska they mostly worked the lower Chatham Straits area, and Larch Bay. As they wiped those areas out, or at least to a point that the production wouldn't justify the effort, they moved down to Warren Island, or sometimes up into Frederick Sound. That particular fishery soon came to an end, and I suspect economics was the big reason. It didn't take them long to thin out the amount of herring in those areas.

When the fishing slowed down, we moved back across Chatham Straits to the Kuiu Island shore, and I spent most of the rest of the season between Table Bay and Pillar Bay. There would always be two or three packers in the area, and you never had to run very far to unload at night. Cal and Jack and the Piatt family and myself would usually be in the same area, and if the weather was bad there would be pinochle games, or beach combing, or maybe trout fishing, and a picnic on deck, afterwards. In most of the bays, a couple crab pots in shallow water would provide more than enough crab to go around. There was lots of visiting on the packers, or aboard the boats, during the harbor days, and that first year I met friends I would have from then on, which would be one of the best parts of the season.

In the earlier part of the century there was quite a little population outside the main towns. Much of this was in outlying canneries, and the various herring processing facilities that don't exist now, and also in hundreds of fox farms, spread all over Southeast Alaska. I'm not sure if they existed further north and west but later on we did see fox on Sanak Island, and I doubt that they swam out there. On many of the smaller Islands, remains of these old fox farms still existed, and it was always interesting to go ashore and look around. If we weren't looking over some old reduction plant or cannery, there was always a whaling station, these fox farms, or an old Indian village site to look at. There were also places where some trapper, fisherman, or maybe just some guy craving some solitude had carved his niche along the edge of some harbor. I always enjoyed the time ashore, no matter what the mission of the day happened to be. Now I wish I'd spent more time on the beach.

One highlight that year was along in September in one of the bays. I was fishing mainly for silvers but there were also a few kings, and this was what I thought I was bringing up to the boat one afternoon. A little closer and I could see it was a big silver, much bigger than what I was used to seeing. When we weighed him that evening he dressed out at 19 ½ lbs. Years later I got another in Sitka Sound exactly the same weight. I never did break 20 lbs. dressed, on silvers. Lee had one, fishing down at Coronation Island, that dressed 25 pounds and that's the biggest I've heard of, from anyone I've known.

I didn't see Ernie again till I got home. On his way to town with that coho trip, he had sampled a spot in Frederick Sound, and had done well on king salmon. When they came back out, they fished two more nice trips there, and headed south. He had a certain dollar amount that satisfied him for a season, and when he reached that amount, he headed home to Sequim Bay. This was an attitude that is scarce now. I fished on through early September, but when the fall storms started being a little closer together, and quite a bit harsher, I decided to call it a season. Tommy Thompson offered to put the Judy up in the cold storage loft, which really helped my cause. I sure wasn't looking forward to the ride home in that little boat, and then to have to turn around and bring it north again in the spring.

So that ended my first season in Alaska. A ride to Ketchikan on the Ellis Airlines float plane, another short shuttle flight across to Annette Island, and my first ride on the big jet, down to Seattle. 1958 was a great year!

# Chapter 5
# Ray Lee

When I was in school they used to have the National School Assembly Program, which was a once a month show, put on for the entire student body. Most of the time there were musical programs; sometimes a concert by some college in the state, or some other group, but there were also some great programs by only one or two people. I can remember a violinist, some great vocalists, and an archery program where a guy shot an apple off his partners head. (he used a hollow arrow with a wire running through it.)

The program I remember best was an old sea captain, who fascinated at least one person in the audience with a few stories about boats and the sea, and then a section on various gear and equipment that he had used. One of the items was a small sea anchor. They were used to hold a small boat into the sea while drifting, turning what could be miserable conditions into better, or pretty darned nice. When all other means of propulsion were lost, one could also be used to move forward by throwing it ahead of the boat and pulling the boat to it. Preferably with not too big of a boat.

The second year I fished in Alaska, I went out to Gedney Harbor and helped the packer owners set up the fish scow for operation. The wind and poor holding ground in Gedney makes it a poor storm anchorage, so along with anchors on the scow, there were shorelines to trees, and more shorelines to deadmen, buried deep in the sand. A deadman is a good sized piece of wood, say eight feet long and a foot or more thick, that your cable from the scow is attached to in the middle, and with the log buried down four or five feet, and a trench dug out aways for the cable to lay in, your scow should be pretty secure. Anyway, this one never budged. In a few days they were ready for the fishermen.

All they had was me with my two hand troll lines. I set out the next morning into Chatham Straits, threw out my gear, and was ready to do battle. It had looked good when we came down a few days earlier, and now there was quite a little bird life and the occasional herring flipping. I had fished down past the entrance to Explorer Basin and was towards the bottom end of Windfall Islands when I got my first bite. I let him work on the pole for a bit, hoping maybe for another, and when he finally tired I brought him up and captured my first king of the year, a little under thirty pounds. It looked better the further down I went, lots more birds and sometimes the herring were so thick that they'd chatter my lines as I moved through them. Before too long I got another, about the same size as the first one and had barely put my line back out when the engine died. No missing, no nothing—not even a sputter.

Hopefully, I pushed the starter. Nothing. I went out and started cranking up my two lines and once they were aboard, went back inside and tried cranking the engine by hand. Still nothing. A little investigating showed the problem to be that I had nothing in the battery. When we came out, I had tied a line on the scow, and we towed the Judy down behind it. Apparently the battery had lost a little ground during the winter, and without the run out from town to charge it up, my morning of trolling took it down to nothing. The little generator didn't cut in till 650 turns, and the less than that trolling speed, was a withdrawl, rather than a deposit. I waited awhile, thinking that the battery might recoup enough that I could still get started with the crank, but no dice.

The tide had changed, and a light southeast breeze had picked up, maybe fifteen or so. The tide would still offset the wind, so I figured I would be moving slowly back up towards Gedney. This wouldn't be so bad if I had been in closer, but where I fished the flats at Tebenkoff, I was two or three miles from the closest protection at Troller Islands. The wind picked up a bit more, and I began wondering if I might have a fair sized problem in the making. At that time, it had only been two or three years since that old fellow had came to the school, and the memory of his talk on the sea anchor was still fresh in my mind. I didn't have a sea anchor, but I did have a square pan that I kept my flashers and spoons in. I punched four holes in the sides, and attached a two foot wire from each side, up to a shackle that had attached the anchor chain to the main anchor line. The Judy, being only nineteen feet long, didn't need real heavy anchor gear and this light anchor line was something I'd be able to throw pretty well.

Now the wind was around twenty southeast, which is no big deal unless you have a big rig like I was on. Also, with the wind and tidal current colliding, the chop department was getting a little sharper. Not a boat in sight, and definitely not a lot of traffic in the neighborhood, at this time of year. It looked like I needed to try out the sea anchor business, the sooner the better.

The boat was laying sideways to the chop, and the bow was aimed out into the straits. The first thing would be to try to get it turned around, and this turned out to be harder than I'd expected. I had tied myself to the bow cleat, and was sitting straddling the bow, a leg over each side, and when I threw the pan out, and tripped it to where it was holding, I'd get the bow around, almost to the point of falling off the other way, heading inshore. Then when I went to throw ahead again, the boat would fall off and I'd lose what I'd gained before I could pull it on around.

After a few seconds I was drenched, and after several more lost tries, I was developing a poor frame of mind. Finally, I shortened the throws by half, and tried to get the pan back out quicker. The bow came around, and I was headed inshore. I had taken off gloves I was wearing, and that helped a lot, too. The pan sailed well, and with a little practice, I was getting it out to the end of the line, around forty feet, and as I was pulling I could see that the boat was moving through the water quite well—considering.

The sea conditions seemed to be about holding their own, but it bothered me that a certain amount of water was splashing into the boat. I'd have to untie myself now and then, and go back and pump out. I didn't like time spent away from my progress, but I couldn't let the boat get too heavy, as it would make it more likely that I would take some serious water into the boat, and I didn't need that. I worked steadily for awhile, and then untied myself, and went back to see how much water I'd taken. Too much. I'd have to cut the pan pulling time in half, and this bothered me. It wouldn't have seemed quite as bad if, there had been a few boats around, because someone would eventually come by, but it looked like I was my own answer at this point.

I tried hand cranking the machine several more times but no go. The battery must have really been dead, to have not kicked it off when the machine was still warm. When the machine stopped, I was pretty much down towards Point Ellis, so now I let the boat stay in the trough, which was where it wanted to be anyway, and let my part of the progress take me straight inshore. The tide would move me back up the straits, hopefully not too far. I had pulled for about half an hour, and it seemed like I was in a bit closer, still nicely below Windfall Islands, but still quite a way out in the Straits. I wished I'd been fishing in closer, where someone with a boat the size of "Judy" should have been in the first place.

My hands were getting sore, so I tried the gloves again, and found it awkward. I tried just one, which was faster, but before long I had both of them on again. Ruining my hands wouldn't help anything, and it looked like I would be doing this for hours. To accomplish anything, you had to keep up a good steady pace, trying not to lose the boat's momentum between pulls. I was twenty at that time, and in pretty good shape, but I knew there would be a limit, as to how long I could keep up at this rate.

The folks at the scow would be looking tomorrow, as I'd told them I would definitely be back in that evening, but I also knew that Bob was used to me staying out late last year, and wouldn't be surprised if I came in right at dark. If I could work my way in behind the Islands in Tebenkof, there would be all kinds of protection from weather, as there were lots of Islands, and some fair spots to anchor. I could either stay put, and wait for someone to come along, or work my way up through the Islands to Explorer Basin, and from there, back out into the straits, and a short jump on up to Gedney, maybe on a little nicer day. Lots of big ideas.

As the afternoon went by, the distance from Windfall Islands definitely became shorter, partly because the tide had moved me back up that way, and also, because I was definitely gaining ground with the new power unit. I had stopped several more times, and hadn't had as much water to pump out as there was the first time, so I felt better about that. My hands though, were another matter, even with the gloves on.

Hours later, I was in to where I could see that it had all been worthwhile, and that barring some other jackpot, I should be able to make it. Another quarter mile and I would be getting some lee from the islands. Windfall Island was the furthest into the straits, and it would have been nice to have came in just below it, but nothing I could do about that. It would still break down the chop.

There was an area ahead that was always more prone to tide rips, and once through that I should be fine. The boat did a lot more jumping and wallering, while moving through the rips, and I wasn't fortunate enough to get through it before having to go back to pump. I had taken enough water in the boat that I used the deck bucket to bail with, instead of the bilge pump. I could see that this could get a lot worse quick, so I took both gloves off now, and when I started pulling and throwing again, this new awareness lent a little to the speed department.

For the second time since I'd owned the boat, my arms had swelled to the point that they had that dead, sort of numb feeling. Slightly damp too. One way or the other, I was drenched.

Before long, I was through the tide rips, and it was a lot better going—even starting to realize a little lee from the Island. The wind seemed like it had gone down a bit too, but now I had thought of something else to worry about. The tide would change sometime soon, and I definitely needed to be in there somewhere, before it changed. Losing everything I'd gained didn't much appeal to me. I really went for it now, long hard pulls, leaning into the line tying me to the cleat, and every throw with the pan fairly sizzled. I was just getting well into the lee of Windfall Islands when I heard kind of a rumble and looked over my shoulder to see the "Curlew", a halibut boat from Petersburg, coming up behind me. The skipper, Andy Wikan, looks down from the bridge and says "man, what in the hell are you doing?"

For a small town, there probably isn't a more squared away fleet in the world, than the Petersburg halibut boats, so this wasn't exactly a high point for me, but I didn't refuse a tow in behind the islands. He told me to put the machine in neutral, and leave the switch on, and he'd see if he could tow me fast enough to turn the prop over when I threw it in gear. It didn't work.. The prop was too small, and the machine too new. After they'd anchored they packed over one of their batteries, a big 8-D, and before long I was running at charging speed alongside the Curlew. Dinner was boiled halibut, and I forget what else, but nothing was ever so good. If you're not hungry at meal time, an executive position on a halibut boat might be a good idea for you. But I managed to hold my own. They had some stuff for my hands, too, and soon I was in my bunk, probably dreaming of installing a trolling generator, or something. After running at charging speed till daylight, the battery would be in fine shape.

The next morning they filled my cup with coffee, and I headed out through Explorer Basin, on my way back up to Gedney Harbor. I rode in to Petersburg on the Chacon with Bob, and while we were in town I bought an extra battery and a generator that I could set up to charge at the slow trolling speed. It would be over five weeks before my hands got back to normal.

So, I guess I lucked out of that one. I did the only thing I could think of at the time, and was able to move the boat to a point that I was pretty much out of it, but suppose it had been just a little worse for weather. You go with what experience you have at the time and I certainly didn't have much. Listening to that old fellow

61

at the school assembly probably saved my bacon that day, and there's nothing like going through what I endured that afternoon, to make you more attentive while listening to other peoples experiences, and how they coped with them. You never know when some little thing might apply to your situation.

Bear with me while I get out of sequence, and move ahead to look at something else. It's 1967 and Trish and I had just been married in March. We had the "Camelot" pretty well ready to go, and left for Alaska within a few weeks, running up with Bill and Nada Small on the "Seacrest." After that, she always claimed they'd went on our honeymoon with us. This was my eighth trip north, but the Smalls had been up and down over thirty some years, and running with them, you were always picking up something, maybe a new harbor, or a different route down some back channel. Maybe just a good, common sense, suggestion on how to run a boat.

I remember running up with them a few years earlier, and mentioned the river that was pouring in at the other end of this harbor. Nada said it looked to her like it might go dry in an hour or so. Sure enough. They'd apparently used the harbor quite a few times, and she was right. What I'd thought was a river turned out to be some salt water rapids. Then the next morning I saw my first U.S.O.? When I started telling them about it that night I said "I don't know if

*Nada gives Bill a haircut*

you guys are going to believe this or not" and about five words into my description, "saw a elephant seal, huh?" She was always way ahead of you.

Back to wherever I was, now we were in Alaska and after we went through Snow Pass, they turned right, heading for Petersburg, and we went on out Sumner Straits, trying a few spots here and there, but not getting much of anything. Chatham Straits was the same and we just kept on going, sometimes trying four or five spots in a day with only a few fish per spot at best. We hit the hot tubs at Warm Springs, and went ashore at Pavlof Harbor.

The third member of our crew was Tiny, a little "mutt" that Trish had belonged to since she was nine years old. Tiny was the happiest critter in the country when we went ashore, and that afternoon we took her up a short piece of river to a good sized lake, and by the time we got back to the skiff, she was one of the tiredest critters in the country. In good company. We poked our way on up to Icy Straits, and into Juneau, still not much fish, but aside from a lot of water over the bow in Chatham Straits and Lynn Canal, it was a pretty nice trip.

A week or so later we had drifted back out and were at Elfin Cove, just through the two Inian Passes that join Icy Straits to Cross Sound. The next day we joined the folks on the Coronation, and went around Cape Spencer to try the bays on up towards Icy Point. The same deal here, only a few fish at best, although the beach combing wasn't too bad. We decided to go down the beach below Cross Sound, and try around Deer Harbor. Before we got down to Cape Spencer two flocks of trumpeter swans flew by, the first ones I'd ever seen while trolling. They were pretty few and far between then, and it would be another fifteen years before I saw another while on the boat, this time just one swan on the water, paddling around with a bunch of seagulls and fish ducks. Probably quite a story there. Along those lines, your library should have "Crusoe of Lonesome Lake," by Leland Stowe. Quite a story there too.

This area just below Cross Sound was a spot I hadn't fished before, so after an afternoon of nothing, Van called and said get my gear aboard if I wanted to follow them in to anchor. Deer Harbor was a fine anchorage, once inside, but you had to wait for the tide before going in. Van was waiting for us out in front of the harbor, and when we got close he started in, but went only a short way before going out on deck, and scooping something aboard with his dip net. Then they moved ahead, and scooped something else up. I wondered, but didn't think too much about it until we got in further, and started seeing what looked like a piece or two of boat, in the rocks. A little further in and there it was, spread over a little area in the rocks, and pretty well demolished. We went on in, and while Van was anchoring, some guy came down on the beach. I went in with the skiff, and brought him out to the boat, and we listened to quite a story over dinner.

He'd been in there lots of times before, but this time the weather was good, not much surge, and he thought he could push the tide a little. He soon found out that he couldn't, and was high centered part way in. Then the surge picked up a bit, not much, but enough to give the "Lox" a few good bounces on the rock bottom. At that point he started getting things together for a quick departure in the skiff. The skiff left without him. He didn't know exactly what happened but apparently in the confusion and excitement of the moment the line came loose from whatever he'd tied to, or maybe not tied to.

Many years earlier, he had lost another boat on some south seas Island, and had used the wreckage from that boat to build a raft that he sailed to another Island, this one inhabited. From there he eventually got out. This was on his mind now and the channel into the harbor being quite narrow, he threw things like a hammer, handsaw, pry-bar, and a bag of nails at the beach, with the hope that he might be able to retrieve them later, at low tide. Then he put some extra clothes and canned food in a bag, and made the short trip to the beach. He set up camp in the harbor next to an old scow that was on the beach, and a good fire and some hot food later, began planning his way in to Pelican.

There was a cold storage worker strike in Pelican at the time, and he knew that the chances of any boats coming into Deer Harbor were pretty skinny, so he intended to build a raft, and when the weather permitted, sail, paddle, whatever, down to South Lisianski, and let a flood tide take him on up to the junction with Lisianski Inlet. From there he should see the odd boat, and if not, the tide could take him on into Pelican. The next morning he walked the beach at low tide, and retrieved the saw and bag of nails, but the hammer was another matter. It threw a lot better than the other stuff, and he thought it might have went into some trees. Either that, or down a gap between some rocks.

The weather had picked up a bit from the west, and the boat was gradually moved up into the rocks as it came apart. The next day he intended to start salvaging raft material. We came along that next evening. He declined our offer to stay aboard, so I took him back to his camp, armed with cookies and a quart of home canned peaches, in case he developed a sweet tooth in the night.

I got up early the next morning, and rowed around the shore, inside Deer Harbor. I found his skiff in a little niche in the rocks. The tide must have carried

*Ray Lee upper left—"Lox"—Van Vanderpool on right*

it in, and a breeze moved it in to a spot it didn't get out of. It hadn't been visible from where we anchored or from his camp on the beach. I brought him out from the beach, and after breakfast we took all three skiffs in and set about salvaging everything we could. This was no small deal as he had a spare or two of everything, including an extra main and intermediate shaft with bearings, two spare anchors and gear, two extra banks of gurdies, and enough stuff for rigging to have set up at least one more boat. Plus enough other stuff to deck load both the Coronation and Camelot. Nothing like being prepared. Most of the heavier stuff was right at the spot where the hull had wound up, but there were other things that floated up and down the shoreline, that Trish gathered up. One of the things that Van had scooped up was a satchel of pictures he had taken in the south seas, which meant a great deal to him.

A long, long day later, we were loaded, everything except the machine, and what was left of the hull. The next morning we took him up to Elfin Cove and unloaded his equipment on the dock and his other boat, a tri-maran. On the way up, he gave Trish a little bongo drum that he'd gotten while in the South Seas, and now it's a good reminder of an interesting time, and a delightful man. It was experiences from his past that guided what he did, and what he surely would have succeeded in doing, if we hadn't come along.

Here's another one that I don't think past experience had too much to do with, but desperation and a good dose of imagination may have helped. I never met this guy, but several of the old timers told me about it. He had anchored in some bay, I think somewhere in the northern Clarence Strait to Myerschuck, to Zimovia Straits, neighborhood. I don't know what he was doing, but it was in the winter, so I suppose either trapping, or fishing winter kings. When he went to leave the following morning, he didn't. The clutch engaged, the shaft went around, but the boat didn't move. He had lost his prop. So he re-anchored, and sat there, thinking what to do.

Not much boat traffic at that time of the year, and this was back when there were no radios on the boats. Being there in a boat that was helpless didn't much appeal to him, so finally he figured a way out. A trip to the beach and some looking around provided him with a suitable piece of drift wood, and once back to the boat he went to work. He made another prop, probably a two fluker, slash grained, with not too much pitch and I suppose a little extra thick. I don't know what kind of an engine he had but if it was one of the old stampmills, maybe even with some kind of a reduction gear, turning the shaft at a slow speed shouldn't have been a problem. At slow speed it would probably stand up fine, and once the boat was under way he could move along, especially with the tide. Using his skiff, he maneuvered the boat in to a sandy spot on the beach, and when the tide went out, attached the new prop to the shaft. I don't know how he held it there, because he must have lost the nut with the real prop, but maybe the shaft was bored through to allow a drift pin through the old nut? Then he could have wired it on. Whatever, this was how Wooden Wheel Pete made it back in.

Years later, the steering went out on our last boat when we were heading in to Neah bay, still about 5 miles out. The cure would be another truck steering gear, at the end of a shaft in the trolling pit, but in the meantime, we needed to get to the dock. Rather than taking time to rig up some kind of a tiller, we tied pants and shirts in a clump, above the lead on a trolling line on one side, and a small bucket on a line on the "heavy" side, opposite the side the boat liked to turn to. In no time we were under way. By using the gurdies we could vary the distance out on the poles, and by working each side, against the other, we could steer the boat. Nothing fancy, just something to correct the course by letting out or bringing in the lines to create a slight pull, and after awhile we were in Neah Bay, where Joe Gowdy came alongside, and deposited us next to the dock. If a guy had a long way to go, he could rig up something a little more elaborate and enduring, and move himself along quite easily. In our case, trolling poles made it nice to pull from, but a short boom, or your imagination——who knows? A tiller bar, built to fit over your rudder shaft, might be a worthwhile winter project, and can come in quite handy when the occasion presents itself. The pitch in the prop turns many boats one way or the other, and a lot of them will move along quite nicely with only a small amount of pull on the "heavy" side, but whatever the cure, it's nice to have it thought through ahead of time, and the necessary stuff, ready.

My boys fished with me on a few short trips, until they were ten and twelve years old, after which, they were my full time crew, when they weren't in school. This always worried me, as to what they'd do if something went wrong, with me, or the boat, so I made sure they new how to use the radios, loran, and everything else they needed to move the boat. They had their own survival suits, and knew how to use them, and once in awhile, at some choice spot, I'd say "Okay, the boat is going down, I'm not here, there's no other boats around. What are you going to do? What if you didn't have a radio?" I tried to select these choice spots where trouble "occurred" to make them think about where they were and what would be their best option to get back, or maybe just get to some spot with more boat traffic, where they might build a fire on the beach and catch someones attention. "What are you going to take with you?" My thoughts were, that at least they'd have thought about it before, and that at a time when they might need to be in a hurry, they could make some better choices. Chris fished winter kings with me for two years, and when we were in some area I tried to make sure he was aware of the few spots where someone lived, and there were darned few trappers shacks and old cannery sites that he wasn't aware of. Happily, they never needed this way of thinking, but it was there, just in case.

Most people that wind up fishing in Alaska have a pretty fair understanding of their boat, and its equipment, but one thing a lot of them come up short on is the need for overkill on anchor gear. I would have qualified as one of these people during the first years we had the Elusive. There's no month of the year that can't treat you to 70 mile an hour winds, and August through May can provide much, more. There's no good reason not to have major overkill in anchor gear.

With the S.C. Hall or the Camelot, and not fishing real early or late in the season, I got by with a 100 pound anchor and 100 feet of three eights chain, plus backing. This was fine, unless I happened to anchor on some exceptionally poor holding ground. That's mostly what Southeast Alaska has, sort of a talcum powder silt, that given enough wind, your hook will plow quite easily. You have to learn the good spots. There aren't very many good storm anchorages in the bays, but you can look around when it's blowing, and sometimes find a real gem in the lee of something that you might not have thought about while looking at a chart. Some of these spots have allowed me many hours of much needed rest. Not knowing some of these spots has put a few boats on the beach.

If I can skip ahead once more, here's a "less than adequate anchor," story. In 1979, Ken Singhose and I had left Port Angeles on the Elusive, after selling a trip there, and spending a day at our homes. My intentions were to go out the straits, and down the beach to Pt. Grenville. We got outside Tatoosh Island about midnight, stiff southeast wind, and a lot of water over the bow. We turn around and in about an hour we are anchored in Neah Bay with at least 50 other boats. Strong winds here too, and we are watching to see that our hook has held, when Ken notices a mast light moving down through the fleet. Against the lights from shore, we can see that it is a big boat, probably a dragger, (trawler) and we watch in amazement as it drifts through the fleet, missing one boat after another. His anchor never does catch again, and unbelievably, he never touches a boat as he moves sideways through the fleet. One guy blows his horn as he goes by, then shines his spotlight in his windows—no response. In a short time he has drifted through all the boats, and is on his way to shallow grounds, kelp, and rocks.

We have a 12 foot aluminum skiff on the bridge, and in a few minutes it's in the water, and I'm rowing full bore, downwind. Lots of adrenalin flowing and about a hundred feet below the Elusive, I break an oar. This happens when your brain isn't engaged. Ken yells, "now what are you gonna do?"

"Keep going." I didn't think I could get back against the wind. So now I had some problems of my own. We had anchored towards the bottom of the fleet, pretty much out of line of the boats immediately above us, and with Ken aboard things were in good hands. We sure didn't need any more screw ups on my part! I got up towards the bow, and using the one oar like a paddle, aimed at the dragger which was already getting into the kelp. In a few minutes I started yelling my head off, and when I've got pretty well up to them, a guy runs out on deck, then back inside, and their machine starts up. Soon a couple guys are pulling their anchor, and another comes on the back deck, takes my line, and hands me another that I can pull myself aboard with. The skipper has started idling the boat into the wind, and just in time. Using their VHF radio I call Ken and tell him I'm aboard, and that they will drop me off, just upwind of the Elusive. I ask him to blink the mast light a few times so we can see where he is. The skipper wishes me no bad luck, but hopes he's around if it happens. They drop me off, and in a few minutes I'm back aboard the Elusive. I think they went in and tied to the dock. Lucky all around that time, but it doesn't always work out that way.

Another source of trouble is people looking at a chart, or Captain Handy Dandy's book on how to get around the country, and seeing an anchor in some nice enclosed bay, they assume that this must be some tried and true storm anchorage. It might not be. When you look at the hillsides around this haven, and see all the trees on the ridges around you mowed down from the southeast, it might be best to watch where you anchor. Sometimes in addition to anchoring, a long line to the beach, tied around a tree, will make all the difference in one of the really hard blows.

I was talking to Fred Grant, who runs the "St. Lazaria," a big packer out of Sitka, and up to that point they had never drug their 500 pound anchor. Overkill?—No, Just right! The biggest improvement I made in the anchor gear on the "Elusive" was going from half inch chain to three quarter, with a chunk of boom chain from the anchor to the winch. Also, if I had it to do over again, I'd have welded a few inches of width and depth to the flukes.

Not having a good set of charts has put a lot of peoples tails in cracks. Too many people have talked themselves out of spending money on charts that may have made all the difference in their world. Getting from Blackfish Sound or Pine Island across Queen Charlotte and up into Fitzhugh Sound is easy in good weather. If the conditions change, that great unknown in on the beach becomes some very welcome anchorages when you've got a good, detailed, chart collection. Then, when you get the charts, learn how to use them. Know how the tides and ocean currents affect each area that you're in, and you'll save a lot of money on fuel, get there quicker, safer, and maybe catch more fish.

The fish part would be another book. If you know what the weather's going to be, it might make a big difference as to what you do, or when you get where. When there's a big lump running and its blowing hard westerly, its not as much fun going by Cape Caution on the ebb. Especially if you're heading north.

Let's look at those same conditions well offshore. More than a few people have got into trouble running too hard to get to a harbor. It's probably a good choice if you think you can get there in one piece, and that might mean slowing down to do it. If going over a bar is a consideration, getting there on the flood obviously makes more sense than on the ebb. If you're worried about any portion of getting in safely, staying out might be the best option. Just don't get excited, and try to get in when the conditions aren't, or won't be good. You might be better off jogging into it, running slowly before it, or just shutting down and drifting, than running towards shangri-la, in a high steep trough. You'll be amazed at what some boats can drift comfortably in. This is with work boats in mind, their hatches tied down, and everything secured before———.

Eddie Grotting and I were fishing tuna quite a ways out from, and above Vancouver Island when a fairly strong southeaster came along. Some of the guys were talking about heading in, either down the inside, or into Winter Harbor on the outside coast. Some of the south seas boats were there, with the weather chart machines, and suggested that they might be better off staying out, as the main blast would be more inshore. Wind and ocean current were going the same way, so we stayed out, ran a line back to the trolling pit, and fished through the southeaster, mostly just riding along on top of a very large swell with a moderate chop. I don't think the wind ever got over 35, mostly less. Some of the guys that went in did a little damage to their boats, poles lost, and other stuff. No loss of boats.

About the middle of the second day the wind changed to northwest, against the swell. Before long, all fishing stopped, the swell coming down but replaced by a high, stiff slop that we couldn't begin to make jig speed in. Everybody shut down and was drifting. The wind kept building and during the night, one hit awfully hard, coming down the starboard side from the stern, even onto the bridge. Eddie was coming up into the wheelhouse just as I got there, "Captain, lets get the hell out of here!" A few seconds later we are idling before it, Ed watching through the back window, and I stayed at the wheel for hours. By mid afternoon we are in light wind conditions. So going in seemed like a poor option, fishing and drifting worked till it didn't, and idling before it was just dandy. We had a parachute aboard, and that would have made for a good drift if we'd wanted to stay, but the area's reputation for September weather made leaving sound better.

When traveling in Alaska or British Columbia, I always liked to use the back eddies when I happened to be bucking the tide. I'd go along with one hand on the beach, and in some spots, would move along at a much better speed, than if I were out in the main channel, grinding into the current. You have to know the various high spots and I'm happy to say that I never met any of them first hand, but I do know a few folks that did. One acquaintance of mine "bumped' while scraping the edge in Grenville Channel, and that evening, backed into a rock while anchoring at Lewis Island. He was poor company when he got to Ketchikan. Most of the spots you might hit are marked, if you look closely enough at the chart, and closely enough might mean wearing your reading glasses. Then again, they're not all marked, especially if your charts are pretty old.

By looking at the hillside that you are running along, you can usually get an idea of what will follow on down into the water. But not always. One big disadvantage that I often wondered about, was just suppose something went wrong while I was in there, making faces at the bears. You would naturally turn out at a moments notice, but this wouldn't give you much room if there was even a slight breeze blowing. With any wind at all, I always figured, drop the hook, and tend to the problem. Without any wind, your chances of hitting the beach while in some channel, are pretty skinny. Anyway, that's what I did for years. I had a couple good teachers, and practiced, and fine tuned until I was pretty comfortable with it. It cut the running time down a lot, and made for a more interesting trip. You see a lot more on the beach, too. But this "sure isn't" a suggestion that anyone else do it.

The Mink Trail is a path of water that the boats use in poor weather to move between Icy Point, and on up past Cape Fairweather. Once in it, the sea conditions can change from grim, in the area outside it, to pretty acceptable once inside that magic line. It can provide a much nicer ride for six, or more hours of running, moving along that area of beach. The color of the surface water will change to a turquoise or maybe a muddy color, depending on the weather and conditions at the glaciers at the time. The width of the trail might vary from 100 yards to half a mile. I've never used it much on the Alsek side of the Cape. I don't know how much farther uphill it could be used.

Since I'm in the neighborhood I'll mention this but I'm not completely sure about it. We were going up to Yakutat in some poor weather, and directly in front of the Alsek we noticed a series of 3 or 4 breakers, over what might have been a hundred or more yards wide. We weren't in that close, and I couldn't see anything on the chart that might have caused this. The depth we were in, pretty much agreed with our loran position, but its not impossible that I might have been getting a little distortion, being in that close. What really threw me, is there was quite a long stretch of water between these breakers, and the river entrance, that wasn't breaking.

We were nicely offshore, and it wouldn't have been unlikely, to have been in enough closer to have run through, or even inside that area. Wouldn't that have been something to have ran into in the dark? Like I said, it was directly in front of the river entrance and the amount of non breaking water inside it intrigued me. After that, whenever I came through there in the dark, I was well outside the spot. The river mouth, this spot where it was breaking, and the canyon outside the Alsek, are all in a line up, but I can't see where the canyon is close enough to affect anything, and I don't think it's likely that any current coming over the inside banks, north or south, would have caused it to break there. Who knows????

Here's something I thought about since. This was probably at the spot where the shallower beach shelf and the deeper water at the edge of the canyon meet. Maybe combined with a strong ebb and miserable weather? If anyone should have thought of this the first time through, it should have been me. Whatever, it's still a spot to keep in mind. I'll tell you of some other of these spots, or alternative routes, in other chapters. Being aware of them can sometimes make a world of difference.

You can't beat being prepared. A clean bilge that might otherwise plug a pump, an extra good fuel filtration system, a well maintained collection of spare parts, plenty of fresh water and supplies including a good emergency kit, and having a good chart collection and a tidal current table and knowing how to use them, only makes sense. Having a well thought out travel plan, and some alternatives is a lot better than -what now? This doesn't touch on all the mandatory safety equipment, or stuff that just makes good sense to have together, ready to grab, and leave the boat with in an instant. Have you got spares for this or that? Belts - hoses? How about spares for your spares? A few sections of good inner-tube, cut in strips and rolled up, rolls of soft monel wire, lots of electrical tape, and a few spools of this braided nylon or poly cord makes a dandy band aid kit for hoses, belts, and lots of other stuff. Maybe you'd ought to read this paragraph over?

Successfully operated boats have one common denominator, and that's the guys running them. That's not to say that some tremendous boatmen haven't ran into trouble, because sometimes the cards get stacked too high to deal with, but still, that boat that operates year after year, successfully, was in pretty good hands. After awhile "the feel" people get for their boat, like how to load it or handle it in tough weather, or when to back off, and then dealing with all it's other little quirks, mean the difference in a good operation, or not.

When you really come up against it, some of the best help you will have is yourself, and how you've prepared ahead of time, before the problem happens. Be ready. If you're out there long enough you'll likely get your turn. Not being able to fish tomorrow, needs to be for some good reasons.

# Chapter 6
# Rickie's Fish

Anyone who has spent much time fishing steelhead will have a few special memories, and this one will always be on my mind. It was a crisp, sunny fall day, with all the color that time of the year brings to the foliage, and I had the river to myself. The season for steelhead wasn't due to open for several more weeks. I was at a spot just below where Coleen had lived and the river was just right, up a little, with the rusty color that often comes with the rains in the fall. I'd caught a couple nice, bright, steelhead, and had released a few red sided silvers. They liked to take the fresh eggs I was using for steelhead, but I guess they'd have hit at anything I used. The river was full of them.

The last spot I was going to fish was a long drift that deepened just before going into a short riffle and into the next hole. High water had left a small log jam on my side of the river, most of it on the bank out of the water. I didn't have a casting reel yet, so I was still stripping the line off by hand, and swinging the bait out with the tip of the pole. I'd only made a couple casts, and was lifting the bait out for another, when a fish followed up behind the bait. He hadn't touched it, and I hoped he'd try again. It looked like a big fish, what little glimpse of him I'd had.

A few casts later the line hesitated as it drifted downstream, and I set the hook, and although I couldn't see him at first, I could tell it was a nice fish. He charged around in the hole for a bit, then almost down to the riffle, across to the other side, and then full bore upstream. I held the pole out over the river with one hand and using the other, climbed up on the jam. Once there, I was able to pressure him until he finally turned around. He'd made it about fifty feet up some faster water, above this spot, after all the running around up through the lower part of the hole, and that takes a pretty strong fish. I finally got him down in the main part of the hole, and was able to climb down from the jam, but then he decided to charge back upstream, so I'm back on the jam again. He didn't go as far this time, and before long I had him back down where he belonged.

He was getting tired now, and I was thinking about landing him. I had a perfect spot, with a gradual sand beach, just downstream from the log jam. I had seen him several times by now, and he was a dandy, a buck, eighteen pounds or so, and beautifully speckled, the way the bucks usually are. A few more short runs, and I was easing him in to where sand and belly met. I eased my foot alongside, to push him a bit further up the beach, and when I went to shove him I lost my balance. A second later I was laying on my side in about ten inches of water, between him and the river. I still had him though, as he had to go right by my hands, the way he was aimed, and that would put him almost on the bank. He turned around, and went past my feet. He wasn't on the hook anymore, either.

That evening I was visiting friends I had worked for while in high school, and was telling them my tale of woe. My lower lip had receded a bit, and I could laugh about it now too. Sort of. Their oldest boy, Rickie, was about seven years old, and about then was all eyes, ears and freckles. I really had his attention. I could see it coming, "you going tomorrow Vince? Can I go?"

When I was working for his folks, Morrie and I had had a few discussions about my one man field trips to the river, during school time, but he and Pauline talked it over, and at daylight the next morning, Rick and I headed for the river, across from their place. This is about two miles down stream from where I'd fished the day before. We went through Alfred's field, then some woods, across another field, and then down a trail through more brush and trees, to the river bank. You didn't have to wait for Rick. He'd run ahead, then run back and jabber, then run ahead again. "Do you think we'll catch any, Vince? What if they're all upstream? If you hook a big one, can I land it?" Then he'd tell me about some other time, when we'd went fishing. It was another perfect, crisp fall day, with a million maple leaves to run through, lots of fish in the river, and today he wouldn't go to school. Rickie was a happy, young feller!

We fished upstream, which is my favorite, even with murky water. In clear water, it's a must for me. You'll see way more fish, and catch more, if you approach each spot from downstream. (Carefully). There were some steelhead along here, too. I had hooked a couple six or seven pound fish, and Rick had landed them, and he was really wound up. I told him he'd have a lot better chance of hooking one, if he fished ahead of me, instead of fishing water I'd already fished through. "Just fish the next spot up, and if I hook one you can always come back and catch him."

The next spot was a bunch of logs and brush in the river, so while I dabbed around the bottom end of that, I sent Rickie up to a likely looking spot about fifty yards upstream. He'd hardly got there, when I heard him scream, and looking up that way, I could see he had one on. Even at his age, he'd handled quite a few fish that his dad and I had hooked, so by the time I got up to him, he had things pretty well under control. The pole was up nicely, and he knew about thumbing the reel spool as a brake. Right then, there wasn't much I could do to help him.

"It's a big one, Vince."

The fish wasn't going crazy the way some of them will. He just kept leaning out into the current. There was some brush on the other side of the river, but he stayed out of it. A bunch of willows in the river, right next to the bank on our side, had me worried. They were below us, and the fish could run right into them, as it was deep water right to the bank behind them.

We had a good spot to land him, where we were, and just below the willows was another good spot. Below that, the river picked up speed, and ran about thirty yards, right into the log jam. The bank on each side of this fast stretch was too steep to walk along, so you were three or four feet above the water to be able to walk up, or downstream. If the fish got into this fast stretch our chances to get him would thin out a lot, and if he got into the log jam, he was gone.

"We better try to land him here, Rick."

"Okay Vince."

The fish was being nice about it. He never jumped, or any hard runs, or anything really spectacular. He did finally come up and splashed on the surface and Rick was right, it was a big one. It looked like a twin to the one I'd had upstream, the day before.

"You want to put a little more pressure on him if you can, Rick."

"Okay Vince."

He leaned a little harder on him for awhile, but he was getting tired. He'd had the fish on now, for almost ten minutes, and it was really starting to show. I doubted we could land him where we were, as the fish was gradually dropping downstream, but staying nicely outside the willows. It looked like our best bet to get him, was from the small beach just below the willows.

"Rickie, what do you think if I take the pole, and get out on the willows, and you run around below them, and I'll hand it back to you just as soon as I can reach you, downstream."

"Okay," and away he went. It was quite a trick. I managed to get all the way through that mess, keeping the pole and line clear, and the line sort of tight, and didn't slip or step through the willows. I'd have been belly deep if I had. On the downstream end, where they were smaller, my weight finally took the willows to the bottom, and I had only inches to go till I'd go over the top of my hip boots. Now, staying on my feet with all the willows around them was impossible, but I did it. Rickie had hip boots on too, but the top of them only came to slightly above my knees. He had waded up towards me as far as he could, and pretty soon the battle was on again. The fish hadn't gone too far downstream, and the short break had given Rick a second wind. He leaned on him pretty good for a few minutes, and I started having hopes. Before long, though, I'd see him turn sideways, or shift his feet, trying to get more leverage. The fish was tired too, and the current was gradually moving him down below our, last chance, gravel bar.

Steelhead usually won't run downstream, out of a hole, and over the riffle, if you handle them right. By simply easing the pressure when they get towards the bottom of the hole, they'll usually turn and ease back upstream. Usually. But this wasn't that kind of a spot. There was no riffle, just a fast drift with a bunch of brush here and there, that picked up speed and ran into a log jam. It didn't look too good.

Finally he got too far below us, and we had to leave our little sand bar, and get up on the bank to move down with him. If he went much further he was gone. I wondered if he had practically no pressure on him, if he'd move back upstream, to where we might get another chance. I could probably pull it off better than Rickie, as he was about as tired as a little guy can get. With another rest he could go again. I told him what I had in mind.

"Okay Vince."

So I took the pole, the fish turned a bit sideways, and the hook pulled out.

# Chapter 7
# **Statehood**

In 1958, Ernie Erickson's oldest boy, Rodney, bought a 26 foot double ender named the "Laura K" and rigged it up as a troller. I threw some supplies in the fish hold of the Nira to fortify my boat, the "Judy," and rode north with Rodney that spring. Cliff Heath would be with Ernie again. We had an easy, enjoyable trip up, re-catching quite a few steelhead, and arrived in Petersburg to find the "Judy" already in the water. They had moved her out to make some more room in the cold storage loft.

Bob had lost the "Pt Reyes" in a fire the previous fall, and replaced it with another big packer, the "Chacon." This year, instead of just buying off the packer, they will anchor a buying scow, the Nefco 11, in Gedney Harbor. The "Chacon" will buy in some of the other harbors further away, and do all the packing from the Nefco 11 to Petersburg.

I ask Bob if I can tie the Judy behind the scow when he tows the Nefco 11 down to Gedney, and he readily agrees. An extra hand aboard probably looks good to him, while towing the scow. We have a nice trip down, and I spend a few days helping them anchor the scow, and then start looking for a few king salmon. I've already mentioned my first venture on the Tebenkoff flats this same year, but there were a few other interesting moments.

Here's one day that stands out from that spring. I had come in to the scow the night before, and was told about a few guys that had fished down the straits from Cape Decision, and fishing 35 fathoms, had done quite a bit better than I'd been doing. Cranking by hand, I liked to fish in skinnier water, especially in the condition my hands were now in. The next day started out slow again, so I moved out and dropped my gear down. Before long, yank yank, and number one, the nicest fish so far that season, started out the day. Then a few more, smaller but still good fish, and I was feeling pretty clever. Then I brought one up behind the stern, and when I went to stun him, he ducked, so I wound up just grazing him. Rather than lie still so I could gaff him, he went into a big circle shimmying on his side, around under the boat, and under the prop. Now the fish is gone, and my leader and running line are disappearing over the stern and into the prop. I finally kick the machine out of gear, try reversing and get the same results, and the machine nearly dies when I throw the clutch into forward again.

The other boats that had came through yesterday are barely visible down the straits, off Pt. Ellis, so it doesn't look like much help from that direction. It looks like going under with a knife will be my best bet. No big deal, but then I'm not much of a swimmer. I spend awhile getting my fish knife extra sharp, strip off all my clothes, and rig a tie up line, with just enough slack under my arms to be comfortable. Then I tie it off, so I won't keep pushing myself away from the boat. It's going to be cold, and I don't want this to be a long term operation. I do a frame of mind adjustment, and slide over, the line length is good, and I'm happy to find that I can reach the prop without having to get my head underwater. It was cold!

I get a feel of my wrap up, and start cutting, always on the one side, which lets me cut with my right hand, and hang onto the prop, or pull out chunks of gear with my left. I hear the shushing sound sea lions make as they break the surface of the water, or is it water noise under the boat as it rocks? It doesn't matter now, keep cutting! Finally, its free and I throw the knife up over the stern, and into the boat. I think hard about a sea lion chewing on my butt, and over the stern I go. It was about as cold as I thought I could stand, and seems even worse when I get out of the water. I get my clothes back on, plus some, and after a while I'm fine.

A few experiences since, either while in the water myself, or pulling others out of it, make me wonder how getting back aboard went so well. No clothes on undoubtedly helped, and maybe hearing the sea lions helped too, although I've never heard of them attacking a person. Maybe thinking about it helped the adrenalin department. When I was getting my clothes back on, I heard it again, and there were four of them there, waiting for me to put the gear back in, so they could eat. Getting just one at a time as I'd been, plus cranking by hand, which is quite a bit slower, I knew I'd be lucky to get anything through them, so I called it a day. Looking back at it now, I know just how good a day it was. Pulling myself over a two and a half foot stern wouldn't be so easy now. It was great to be young, and like so many, I didn't fully appreciate it until I wasn't. Now I think that's probably a good thing.

This early part of the season, also gave me a good look at what other people in the industry went through. I liked to have some boats around, but then, I sure didn't mind fishing alone. Sometimes I'd see Andy Wikan on the "Curlew," fishing halibut out of Petersburg. They generally worked further out in the straits from where I fished, but sometimes I'd see them in some harbor, or they'd be anchored along the beach, and we'd compare notes. What they considered "a poor day" on halibut would have sank the "Judy" so fast there wouldn't have been time for a bubble.

Skip and Marilyn came out and were fishing halibut before starting their troll season, so I got my first close look at longlining, going out with them one evening, to pull a set. They got a nice amount of mostly good sized fish, and I was impressed, but it would be years before I would become a longliner.

A few trollers would go through and try it, and occasionally get a few fish, but nothing that put much poundage on the Nefco 11. There wasn't quite enough to keep bigger boats around, and Bob needed some boats in the area. I didn't cover enough water to give a very clear picture of what was really available, and those fish in the deeper water were a good example. Some of the guys told me later, that I was probably the most famous troller in Alaska, as it was on the air several times a day, "this little 19 footer, only two hand lines, and he's getting really nice fish." Most of them knew about as well as I did, how many fish I'd caught in the last month, but twenty times what I was catching wouldn't have shown Bob's packing operation any profit.

Finally I had a little better fishing than usual, three or four days in a row, and here came the boats. A lot of them. It wasn't good fishing, but my catch stayed about the same, and a few fish each from a lot of boats, looked good to Bob. A few weeks later the cohos started to show, and I think the scow had a pretty good season.

The "Amazon Fleet," Frank and three other boats from Kake, showed up about this time and Frank, or one of the others, towed a little rig down behind them. It belonged to an elderly Indian couple from Kake, Mr. and Mrs. Bean. They set up camp on the beach in Gedney, and spent the summer drying fish for the next winter. He would fish out in front of the harbor and the four Kake boats would bring in the occasional short salmon or bottom fish for them. Before long, quite a few of us would bring something in for their drying racks, or if the weather wasn't right, for their smokehouse. They would set them aside at the scow, and each evening they'd come over to the scow, or one or two of us would take them across, and spend a few minutes visiting.

One of these evenings, Mr. Bean asked his wife to make some ice cream. I don't remember the exact ingredients, but she took a big bowl of blueberries and sugar, and crushed them down, then canned milk, and there was a couple other things, but I forget what they were. Then she starts whipping it with a big spoon and gradually it turns into a blue froth and was really good. I do remember that the whipping time was no quick thing. You never know what will make some of your better memories.

Later in the season I was fishing down off Malmesbury, in quite close to the shoreline, and was getting a few really nice kings. If this phrase is getting familiar, almost all lower Chatham king salmon are nice fish. The May thru August catch runs bigger yet, so—"really nice fish." Another boat had seen me catching them, so they joined me, and had also picked up a few. I was going down the beach, (beach on my starboard side) and a "Really Nice Fish" started working the inside pole. He kept it up and before long had pulled the boat around, to a point that I was aimed straight in at the beach. I had held the rudder against him, but it didn't make much difference, and I decided to keep going on around, as I didn't want to put that much more strain on things. Soon I'd made half of a circle, and headed offshore to get some elbow room. He was still raising hell out on the pole, so I decided to drop him down slowly when he eased off. I dropped him down ten fathoms deeper, and pulled the other line aboard to take away the chance of him tangling with it. Then I started him up, and in a bit he was on my running line. Just in time too, as he felt the need for a really long run. After the tangle with the prop, I had put plenty of line back on the spool, and now I was happy, as he went through quite a bit of it. Then back towards the boat, a little more commotion, thunk! on the top of the head, and over the stern. It dressed 61 lbs. and although I fished for over thirty more years, this was the biggest king salmon I'd get.

Alaska has become a state, and on July 4 there is lots of celebrating, and not surprisingly, some pretty disgruntled people, but they celebrate anyway. Any old excuse will do. Not being too aware of the political situation, the big thing to me, is that they are going to take out the traps. Cal had worked on the traps, and told me about having to go out in the mornings, and using a big scraper, shearing the heads off small salmon fry to relieve the strain on the trap, because it caused so much additional drag from the current. He said that at times, it seemed like there was a small fish in every hole. So, very high humidity in all Alaskan towns, and in most harbors, over the fourth. A bunch of us go trout fishing, and a picnic on the boats afterwards. Lots of trout fishing and beach combing that year.

Along in August, we started getting southeasters, one after another, and it pretty much shut the fishing down for the fleet, for days at a time. Gedney is a poor storm harbor, with very poor holding ground, and most of these blows were in the 40 to 70 MPH department. Most of the boats would be dragging anchor, and after each storm was over, quite a few boats would have better, or at least other spots in mind. You'd get in a day or so of fishing in between, and then it would blow southeast again. The old timers said it looked like one of "those" falls.

Being cooped up on a 19 footer was getting on my nerves, and one evening at the scow I was talking to this guy, and he mentioned that he was ready to head south, as soon as he had fuel money. I had been wondering how I was going to end the season, as I wanted to either sell the boat up there, or bring it home and sell it. I definitely needed a bigger rig.

I said, "look, how much are you lacking in those fuel tanks?"

He told me, so I suggested me throwing that in plus a bit more on the fuel, go in with him on some grub, do the cooking, split the wheel watch, and we throw a line on the Judy, and pull her along behind.

"Lets go."

I'd had an invite to dinner that evening, and told them what we had in mind, and they asked if we needed some company. They'd about had it, too. I knew they were ready as I had spent a two day blow tied alongside them, and we had plowed and re-plowed our little strip of the harbor. He didn't have real good anchor gear, and it was a good thing because we had to haul it the hard way. Being in their sixties, I didn't think they could have stood up to it alone. There's only the one good spot in the harbor, and it only held a few boats. Nearly everyone else drug their hook, no matter what kind of gear they had.

So the next morning, away we went for Petersburg. I ran the Judy, since we wanted to try a few spots on the way in, but there was a strong pull to the south, and a lot of the spots didn't really look good enough to throw the gear in. Maybe something like a 40 pound king jumping over the bow, might have slowed us down. The weather had turned nice, and we make a long days run of it.

Not much wind at all, the next day, and the "Judy" is riding along nicely, on the third wave back. Positioning a tow is important, but it doesn't take long to find a happy spot. We have a fine ride, and I get a little comic relief before we get into Ketchikan. We've just passed Guard Island, which is a lighthouse on a big rock just north of town. He's at the wheel, and I'm sitting at a sort of settee at the back of the cabin. ARROOM!!! Almost deafening.

"Take the wheel," and he disappears down the steps, and into the engine room. One of the gooses (Grumann) used by Ellis Airlines then, was on its way into Ketchikan, and had flown low, directly over the boat. I'm laughing so hard I can hardly stand at the wheel.

He comes back up in about five minutes, and says he can't find anything wrong, and I crack up again. I tell him what it was, and he doesn't believe me. What do you do with something like that? He's probably mid 50s and definitely wasn't in a mood to be laughed at by this dumb kid. I shut up. Most of this mood was because he'd had a really poor experience on what should have been a reasonably profitable, enjoyable year. This involves the arrangement on his buying the boat, which is at least another chapter, and no point in getting into here. When we get into Ketchikan they tear the machine down, and can't find anything wrong. I get a little exercise, walking around town.

Good weather all the way south, and we separate at Friday Harbor, after entering customs. I run across to Dungeness, rig an inhaul on the anchor line, and give the Judy a shove. When it's out far enough I jerk the line and the anchor falls over and I tie off the inhaul on a beach log. The next day, Judy rides home on a trailer. I go down and see the Ericksons and Lee, and learn that they'd spent nearly the whole season in Frederick Sound. Lee had been down in lower Chatham several times in the early summer, and we'd had some good visits. Always lots of stories, pointers on how to fish here or there, and of course, lots of cookies.

# Chapter 8
# **Bigger Boats**

After fishing the Judy for two years in Alaska, and that first season off Washington, it was time to get a bigger boat. This next one, more of a troller, something I could ice fish in and some kind of living quarters. And power gurdies. I'd had enough cranking by hand.

Hal had moved back to California, so I was pretty much on my own in the boat hunting department. I spent a good deal of time just looking, comparing, and talking, most of this at the boat haven in Port Angeles. I'd look at the few boats that were for sale, compare them, ask questions, and listen. I'd call Ernie that evening, and what did he think of electric gurdies, an anchor winch on the bow, no bow poles, have you ever seen this boat or that one? Sometimes Lee would be up at the house and I'd be able to talk to him, and other times I'd go down and row out to the Eel and talk it over. Nothing I looked at really took my fancy, so I kept expanding my travels and my list of available boats. I'd be up in Seattle, Bremerton, or maybe Poulsbo, chasing down boats in some pretty remote places, and looking at too many boats that someone would have been willing to sell at any price.

I was waiting at the ferry dock in Seattle, after another day of boat chasing, when this guy taps on the window, and asks if I'm going to Port Angeles?

"How about Sequim?"

"Great, could you take me that far? My wife can meet me there."

This was my introduction to Bill Wilcox who just happened to be a troller and owned the "Lilly," which he kept in the Port Angeles harbor. He had been working in Seattle during the winter, as a machinist, and would head home Friday evenings. I described my boat hunting adventures to him, where I'd been, what I had to spend on a boat, and—did he know of anything?

He mentioned that I might be interested in his old boat, the "S.C.Hall." He said it was old, but in good shape, and that he knew the guy that owned it before him had spent some money on the boat, as well as the folks that owned it now. When Bill had owned it, he did quite a little with the drive system, the machine, and a few other things.

The next day I was back in Port Angeles, looking at the boat from a different perspective than I had before. I had taken Bill on home, and after hearing him talk about the good points the boat had, what I'd thought was overpriced, didn't seem quite so bad. It had a Chrysler Royal, that's an inline 8 cylinder gas engine, a radio, fathometer, and an auto-pilot. There was a belt drive, to a pulley and shaft system that powered the capstan for pulling the anchor, and there was an electric motor that turned the gurdies—two speeds and reverse.

A low trunk cabin, maybe two feet above deck level, extended back from roughly five feet back of the bow stem, to the middle of the boat, providing head room while standing in the focsle, which is where the living quarters were in most boats built in that time period. Two bunks were in the bow, one on each side, and the stove and sink were on the port side, between the bunks and the engine. Storage was under the bunks, and in lockers which you sat on while at the table,

*The S.C.Hall. Photo courtesy of Bill Wilcox.*

which folded up. The oil stove and the sink were across the focsle from the table, with more storage under each. The focsle was from the fish hold bulkhead to the bow stem, so this included the engine which wasn't too bad for company. After shoving the boat around all day, it made a pretty good heater.

A short set of three steps put you up in the wheelhouse, which was set into the back of this trunk cabin. It was big enough to hold a comfortable seat, and for two people to stand, if nobody moved. It was a little unique, in that the wheelhouse set slightly right of center on the trunk cabin. It was a 34 foot double ender and instead of the round belly most of that type boat had, this was more of a V bottom, and had rolling chocks. It proved to be an exceptionally good sea boat.

I ran north with Lee that spring, and had an enjoyable trip up. Half the elderly ladies in the Sequim area had baked him at least one coffee can full of cookies, and there must have been enough to fill two lockers. Each morning before we started out, we'd have coffee and cookies. Over the years, eating cookies was about the only thing I would really get good at, and running with Lee was good training.

He was impressed with how good the S.C.Hall was in a following sea. Double enders aren't the best in that category, but this one held her own. Lee had known the old guy that had either built it, or had it built. He couldn't remember which. Shirley Charlie Hall. Lee said there wasn't anyone in the fleet more fussy about how his boat was kept up, which made me feel good. It was built in 1918, so it must have had a little TLC somewhere along the line.

I fished the Stikine run out of Petersburg that spring, and did quite well, by my standards. The boat didn't have bow poles when I bought it, so I had cut a nice set before I left home, and now fished four lines, one off each pole. The bow poles mounted just in front of the trunk cabin, and when lowered, angled ahead of the boat to about 10:30 and 1:30. They were 24 feet long, and fished with 50 pound leads, with 20 or 25 pounds off the main poles, they separated the gear nicely.

The Chrysler Royal was a perfect trolling engine, as it would run smooth at 400 turns, and I could get the speed down to perfection on the choked herring.

I'd sleep through the alarm each morning, and then try to make it up by fishing till after 11:00 that night. Then the same thing next morning. I mentioned it to Andy Grenier who had the "Ginger" then, and he said, "I'll get ya up in the morning." Next morning I woke up from a peaceful sleep behind Sukoi Island, a foot above my bunk, literally clawing the air. The Ginger had pulled right up to my stern, and Andy didn't take his finger off the air horn button until I was in the doorway. Same thing the next morning. The following morning I heard his machine start, and was dressed and pulling my anchor when he went by.

I spent the summer months in lower Chatham Straits, with on and off fishing. Probably I could have gone any direction, and done at least as well, but didn't. I was slowly getting my feet on deck as a fisherman, and up till now, there had only been one poor move that might have been disastrous. It wasn't, and happened along about this time. The packer had came back from town, and had gone into a place they called "Gods Pocket," rather than come on out to where we had been fishing. It looked good in this area, and he thought we might improve our lot with this slight change of address. We got up there after dark, and he came out and led us in with a flashlight, the tide being out enough to show the reef.

Going out in the morning was easy, since the tide was still out, and the break in the reef, which you came in through at an angle, was no big challenge. Bob had mentioned a couple prominent trees and snags that would work well for lineups and after I got outside the slot, I stopped and found that the trees weren't quite exact—but if you held to the one side, just a bit—. The fishing was an improvement, and although none of us had fished here before, we all felt good about the move. My catch included one fish that dressed over 50 pounds, which you didn't see many of, along in September.

A fog bank was moving our way from up in the sound, and rather than fish around these reefs in the fog, we all went in, the reef showing nicely at half tide. The fog came and went, and we all started back out, hoping for a few fish at high water. Looking out the back door at the lineup; it looked pretty good. I should be okay.

Thump! I'm on the end of the reef. Hadn't missed it by much, but that didn't float the boat. Full reverse wouldn't get me off so Bob came out, and the heavy "Chacon" pulled me off with less effort than when I'd got on. It took a bit for him to pull the anchor and get out there, and I suppose the tide coming in that extra bit didn't hurt anything. Water was spraying in along side of the engine so I ran to the end of the bay and eased the boat onto a nice sand beach. The fact that there was one here, was nice.

The water was coming in where the elbows to the heat exchanger had been jammed thru the planking, and a few towels stuffed in this spot slowed things down nicely. Bob had a portable pump, which I used a few times until the tide dropped, and before long we were able to check out the damage.

The inlet to the keel cooler seemed to be the only leak, so after smoothing up the ruptured planks we put a plywood patch over the area, with the fittings to the cooler going up through the patch. Then we cut off the damaged ends of pipe, and patched them with hose. Other than a small scar on the keel, everything looked good. When the tide came in enough, I started up, and no problems. In the morning we went fishing.

And, I'd met a new friend. Bob Bell had ran the "Missouri" across the Sound, on the chance he might have that piece of something that might make the patch up go better. He had me over for dinner, and gave me some great tips on refining my gear. Some of the Sitka boats were way ahead of us on that score.

Next winter, a couple new planks and a new keel cooler. When taking the planks out, the nails and caulking caught our attention, so before going back in the water, we re-nailed and re-caulked the whole boat, below the waterline. And, I had decided that this way of thinking,—"just a bit to the side of a line up," might not be quite good enough.

The next year, Lawrence made the trip north with me. He was over seventy years old and lived in Los Angeles, but had been raised in the Sequim area. There were six boats of us going up at the same time, and by coincidence, two of the friends Lawrence had chummed with as kids were on the Lena O. Cliff had fished with Ernie the first two years I fished Alaska, and his brother, Orville, had fished off the Washington coast.

Lawrence intended to ride up as far as Petersburg, and then fly on up north, to go by train into the Whitehorse country. The trip north was one of the nicest ones, weather-wise, which I was happy for, because at his age, and not being on boats since the navy, I'd hoped he wouldn't get banged around too much. We tied together in some nice harbor each night, and the three of them caught up on the last 50 years. Lots of stories, long into the nights. The first evening out, Orville asked Lawrence if they had ever had a family and this was the only hard part of his trip.

He and Hulda had two boys, and when they were still quite young, they'd had a paper route. They rode together on a small motor bike, and one Sunday morning some drunk woman ran them down and they both died. He broke down while telling them about this. Hulda had never been able to handle it, and never would move from the Los Angeles area where the kids were buried. They each lived this until they died.

We tried a few spots around Ketchikan without much success, and moved on up country, now just Cliff and Orville and us running together. A little better

87

fishing up towards Wrangell, so we spent a few days in the area and each evening Lawrence would fish with the sport pole after we'd anchored. I'd told him about the really big halibut we occasionally got, and he had his heart set on a 200 pounder, at least. I was getting some dinner together when he started yelling for help, and pretty soon we had an eater aboard, maybe 30 lbs. I mentioned that this would be gobs to eat and the line went back out, "I'll get one for Cliff and Orville." I had barely got back into the focsle when, "hey, I got another one." Pretty quick there was another, about the same size, and when we got it aboard I suggested dinner. He wondered if we couldn't sell them, and I told him the season wouldn't open for another ten days. Then he wondered how long we could keep them on ice. I told him to forget that! I think he had a ten day halibut derby in mind. Then it was—maybe we'd run into Bill and Nada when we got to Petersburg. "I'll get them one." I told him he already had, but felt bad about shutting his fishery down.

On the trip up through Canada, after we had crossed Milbanke Sound and started up Finlayson Channel, it had been a clear sunny morning and the mountains on both sides, and as far as you could see ahead, were covered with snow. Scenery wise; about as good as it gets. He said, "If I had known this existed 50 years ago, I'd have spent my life here." I always wished they could have.

I stayed on the Stikine fish again that spring, and had done quite well, but had thought a lot about going down into lower Chatham Straits for the summer. Frederick Sound had been good for kings the last two summers, and I decided to give it a good try and at least learn the area a little better for future reference. It was a decent summer season, but nothing compared to the previous two years in the Sound. On the other hand, it would prove to be a great investment for future seasons. I was able to put what I had learned about the area to good use for nearly another 30 years.

Petersburg would have been called a close knit community at that time, and striking up a conversation on the dock, sometimes made for a one sided visit. One group that caught my interest was an old bunch that were always on the dock, re-catching yesterdays halibut trips in verrry tough weather. I came into town one evening, fairly late, but still good visibility. There was a heavy mist in the air, but that didn't stop this bunch, who were gathered near the spot where I was nudging the boat into the dock. I hoped I wouldn't make one of my usual landings in front of this bunch. This was before they had put in the finger floats between the boats, so I kept the machine in gear against the dock and a piling, and went up on the bow. With no offers to take my bow line, I grabbed it and jumped over onto the dock, taking care to miss a substantial pile of dog shit. The wooden dock was like grease from the rain and I found myself on my back, the wind knocked out of me and these guys are laughing themselves sick.

My first breath, when I could, told me I hadn't exactly missed and when my audience saw this, it got worse yet. Two of them were sitting on the tie up rail in that kind of hysterical laughter they'd been saving up twenty years for. I had it between my shoulder blades, in my hair, and then down one side when I'd rolled over in it to get up, and they were still laughing. It could have been worse, but not much. I got the boat tied down, before bucketing water over my head till I thought I was rinsed off enough to go inside and shut the door. Slam!

But it wasn't all bad. It was tough to see someone coming down the street half a block away, look closer, recognition, and then start laughing. Before long though, these same guys who had looked through me for three years, now stopped to talk on the dock, even coming aboard for a cup of tea. Either they were feeling a few pangs of guilt, or had decided to be friendly. I would bring in the odd fiddler (small salmon), or maybe some bottom fish, and before long, my cookie canister was in a good mood.

They had all fished for years, and of course, they all missed it. One of them kept telling me that he wanted to make a trip with me. He was always good company when he came aboard, but on the other hand, there was always something, or two or three, things, wrong with my operation. Probably more than that, but I was developing my own way of doing things and always hesitated in asking him to come along for a few days.

Lee and I are talking about him a couple years later, after I've got out of the service. He tells me about the old guy getting one of the smaller boats in the fleet, and rigging it up to troll with, in Frederick Sound. He has a heart attack and they find the boat on the beach. I tell Lee about him asking to make a trip with me, and he says that he had always wanted to go with him too. He says, "I never was sure I could get along with him." Now we each wish we had taken him along. On the other hand, what a way to go. I always hoped he'd got the gear out and was getting a few fish.

During the season, it had become obvious that I needed a bigger boat. You could fill the S.C. Hall, and still not have a really good trip. The big problem was my age, as there was no reason to think I wouldn't be drafted into the service in the next year or two. I expected it could happen any time. It was a poor time to jump up and get involved in a new boat, and then get my draft notice. I'd pretty much decided to sell the boat when I got home, volunteer for the draft, and get it over with. Volunteering for the draft meant two years active duty, compared to a minimum three years if I enlisted in the army. When I got home one of the first things mom said was, "hey, you got a letter." Sure Enough.

I went up and took the physical, and they thought I might do, starting Nov. 13, 1961. Now I had to find a buyer for the boat, and that was no problem at all, except nobody had any money. I decided to sell it to the one of four potential buyers who had taken extremely good care of his boat. Nothing down, three equal payments a year apart, with interest on the balance up to that point each year. At least the boat would be well cared for, and I was happy with the arrangement, since I didn't seem to have a lot of choices.

The boat was hauled out with only a few days to go before I left, so bottom paint and zincs, plus a good look over by the new owner. After the previous season I had re- caulked and re nailed the boat below the water line, and everything was in fine shape. When they dropped me back in the water we had a slight problem. I was on the forward ways, with a larger boat behind me on the rear ways. The boat behind me got back in all right, but being on the forward cradle, the S.C.Hall didn't float free. We had thought there would be enough water, but that didn't seem to float the boat. The tides would keep getting smaller and Bob Nelson, the guy that ran the yard, knew the bind I was in time wise, so he got a brainstorm. He grabbed half a dozen guys from the yard, and off the docks, and brought them out in a skiff. They would all stand on one side, listing the boat off its keel and as soon as we got over far enough, off we'd go. It worked. Everyone to the side along with a little reverse, over and off. The next day I drove into the yard, and mom runs out, yelling, "get into Port Angeles quick. Your boats sinking at the dock."

Bert had gone down to check the boats, and as he was getting on his other boat, he glanced across and saw the S.C.Hall, down a bit in the bow. He had the key, so ran over, and a quick look into the focsle told him he needed help. He ran up to the phone at the top of the dock, and called the Coast Guard and the Fire Department. He said the fire department nearly beat him back to the boat. He never could figure out how they had done that, even though the firehouse was just up the street. "I'm not kidding you Vince, I came right back to the boat. They were almost here." He had grabbed the deck pump handle and started pumping, and they were climbing across the stern with a portable pump.

Joe Ferris, the boat haven manager, found the problem. Looking down along the hull from the next boat, he saw an old thru-hull fitting that appeared to be slightly separated from the hull. This had been an old fitting like one of the old exhaust discharges that were cupped and protected from the front, the outer part, out about an inch from the hull. It was above the waterline and someone had capped it off on the inside, maybe thinking someone might need the thru hull for something in the future. Apparently, with everyone moving back off the rail, the boat rocked a bit, and it must have been on just the right tilt as it went past the last upright on the ways, to put this fitting out slightly farther than the guard. It apparently clipped the upright on the ways, rupturing the wood around it enough that a serious leak was available. All it needed was for this spot to get under water, and a tie up line, maybe hung up on some piling barnacles at low water, must have accomplished that. I had stayed with the boat for awhile, after I got off the ways, and there wasn't a drop coming in anywhere.

We threw another little list on the boat, and took out the fitting, temporarily patching it with a sheet of lead. It would only have to move back to the ways, this time the rear cradle. I called the lady at the local draft board and explained the situation. There just wasn't time enough before I had to leave, to get the work done. "Can I possibly have two more days?" She said that this was something I could try to put off indefinitely. Be in Seattle the 13th or I'd be talking to the Feds. I went back and told Bert, and he said not to worry about it. "If you'll catch the shipyard bill I'll do the cleaning up." I helped him change the oil, and we took the boat back over and put it on the ways, this time the rear cradle. He had them put in a new plank, and then, back at the dock, was able to take his time with the clean up. I hated to leave him with a job like that, but he said, later, that it wasn't that bad. A little water had got into the oil, but no oily water had got out of the machine.

So, I was in the army now. Two years later I was out. That's another story, or quite a few. A few days before I got back home, mom answered the door, and here was Bert with a check for the boat, which he had just sold. He hadn't done that well while I was gone, and one of the reasons is worth mentioning here.

He had replaced the capstan for the anchor gear, with a small electric anchor winch, which he installed behind the cabin. He and a few other boats, had gone in behind Destruction Island to anchor and during the night the wind changed to southeast and their protection was suddenly behind them. Everyone started pulling their hooks with the idea of moving offshore a bit, and running the twenty miles up to the Quilleute. (La Push.)

Bert had some kind of a board, or handle, that he used to fend the anchor gear evenly onto the winch, but he couldn't find it. He had an old welders glove on the boat, so used it instead, and sure enough, got it under the chain. The switch was on the back of the cabin, just above the winch, but in the excitement of the moment he grabbed the glove with the other hand, and got it involved, too. His arms were going down over the back of the winch when he made one desperation jump, bashing his head into the switch and shutting it off. Then he was able to work one hand free, and reverse the switch, freeing the other. The Coast Guard ran down from La Push, and put a man aboard to take the boat back, after putting a splint on Bert's arm, which was broken in two places. I took a short leave, and went up and fished with him for a few days, but he hadn't been able to get good help, and the season was pretty much of a wash for him. Could have been a lot worse though. Then, after the next season, he decided he'd had enough of fishing.

Now I was looking for another boat. Ernie knew of an old fellow that built boats in Port Townsend, and he thought there was one of his boats in the water now. He and Lee and I went down and looked it over and liked what we saw. The hull and house were finished, and he'd put a 200 gallon fuel tank on each side of the engine compartment. There was a 100 gallon water tank in the stern, and the rudder, main shaft, and the prop had been installed. The mast was up and rigged.

We were sitting in the car, talking it over in front of the little dockside cafe, and some guy runs by, pounds on the car roof and shouts, "have you heard the news?" Then he ran inside the cafe. When we got back to Ernie's, we went inside, and the TV was on with some footage of water breaking on the beach, and some peaceful music. Then Margaret came out of the kitchen and said, President Kennedy had been shot.

Some inquiring got me the name of the builder, Jake Herwick, who was building another boat near the waterfront in Port Townsend. Jake had worked in the boat yards in Seattle, and after retiring, had built a boat almost every year. He hired only a little help when he was bending ribs, and a few of the heavier jobs. Otherwise, it was a one man show. He was very hard working, frugal, and one of a group of people who get scarcer every year. That generation of woodworkers who did all the building and repair work, on what was then an almost completely wooden boat fleet, are pretty much gone. A few who were drawn to the trade still work in a couple small yards in Port Townsend, but otherwise, skilled people who turn wood into a boat are few and far between. Good boat lumber is getting pretty scarce, too.

He gave me a tour of the boat in progress, pointing out ways of doing things and answering a slew of questions that popped up as we looked. All of the boats he had built since retiring were from 34 to 40 feet long, and the one down at the dock was a 40 footer. He liked to fish most of his boats for one season, because of tax purposes, and always had the boat spoken for, by the end of that season. When he first came to this country as a boy, he had sailed on various east coast lighthouse tenders, which were all named for flowers. These boats he built now, had the same names. Gardenia, Larkspur, Tulip, Larkspur II, and a few others that may have been renamed since then. Juanita H, Sea Wife, Gorm, Chance It, and several others, that I can't remember now.

He told me that the boat at the dock had already been bought, but said that he didn't know if the people would be able to go ahead with the project. Their house had burned down, and finishing the boat might be more than they needed at this point. He gave me their number, we met, and I bought a boat.

The first order of business was to get a machine in the "Camelot," so I could move her up to Port Angeles. It would be nicer to have her closer to home and my scrap pile, while I put things together. I had met Bill and Nada Small the first year I went north, and had fished around them a lot, as well as tying across the dock, when I had the S.C.Hall. Bill was one of those I always listened to, since he had over 30 years of fishing behind him, and was one of the really good, all around boat men I would ever know. His experience was largely without all the new fancy stuff, so learning from him was like laying a sound foundation. When he suggested I get a new diesel engine for the boat, instead of gas, I didn't blink. He said, "get a Jimmy. They catch fish, everyone's got one, and you can always get parts."

I put in a 4-53 GM, and enjoyed eleven trouble free seasons with it, but the reduction gear behind it was another story. The company I bought the machine from, backed me on the financing, plus another $2,000 to go towards what other equipment I would need. Among these items, was a 65 watt Raytheon radio, a Bendix fathometer, a Neptune 2—oil stove, hydraulics for the gurdies, and anchor gear.

Hydraulic and electrically powered equipment are a wonderful thing, but now I think back at some of the mechanical drive operations I saw over the years. Many of them were masterpieces in simplicity and durability, and several times I saw a bow pulled down, trying to free a hung up anchor, to the point that hydraulics would have been screaming, well short of that point. Belt drives and P.T.O.s, belt tighteners, clutches, chains, and sprockets, and shafts and bearings, and gear boxes. And injury. As beautiful as some of the systems were, you had to stay out of them. Anyway, I'm glad I came along when I did. Getting to see, and use a bit of what was, helped me in setting up the Camelot's steering system, as well as a dandy belt tightener for the hydraulic pump. And a good many other things, over the years.

So here I was, in my usual state of nearly broke at the first of the season, and with monthly payments on the note I had, plus a monthly insurance payment. After trying it around Petersburg I decided to give up on the Stikine fish, and Cal and I had been wondering which way to go. Skip had brought in a good trip on the Nohusit, and that afternoon, came aboard with a tip, as to where some king salmon could be found.

It really helped, going right to a spot and start catching fish as soon as the gear was out. Now I could breath a little easier. It was an enjoyable trip in a way, in a spot I loved to fish. "Some really nice fish," and not much in the way of boats. On the second day, my brand new fathometer packed it up, and this isn't the kind of place you can fish well, without one. Out on the tip of a peninsula, line-ups were non existent for most of the crucial areas along the reefs, so by the end of the trip, I had left considerable gear there. I was fishing along the reef, apparently too close, and had several fish on the gear. I was working the other side of the boat when the line nearest the reef suddenly broke off, halfway between

*Camelot—A very easy running boat*

the boat and the float bag. I got the fish and gear aboard, circled around and came up into the current below the float bag, threw the machine out of gear, fished the loose end out with the pike pole, and ran it through the outside block. I put a clamp at the first marker to keep it from getting past the block, and splice into a loop I've already put through the inside block. Take off the clamp and I'm ready to go. Back in gear, and there's a nice fish on the gear, because I can see the line surging away from the boat. It dresses out at 56 pounds, one of the best in the trip. I always wonder if it was already on the line, or if it grabbed the plug as it was working in the current. It joins a larger one in the trip, and two more that dress over 50, a size you were beginning to see less of. The most obvious thing I can think of, is the power dams across the Columbia and Snake Rivers. This was in 1964, and between 1953 and 1961 they had put in eight dams, and they'd build about that many more.

Cal had his own set of problems, funny to everyone except himself. The boat was over fifty feet long, and powered with an old Hercules diesel. There was scads of cruising speed, but slowing down was another story. To get even close to trolling speed, he towed a five gallon bucket from each pole, and a small wash tub from the stern. " I've never seen so many gul durned kings, trying to get into a wash tub!" Even with the tubs he'd make three passes to everyone else's two. That next winter he'd have the wheel re-pitched.

In July that year, we were at Port Alexander fishing cohos, and got a fish tip from an unusual source. Fishing had dropped off, and fishing alone on the boat, the afternoons got awfully long. The weather was clear and warm, no wind, and looking across Chatham Straits, you would see quite a little contortion and shimmering in the water, seemingly all the way across Chatham. Out of boredom I had fished a little further up the straits and after turning around, and looking back across, I can see seven or eight trollers working against the shoreline. The distance, from my location to where they were, was about ten miles, so I was getting help from some sort of a mirage condition. For awhile, the boats were distorted, appearing at least as tall as they were long. Then for a minute the conditions changed and I could see clearly enough to identify two of the boats. Time to move! I talked to Cal when we passed and soon we are heading back across. The boats go out of sight on the way over, then re-appear for a bit, disappear, and finally come into sight for real. My tip was a good one, and we realize some nice fishing.

This isn't an uncommon thing in clear weather, usually warm, but not necessarily. I remember sometimes during the winter in Port Angeles, you could look across the straits at Victoria, and see the windows in their office buildings. Most of the time you couldn't see the buildings.

Bill and Nada were fishing just outside Pybus Bay, in Frederick Sound, and had another of these experiences. At any time he was working in the stern, she would be running the boat from the cabin, probably better than most guys in the fleet. Glassy calm, hot, weather, and when she happened to look up into the bay, she sees a boat on a rock. She yells back at Bill and he doesn't see it, and by the time he gets up on deck, she can't see it either. Considering the weather conditions, he knows there has to be a boat there somewhere, so he pulls his gear and they start running over towards the bay, and on up into the big arm. Before too long, a boat comes in sight, and as they get closer they see it's Fred McGilton. At that time Fred had the "Rainbow." I don't know if they ever did a new chart that shows that rock, but if you go very far into the bay, on the left hand side, pay attention. Fred still had the gear out, and said that it got shallow and he sped up to raise the gear, then some more, oops! They stuck around till high tide and he got off okay, and without too much damage. This was back when hardly any of the boats had a fathometer.

Another interesting thing you get, weather wise, is the localized blows in clear weather. When it's clear and cold, you get the northeast winds that will blow out of just about any inlet, river entrance, channel or strait. This gives you something else to consider when moving around in the winter. Then, when it's clear and warm, you can get areas where it blows northwest, sometimes for hundreds of miles up and down, and across. Sometimes not. One of the smallest, most defined spots I can think of is on the bottom of Baranoff Island, from Puffin Bay down to Cape Ommaney. During warm summer weather, if it bothers to blow at all, it will get to around 40 knots and sometimes much more, especially off Larch Bay. Then it tapers off as it gets out into Chatham Straits. When you get up towards Little Puffin, fishing north, you'll get to a point that you can look ahead and it looks a little better. A hundred yards more and it's definitely better and before long you're above it.

This first year with the Camelot was kind of hit and miss, maybe a bit heavy on the miss, and I was thinking a lot about how to improve my operation. I'd already figured out that I didn't like fishing around crowds of boats, which shouldn't be a problem because Southeast Alaska is a big place. It seemed like there were quite a few boats that ran right on through spots where I was fishing; probably for good reason. I felt I definitely needed to expand my horizons. Like Bill Small said, "first, get where there's some fish."

Before the season is over, Pete Peterson who has the "Clift" writes, and suggests I get up to his neighborhood, so I spend most of the rest of the season between Cross Sound and Lituya Bay. Fishing has dropped off, but I grind it out, and learn an area that I'll fish a lot in the future. On the way home, I stop in Wrangell and pull alongside the "Irish" and before long, Steve Prader and I are on the way south. Walt has asked me earlier in the season if I'd mind stopping on the way through, and having Steve ride down with me. They are going to get another boat and this will give Steve a good chance to look the trail through British Columbia over, prior to coming back north. The next season he and his dad are on an old Forest Service boat, which they've re-named "Lochinvar."

With my seasons, up to now, being on the slim side, I had figured out that any step of my operation that I could do myself, was about like catching a few more fish. Over the years, I watched a few very good fishermen spend themselves out of business. Generally, the ones that survived were the ones that did as much as possible of their own work, themselves. Accordingly, I became more interested in how things worked. Or why they didn't. I had got to where I could make a gas machine purr to perfection. Diesels were another story. Bill Small pretty much summed it up—"give them clean fuel and air, and run them right, and they'll pretty much run forever. Check your filters and fuel sump daily and you won't spend a lot of time wishing you did. Then, after 10 or 12 seasons, get the best man you can find to overhaul it." I got to where I could pretty much deal with the stuff hanging on the sides of the engine, and had a fair idea of what was going on inside.

It's easier to make good moves, during seasons when there are more fish around, and once you've had a taste of this better fishing, your expectations get a little higher. You have to learn to balance these expectations with the realities in any given season, and this is where experience starts making a difference. I'm not going to lead you step by step through 34, yaaaaawn, seasons, but a quick peek at the next couple years, might be a good idea. I thought I'd come a long ways in six years, but looking at it now, I was just getting started. I'd have been way ahead at this point if I'd learned on someone else's boat, but I hadn't wanted to do that. Look what I'd have missed.

With the previous seasons thoughts on expanding my horizons in mind, I started 1965 up in Icy Straits, in an area called "Homeshore," by the locals. I spent most of my time off to one end or the other of this small fleet of boats, and finally did manage to get a pretty good trip. That and seeing my first brown bear, and later on, a lynx running along the beach at Homeshore, were pretty much the highlights of that expedition. After the "pretty good" trip there didn't seem to be much alone-ness, so before long, I was moving back down through Chatham Straits. This would be one of those lower Chatham years, and it was hard to make a poor move; lots of kings and good coho fishing that stood up for months.

I am anchored in the outside harbor at Malmesbury one evening, and Ernie came in and anchored just slightly to the side, and ahead of me. He came out on the back deck when he'd finished, and said that Lee had died. I had been up to visit him in the Marine Hospital before I left that spring, and remember thinking when I left, that I might not see him again. One of the good things in my life, was meeting him and his family.

I always remember him going by when we were fishing, hobbling out on deck, and hanging onto the shrouds as he yelled across the water. He'd still be hollering when he was 200 yards away. Or the mornings having coffee and cookies before we went out. Another older fellow from Ketchikan buys the

*Lee Harbaugh*

"EEL," and I wave when he goes by. He doesn't come out of the house. Of course, he doesn't know me from Adam. Twenty five years later I was walking the docks in Ketchikan, the last time I was there, and here was the "EEL." It looked like whoever had it then, was keeping it up pretty well.

Another memory from later in that season is going into Petersburg on the plane, and coming out with a good fish tip from down in Sumner Straits. Joe Cash was at the scow when I got in, and when I told him about it, he was ready to go, as fishing in lower Chatham had been falling off. We ran down to Table Bay that evening and the next morning, found ourselves moving around Cape Decision and up Sumner Straits, in

pea soup fog. Even thicker than that. I found my way behind the Flicka's stern, and we moved along at not much over half speed.

Flat calm, not a breeze, and massive kelp Islands which looked like the beach and everything else, in these no-wind and gloomy light conditions. You couldn't tell where water and sky met, and sometimes it looked like the kelp was in the sky. We had to be constantly turning to stay out of the kelp. It didn't mean shallow water, but going through kelp that thick would get it wrapped around the rudder and prop. Then the stern would start shaking.

We never did see the buoy off Pt St. Albans, but when we went by the one off Amelius, Joe stepped into the back doorway, and pointed off to his right. Sure enough, there it was. A little further along, the fog lifted, and just ahead of us, on our right, was the buoy at Calder Rocks. Joe would have passed it perfectly. We dropped the gear in, and had quite a good afternoon on some big silvers.

I could see that this was one area that I needed to practice in. Joe had moved up country like he had a radar, and if I was going to be able to move around at all, I needed to be able to move through the fog with a little more confidence. School started taking place nearly every time I moved. Make out a course, think about the time to go, tides and currents and what they'd do to you, and then see how you would have come out. Eventually you have a better feeling for what to allow when going across, or into the current. Gradually you get better at it. If you are going across the bottom where the soundings might change as you move across, that might be useable. I fine tuned my hull speed at certain machine turns, and practiced applying it to what's happening with the water.

Going through water might not be going over as much land as you think you are. The water makes it a little smoother, but you're running your canoe over land. Lots of guys have gone around some reef in the fog, until they found out they were going over it. Take your time! If there's any doubt at all, stop the boat and think it through—slowly and thoroughly. I was still practicing this stuff nearly thirty seasons later. As long as I fished. Eventually, I would have radar and loran, which are each a wonderful thing, but the way of thinking required to move the boat with just the compass, the chart, and a clock, was a tremendous benefit on a good many occasions.

Joe and I spend several weeks in Sumner Straits, and then I go back around into Chatham. We never do hear of any good fishing, like what was available in lower Chatham all summer, but they can move quickly. A few days of a southeaster, and fish can move a long ways. I've got my mind set on Icy Straits, and several of us take off up Chatham.

Skip hears that it is dead, and wonders about turning back towards Frederick Sound. He does, but I've got my neck bowed, and have to go up and give Homeshore and Pt Adolphus a try. A few days later I'm heading back down to the Security Bay to Port Camden area, and find only an occasional fair day, at best. Skip hasn't been feeling well all season, and the kids and Marilyn have been pretty much fishing the boat. It didn't seem possible to me, that a man like him could get sick. They decide to bunch it, and head into Petersburg, but I and a few others grind it out for awhile longer. Finally, enough is enough. I stop in Petersburg and Skip comes aboard and says, "Hey, I got ya a job. We're construction men." I tell him he's nuts, I've never done anything like that in my life, and am pretty well set on heading south. We visit for a bit and after awhile its time to catch the tide in the narrows. Skip passed away that winter. So what was a good season was also a horrible one.

The next season started out well, and kept up a nice pace all season. I spent most of my first two trips at one of my former hot spots, and although the fishing was fine, the sleeping wasn't. I'd nicely get asleep and the wolves would start their serenade, gaining volume until I'd get up and spend a minute banging on a cast iron frying pan, with a big spoon. Sometimes that would do it, but more often than not, they'd start up again, about an hour or less before the alarm clock would go off. Howling is better just before daylight, and they knew I probably wouldn't get back to sleep. Sometimes I'd shoot the shotgun out the back door, and that would sometimes get me through till daylight. 1960 and 1961 were definitely at a peak in the deer population cycle on Kuiu Island. I'm fairly certain, that 1966 was at, or near, the peak in the wolf department.

I had fished several trips before Steve Prader showed up, and we fished several more together, in lower Chatham. I had met Steve's folks the first year I fished Alaska and had fished around them off and on, since then. Mrs. Prader was a highliner. When she was in the area she would be the high boat, or in a big fleet, one of the top few. When everyone else was still using what amounted to cave man gear, the Praders weren't missing a trick in streamlining their operation. This was when monofilament leader was still about as thick as spaghetti. To have your gear work effectively, and still handle the bigger fish, was a bit of a balancing act. In a few years, the quality of the leader material would start improving. Most, or maybe all of it, came out of Germany or Japan.

Mrs. Prader passed away when I was in the service, and Steve had started fishing with his dad. Walt had quite an arthritis problem, but was an excellent fisherman, and they made a good team. After the 1965 season Walt retires to warmer climates, and Steve and I fish together for years, or from then on if we're in the same area.

A good portion of this 1966 season was between Sitka and lower Chatham Straits. The whole fleet was selling to the old Sitka Sound plant, and the lineups to sell fish, or get ice, were awful. You could be on the list early in the morning, and still not be unloaded until late that evening. The quality of the ice was poor, since they couldn't make it fast enough to cool it down, and when you took ice up to the deck beams, it would be a foot lower the first morning, and your bilge would be full of water. This, along with a nice amount of poundage, made for short trips since you'd normally be out of ice in four or five days. My forty foot boat was beginning to seem pretty small.

I've met lots of people who like to beach comb, but none more than myself. Except Steve. Any old excuse would do, and he'd be heading for the beach. The possibilities were endless, and you never went on any of the beaches we used without finding some kind of treasure. Sometimes glass floats, or the halibut buoys that had marked the ends of a set. Until I started longlining we used them for bumpers between the boats, or when we tied to some dock. In some areas, a lot of fishing plugs would find their way into shore and you took them all back out to the boat. Then, on closer inspection, some would get thrown back in for some other lucky devil to find. And there was lots of other stuff. If it floats, it will likely find some beach.

When I say "beach," don't visualize the nice sandy beaches that are in Oregon and Washington States. The sandy part is usually just a small strip, or patch, here and there, between the trees and a bunch of rock leading into the water. But we loved it. Beachcombing and clam digging. If I told you how many clams were in some of the spots, you wouldn't believe it. Now I find myself wishing I'd spent even more time ashore. Each time was enjoyable, whether in the woods, up some creek or river, or on some beach, those are the memories that keep coming to the top. One place that sticks in my memory, was one of those spots

*Lots of butter clams*

that had just been fishing on the one tide. Judging from the last few days efforts on the (off) tide, it wouldn't make much difference if we weren't out there before noon. We went on the beach and found 33 glass balls between us, and could see that someone else had been there ahead of us, and creamed it. Back in the woods, sometimes thirty feet back, you'd find a nest in the moss where this guy had picked out a big one, the 12 to 16 inch kind. Whoever it was, he'd got quite a few of them. Looking into the trees at the beach edge, we saw driftwood hanging in limbs ten feet up. We were glad we weren't anchored there, at that time. A good fire, and some hot dogs and potato salad later, we go out, and have a very nice evenings fishing. There's a day you remember.

The outer Baranoff coast has some exceptionally nice salmon in the summers, and it was a pleasure to handle them. That's putting it very mildly. You wouldn't get that many, but every few days, or maybe once a week, there would be a fish that you were lucky to catch one of, during a lifetime.

For nearly two trips, one of the spots we were fishing would put a few fish on the gear every time we went up to it. Then you would turn when a snag and a certain tree behind it, started to line up, and head straight out along this reef, often resulting in a few more fish on the gear.

I had a nice fish on, and was coming up towards the lineup, so I had gone back to start it up, hoping to get it before I started the turn. When I started bringing the line up, I noticed that it was holding in towards the boat, more than would be normal. Several possibilities here. I was using plugs, and if a fish is hooked on the left side of his mouth on a plug, he will lead off to his right, much more than if he were hooked on most any other kind of a lure. Opposite this, if it were hooked on the right side.

The other possibility had happened to me a few days earlier. A big fish had picked up the line, complete with a 50 lb. lead, and carried it far enough to the port side that it had tangled with the other bow line. The way the line was holding in against the side now, it looked as if that might have happened again. I looked up at the other bow pole, and it didn't show any sign of a hitch hiker, so I started the line up again, and kept feeling the line as I continued taking off leaders. The mainline was literally wrapped under the boat, not pulling straight back like I would have hoped. It looked more and more like a tangle, but still no sign of that on the other bow pole.

Line up time, so I started a nice, steady turn out along the reef. There were only two leaders to go and the mainline is still holding in tight against the boat, where it should have been out about eighteen inches and pulling slightly back. Rather than risk a line in the wheel, I grabbed the mainline with both hands, and eased it back over the stern, making sure it was behind the prop. I thought that if I had to, I could move offshore a bit, and be free to turn the opposite direction. This would get the line away from the boat long enough to bring it up, and maybe get the line snap on the running line.

Now the line was pulling less to the side, so I eased it back around the stern, and for a moment it hung down normally from the block. Then it started pulling straight back and then back some more. I dropped the line down a bit with the hydraulics, and when the fish appeared to have eased off, started it back up, still hoping to get him on the running line. The last snubber was only down about a fathom when the line pulled back hard, and I saw the lead only a few feet under water and the snubber stretched out as far as it would go.

The biggest salmon I would ever see, was swimming lazily off across the top of the water. I had eased the hydraulics back into reverse but it was too late. The 130 lb. test leader popped like a 22 shot and it was all over. We had been handling a few fish that dressed out in the 40 to 45 lb. department, with the occasional fish going well beyond that. I had thought it was one of these. If I'd had any idea how big it was I might have tried getting all the other gear aboard, and maybe a long, slow turn to see if that straightened the line out. Even then, something might have gone wrong. I only had around six feet to go before I could have put him on the running line, and then I might have caught him. But I didn't. Not much point in suggesting his size. I'd always wanted to catch a really big king salmon, and I had my chance.

It helped, having two seasons where there was a decent amount of fish wherever I went. I'm sure that luck was occasionally with me, and maybe once or twice, I might have thought it out and made a good move. These good moves were likely from spots that were incredibly hot tomorrow, but that's the nature of fishing. Many things affect each individual fisherman's operation, and for those like myself—I wonder what's going on up at— ? Chuck said "over the top of the tides." I could run all night, and be there for hi-slack in the morning. If that doesn't work out I could go on up to—. Or grind it out here? Well,—nothing ventured, nothing gained.

After awhile, running all night, on "I wonder," would become a less frequent thing, and I'd try to have a little information to justify the move. There's sure nothing wrong with spending a little time looking, on the way to some mother lode, and, in the back of my mind as I'd head off into the unknown,—a place that has been maintaining a good scratch might be a poor area to leave.

Later that season we sold some trips in Tokeen and happened to meet some folks who had just moved to Port Angeles. We visited a bit, and they mentioned that they were going to go up to Icy Straits for cohos, which was what Steve and I had in mind. Later, when we happened to be in the same area, we tied together and after listening to the roar my exhaust system made, it was suggested that I come up to their place during the winter and he'd build me a new muffler. I did, and happened to meet their daughter, who has been Mrs. Cameron since then. That was my best season!

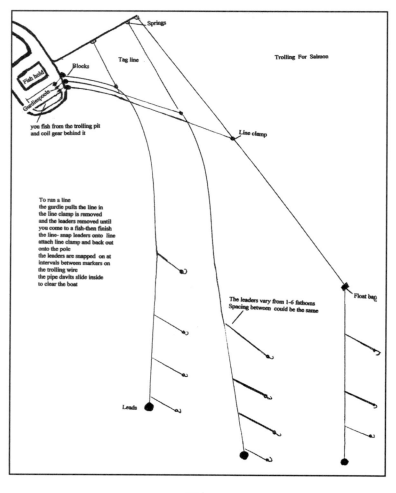

Springs

Trolling For Salmon

Tag line

Blocks

Fish hold

Gurdiespools

you fish from the trolling pit
and coil gear behind it

Line clamp

To run a line
the gurdie pulls the line in
the line clamp is removed
and the leaders removed until
you come to a fish-then finish
the line- snap leaders onto line
attach line clamp and back out
onto the pole
the leaders are snapped on at
intervals between markers on
the trolling wire
the pipe davits slide inside
to clear the boat

Float bag

The leaders vary from 1-6 fathoms
Spacing between could be the same

Leads

# Chapter 9
# Ernie Brannon

It's hard to tell you about the Dungeness without thinking of Ernie Brannon. He was the Superintendent of the Dungeness Salmon Hatchery, and spent most of his 52 years in state fisheries, working there at that hatchery.

Quite often I would ride my bike up to the old Duncan Bridge site, and fish upstream from there. One morning I saw him walking up below me, carrying a big bucket, and a long pole with a gaff hook on the end. He stopped to talk, and said someone would drop him off most mornings, and he would walk back up to the hatchery, taking the eggs from a few king salmon each day.

Salmon could go upriver as far as the hatchery racks, and many of them were diverted from there into a large holding pond, until they ripened. Those that never found the pipeline into the pond would stay in the river, and some of these would drop back downstream, a short distance. Some would spawn later in the river, and some would be taken as they ripened, their eggs packed up to the hatchery by Ernie. His morning walk also helped him keep tabs on what was in the river. This was a lot of effort that most people wouldn't have taken, but to get the extra eggs, he did it. He was more interested in the end result than any amount of work it took, to get there. There aren't too many Ernie Brannons, but there is a second edition out there, somewhere.

Over time, Ernie and I got to be quite good friends, to a point that I'd put aside the fishing on some mornings, and carry the egg bucket. I offered to carry the gaff hook and even went so far as to suggest that I get one for him, "That ones a female. Here, hand me the hook."

"No, Cameron, I'll get her. Maybe next week. She's not ready yet."

I never did see him take one that wasn't just to the exact stage of maturity, waiting the extra bit of time till each fish was just right. Some years, even back then, there wouldn't be that many fish, and this was one way that he could maximize the results from the hatchery's operation. If I didn't run on to him back on the river I'd go over to the hatchery, and they'd often have some project going, maybe taking eggs or building something. Like as not it would be with material that they had pulled the nails from and carefully stacked behind the hatchery, to be used again, and maybe again.

I remember one year, he was telling me about a big percentage of bruised eggs in fish they were seeing at the hatchery. The problem was down towards our place at the diversion dam, where the ditches were taken out. There was an apron that went across the river at the bottom of this dam, and apparently the fish couldn't see it because of the turbulence made by water running over its edge. The river had changed slightly below the dam, and there wasn't enough water for the fish to get over to the fish ladder, so they were jumping into the apron, and bruising the eggs when they'd slam their bellies into the edge of it. I was down there with him when some guy from the Fisheries Department came out, and they had a couple loads of big rock dumped just below the fish ladder, enough to make a big pool below it. This raised the water below the fish ladder enough that the fish could go right on up, and also diverted the water into one concentrated stream, to where the fish would move into the pool in the first place. I was impressed. This apron caused trouble almost every time some high water would change something about the flow at this diversionary dam.

When I mention that over time we got to be quite good friends, I mean that it was no instant thing from his part. Even at twelve years old I could recognize that here was someone doing something I could really respect, and about then I probably needed one of those. On his part, he'd probably never seen a tree high enough that he thought I might have fell out of.

I never did get to carry the gaff hook, but after several years of seeing me get darned few summer run steelhead, he showed me how to catch them. The first thing he did was take the time to explain the river portion of their lives to me. Everything he'd tell you about was that way. He took the time and completely explained it. He should have been the one teaching the fisheries class at the U.W. Then, heaven forbid, the class would have been allowed to explore the whole subject.

In a few years I asked him about coming to work for him after I finished high school. He said we'd have to see at that time, because they could only have so much full time help. If something opened up not too long before I graduated, he said he would keep it open until I finished school. So up until the summer before I became a senior in high school, my plans were to go to work there, even if it took a little waiting until things opened up.

One day on a summer run steelhead expedition I parked outside the hatchery office, and went in to visit. Several times, I'd heard him mention that he wouldn't be able to use the hatchery at full capacity, because of lack of funds to pay for this or that. Usually, it all came down to feed for the fish. On this particular day he was in an especially black mood, and made the comment, "Cameron, if you ever go to work in the state hatchery system, you'll spend the rest of your life fighting with politicians." I had never seen him so upset before, and it threw quite a shadow on my wanting to go to work at the hatchery. I've silently thanked him many times since, for being so honest with me that day. Even so, I think I would have enjoyed spending my life at the hatcheries, especially, working with him at the Dungeness. As it turned out, I wouldn't exactly avoid the politics of fisheries later on.

# Chapter 10
# The Elusive

Trish and I were married on St. Patrick's Day in 1967, and within a week or so we are on our way north, running up with Bill and Nada Small. I've already told you about the first part of this season, when we ran across Ray Lee at Deer Harbor.

After taking Ray into Elfin Cove, we went back through Icy Straits, and then down to lower Chatham to investigate some of my hot spots. I hoped they might be a little warmer than they'd been when we had tried them earlier. One of them

*Another "nice" fish*

was, and we had a decent trip on "good sized" king salmon, in nearly flat calm water. Also, we had 33 eagles and a bunch of seagulls in one picture. When we got in to Petersburg the old guys on the dock would try to get Trish to give them a hint as to where that (big) trip came from. Petersburg is right at the north end of Wrangell Narrows, a beautiful channel about twenty miles long, that runs from Frederick Sound to Sumner Straits. She'd point out through the narrows towards Frederick Sound, and say, "right out there."

Of course, it was a fifteen hour run "out there" to where we'd been fishing, but they knew that. They got a big bang out of it and even on trips where we hadn't done all that well—"where were you this trip?" They'd give her great advise on how to do dishes on a boat, "put em in a sack, and tow em behind the boat when you're fishing." Or how to wash clothes, "tow em behind the boat when you're running." She loved it and so did they.

She had a little trouble with the seasick department, but did fine when we were in the bays or further up inside, out of the ocean swell. As luck would have it, this happened to be one of those years when you could find kings on the inside. On the way in to town one trip, we had stopped with the intention of anchoring in this bay, and running on in the next morning, right after change of tide. Trish wanted to sleep in, and said she'd get up and get some breakfast going as soon as I got the gear aboard.

Tiny had woke her up about the time I was going to holler at her, that we wouldn't be heading in that day. I had caught almost 30 nice kings, and had decided to fish out the day and go to town tomorrow. But breakfast still sounded good. When she thought Trish should get up Tiny would get into the opening, going down into the focsle, and move back and forth to make shadows move around. Pretty quick, Trish would peek around the end of the bunk at her, and the tail would start to wag. When she first got up, she'd get a cup of coffee, and sit in the wheelhouse seat, and Tiny would sit beside her. She'd had her since she was nine.

On the way into a harbor one evening, she saw a black bear on the beach. She'd been sitting on the fish hold hatch and after she'd barked at it, the bear whirled around, so she dove off the hatch, into the house and worked her way up to the seat, across the console and barked her head off in the security of the wheelhouse. When we'd pick up some porpoise, Trish would take her up on the bow and they spent a lot of hours watching the show. I don't think it was my imagination that the porpoise favored the side they were on. Tiny certainly cheered them on.

*Tiny—almost grinning*

If we went somewhere in town, and didn't take her with us, Tiny would get up on the wheelhouse seat, then up onto the console, and walk across in front of the windows to stand on the horn button. She wouldn't budge, either. Guys would go aboard and move her, but she'd go right back the moment they were off the boat. Then they'd go back aboard, and throw the main switch on the batteries. We tried putting a coffee mug over the button and she'd nudge it off, out of her way. In Petersburg this passed for mystery, intrigue, excitement, and there was even a small plot. Or plotter. Almost better than snoose. She started going with us when we left the boat.

It was a fun summer, and pretty fishy. That was when they still had halibut seasons, and Trish would jig in the harbor for a few minutes each evening after the anchor went down. If there was a few agreeable fish around, she'd keep right on jigging. Dinner might be a little bit late. She liked to keep those fish separate, and at the end of the season she had a nice little stash to outfit a kitchen.

Pretty often during the off tide, we'd throw the skiff in, and go on the beach. Tiny loved it, and would really come alive the moment I started getting the skiff down. The long hours on the boat always made going ashore welcome. Some spots would have some decent beach combing, or logging roads to walk on, or you might go up some creek or river to a lake. If we were in Saginaw we'd go in and tie to the dock at Mac's, and have a cup of coffee. We always brought him

*Tiny almost indignant*

110

in fresh fish of some kind, and we pruned his rhubarb frequently. They had a NOAA boat there for part of the season, and the next year there would be a much better chart of the area.

Steve had spent most of the season in the Cross Sound neighborhood, but came down when our king numbers started sounding pretty good. One afternoon was spent looking over a spot that had a certain legend attached to it. A Sun God, a planned attack by one tribe on another; and a rockslide that mostly covered a small cave or overhang, killing or injuring enough of the would be attackers that it saved the tribe that would have been attacked. Trish was a sissy and wouldn't go in under the slide area, but Steve and I did, and after looking the situation over, decided maybe just a burial spot, and a few good, story telling natives in years past. No use elaborating on it here. Too many have been there already.

There are spots in some of the bays where the beach rock is almost solid fossil, and this made for some enjoyable times ashore. And petroglyphs. Years later, Chris and I went ashore and saw some of the more common figures they used to do. Fish, two figures facing each other, different animals, birds, fish, and the like. Some variation of the opposing figures is found in petroglyph all over the world, and it would be interesting if you could know how they came to be in the rock here. They are cut into stone, in this case, solid sections of beach rock. The cutting is not too deep, say ¼ or ⅜ inch, and slightly wider. The thing that interested us the most, were the long lines that seemed to section the rock into long strips, maybe fifty or more feet long and I forget, but it seems like about six feet wide. We looked the immediate area over, and then spreading out, saw other work. We came onto a beautifully done swan, about the same size as the other smaller drawings. Then, not too far away, FULMER 1948. You couldn't see much difference in what he'd done, and what the natives had done, who knows how long ago. For me, that's a good enough reason not to elaborate on where, or what, in certain instances. It's all going to be ruined soon enough anyway. It's not that I wouldn't like people to see and enjoy these spots, and I've made certain that a few have, but to provide an open key—I don't think so. There's always that glad jackass that comes along and spoils it from then on.

Along towards the end of the season, we were fishing kings in Frederick Sound, and Trish got the urge to call it a season and head south. We only had a few days on the trip, and I wanted to fish a few more, but she was persistent. Luckily, we went with her instincts, or feelings, or whatever it is they use, and headed south. We stopped in Wrangell and had dinner with friends, a quick stop in Ketchikan, and down the line we went. When we were going across the straits to Port Angeles we were listening to a radio station in Victoria, and they were telling of this big storm in Southeast Alaska. I mentioned to her, that you didn't normally hear a southern B.C. station talking of weather up there, and that it must have been a dandy.

When we got over to Port Angeles, Bill and Nada were awfully glad to see us. They had been worried we were in it, because that's right about where they knew we would have been. The wind gauge at Kake, and Mac's, both pegged out at 150 MPH. which was as high as either of them went. At the logging camp across the bay, boats were sunk at the dock, and one lady was hurt when the building she was in blew over, or down. One of their buildings was a quonset hut, and I was told later, that it had pulled the deadmen anchors enough to move the quonset hut sideways four feet. Something stretched, anyway.

The boats that were at Mac's left a bow line on the dock, and ran against the dock to keep it in place. Mac thought the wind would have put them on the beach in seconds if they'd tried to leave. It was the worst he'd ever seen there. A couple others got loose from the dock before it got to blowing too hard, and tied to the log boom behind the island. One of the Petersburg seiners sank in the harbor at Tyee, and another boat that had its anchor up and was just jogging, picked up the crew. Other boats further up towards Juneau were also lost. We didn't realize it at the time, but Keith, our first born, was riding along with us, and maybe the nesting instinct saved us a real ordeal, or worse. I'm sure glad we weren't there.

Right after getting home, we rented a little place outside of Port Angeles, and during the winter, bought a place out by the river. The big cottonwoods I'd used as a marker to show me where to cut up through the woods, were right behind our place. A few years later we would buy the property behind us, and later on, the property the cottonwoods live on. This is directly across from where my favorite piece of river had separated, and gone down through the woods on the east side.

Now with a family en route, we began thinking of a different program for the fishing seasons. We decided that first year, that I would go north early, and fish till about the end of June, then come down and put in the rest of the season off the Washington coast. I flew down before Keith was born, ( on my birthday) and stayed until Trish got settled back at home, and then flew back north. One quick pass through lower Chatham, around Cape Decision, and I was headed south. This was one of the realities I would have to face in having a family and being a fisherman. Me and a lot of other fishermen. Trish and a lot of other wives and mothers. A tough situation, and I'm certain it was much worse for them. The guys at least knew what was going on, but at home they'd be wondering every time a good storm went through. We did this the next two seasons, up early, and back south around the first of June. Chris (Christopher Lee) came along about midsummer of the third season and Deann would show up in 1977.

Starting in 1971 we started fishing full seasons in Washington, which made it nice. I could spend more time at home and fish kings before the June 15 opener for silvers. Then, when the silver season

*Trish, Keith, and Tiny*

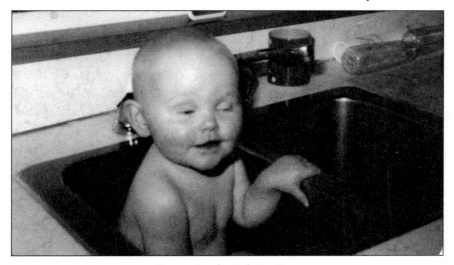

*Deann in the "Elusive" spa*

113

started, the trips would be good, an open fishery for kings and silvers, and anyone who put out a good effort would see a decent season for their efforts. There's no good reason why Indian fishermen couldn't have had good seasons then, too, if they had came out and fished "In common" with us. I'll never understand why the Alaskan Indians worked so hard at fishing, or at jobs ashore, when so many of the Washington Indians, didn't. This isn't all inclusive, in either case, but the contrast is just about blinding.

*Chris fishing behind lighthouse at Dungeness*

What a wonderful thing to be able to go home at the end of the trip. The season stayed open till along in October, and with the season so long, you could afford to take time off when the weather was bad, or when there didn't seem to be much fish around. There was very little loss of boats or life then. So we were Washington fishermen full time, from 1971 on through the 1975 season.

I had to adapt my operation to fishing around many more boats, than I did up north. I received some great coaching from Bill Wilcox, and Lloyd and Joe Gowdy. It started making a good difference in what I put across the dock. I don't know how many times I heard "you've got to refine your gear" from Bill. Each time I'd go back out and fine tune a bit more. This was during a time when there was some big changes being made in leader, hooks and the various lures, which made it an interesting time in the troll fishery. These guys weren't afraid of experimenting, and they opened my eyes to the possibility that what works today might not tomorrow. I started thinking a lot more about what was going on down the lines, where it ultimately happens, and applying it to ocean and feed conditions, the weather, the nature of the fleet I might be working around, and anything else that I thought might affect the operation.

Gradually, I became a better boat handler by listening to them, and quite a few others, and got the best of coaching from Lloyd, on taking care of my fish. His quality was right at the top, always, and not many handled the amount of fish he did. This expanded way of looking at things, started making a difference on a daily basis. The depth you set the gear at, especially when fishing in very deep water, and how you arranged the gear on the lines, were both things that made a major difference in what went across the dock and it kept you experimenting.

I always enjoyed fishing right up till dark, especially off Washington, and when fishing way offshore, it made more sense to drift at night, rather than run in to anchor inside 25 fathoms or maybe behind Destruction Island. Several times I would wake up from a comfortable snooze, and be amazed at the sea conditions I woke up in. The Camelot was the best boat for drifting in poor weather that I've ever seen. Rather than join the fleet behind the Island I'd tie down the fish hold hatch, trolling pit, and gear covers, turn on all the lights and hit the sack. I'd get up to check off and on all night, but still get more rest and fish earlier and later, doing this.

Experimenting with gear patterns while fishing in deep water, became one of my favorite pastimes. Sometimes they were on the top, sometimes on the bottom, sometimes both or neither, and sometimes in between. Fine tuning your gear to depth and patterns could make or break your day.

I had been fishing silvers further than usual offshore, and had ended the day in nice conditions, to wake up to a very big swell and 20 or so westerly. There had been a few boats around during the night, but I couldn't see any now, and the size of the swell was likely part of the reason. I threw the gear out, and started fishing up and in, with only a few fish now and then. It had been good fishing, especially in the mornings, and I was wondering what would be the thing to do. After another hour of scratch fishing I'd moved in to where the swell had over doubled in size, and although it was big enough to be safe, it was a bit intimidating. You would have the stiff wind towards the top of the swell and calm when you were down in the valleys, and now the only boat I saw was a freighter moving uphill, and that scared the hell out of me. We were only one long swell apart when we passed, but when we were both in our respective valleys, all I could see was the top few feet of his mast. A few swells later, I saw his entire front deck take a bath and being on the Camelot seemed a little better. Being tied up in

La Push sounded better yet. Before long I had the gear aboard, and was moving up and in, not too fast.

The swell had gone down quite a bit as I moved further away from the edge, and a few hours later I was throwing the gear out again. What fish I'd had further out were deeper than the day before, and I'd decided to try a couple lines a bit deeper, now. After awhile I moved into an area of fish and deeper was definitely better. I finally set all the gear from 30 to 50 fathoms and had all the fish I could take care of. They obviously didn't like the movement or commotion caused by the big swell, and had dropped under it.

One of the pastimes, if we were blown into La Push in any northwesterly weather, was the ball games. The Indians had kind of a mediocre team, and we could always find enough bodies in the fleet, so we had some fine games. To be a bit more accurate, they had a lousy team, but they always beat us.

Loser buys the beer! If it looked like they were losing they'd set a couple cases by the backstop and before long, some of our team couldn't find second base. Then one game when the fishermen actually used a little self control, and we were showing them what baseball could be, I started noticing a few subs on their team. Before long we were playing a bunch of ten or twelve year old kids. I couldn't remember seeing one of their original team leave, but they were all gone.

While I was quite young, I had started having migraine headaches, only a few at first; but they kept increasing until they became quite a factor in my life. I'd been to several Doctors over the years, in the army and otherwise, who told me that migraine meant split, or one sided. They said the term "migraine" had nothing to do with severity. The particular type of them that I had were stoppers, at least in my case. If I had time, I'd get in and tie to the dock, or anchor and try to get things squared away before it got going. If one came on in poor circumstances, I went through hell. You craved complete darkness and quiet. Usually, once they were started, nothing helped. The Doctor in Port Angeles, said they could take a migraine away, or cover it up, with a shot of Ergotamine, but he was reluctant to start that, at my age. We would watch them and see how it went. Now it seemed like they had finished with me. I had only had two of them all season and that was pretty much the end of them. Who knows?

Fishing means different things to different people. Probably there were other things I could have done during this time period to have made a living, but working for someone else wouldn't have been a very good option. You can either do a job or you can't, and too much of the time, I couldn't. I worked nights for two winters at the lumber mill in Port Angeles, but if Rodney Erickson and Kenny Chace hadn't picked up the slack on a few bad nights, I never could have stayed. At their worst, but for only a short time, I had three separate ones a week, and no employer could put up with that. Usually they spanned around ten hours, but one lasted over two days, and I was useless for days afterwards.

So where this affliction didn't amount to much when I started fishing, it later became quite a problem. I could still make a living fishing, but it was never what you'd call a good one. Sid had crushed an elbow, and ended up with an arm that wouldn't bend, and there were others who only had one leg or one arm, and still figured a way to get the job done, and went out and did it. Just about anything that could be wrong with someone, was in the fleet somewhere, but when you're your own boss, and the seasons were long enough, you could make something like fishing work. Now it looked like we might be able to stick our neck out and get into a bigger boat. With a growing family it had been more than we had wanted to chance, but now anything seemed possible. You can't imagine how a near migraine- free season built confidence.

This made another change in our lives possible. Before I started milking cows, I had made most of my spending money, selling steelhead and silvers I'd caught in the river. This stopped for years after I started fishing commercially, but after marriage and a family, there always seemed to be a need for a few extra bucks. When the silvers came in the river each fall, a few of them got diverted towards which ever area we felt needed it the most. We felt that now, we shouldn't need to do this again, and didn't. Later on, they legalized taking salmon on sport gear in the river, and our smokehouse finally saw some legal salmon.

One of the guys from Port Angeles had gone down to California and had a 54 foot steel boat built. When he brought it home there was a lot of interest, and before long four of the guys went down and ordered boats. Ray Balch and I were two of them.

We went through an awful lot to get the Elusive. Another fisherman from Seattle, named Ted, was also having a boat built in the same yard, at the same time. Four boats, five buyers. Ted and I were buying the same boat. He wasn't there full time either. We would both go down with equipment, and check on how things were going, then back to fishing. We both started hearing about each other. Each of us made calls to the builder on this one subject, and each of us were told the other guy didn't exist, or—"he's nuts, don't worry about him. That's your boat!"

Finally I received a letter from one of the other three guys, saying I'd better get to the bottom of this, because being there full time, he knew for sure that I had a problem. This other guy named Ted thought my boat was his boat. Ted had helped someone else run their boat down the coast, and they had stopped in and unloaded a bunch of major equipment for "our boat."

I called Bill Hammer, who I knew was also a friend of Ted's, and explained the situation.

"I know, Vince, he thinks it's his boat."

"What is he, some kind of a nut?"

"No. No more than you are, Vince." Great!!

We talked it over and he suggested I call Ted and get to the bottom of it. We'd both screwed around long enough. Ted said he'd been hearing about me. We talked a bit and he said to stick by the phone, he'd give the builder a call. He called back in a few minutes and said, "I'm sorry Vince, he still says that's my boat."

I told him to sit tight, I was going to call down there and I'd call him right back.

When I called Ted back, I told him, "Just about word for word, what he just told you. We've both got to go down there and look him in the eye at the same time. Then we'll see what he says."

Ted asked where we lived, said he could be there in two hours, and we'd go get to the bottom of this. We had lunch ready when he got there, and showed him our slip of paper, which was the most the builder would agree to signing, basically saying he agreed to build a boat for costs plus materials. It was dated, and the amount we'd advanced was receipted.

He read it, and told us that before we went any further, as far as he was concerned the boat was ours. We had put quite a bit more down, about six months before he had. He said he'd still like me to ride down with him, as he was going to get his money back. So away we went. Lots of fish stories, and I would be a better tuna fisherman afterwards. Tuna were Ted's specialty, and at one time he had the "Maureen" which was one of the fishier tuna boats out there. It's never just the boat though, and listening to him talk about it, you could hear the little things that made a big difference at the end of the day.

We drove straight through, and stayed the night with friends of Ted's. With a good breakfast under our belts, we were at the yard first thing in the morning. There was an awfully quick offer to lay a keel for Ted the following day, but he just told him that he wanted his money back, by noon. Actually, he said a bit more than that. He did get his money, and we were on our way back home. He could have had the guy thrown in jail, but realized that would have sunk the rest of us. After what he'd been through, and what it had cost him, you couldn't have blamed him. Now and then you get to see a class act, and Ted's was.

Dave Meneghini, the fellow that had bought the first boat, prior to the group I was in, told me I might be making a big mistake if I expected to have the boat fishable for that next season. I stewed and fussed over it for several weeks, and in the end, decided to fish the Camelot that next year. Dave's tip was a good one. It put another decent season under our belts, and lots of time afterwards to transfer the Camelot, and then concentrate on the Elusive. There were two brothers in the group I was fishing in and they had spoken for the Camelot. They sold the boat they had been fishing, and Guy would take the Camelot, and Al wound up buying the Showboat, so they had the equipment now to do quite well, and did. In several seasons they each moved up to the fiberglass Hoquiam boats which, were around 46 feet long. Good boats.

They'd stopped work on the Elusive in order to speed the other three boats along, which I had agreed to, so when I got back down to the boat yard, we had quite a ways to go. Most of the metal work was done, but the foaming and fiberglassing in the fish hold, setting up the machines, steering system, and installing enough equipment to move the boat home, was waiting for me when I got there. I'd start it up the beach, as soon as the boat was moveable.

We had bought a new 8-71 GM for the main, and had decided on a Twin Disc 514 gear with a 4.13 to 1 reduction. The prop was a 50-36 Michigan, a 3

*The Elusive under construction*

119

inch monel main shaft, and the intermediate was a 3 inch cold roll. The alternator on the main was an 85 amp Leece Neville. These all proved to be good choices. The gen set was sideways to the front engine room bulkhead, and was a 4-53 GM with a 50 KW Kato generator. Poor choice. Both fine pieces of equipment but a poor match-up, and even if they'd been a better match, it was a poor choice for the boat. Turning the system at 1200 turns appealed to me, but never having owned a gen set, or knowing the subject, made for this poor move.

The old radio on the Camelot wouldn't be licenseable for new owners, so I had it as a way to communicate in an emergency. We had a "hunting type" Wood Freeman Auto Pilot, a Mieco Loran, and an old Apelco fathometer. Once again, I needed to get home, next to my scrap pile and salvage yards, so that outfitting the boat wouldn't be as draining as this was proving to be. I put 4000 gallons of diesel in the boat and filled the freshwater tank. That put her down in the water where it felt more like a boat. The next day we took it out for a boat ride and, two days later the Elusive was going up the beach. It was easy not to look back!

Using up some scraps, I had nailed a sort of bunk together against one wall, and had a Coleman gas stove, mounted on a crate, fastened to the back wall of the cabin. There was a piece of plywood from floor to ceiling, at what would be the back of the wheel house, and the gauges for the machine were mounted on this. Otherwise, from the back door, to the console across the front of the wheelhouse, it was wide open. Not much to brace against.

It was a nice day to start on, and as part of breaking in the machine, I was running at 1600 turns which would generally get around 10 knots. You started paying for the last two or three knots in diesel consumption, and after that I would usually turn the machine slower, but occasionally you wanted the power, and it was wonderful to have it. Being able to buck through a little tougher weather, or make it to some spot in time to jump on a tide, was nice. The stern didn't start to pull down till after 2000 turns and, by by-passing the governor, the machine could turn 2300. There would be a few times, when getting to some good spot in time to fish high slack, would easily pay for that trips fuel. Enough power is better than too little.

The current was heading to the north too, and the next morning about daylight I was coming up on Cape Blanco, on the southern Oregon coast. I was pretty pleased with the progress, but a blanket was thrown on that, when I listened to the weather, which said it was going to blow southeast that afternoon. Being alone on the boat, and the boat being pretty much untried, I was thinking about where to pull in. I was already tired, and didn't need to do something dumb. Tatoosh was still a long way off.

For some reason the Umpqua looked like a good spot. Nice and handy. Coos Bay would have been a better choice, in that it would have been easier to get back out of, but I didn't know that. Newport would be better yet, but it was still a long ways up the beach, and it sounded like I'd have weather by then. All I had was running charts, and they gave no detail at all of what I'd need to see my way upstream, into the harbor. I called the Coast guard Station at the Umpqua, and asked them if they could give me an idea what to expect, once I got up there. They had a boat on bar drill, and when they saw me coming they would come out, and hold my hand on the way in.

When we got in, a couple of the young Coasties came over to do the inspection, which is usual whenever they provide any assistance. I didn't have the boat papers, but was traveling under the master carpenters certificate, which got me by. I forget what all I didn't have on the boat yet, horn, bell, ? two or three items, some which had been ordered, and some not. Nothing that amounted to much. That afternoon it started blowing from the southeast, and I was pretty happy to be where I was.

The next morning I heard a machine running close by, and looked out to see a little Coast Guard boat pull along side. They said, the skipper says to come on over if you get a chance. They were going back now, and if I wanted I could ride over with them. When we went in, there was a sort of day room, and the walls were lined with guys, with an instructor in the middle of the room, giving a class, so apparently this was a school as well as a Station.

Meeting the skipper, you liked him. You knew, to get where he was, he had to run on salt water instead of blood. "Hi, what'd you come in here for? I know you want to get home with Christmas and all coming, but this place set a record a couple years ago—28 consecutive days that no commercial boat went over the bar."

He said this one didn't sound like too much, although I wouldn't get out for a few days. When the time looked right, he'd send the boat out, and they'd count waves and get me outside in good shape. We looked at the chart for Newport, and he gave me an extra he had of the Columbia. Then we went down and he gave me a tour of their boats, which were maintained slightly above perfection.

The next day he came down the dock, and said lets go out and look at the bar. We went out in his van, and drove up to where their lookout tower gave a good picture of the whole bar. There were good sized breakers for quite aways offshore.

"Any of those will take out your windows, but we won't even send you down here until we're sure you can go." He pointed out a little spot off to the side, that had a little lee from the surge, and said that was where I'd wait until their boat told me to go for it. Years later I watched a TV documentary about the Umpqua Coast Guard Station, and the skipper. He's about three and a half legends. What a wonderful thing, for me and anyone else out there, that he was there to teach the young people coming up. He'll make a difference, long past his time.

The wind had dropped nicely now, but the bar was still nothing to deal with, and I'd have another day in the harbor. Before we head out I'll tell you a bit more about the "Elusive." I've already mentioned the machines, and the drive, but there's a bit more. She is 54 feet long, 16 feet wide, and with full fuel and a little ice in the boat, drew right at 8 ½ feet. Fresh water was circulated through the keel for cooling, so the keel was divided just forward of the engine room bulkhead, with the front half cooling the auxiliary and the section towards the stern cooling the 8-71. Both sections of the keel were baffled, to circulate the water.

In the focsle, built against the front bulkhead that separated it and the engine room, I had a 200 gallon tank for lube oil, that had its outlet in the engine room. The top of the tank was used either as an extra bunk, or for storage. When I got home, I would add two other bunks, toe to toe at the bow with storage lockers

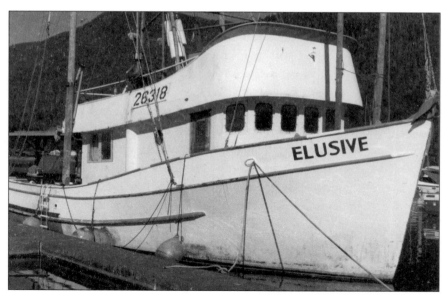

*Looking at her from the front, it looked like she was all house*

*From the stern it looked like she was all back deck*

underneath. A 500 gallon fresh water tank is under the focsle floor, it's outlet in the engine room.

There was plenty of room to walk around the engine, and when working on any part of it, you had easy access. You could easily reach underneath from the sides, and you could put a tall five gallon can under from the front, to change oil. There is a 400 gallon fuel tank on each side of the engine, each having lengths of angle iron welded to the top to secure machinery from, or to hold boxes of parts and equipment between. There are four more tanks in the stern, one that the trolling pit is built into, one on each side just in front of the pit, and a big tank in the middle. This made for a 5000 gallon fuel capacity. You don't use that much fuel trolling for salmon, so to keep the fuel fresh, I used the two in the engine room, plumbed together, as day tanks. At the end of each trip I'd run fuel forward from either the stern tank, the big middle tank, or the two side tanks, ran together. This allowed fresh fuel in each tank, every third trip.

There is an organism, or some kind of a critter that actually lives, develops and multiplies in diesel oil. It likes warmer conditions better, but it does exist in Alaska, and that's where I encountered it. You first notice it when your fuel pressure gauge turns red in the face. When you pull your main filter, you'll have a bunch of slime hanging all over it, and running a bit of fuel into a glass jar will let you look at the individual culprit, which looks like a bit of clear snot with a small dark nucleus. They are absolutely devastating to diesel systems.

Here's what you do about them, and at the same time, I'll describe my fuel system. I had a settler tank, which looked about like a twenty inch piece of hot water tank, cut in two to form a half round, welded to the side of the stbd. engine room tank. Each of the six tanks was valved in at this settler, and there was a line that went to the main filter, which was a 750 lubrefiner with a diesel- pac, and then went over to the secondary filter on the machine. The auxiliary went through the same settler and lubrefiner, but then went into a Racor filter.

There was a drain valve at the bottom of the settler and I could tap this during fueling or transferring fuel, to see what was going on. Also, each morning I drained off a pint or so of diesel and held it up to the light. I'd heard about "the bug" and by using the settler and a glass jar, saw it coming before there was a population explosion. This might seem like a lot of trouble, but nothing compared to plugged fuel systems and injectors.

I didn't have one plugged injector in either the Camelot or the Elusive in 28 years of diesel engines. A good settler is a nice thing. Likewise, a fuel pressure gauge. You can get water or dirty fuel as well as "the bug," and by checking the settler you will know about it, and be able to deal with it before it causes problems. Even if it got into the filters, the gauge would have told me in time to deal with it, before I had bigger problems.

They make a product called Bio Bor that you mix into the fuel, and it will kill the bug. You'll likely have to change filters after treatment to get "the bug" carcasses out of the system, but at least you'll have licked the problem. Probably lots of places handle Bio Bor, or something like it, but the only place I ever got it was Ballard Marine or Ballard Fuel Dock, whatever they called it, in Seattle. With so many non boat fuel tanks being installed above ground now, this will probably be more and more of a problem.

I was comfortable with my system, and it worked well, but I think a clear system you can see into, like the Racor, would be a good thing in any installation, or especially where lack of room might be a consideration. I know Racor makes bigger units than what I had on the auxiliary, but I still like the settler idea with a big filter, in the front lines.

There were four 8-D batteries tied together at Pos- Pos, Neg- Neg to make two separate banks of 12 volt, with more backbone per bank. It took two of the 8Ds to start the 8-71 effectively, using 12 volts. I alternated the two banks daily.

The batteries were in a fiberglassed box that wouldn't allow any leakage of battery juices to go astray. The auxiliary had its own private battery and box, and all the batteries could readily be charged from either machine. Later, I would install a constavolt system, that would charge the batteries using shore power.

An alarm system monitored engine room, and above the stove temperatures, engine coolant temperature, oil pressure, and water levels in both the bilge, and the expansion tank for the main engine. A green light showed each system to be working, and a red light immediately pointed out the culprit. Sometimes you already knew. Along with the lights, the unit made considerable noise if you had a problem.

But darned little was in place when I took the boat up the beach. Just enough to get it there. The next morning saw me over the bar in good shape, and I was on my way up the beach, again. The wind had gone down to 15 or 20 southwest, with a pretty fair southwest swell running that would liked to have made for a miserable ride, but the Elusive seemed to enjoy any version of a following sea. Daylight the following morning had me between the Columbia River and Westport, and along towards noon, one of my favorite trees was coming in sight. It's a dandy, and lives up behind Split Rock. I've never been up close to it, but my guess is Douglas Fir (red fir.) Late that night I tied between the pilings in Neah Bay. They had pulled in the floats for the winter. A stiff northeast blowing out of the straits the next morning, so lots of water over the bow on the way into Port Angeles. Trish and the kids were waving at me when I went around the end of Ediz Hook. I was glad to be home.

At this point in a boats life, there are several ways you can go. We were already nicely in debt on the venture. We could have borrowed more, and went first class in finishing the boat, borrowed less and went somewhere short of first class, or not borrow anymore at all, and just go fishing. We had gone first class, as far as I was concerned, on the 8-71 and the Twin Disc gear, and now it looked like the thing to do was play it safe, and close to the belt. I remembered what Bill Small had told me. "Put the best machine you can in the boat, and after that, all you need is a pair of gurdies, and something to pull the anchor. Everything else can come later." The gurdies, stove, and a few other things were already home in the garage, and the anchor winch was sitting on the bow. We had a few bucks left to get us through till spring, and decided that sharpening the pencil and getting a job for a few months, and putting all of that towards bare essentials, would be the best way to go. The migraines were still in the back of our minds, and were likely a big part of this decision.

I did a little job looking, and wound up working for one of the dairy farmers, helping install a liquid manure tank. He had hired a contractor to install it, so I and the farmer, who helped between chores, were extra help. I heard bits and pieces from the farmer, and the guy building the tank, but never did get it clear in my mind what all was happening. It seemed like the more you heard about it, the less sense it made.

There was a Sheik, or whatever they go by, that owned quite a bit of desert and oil wells, and he decided that when he sent a tanker full of oil across to the U.S. they might as well take something worthwhile, back. A pay trip. He sent his son over to put things together, so when it was arranged, farmers in the Sequim area were going to provide liquid manure in volume, to be loaded into a large barge, and towed down to some Gulf Port destination, to be pumped onto the empty tanker. Obviously they knew that any fertilizer from the southern states wouldn't compare to Washington State B.S.

Probably even in the mid-east, they had heard about some of our northwest politicians. Once home, they'd add seed, pump it onto the desert, and everything would turn green, one way or the other.

Farmers in the area suddenly needed a liquid manure tank. Others that already had one, needed another. My main job was bending re-bar, plus a little bit of everything else. For that time of year we had good weather. It went fairly well, and was interesting to someone like myself who hadn't been around anything like that. When we finished, the contractor offered me a job, working with them on the next tank, which would do me nicely until time to start putting the boat together. They never did ship a gallon of liquid manure. Since then, I've heard a dozen more stories, or versions, but I don't really know what happened.

Now we had about a month to go before we went fishing. Larry Peters was going to fish with me that year, and had fished with me in 1973. Then his brother Don had got the "Duwam," and they had fished it together in 1974. Their dad was a troller, and they had raised kids that knew how to work. Years earlier I had bought some yellow cedar logs from the west end, with the intention of using them in a wooden boat project that I hadn't gone ahead with. We hauled these to one of the small mills that there used to be quite a few of, and had our upright posts for the fish hold, bin boards, and some other material for a quick put together, to get us fishing. My scrap pile, lumber which had been kept under a roof, and stripped between layers, and a nice assortment of scrap metal, pipe, and brackets, became a close friend.

I had worked several winters with Kenny Chace, at the lumber mill, and he was there most of the time, making a hay rack in the stern for the blocks and gurdies, out of my pipe collection, and spent days making brackets and gear for rigging poles, or to mount things on.

In the week before we went fishing, Trish came down the dock with a VHF radio under her arm. She'd been squirreling money aside, just in case, and figured this would be the best place to put it. If a guy happens to make a success of something, it's pretty often because of the people behind him. What a home team I had!

The first season with the Elusive wasn't that good. Sometimes you don't connect. This was one of those years, and we had the odd problem, boat wise. They had used a steering gear out of a truck to go from the end of the steering shaft in the stern, over to the rudder. I had trouble with this three separate times before giving up on the idea. The last time, I happened to be backing out of a slip in the Port Angeles boat haven, when it collapsed. Bill Wilcox was in town, just winding up his season, and suggested making a quadrant, putting a small drum on the shaft, and running cable from it to blocks on each side of the trolling pit, and back to the quadrant. He helped Kenny and me design a quadrant using the rims used to secure a lid to a 55 gallon drum, and his parting comment was, "this'll work fine for now. If you want, you can put in something more elaborate during the winter." I wound up using it the rest of that season, and for years afterwards, not taking it out until we decided to go longlining, and installed hydraulic steering. Like I said, Bill is a machinist.

The first season would allow very little improvements on the boat, so I took care of a few of the worst bugs, and decided my time might best be spent in the engine room. They had only primed it before putting the machines in, and now I spent a good portion of the winter cleaning, preparing, priming, and painting every inch of the engine room, bilge, and inside the air ducts, and the stack. These last items took forever, using an extension handle, and tying a wire brush to it, or a paint brush with primer or paint. On the other hand, I had lots of time, and got a good job. I used a light grey up to the top of the tanks and white above that. I was proud of my engine room.

After that first season, things started looking up. The next year I started in Alaska, and had a dismal start on the season until I finally moved up towards Sitka. Late one afternoon, on what was one of the better days of the spring, I got a call on the marine operator from Trish. She said Joe Gowdy had called, and suggested that if I wasn't doing really well, I ought to get on south. I thought about it for a few minutes, went out and got the gear aboard, and headed south. I did quite well that season, and had room that next winter, dollar-wise, to make some major improvements in the cabin and wheelhouse. I stripped out all the scrap pile material, put a tent over the back deck, and put things together like I would have liked to in the first place. The season also allowed quite an upgrade in other equipment.

Each year after that I would finish the season with at least a two page list, some of it small, few hour jobs, and some that were major projects. It was nice when working with something that wasn't quite right, to think it out as much as possible while in operation, and the notes taken, would often eliminate a lot of trial and error when fix-it time came. Without the list you would start the next season, and the first thing that wasn't quite right was one of the things you had vowed to fix during the previous winter,—and forgot about.

# Chapter 11
# Eagles

In all the years of trolling for salmon in Alaska, I saw jillions of eagles, but none come to mind more than "our" eagles at Snipe Bay. We spent a lot of time at Snipe when the boys were young. It was great fun to save a scrap fish, and when our circle of the bay got around to the eagle's nest, we'd throw it out. One of the eagles would swoop down, feet extended, and take it up on the rocks to eat, or when the nest was full, they'd drop it in to a bunch of always hungry, critters. Sometimes if their aim wasn't too good, the fish might bounce off the nest, and then the limbs would shake, as the little guys would follow it to the ground, screaming all the way. What a commotion! I wondered if this wasn't deliberate, because then they had to fly back up. They weren't exactly little either, at this point being about as tall as their elders, but not nearly as heavy. As well as they ate while we were there, mom and dad looked like a couple military cargo planes. At first, the boys would holler out their version of an eagle call, then throw the fish. After awhile it was obvious that the call wasn't necessary. Most of the time, we'd see them on their way out, as soon we'd thrown the fish.

To separate our gear, large floats were attached to two lines, and these were pulled along about eighty feet behind the boat. Two more lines were fished directly from the poles at the boat. One day, one of the eagles got careless on his approach, forgot about the wire angling back to the float, and was swooping down to pick up his catch, the wire directly in his path. When he saw it he reacted instantly. To drop under it would likely have put him in the water, so he put on the brakes, feet forward, mouth (beak) open, every feather on those massive wings fanned down to slow himself. Then full power, up, barely over the wire, and with almost all of his momentum gone, he dropped down, grabbed the fish and turned back, flying low between the floats and then up to the nest. In all the hours of watching eagles, that was the best I ever saw.

On another day we saw him (or her) head out to a boat well outside of us, far enough that we couldn't even see him after awhile. You knew that with his vision and his perch high above the water, he knew there was something worth going out for. Soon we could see a little black dot coming back in, low to the water, and before long we could see that he had a fish. He was flying hard, but he had a long way to go, and he'd already came a long way.

We were in by the rocks when he got in close, and I wondered if he had enough oomph left. He had to get himself and the fish to the top of the rock wall that makes the outer shoreline for that side of the bay. He poured it on and gained enough altitude to barely clear the top, dropped the fish, and landed, exhausted. The fish flopped, went past him over the edge, and down into the water thirty feet below him. He studied it for awhile, but didn't risk picking it out of the ocean surge, against those steep rocks. So that one got away.

Each of these incidents brings up an interesting point. I've seen eagles in the water more than a few times over the years, and I never did see one get back into the air from the water. In each case they'd fly as hard as they could, with their wings never quite getting out of the water till they finally got their feet on the beach. Several times I saw one stop to rest for a few seconds, and then away he'd go again. I suppose mis-judging choppy water knocks a few of them down, and like the one that jumped over our float line, they occasionally screw up.

# Chapter 12
# Tuna

During a stretch of slow salmon fishing in 1969, I decided to go tuna fishing. If there was any salmon to catch, the difference in price between the two, and the long runs usually involved in getting the tuna, had kept me on the beach up until then. This time they were only forty some miles off the Quilleute, and with only a poor scratch on salmon, it seemed worth a try. Joe Gowdy drew me some pictures of how to rig up, and along about midnight we slid out of the Quilleute, and moved out towards this spot of fish about five hours offshore. We went past a few boats before we got to yesterday's hot spot, and he suggested we shut down and drift till daylight, and check this area before moving further out.

Rather than shut down, I decided to put together some lines so I'd be ready at daylight. I set the speed at a slow idle, and went to work under the lights in the trolling pit. In a few minutes I had a short line hanging off the stern, one that placed the jig about thirty feet behind the boat. Then I decided to start on the back lines, ( long lines) and work my way back in towards the boat. One long line off each pole, around 120 feet of tuna cord to a swivel, then a nine foot leader to the jig or tuna skirt, the leader tied into a sturdy swivel on a barbless, double tuna hook, the jig sliding free on the leader. A three way swivel on the boat end of the tuna cord, sent the other connections to the tagline off the pole, and to the in haul line, which led to the stern. The length of this inhaul line determined where, in the boat's wake and turbulence, your jig was pulled.

With a lot of experimenting, we'd find out that placement of each jig was very important. After the long lines came the mid lines, (short long lines) these being identical to the long lines, except only about half as much tuna cord, and they

131

used a slightly longer inhaul. This enabled you to pull a long line fish down the middle, with less chance of tangling with a fish on the shorter gear. Also, each shorter line was attached further out on the pole, enabling you to handle a fish on the shorter line, by pulling it under the long lines. Separating the two with the in hauls let the shorter line fish better, without the long line trailing too near it. A chain line, actually just another short line, with a piece of chain attached between the tag line and leader, was especially effective, because it surged in the chop, or in the wake from the boat. These hung from the tips of the poles, and were fished the furthest out from the boat. A short line from each corner of the stern, and the two chain lines, were all we fished at the boat when we started with the Camelot. Later we would add two lead lines, fished about three feet deep, and only a few feet from the stern.

While I was rigging these short long lines, I noticed a funny, droning sound, but couldn't seem to find a quick reason for it. My deckhand started tracking it down, and after he'd gone all over the boat, from the bow to the trolling pit, he said it was coming from the stern. The stern on the Camelot wasn't a very big place, but we still didn't find it, and having heard how some noises bothered tuna, it had me concerned. I finally got out of the trolling pit to see what he'd missed, and a few minutes later was back in the trolling pit. The noise seemed even louder now. Especially behind the pit. My hand finally touched the short line that I had first put out, and it was down, our first tuna, and in the middle of the night. When they are first hooked they sound, (dive) and the tension of the line in the water was what made that heavy, droning sound. Before long I was completely rigged up, but we didn't get another droner till about daylight, and not a great deal then. We did get a few fish, but could see other boats doing considerably better, and after comparing notes with Joe, it was obvious that something wasn't quite right.

Tuna are a little different to ice than salmon, so I had told my deckhand to put them down on the ice to chill off a bit, and I'd go down with him to help figure out a way to get them put to bed. They're shaped more like a coke bottle, and come out of the water warm, so you have to lay them on the ice to take the body heat away, or you'll melt a hole in the ice, around each fish.

Once iced down, the crushed, or flake ice around each fish will solidify, and form a foundation to help support the next layers of fish. Without a good foundation of ice, especially on the bottom two thirds of the bin, the weight of more fish will crush the fish on the bottom. Not going too deep with the first few layers of fish, allows the ice to set up, and once this has taken place, you can go on up with more layers. The same method is used in icing salmon, except that you put ice in their bellies and the gill cutout, and that you place them differently in the ice, than with tuna.

I noticed a sort of chattering sound, and asked the deckhand if this "new noise had been going on for long. "Yeah, since we've been out here, I didn't notice it much when we were fishing salmon."

We fished salmon at a much slower speed than tuna, so the noise wouldn't have been there when we had the salmon gear in the water. We iced the fish and shoveled all the ice off the shaft alley,

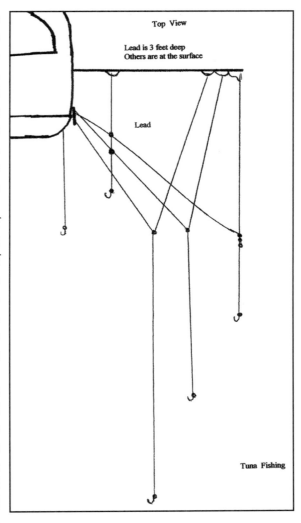

Top View

Lead is 3 feet deep
Others are at the surface

Lead

Tuna Fishing

and attended to the problem. A bearing for the intermediate shaft had a slight chatter, and apparently was putting noise through the hull. I hadn't been able to hear it from on deck, or in the stern, but remembering all the "boat-noise" horror stories I'd heard from the guys that fished tuna, this noise had to go! The bearing would have been a quick fix at the dock, but it seemed like the best solution now, was to just take it out. The shaft had plenty of bearing anyway, so soon we were under way again, minus one shaft bearing. It was as if someone had thrown the tuna switch.

Now the short lines, which had only caught a couple fish, were going down all the time, and the Camelot was what appeared to be a very fishy boat. On the other hand it wasn't a tuna boat. It's carrying capacity wasn't great, probably less than most other forty foot boats in the fleet, so four and a half tons of albacore had you looking at the beach. You couldn't justify going a long way for fish, and unless the fishing on the beach for salmon was very slow, or the albacore were close and hungry, tuna fishing wouldn't be a good option.

There is no fishery that I've been in, that's as exciting. When the lines went down, you pulled your heart out, empty jigs being the only reason they would keep coming. If they stopped, it could all be over in a few seconds. Pretty often you could see fish come up and take a jig down, and when they were coming on the short lines, they were the first line you would grab, since that would be the quickest fish. Before long I figured out that a duplicate shorty, coiled up and ready to throw, would put an immediate jig there for them to grab, and this would occasionally mean quite a few repeats, before grabbing the next line.

During the first tuna trip, I was asleep one night and, through the cobwebs, I thought I felt something moving on my chest. I didn't wake up completely, and didn't feel the movement again right away, but when I did I was wide awake. I'd watched a rat run down the tie up line from a freighter, to the dock in Petersburg, and had thought at the time that one could get on the Camelot without much trouble. This, and adventures during my first milking job, took over my mind. The skylight in the focsle was directly over my bunk, and I had it open slightly to allow a little fresh air, and it went through my mind that the rat had probably got into the focsle that way. I was thinking of hundreds of rats swarming over the deck, when it moved again, this time just under my chin. I finally reached up for the switch on the reading light, and here was this dumb looking bird trying to get focused in the bright light. I grabbed him and put him out on deck, and closed the skylight. He and his buddies were still there in the morning.

I was fairly foaming at the mouth, when I came in with that first trip. I told Trish, that if I happened to croak, and hadn't cooled off too much, I'd be back up and pulling when the lines went tight again. This isn't the bait fishery that everyone has seen on TV, with a bunch of people around a stern, each with a pole, and tuna flying through the air. In the "jig" fishery, the fish are mostly pulled to the boat hand over hand, or pulled up to the boat with some kind of a powered hauler, and then swung or gaffed aboard by hand. The jigs are trolled behind the boat at a speed of around five knots, maybe slower early or late in the day, and sometimes faster depending on conditions. You only have 8 or 10 jigs out, and at first we only used eight on the Camelot.

Like I said, to keep a bite going you have to keep empty gear going back in, as fast as you possibly can. Let the hooks fill up and you'll probably lose the bite. You might get them to go again quick, or you might go awhile. Sometimes, quite awhile.

If there were a few fish around, you would put the boat in a big circle when a few would get on, and sometimes you'd still be going round and round, hours later. The size of the circle would vary depending on the weather conditions, or maybe the amount of boats in the area, but usually 70 yards across or more. Maybe you'd make a few revolutions with nothing, and then they'd start going again, or other times it would just be steady, a few fish at a time for a little while, or quite awhile. Sometimes a small amount of finely chopped herring or anchovies, thrown straight into the wheel wash, would bring them up again, or sometimes pieces of boiled macaroni. Sometimes it would be too sloppy to maintain a good circle, and straight tacking would work well. Sometimes nothing worked well. One thing that stands out in the albacore fishery, just like every other fishery, is the guys with the experience and the equipment, day in and day out, will have the numbers. It isn't just towing some jigs around.

Another big incentive to go out for a tuna trip, is the eating part. Albacore that you've caught and canned yourself are a different item, entirely, than you purchase out of the store. The fact that we bled the fish, and took the extra bit of care, either when we were icing or years later, when we were freezing them, made for a better product when we got to the dock. We always took the bigger fish for canning, simply because the recovery of useable meat was greater with the big fish, which meant a lot less work per lb. Then we skinned and trimmed "every" bit of dark meat from them, before putting them into jars, and then the pressure cooker.

People living along the west coast in the U.S. and in Canada can purchase an excellent product in many ports, for home canning or to eat fresh. Watch for the "Albacore for sale" signs, between mid July thru October or later. You'll be glad you did. Albacore, filleted, cut into strips about ¾" thick, and then marinated in Italian dressing, along with a few cloves of finely chopped garlic, and then barbecued, are fabulous eating. Just put some aluminum foil on the racks and serrate through it every few inches. Turn the fish once, and after a few more minutes take it off. Most people will have no idea what they're eating. We've tried various lengths of marinating time, and I'm beginning to think that out towards 12 hours, or more, is perfect. I thought 6 to 8 hours was perfect too.

An enormous amount of trouble was handed to the west coast albacore fleet, by those people who jump on any cause that comes down the pike, and then use their position or fame to publicize a subject which is all too often, something they know little about. When these folks were encouraging everyone to boycott tuna, no distinction was made between the tuna seiners, which frequently find porpoise in their nets, and the hook and line fleet. At that time, almost all the effort on albacore tuna from California to Alaska, was by the hook and line fleet.

I've never been on a bait boat, but haven't heard a thing that would lead me to think that it isn't a clean fishery. I've participated in the jig boat fishery for quite a few years, and in all that time, while fishing in actual blue water conditions, I caught one pomphret, and during the last few years we got a couple skipjacks. I had what must have been a yellow fin tuna on once, but being alone on the boat, he was too big for me to pull. I certainly tried. Except for those, everything else has been albacore tuna. This is what I would call a perfect fishery. For the do gooders to blast away, and when confronted, skip off to the next outrage without looking back, is hard to take, especially for those looking at the resource as a livelihood.

The Elusive broadened our tuna horizons a lot. We were still limited because where other boats could freeze their catch and stay out for whatever time it might take to fill up, we were still icing. But now, finally, we had plenty of room to put fish.

I had sold a salmon trip in Astoria, with albacore in mind for the next trip, and was looking for some help. You needed more man power than I was capable of if you happened to get into some decent fishing. That's how we met Admiral Grotting. Ed's dad had been a gillnetter in Bristol Bay, and also the Columbia River. Ed had fished with him, and had also fished all over the Pacific on other boats, for albacore. Soon we were headed up and out from Astoria, with the intention of being at the upper end of Vancouver Island in a few days. We had heard some good reports from that area.

Sometimes there will be an area of ocean where the wind will blow steadily for a week or more. Sometimes lots more. More often than not, it will be during nice sunny weather on the beach, and the wind direction will be from the northwest. Water and weather temperatures, ocean currents, and the fact that the Elusive might want to go through these spots, are some of the reasons for this.

If I had thought, I'd have gone up the inside, and came out at Queen Charlotte Sound, but I didn't. I should have, because I had listened to a few other boats pounding their way up through it, but I guess I was brain dead. It'll go down before we get up there. Absolutely! We took water over the bow for well over two days and sometimes it was stuff you slowed the boat down to nothing for, and still the occasional green out. When those came through at night, you hoped you were braced. Plexiglass and lexan, over the windows, is wonderful stuff. We had some of each. Finally, late one afternoon, the boat that was chartering for the Tuna Boat Association gave our position, and asked who we were. Each year the association sends a boat out to look over the different areas that might be of interest, reporting in, several times a day with fish counts, water temperatures, and anything else that might give the fishermen a better feel for the tuna picture. It's a big ocean, and a boat scouting a pre planned trail, helped the cause. He was on his way back down hill, and running with the slop, so he was able to see us on his radar, where we couldn't see him because of sea clutter. He told us that in a few more hours we would start to break out of this, and we should start picking up a few fish about the same time. A few hours later it seemed to be a bit better, and the occasional tight line. When we shut down that evening it was nice weather, and we had gathered up a nice bit of tuna for the evening. Captain Cameron and Admiral Grotting were looking forward to tomorrow. The trip went quite well, and we decided to try something different when we sold it.

They had had a reciprocal arrangement for the tuna boats from the U.S. and Canada, with designated ports in each country where the foreign boat could sell his trip, and outfit and provision for the next trip. It might save a Canadian boat a run all the way up our coast, or likewise, it would save the Elusive a trip down to Bellingham, La Push or Astoria from the other end of Vancouver Island.

During a storm years ago, some American boats had gone into Winter Harbor—party time—and from anything I've heard it was a mess. Canadian authorities were called in, and the outcome was that both countries lost this privilege. The usual deal of a few spoiling it for the rest. Anyway, the agreement was back in effect now, and Ed and I were thinking hard, the trip uphill still fresh in our minds.

We got some coaching from some of the Canadians we'd been fishing around, and before we could make a call, a Canadian buyer from Coal Harbor called us, and after talking a few minutes, he agreed to take our trip. One of the Canadians must have put a bug in his ear. They would be unloaded at Port Hardy, which is around the north end, and a few hours run down the inside of Vancouver Island. As they were unloaded, they were weighed, re iced in a big refrigerated truck, and when the last fish was in the truck, they were on their way to some Canadian market. Possibly in the U.S. Who knows? I didn't ask.

The fish company put a crew aboard to take the fish out, and we scrubbed the bin boards and ice blankets as they came out. After unloading, we took out the old ice, cleaned up the hold, and they had another truck, this one full of ice. It had to be dumped into the hold with the hoist and totes, and as it came in, Ed and I shoveled it into the bins.

The Canadian crew was a bunch of hard working young kids in their prime, and there was no way the fish could have gotten out quicker, but shoveling 10 tons of ice into those bins after shoveling the old ice out, plus the clean up, about killed Ed and me. We were able to use a piece of plywood to divert quite a bit of the new ice into the bins, but even then, we were about dead when the boat was loaded. Ed looked like a strand of last weeks spaghetti, and I was more like a dead sea lion. On the other hand, there were nice stores and facilities in Port Hardy, even an airport, and we were soon going out the channel, and listening to someone pounding his way up through the slop. It sounded like he had about a day to go. One more trip, which we ran south, and it made a nice end to a season.

After talking it over all summer, we decided that refrigeration would be one way to get a better summer season. We put in an air blast refrigeration system that winter, taking out out the old gen set, and installing a new 35 watt Isuzu. When it came time to try the unit out, it was obvious that we had a long way to go. Some small areas of the deck iced over, and there were places all over that were costing us cold.

We had extra foam insulation sprayed in, faired it out with sanders, and then became fiberglassers. The guy in Port Townsend who did this fiberglassing work was swamped, so he looked the project over, sold us what materials we would need, and told us how to go about it. Fiberglassing over head had me worried, but once he told us how, it was simple, and we were very pleased with the outcome. We had also built new shaft alley covers, and had rebuilt the fish hold hatch, and hatch cover.

The greater range we had with the refrigeration made a big difference. Now you might be running around four or five hundred miles off the beach when fishing tuna, and if you heard about fish someplace, you thought about going, instead of counting the number of days you had left on your trip. The numbers of fish were greater offshore, and it became obvious that our freezer wouldn't handle production that we occasionally would get. I had thought that a unit that could handle a ton and a half a day would be fine, but over four tons in an afternoon choked us. It would be okay for salmon but came up short on albacore. Luckily, we had ice left over from salmon fishing, and were able to put that up on deck and ice them down for a good pre chill.

I enjoyed fishing further offshore. It was different, going over some mountain top, 300 or more miles offshore, and being in no more water than if I was in against the beach, fishing salmon in Alaska. You'd see quite a bit of upwelling around the different seamounts, and we usually got fish, but never did really well when we were close to them. I'm sure others have, though. You didn't have to be on top of a seamount to have lots of current action and upwellings.

You always had an eye out for glass balls, and some years you'd get a few, others not. The year I looked the hardest, was for logs. There had been some fierce flooding in California and Oregon that winter, and the ocean was full of trees, root systems and all. Some of them were the real biggies from the Redwood neighborhood. There were enough of them that no one would run at night, and you paid attention while you were fishing. It's easy to forget about that tree off to the side while you're pulling fish. They were worth going fairly close and looking at though, because the albacore would lay under them. If you didn't see any limbs sometimes it paid off nicely to drag the lines by, fairly close in. Aside from that, you saw an occasional big turtle and birds. Lots of birds, and more often than not, that's when the lines would go tight.

The last year we fished we heard of some fish out 600 plus miles, and since we hadn't heard of anything else worthwhile, we decided to go for it. Starting at about the Dumping Grounds, which is about a hundred miles off the Columbia, we rode a stiff northwest slop in the trough for nearly 300 miles, and then it got nicer, and we started getting occasional dabs of fish. At one point that trip we got out around 700 miles offshore, which was the farthest out either I, or the Elusive, ever got. We handled quite a few fish that were pretty well roughed up, apparently from swimming alongside high seas gillnets, which we heard were just outside of us. Out here, we had 67 degree water, different seabirds, and fog. Fishing at jig speed in the fog, among a bunch of other boats doing the same thing, is no fun!

Another strong blast of fish that trip, had us shut down, trying to get the freezer a chance to catch up. I mentioned our address on the radio and several boats used us for a marker and did quite well. After coming through all that slop to get there, I had a lump in my throat the size of a watermelon. If I'd had a bit more experience in the refrigeration department I'd have put in a larger unit, but I didn't. It would be fine for most salmon and tuna fishing, but now I came up short. You live and learn. Anyway, you might be interested in how you set up and move the tuna through the operation.

You catch them on jigs, either made of feathers, or more likely now, on lures made out of a soft, rubbery material that are fringed on the bottom like a hula skirt. They come in all kinds of color, and sometimes one color will definitely work better than the other. You use a barbless double hook, quite heavy, and if the fish aren't too big, you can just swing them aboard with the leader, or one that is larger, or poorly hooked, you would gaff in the head. Before you take them off the hook, so they can slide down the chute and onto the deck, you slit them at the gills so they will bleed out. We moved the chutes to separate them in bunches as they came aboard. Then they could go down onto the freezer trays in that order. We kept water sprinkling on them to keep them clean, and so that the evaporation could cool them down. We had a double fan blower against the deck in the front crossing of the fish hold, and had four levels of trays that went across in front of them. We would put down 50 fish at a time on these trays, every four hours, sometimes all day, and all night. Putting down much more than that just raised the temperature too much, and took too long to recover. When you had quite a bit of fish aboard, the added block of cold helped you recover temperature more quickly, after more fish had been put down.

Defrosting, especially when you are handling this much product, was one of the most important parts of the operation, and if you wanted to get the max out of your system, you paid attention. You could adjust the frequency of the defrosts, and the amount of time you allowed, and we had to add some heat tape and other tricks, to help things warm up quicker. Ed had experience with the other boats he'd worked on, and we got some good coaching from other guys in the fleet. One guy suggested we "stop catching so many fish."

To put more of a load on the gen. set, most boats would run big deck lights full time, and this would make for some interesting looking over the side, during the night when you were drifting. With the water running over the fish, there was always something washing off the boat, and this would gather up quite an audience in the form of sharks. Sometimes hundreds of them.

The stretch of 300 plus miles of sloppy northwest weather, was waiting for us on the way in. We put chains on the long lines and they still blew across, so we pulled in one side of the long lines. The wind eased off once we got back towards the Dumping Grounds, and we picked up a few smallish fish, and then on into the river.

After buying a license and scales, so we could sell fish from the boat, we sold over the dock in Astoria for several days, and had one interesting sale, our biggest ever outside of selling to the fish buyers. This guy asked us to pick out 2200 pounds of bigger fish , for custom canning. A well to do friend of his had come up several years earlier, bought some albacore, and was so impressed with the product of one of the local custom canneries that each year he had this friend purchase the fish and have them canned, to be used as Christmas gifts. What else as good and unique could he give friends for Christmas, that he would be sure they would enjoy, and appreciate?

Then we moved on up the Columbia, to a place on the Oregon side called Scapoose Bay. We had bought a license and scales, so we could sell fish from the boat, and after an enjoyable trip up the river, we tied up at St. Helens. We waited there for the tide to get in enough, that we go up to a little marina at the end of the channel. We had talked to the owner of the marina, and he told us how to get in, and that there would be a spot where we could tie, stern to the dock. At low water we would be sitting in a hole that would be plenty big enough to float the Elusive. With this amount of fish aboard we'd need almost ten feet of water.

On the way in, we passed a guy in a small outboard boat, and he waved us down and came alongside. He asked where we were going, and what we were going to do, and said that he would like to visit a bit after he got in from fishing. He was going to try fishing out in the channels that evening.

We went on in and got tied up, even selling a few fish that evening. The folks at the marina had put up a few notices as to when we would be in, and we were amazed when we started selling fish right away. Along towards dark, the guy with the outboard came in, and we nibbled on barbecued albacore, and gabbed for several hours. He was Tom McAllister, the outdoor sports writer for the Oregonian. He asked questions about the trip, and the tuna, the price and the boat. Even the crew. I forgot to mention that Todd Moonbeam fished that trip, with Ed and I.

The next morning we had lots of customers, and at least ten people brought us a copy of Tom's article from the paper. He undoubtedly sold more albacore for us than all the rest of our advertising combined. We hadn't actually ran into the high seas net fleets, as it said in his article, but had certainly caught enough fish that had run up against their nets. The marina owner let us use his wheelbarrow to move fish up the dock, and in four days, Todd and Ed put miles on it. Trish and Deann had met us in Astoria, so they were the bookkeepers and had made a bunch of copies on how to fillet and trim an albacore, and recipes on canning, or just cooking them. Our favorite was the marinated in Italian dressing, and then barbecued, recipe.

One fellow from up around Portland came down to get some to barbecue, and had brought his son in law with him. We had some we'd just cooked, and took the tray back so they could taste the Italian dressing bit. The kid decided he would take a few fish also. He and his wife were back late that evening, and got some more. We mentioned in parting, that we'd be going down the river in the morning, as soon as the tide allowed. The next morning when I crawled out of the bunk and looked over the stern, there he was, waiting on the dock to get a few more fish for their freezer. They obviously enjoyed barbecued albacore.

# Chapter 13
# Eating Fish

I've always enjoyed eating fish. There's a good variety and many ways of preparing them. They are delicious, and one of the more healthful ways to take on protein, so how can you go wrong? Fish oils reduce cholesterol, but the benefits of the Omega 3 essential fatty acids within these oils go far beyond cardiovascular benefits. There seem to be many areas of a persons health picture that benefit by eating fish once or twice a week. Healthier skin, bones, and heart, and all the benefits of weight control are a few, and the list keeps growing.

The ones that will be especially rich in these omega 3 essential fatty acids, are the fattier cold water ocean fish. Ocean caught salmon would be one of the best examples. Other fish from our lakes and rivers won't likely be as rich in these omega 3s. The farmed salmon, while being an especially fat fish, will have a low ratio of the omega 3s, and a much higher ratio of the Omega 6 fatty acids, both a result of their diet. They don't eat the right stuff, and overcrowding in the pens restricts their moving around much, so they put on weight fast.

Maybe if we can kick the subject around a bit, I might be able to give you some possibilities to explore, or at least some interesting ways of looking at the fish department. Say that you're getting your fish from the store, or maybe better yet, a seafood market. This isn't to say that many grocery stores don't have their own excellent seafoods section, but many don't. Take a good, long, look at their fish display. If the display suggests a little pride, then you'll likely be dealing with people who want you to enjoy their product, and come back again. That's a good start. They say if you can smell fish, you shouldn't buy it. Please take my word for it, fish smell. So does any other kind of meat. Most fish have their own distinct odor, but some you can't tell from others. If a fish smells bad, don't buy it. If it doesn't look good, or fresh, it's time to look a bit further. On fish that haven't been headed, a clear eye would be a plus. They say if you push in on the skin, lightly, the dent should fill back out. That's pretty much correct if its fresh fish, but maybe not if the fish had been frozen, and was thawing out. Personally, I wish they'd leave the frozen fish, frozen.

If you've purchased fish close to home, get it home and into the refrigerator as soon as possible. Or lets assume you've caught your own fish, or maybe you've purchased fish some distance from home. The first thing to think of is a means of cooling the fish down, once you've got him. If it's in the dead of winter and you aren't too far from home, this may not be necessary. If you were going to purchase fresh fish very far from home, an ice chest and a little ice will get it home in good shape. In warm weather, one of these little insulated lunch boxes with a cold pack, takes the worry out of getting them home cold. They are very perishable, so you won't get away with sliding much on this. Like so many other foods, when you let them warm up, bacteria counts go up and quality goes down. Quickly.

When you get frozen fish and are taking it home, or maybe shipping it, five or six layers of newspaper tightly wrapped, with the pieces put against each other in a heavy cardboard box, or ice chest, lined with more newspaper should get it there in good shape. We've moved fish several days away, in pretty warm weather, and they got there rock hard. When the old timers put newspaper in their walls, and under the linoleum, they had the right idea. Newspaper is a dandy insulation. A heavy cardboard box or one of the "wet-lock" fish boxes make good shipping containers, and again, good insulation. Some dry ice would be added insurance.

If you are catching your own product, stun the fish immediately, either before or after you get him. We always tapped them behind the nose before gaffing them, as it was over for the fish in an instant, and made for a much better product. All the flopping around, and the resultant bruising and scaling needs to be avoided. Then slit the membrane behind the gills so they bleed out. I've never been able to understand some people, who are so meticulous about the way they handle game, and when they get a fish, they get it home half a day later, un-cleaned. Clean the fish right away, and you'll be well on your way to a better product.

Take every step you can to get all the blood out of the body. After removing the gills, insides, and kidney, cut through the small cavities in the backbone, near the vent on any salmon or large trout, and using a water hose cut off at an angle, flush against the backbone, and back towards the tail of the fish. By doing this on a freshly caught fish, you can remove an unbelievable amount of blood that would otherwise be left in this part of the fish. Using your fingers, or the spoon on a fish knife, you can pull blood showing through the membrane along the ribs, into the belly cavity. Sometimes slowly working the tail back and forth will help pressure blood from along the tail end of the fish. Getting the blood out is one of the most important steps in properly cleaning a fish. If it isn't done, the meat against the backbone, in the tail portion of the fish, will be some of the first to go bad.

Leave the chin strap intact to prevent bruising of the flesh just behind the head. Then lay him in a layer of ice in the ice chest, a bit of ice in the belly cavity as well as all around him, and forget about any filleting or cutting until the next day. They'll stiffen up, and make a much nicer product to handle.

Keep the fish cold until you are ready to cook them. If you intend to freeze them it will be handy to cut a larger fish into the size pieces you will want to use later. If you intend to use the whole fish at one time, don't cut it up until you are ready to use it. Leaving the skin on until you're ready to cook them will be worthwhile, since it's a perfect barrier against freezer burn. Before wrapping, freezing them on a sheet pan and then dipping them several times in water, will put an ice glaze on them that will help them last longer in the freezer. Get them as cold as your freezer will go before you glaze them. Some karo syrup added to the water will make a tougher, more elastic glaze. Vacuum wrapping is great, and if you can't do this, try to get every bit of air away from the fish, as best you can. Freezing fish in water isn't a bad way to go for quite a few species of fish. I'd still leave the skin on until I was ready to use it.

You get some texture breakdown in flesh, once it's been frozen, but it would hardly be a factor in your use of the fish. Maybe slightly less seasonings, and less time marinating, as the flesh will absorb the seasonings more readily after it has been frozen. You'll also find that it takes less salt, or any other ingredient in your recipe, for smoking fish that has been frozen. After a little trial and error, you might decide to decrease the amount of time in the salt or brine for these fish.

If your freezer will get down in the 25 to 40 degree "below" zero, range, you can figure on being able to keep the product quite awhile. Most home freezers go to around 10 or 15 degrees, (above zero) so at this temperature, when you get out towards five months freezer time, your fish ought to be a good memory. It's my opinion that getting the product down to the "super cold" temperatures before putting them in the home freezer, stretched out freezer life an extra few months. At any freezer temperature, vacuum packing will help your cause. No matter what you do, I can't think of one advantage in not using them fairly soon, after putting them in a home freezer. Extended freezer time, unless it's at these colder temperatures I've mentioned, just takes the quality of your product downhill. The cold storage plants use freezer rooms that circulate the air at very cold temperatures, and will freeze large volumes of fish, fast. Then they are kept in large storage rooms, also kept at these very cold temperatures. The end product represents an enormous investment in time and money, spent to provide the best possible product to the consumer.

Now, suppose your favorite store gets in a frozen product that's in the best possible condition. They thaw it, cut it, display it nicely, and some people come along, buy it, and that evening they enjoy a first class seafood meal. At closing time that evening, some of the fish that was thawed, remains unsold. The next day they re-package it, fresh pad underneath, the fish still looks good but not quite as good as it did yesterday. There's something lacking, a certain lustre to the color, and you may be imagining that the fish doesn't look real firm. You may be right. This is what seafood departments in stores have to contend with when they handle frozen fish, and then thaw them, before or while, they're on display. They may get it in perfect shape, but by the time you get it home, who knows? If you buy the fish after its been in the display case for several days, you may have paid a lot for a borderline product. Thawing out in the store isn't likely to improve on the fishes quality. The big loser is you, the consumer. Too much of what you pay for a piece of fish, fresh, or frozen and then thawed, goes to make up for other fish that used up their shelf life, before they weren't purchased.

Along these lines, you may be able to do the industry a favor. When you see frozen, vacuum wrapped sides, or portions that have lost the vacuum, please bring it to the attention of the market employees. When processors knowingly use equipment that is coming up short, there are two groups of people that will pay for the loss, the fishermen and the consumers. There's no reason in the world to allow this to slide.

I know I haven't painted you a very bright picture. Change has been slow, but the pace is picking up. I think as more people taste what good seafood can be, and demand it, the quality level will soar. It's sickening to the industry, that so much of the available quality was lost before the fish was caught, (keep reading) and again, after it left the boat and cold storage, or the fish dock. Other than something you know to be really fresh, the ideal product is a fish that has been

146

frozen at sea, or at the cold storage, and kept frozen until you buy it. The effort by the cold storages, plus an enormous investment in equipment, facilities, and training of personnel, is really starting to pay off. The effort is being made on that end of the line. It's time for the retailers and the middle men to pick up the ball. They're already picking up most of your fish dollar.

Fish that will require filleting before use can be cut in various sized portions, frozen, glazed, and vacuum packed, and then kept frozen in really good display cases. Not too hard to do. Everyone gains and loss of the product is eliminated. This may sound like a big extreme to go to, just so someone can enjoy a better seafood product, but if you realized the difference in what can be, and what is made available to the fish consuming public, you would be all for it. I'd rather help pay for some store's freezer room and display cases, than to pay for the various losses associated with them not having one. It amounts to a big chunk of your fish dollar. Any frozen product will keep better at these colder temperatures, so these "colder" rooms, or display cases wouldn't be an expense just for the seafood products, and down the line, would probably be a money maker for the store. Imagine what this could mean to fish loving folks from the middle part of our country. The markets wanting to provide a high quality product and not wanting to gouge their customers at the end of the day, should be all for something like this. Maybe they can even do better. Mine can't be the only sensational ideas out there.

I've been smoking fish since I was 11 years old. And still learning. Here's a couple things I've picked up that I thought improved my product. First, start with a good product. If you start out with a spawned out dog salmon, you may wind up with a smoked, spawned out dog salmon. And that's what it's going to taste like. Spend the time to get all the slime off your fish, before you put them in the brine. The water hose and a cloth or knife, pulling with the scales, works fine. Get it all off!

There are many good recipes for a brine, or you can just sprinkle layers of fish with rock, or mild cure salt, and let it make it's own brine. I like to rinse the fish quite a bit more if I use the latter, but no matter the system, it all gets down to personal preference. The one I've used on my last few batches is:—a cup of salt and a cup of sugar, stirred into a quart and a half of warm water—a quarter tsp. each of liquid smoke and Tabasco, and then add a quart and a half of cold water. Make enough at this rate, to cover the fish for 10 or 12 hours. Cover and put it in the fridge. Rinse it once and pat dry, and after you've got the chunks on the racks, which you've oiled with Pam on a paper towel, turn a fan on it for an hour or more. Salt and sugar-wise—I've used plain table salt, rock salt, and mild cure salt and white and brown sugar. It was all good. Also, I like to sprinkle pepper on it, which ever system I use, and I like to carefully peel the skin off, after it's about half done. This is when I've cut the pieces fairly small. Using the ten shelf, metal smoker, I like to cut it into strips a little over an inch thick, as I move down the fillet.

After that—trial and error and taste. The little aluminum smokers can get a batch thru in 6 to 12 hours, and you'll probably be revolving the racks every hour or more. Just keep putting the bottom on top, and then drop them all down one. I like to chill a big stainless half moon, by putting it in the fridge, and then cool the pieces, by laying them around the bottom and sides. When they've cooled completely, saran wrap, and then put the pieces in a big zip lock bag in the fridge, unless the fridge is empty. You can taint other stuff, otherwise. When I use alder, I take the bark off. I've also used maple, apple, and hickory and thought it all worked well.

If you're going to smoke whole sides, score through the skin frequently, so that the oil can dissipate. One fall I got the bright idea of cold smoking a batch of larger hookbills (male silvers). I had sampled some a friend had done, and decided this would be a good break-in for my new smokehouse. It set above the creek bank that ran behind our house, with the fire drum above normal high water level, and the smoke piped up into the floor of the house. Ten feet high, by four square, it was my pride and joy.

This all got off to a poor start, back on the river. A bigger than usual silver, got farther than usual downstream, within sight of a talkative neighbors house. No need to advertise, so when I finally got the fish on the beach, I grabbed it and ran up the bank, putting some trees downstream, between me and the house. I couldn't find a handy stick to stun the fish with, so grabbed a rock, and when I brought it down the fish flopped, and it's head came up. My knee hasn't been too happy since then. Worse yet, Trish laughed her head off when I told her what happened.

So get a good stick to stun your fish with. After over six days of constant smoke, low heat, up three times each night, and having to check the fire off and on all day, it's finally done. When I was up on the ladder taking it out, I got a whiff that wasn't quite right. I really gave the piece I had just handled a good sniff over, then the other recently handled pieces. It all appeared perfect. When I went in, I told Trish about it, and we each spent considerable time looking for the

148

culprit, and couldn't find it. We gave fish to at least half a dozen friends, and one of them was good enough to call, and tell us that I had slipped up. He even told me how. Without scoring the sides frequently through the skin, the oil laid above the skin, and without the usual amount of heat to cook the fish, the fat, (oil) on at least one of the bigger fish, had gone rancid. The smaller fish in the batch were great, and if you've got the time and patience, this slow mode of smoking puts out a mighty fine product. Cutting the fish in chunks, would also have solved the problem I had with these larger whole sides, using this slow smoke method. On the other hand, depending on the smokehouse or smoker, 8 to 36 hours puts out a mighty fine product and allows more full nights of sleep.

Seattle is famous for it's Pike Place market. The produce, seafood, flowers, and many other displays, always make a fun stop on a trip to the city. It's obvious that every effort is made to provide the freshest seafood products available, in each of the three fish markets. One of the seafood sales places has become famous for its, run out for a pass, throw the salmon like a football, sales gimmick. Lots of noise, people cheer and applaud. Yaaaaay!

As a fisherman, I did everything I could to put our fish on the dock in the best condition. When we were handling fish, they were supported with both hands whenever possible. As you handle the fish you put them down into the hold, and on ice to cool them down before the actual icing. I picked them up from the chinstrap, using a long pole with a large hooked rod on one end, to lay them down, rather than just dropping them. It's hard to watch this sporting event if you're a fisherman, or perhaps a cold storage worker. You hate to have your efforts compromised for a sales gimmick. These people are "the girl at the front desk" for the industry, and so many of them have let us down.

Here's something I've wondered about. Why isn't fish one of our main breakfast foods? With the millions of people who don't eat pork because of religious reasons, and millions more who either don't care for pork, or perhaps their systems can't tolerate it, fish for breakfast is a perfect solution. When we were on the boat, we had fish of some kind almost every morning. Granted, we had a ready supply and an unlimited variety, but once this has been available it gets to be something that you crave. Any bottom fish, filleted, or in ¾" thick slices, grilled, or pan fried in cracker crumbs or your favorite breading, will make a wonderful treat in these meat-eggs breakfasts. There's lots of ways to go besides pan frying, that will work just as well. My favorites were halibut, salmon, any rockfish, or the silver hake we used to get off the Washington coast. Believe me, fish, eggs,

*Waiting to be lifted into the hold*

and spuds or toast were made for each other. The perfect Sunday brunch. This is in no way a shot at the pork industry, but it's worth mentioning for those who can't, or won't, eat pork.

I don't intend getting into the cookbook department, but here's a couple of the ways we had fish on the boat, or maybe on the beach. Before I go on, it's easy to over season fish, probably more-so than other meat products. The texture is light, and the portions are often not very thick, so you'll need to experiment a bit until you get used to dealing with this. There's many different taste treats available, and it's a shame to cover them up. In many cases, just a very small amount of salt and pepper works fine.

When you're baking salmon, it worked good to take the chunk you were going to bake, and fillet it, leaving the skin at the back intact from the dorsal fin, forward. This way the skin is a sort of hinge. Take out the backbone, ribs, and pin bones, and put in your lemon, onion slices, various garlic or ginger preps, seasonings, and whatever else you like. Then, fold one side over onto the other. Or sheet pan, chunks of fish, that you've dipped in egg and one of the baking mixes, (or your own) and shoot it into a hot oven, then turn it as it starts to crisp. Tastes fabulous and doesn't put the fried fish aroma into your house. A few drops out of a lemon goes great here, or on almost any other fish dish.

When we were on the beach, it worked good to take a fillet, or a chunk of salmon, season, and wrap it in aluminum foil and lay it in the coals, turning it in about four or five minutes, or more, depending on the size hunk of fish you're doing. Put the spuds in the same way, about 30 or 40 minutes earlier. The Indians used to make a rack out of fresh split cedar strips, and the salmon sides were held in place with other thin strips, sort of woven into the rack. Then the racks are stood upright close to a fire with a good bed of coals. One of the guys I used to fish with was raised close to a reservation, and did some fish this way and it was hard to beat. The cedar definitely adds to the taste. Any cookbook will give you a bunch of recipes for barbecued salmon so take your pick. Just start with a good piece of fish!

There's a lot of ways to approach frying or grilling fish, and what we mostly did was pieces up to ¾, or an inch thick, dipped in corn meal or cracker crumbs, and into a fairly hot pan, with a small amount of Wesson, or olive oil, or just a dab of margarine. Sometimes on white fish, I'd dip them in egg before breading. Sometimes just the dab of margarine, without breading.

An easy dinner, was do up the fish (whitefish, seasoned, but not breaded) in the pan and then dump in a bunch of cooked rice over it, and then some veg-etables—broccoli, cauliflower, brussel sprouts, carrots, whatever, and cover it for a bit, pulled back on the stove so the vegies sort of steam. Then a bit of parmesan or sharp cheese, grated over the top just before you eat.

Small red or white new potatoes, in the skin, broken up on the plate with smoked or kippered black cod broken up in chunks over it, then baby peas, topped with a good creamy white sauce, is definitely a good one!

King salmon are so rich that many people prefer it barbecued, baked, broiled, or boiled, rather than grilling or frying, but whatever method you use, it's still a good idea to put it down there with some boiled or baked spuds. But boy is it good! My favorite for salmon is still salt and pepper, a little lemon juice squeezed over it, wrapped in aluminum foil, and baked, or cooked on the barbecue.

Quite a few people in the fleet, liked boiled salmon or halibut, and I had it a lot if the kids weren't aboard. They liked a more zesty approach. A little lemon and vin-egar in the water, along with whatever other seasonings you like, add a bit of flavor, as well as tighten up the texture. The halibut boats did this a lot, as it was some-thing you could get a belly full of, and sleep on. Halibut, and most other whitefish leftovers, can be used the next day in salads, regardless of how they were cooked, and make a delicious meal. We called it "Hallelouie." Leftovers from any fish meal make a dandy sandwich tomorrow, with some mayo, onions, pickles, and lettuce. Or open faced toasted cheese, with the sandwich mixture spread on cold while the cheese is still bubbling, and then eat it before it averages out. I thought I was the smartest guy around, till someone told me the "tuna melt" had already been invented.

If you haven't had barbecued albacore you've missed a treat. Fillet it, skin it, cut out "all" the dark fat and marinate it in Italian dressing for four to sixteen hours. We've had it at each extreme, and everywhere in between, and it's always been a treat, although I lean more towards eight or more hours. A few finely diced cloves of garlic in the marinate won't hurt anything. Then, place chunks about ¾ of an inch thick and an inch or two wide, on the grill, over some aluminum foil that you've

*Some are primer than others*

*Deann and friends*

serrated, and do one side, turn, a few more minutes, and eat. You probably won't have to worry about leftovers. So anyway, there's a couple ideas for a light snack. Just make sure you start with a good piece of fish!

Our salmon fisheries being one of our natural resources, you would think they would be harvested with every intention of making sure they were at their best, as both a delicious and nutritious product. Too often, this isn't the case. For years, the "terminal area harvesting concept" was taught (probably still is) at the University of Washington. The general idea was that it made better sense to harvest the fish near the mouths of their river of origin, where certain runs could be more closely monitored.

*Keith and his first solo effort king salmon*

*Chris lost the bet.*

It was suggested that the fish would be harvested in their prime, rather than at some spot further away from the stream, where they might have some amount of growing yet to do.

I'm told that on several occasions this concept was questioned, and students were given little, or no, chance at all to express themselves. What could they have said? One thing would have been, that nearly all adult salmon caught in the terminal areas, are well past their prime when caught at that point. These salmon have been losing dressed body weight, nutritional value, and all of the things your taste buds relish, long before they get anywhere near the terminal area, at or near the mouth of their parent stream. There are some exceptions, and these are streams where certain stocks of fish will migrate a long way upstream. Their body fat will be fully loaded with nutrient to sustain them over what will be months of extra in-river time, as compared to salmon in shorter river systems. Two of the best examples would be fish that used to go well into Canada or Idaho, via the Columbia - Snake River system, and some stocks of upper river Yukon fish. After that, it becomes more a matter of degree. This will vary depending on the specie, which river, time of year, and a lot of other things.

For an example, let's follow a lady king salmon down the beach from Alaska's Fairweather Grounds. It's August 10th and she's just starting to get the urge to head "that" way. Others will be days, or months, before or behind her, but being the average fall run king, let's assume she's about in the middle of the pack. Their address when they get this urge to move on, and how far they might be from their parent stream, as well as the fact that others might spawn months before or after any particular fish, will determine their place in this migration. Her weight now, dressed out, head on, is 30 pounds, and she is in perfect condition.

Their growth rate since they entered the ocean several years ago, has been phenomenal. As they grew bigger this rate of gain increased, and many of them have more than doubled their size in this last year. At this point in their lives, they are what I think of, as prime, and have been for fifteen to eighteen months. Most of these fish will put on more weight in the next few weeks, others not much at all. As she moves further south, nature starts shutting down her appetite, although she will still be feeding well into September. The energy spent to fuel migration, and to develop the roe (eggs) in her body, will gradually switch to energy reserves stored in her body fat.

Some days they move quite a bit, some, not much at all, and at this point they don't stay anywhere for long. A shot of southeast weather will usually get them moving. Her new temporary address is in Hecate Straits, in northern British Columbia. It's been just over four weeks since leaving Fairweather Grounds, and although she is still ocean bright, and will be for nearly another month, there's a noticeable difference in her appearance from then till now. Her back isn't quite as round and full as it once was and, the sides that were once thick, are thin enough now that if she were laid on her side, dressed out, the side would cave in rather than support itself. Calipers, measuring her from one side to the other, at her thickest point, would be an inch or more closer together, than they were when she left the grounds. The meat is still a deep orange-red, but not the rich, vital, color it once was. The flesh has lost some of the fat content, as she lives more and more from these stored energy reserves.

If she were caught at this point, she would be less than a first rate fish. That's not to say she would be poor, but where her condition at Fairweather Grounds would have put her at 10, or perfect, most fish graders would wonder about a 7 to 8 now. If she were a male she might still go 8 to 9 using that same scale. They'll hold their weight a little better or longer than the females. She could be a good eating fish yet, but each day the quality diminishes, and where she could be very good table fare for some, at this point she might not be for others.

In a vital, still gaining salmon, the fat that is in the flesh, between the layers or flake of meat, and surrounding the fish inside its skin, is of a quality that adds to the flavor, as well as to the food value of the fish. In this fish, at this stage of maturity, the fat has begun to get a touch stronger to the taste. Some people will take the time to carefully trim away all the skin fat and the lateral line fat, before cooking. Others will use the edge of their fork to separate it from the flesh as they are eating it. Those who aren't aware of this will be treated to the occasional bite of stronger tasting salmon. If we use salmon at this stage of maturity, I prefer to take this concentrated fat off first, as I can't see where cooking it adds anything to the good stuff that you intend to eat. Kind of like cooking a crab before cleaning it.

I think you'll notice a difference in the texture of the salmon that are caught when they are still a vital, gaining fish, as compared to ones that have been caught just a bit too late. On the other hand, a bit too late is still 10 + when compared to so many of the fish that are caught at the terminal areas.

On the Camelot, I used to have a measurement for big fish which, over time, proved to be quite accurate. If the fishes nose touched the break plank in front of the trolling pit, and its tail lapped up the length of my hand on the back of the checker, the fish would weigh 50 to 53 pounds, dressed out. This, in Alaska, and at any time prior to their having started their southern migration. The same length fish, caught off the Washington coast around mid September, would dress out between 35 and 39 lbs. That's the loss of a lot of value, from a nutritional as well as a poundage, or monetary, point of view.

A prime fish, to me, is one that's still gaining. One that's putting on body weight, and storing food values in its flesh. Whether it's a 10 pounder or one that has reached 40 or more pounds, if it's still gaining, it's what I would call prime. This isn't taught, or allowed to be suggested, in some of our local colleges.

It seems the professors would prefer the apples you pick off the ground. I think the quality available in a "prime" fish, easily offsets the weight loss in a fish that still has some amount of growing to do. Going to the other end of the scale, the loss of weight and quality of the product, from prime condition to terminal area quality, also recommends taking as much as possible of the salmon harvest, when they are in prime condition. It only makes sense.

Now it's late September, and she's getting towards the end of her time in the ocean. She's still an ocean bright salmon, and although her food value has dipped a bit more, she's still a beautiful fish. The color of her flesh is paler than it used to be, and her two skeins of eggs will weigh almost four pounds. Her dressed body weight is 23 pounds, and it will keep dropping. The weather will be a big factor in what she does now. With sunny, clear weather, she could be poking around in the ocean, or Grays Harbor for another three weeks. A good southeaster and lots of rain, and she could be heading up the Humptulips river in a few days.

If the conditions in their lives after leaving the river as smolts were equal and normal, there shouldn't be any difference in the quality or condition of a hatchery fish or a wild one, while in the ocean or when they enter the river. The ocean grows them the same. This is assuming the hatchery fish wasn't part of any late release program. The tougher upbringing the wild fish experience, compared to those in the hatcheries, might make for some difference, but this would be more like comparing a kid out of the ghetto, to one raised up on the hill. The streetwise ghetto fish might be a bit tougher, or more wary, and have an edge in dealing with any predators, but looking at them as a food product, at this point in their lives, same thing.

Her condition will continue to deteriorate, as she moves into the river and on upstream. Depending on how long they've been waiting to get into the rivers, most of them will still be ocean bright, but some may already have started to change color. By the time Suzie starts to change color, she's really lost a lot in terms of nutrition, yet a male could show a slight bit of color and be something you might consider eating, maybe after a trip to the smokehouse. As the nutrients have been depleted in her body, more water is retained in the flesh, so about the only gain nutrition- wise would be a slight mineral content increase from this water.

If you haven't seen a skein of eggs, picture a thin length of gut, with membrane attached, and layers of eggs attached to more membrane that lays cross wise to the skein. The size, color, and amount of eggs will vary according to the species, and in a king salmon like Suzie, her four or five thousand eggs will be a rich orange red, will eventually get to about the size of a pea, and the skeins in a fish her size will get to be around 17 to 20 inches long. It varies, and the larger fish within any species will carry more eggs than the smaller ones. Silvers and sockeye will have slightly less eggs, of a deeper reddish color, and humpy and chum eggs will be much lighter colored, the humpy having around 2500 eggs and the chums egg load depending on whether she's a 3- 4 or 5 year fish. The big five year olds are really loaded. It's interesting that one of the skeins will be shorter than the other, and just a bit fuller.

Before spawning, the eggs separate themselves from the membrane, and she is able to spew them out into a nest (redd) she has dug in the gravel with her tail. Then she covers them with more sand and gravel. While all this is going on, the male will be doing his part by squirting the milt into the redd. It comes out about like thick cream, but had been solid until just before spawning.

She moves on upstream, past the fish hatchery on Stevens Creek, and some miles further upriver she takes the left side at the forks. Only a few more miles up to the area she was hatched in four years earlier, and she and this fine looking king go through the spawning process. In a few days, their bodies become part of the food chain in the river. This whole process is a wonderful thing to watch, but left to itself, natural spawning isn't going to provide the numbers of fish needed to meet todays demands.

Lets look at another portion of the salmon fishery. I used the "Elusive" to buy gillnet and seine fish for a few years, starting in 1976. Each year, along in mid-September, we started buying behind the lighthouse at Dungeness, and running them back down the straits to Port Angeles. A week or two of mostly silvers, and then the chum would start showing, becoming most of our production by the second week in October. They would all be ocean bright, and caught at this point, they would be in good condition. What they call "silver-brites."

Each year they would close the fishing in the straits, and the boats fishing that area would move inside to Hood Canal, or to areas like Kingston and further on into the sound. Others would move in to the Skagit, or up around Bellingham. At these times there would still be good fishing available in the straits, on fish whose condition would still be largely silver brites, or semis. I would leave the Dungeness area to move up further inside, and the grade would then drop to a mixture of semi brites and darks; fish that were in a much more advanced stage of maturity than those still moving through the straits. At this point, most of the brites available on the inside were the small, three year, hatchery females, not much of a fish. Depending on the individual years that I bought salmon, silver brites would bring from $1.00 to $1.30 per lb. Semis from .55 to .65 cents, and the darks would be around .35 cents.

These fish were bought in the round, (not cleaned) and the more they had matured, or from an edible standpoint, deteriorated, the less dressed body weight would be available. Less dressed body weight than the fish we had been handling at Dungeness, less price per pound—you figure it out. The same fish available in the Straits, at a value of $10.00 or more, might not be worth more than $3.00 taken from one of these terminal harvesting areas, later on.

On our first trip into Hood Canal one fall, I had listened to two seiners talking on the V.H.F. radio. One of them made the comment, "I guess I ought to be happy. I've got more fish on the boat than I've ever had before, but I'm sick about it. They never should have been caught."

Later on that season, I ran the Elusive into Hoodsport for one of the Indian fisheries openings. The buyer said he would come out fine on the eggs, which have quite a value. I could smell that nights catch when the first boat was still 50 feet from the Elusive. This wasn't because the fish had been riding around on his boat for days. They had been caught that night, but their condition was grim before they ever got into his net. We tied him alongside and bought his fish, and then I told other boats waiting to unload that I needed to go ashore to make a phone call, before I could take any more fish. When I told the buyer that his eggs had run out of the fish like water, he said to head on back home. That ended that season.

It's always been hard for me to understand why Washington State targeted such a big percentage of its gillnet and seine caught salmon, when their quality was at its lowest. I understand that the fish move towards these areas and arrive there in considerable numbers, but a much greater percentage of them could have been caught in so much better condition, at points further away from the stream. Monitoring escapement into certain streams sounds good, but if there's enough salmon for the Indians to gillnet, cut the eggs out of the females, and throw the carcasses back into the rivers, it makes me think escapement goals were apparently being met.

Having spent some fall seasons buying fish at Dungeness, I can say that any incidental catch on blackmouth (small king salmon) was not enough to even have been a consideration, but the loss to the industry and local economies, using this "terminal area harvesting" concept, was enormous.

They say "you are what you eat" so whether you're talking about a deer that is in grim condition after a real hard Alaskan winter, or a salmon that has pretty much gone without eating for the last month or so, it still comes down to the same old thing. If you are going to kill something to put on the table, if you've got a choice, get it while it's in the pink of condition—still gaining—PRIME.

The beef rancher doesn't starve his animals for a month or so, before he butchers. They're pushed right till the last, and never allowed to even level off. People who have orchards and gardens follow the same policy—they harvest while their crop is still growing, or just as it has reached prime condition. Yet using Washington State's harvesting policy on it's net caught salmon, the goal seems to be to harvest the majority of them after they have deteriorated to a catfood quality product. Then again, you don't improve something you're trying to eliminate.

It's hard to imagine the farmed salmon operations having virtually taken over the salmon industry in Washington State. Now you can purchase salmon that have spent their lives in a pen of some kind, overcrowding leading to a very dormant life style. Accordingly, they put on weight fast, with a high ratio of body fat which will be high in the Omega 6 fatty acids which, as I've mentioned, we already have plenty of. The ratio of omega 3 fatty acids in their flesh is low, compared to an ocean caught salmon. They are fed pellets complete with preservatives to retard spoilage in the pellet, and antibiotics to keep down disease. Since the flesh has that typical fish pen pallor, this is also manipulated. How about a rich, natural looking orange-red? Like a wild king salmon—(color-wise).

To me, the ocean is our greatest natural resource. It makes life on earth possible, even though we are compromising it more and more all the time. Salmon that have spent their lives in the ocean will reflect the nutrients it has provided them. The same can be said for salmon that have spent their lives in a pen. Ocean caught salmon, each specie having their own unique flavor, will be a delicious, nutritious, very healthful, food source when taken at its prime. It will be rich in the omega 3 essential fatty acids, reflecting the diet it has lived on. As I mentioned, these omega 3 essential fatty acids are a path to better health for the consumer.

So that's a little bit about the piece of fish you eat. The farmed salmon industry would like to drive the traditional wild salmon fisheries out of existence. They haven't pulled many punches. Whether they are successful in driving our traditional fisheries under, in a large part, will be up to you, the consumer. Remember—first start with a good piece of fish.

# Chapter 14
# Look What They Did To My River

The old timers say that the old timers told them, that the river used to go by Sequim and empty into the salt water at Washington Harbor, near the mouth of Sequim Bay. There are a couple possibilities, and there's no doubt in my mind that the river, or maybe some portion of it, did go to the east at one time. It has also been down through Carlsborg and all over the valley in between.

The river bed fills at an amazing rate, and the effect that man has put on it speeds this process all the more. It doesn't take much imagination, to see that what is now rich farmland, or rich housing developments, was once part of a mountain or foothill. Before man came along, the river would run through what was once low ground, until the bed was raised with silt and rock. Then it would find the next channel of least resistance, now the new channel, but what had been high ground 50 or 500 years ago. Or more. Once the Dungeness spills out onto the valley, it runs down over reasonably flat ground, although by most peoples standards, it's still a fast river all the way to the bay. There's the odd bank or bluff here and there, but only on one side of the river or the other. With very little effort or change, the river could assume several different paths on its way to the straits, as it has in the past.

Mastodons used to drink from the river, and one of these either died, or maybe just lost a tooth near its banks. Where I found the tooth is barely out of the foothills, just as the river goes out onto the valley. I was up from the old Duncan Bridge site, fishing steelhead right after a high water, and found what I thought was a petrified rib cage of a small, dog like animal. As big as it was, I didn't think about it being a tooth. It was ribbed and shaped just so, that it looked like a small dogs chest. I took it to school, and showed it to Mrs. Scott, our biology teacher. She said it was a mastodon's tooth, and if I liked, she would send it up to the University of Washington for verification. She did and they agreed with her. Many years later I watched a program on TV, and learned that what I thought might have been ribs, were sections of growth that could be used to determine the animals age.

During that high water there had been some pretty significant sloughing on two areas of clay bank upstream from where I had found the tooth. One was a low bank, only a few hundred yards upstream, and the other, a long, high bank about a third of a mile above that. I always liked to think he was encased in the bigger bank. Again, maybe it just lost a baby tooth while in the area. According to the encyclopedia, it's been about 12 million years since the mastodons got to North America, and eight thousand years since they died out. The Blair kids found a tusk sticking out of the beach bank a few years before I found my tooth, and I know of several other teeth that have been found, one of them also on the river. Lawrence found one down by the mouth of McDonald Creek when he was a kid, and a few years back, there was a major find in an area just south of Sequim.

The river is on high ground in several areas now. That doesn't mean it will take off sideways tomorrow, but there's good potential for the loss of roads, bridges and homes. If it rains hard enough, long enough, there's a limit to any watersheds ability to absorb all the water, but these high water crises that are so common now, ought to tell us we are doing something wrong in the management of our rivers. Here's an example on the Dungeness system.

When we still lived out by the river, I came in from a trip off the coast, and Trish said that I'd better go back and see what they were doing to the river. I went back, and directly behind our place were two big bulldozers, pushing river bottom both directions to form river rock, sand and gravel, dikes. Each of these dikes were being put on what had been the river bed, with considerable more river bottom behind each dike, before you would come to the river bank By river bank, I mean the extreme edge of bank that would normally contain the river, during extreme high water. Sometimes my terms and ideas aren't the same as the experts and developers, and several times I've been confused by what they thought of as river bank. Generally on this portion of the Dungeness, these banks would be 100 yards or more apart. This wouldn't count the stretch of east branch, which ran from the present day Dungeness Meadows, to the big Island, which would have added nearly another hundred yards in much of this section. Two dikes between the two banks, take up a lot of river bed. I wish they'd taught that to a few of yesterdays engineers.

I talked with one of the dozer operators and asked him what was going on, and he said the property on the east side of the river was going to be developed. I pointed out to him that the two dikes would overflow, if they hadn't already washed away, long before the river ever got near flood stage. He said I was talking to the wrong guy.

Of the seven property owners on the west side of the river; those who might have been notified before the bulldozers went to work, only one had been. Of these seven, our property had a small, pie shaped wedge between it and the river bank, so our property at that time didn't extend clear to the river, and I guess we wouldn't have counted as a river front owner, at that time.

We got the county engineer to come out, and he stood on the top of the dike and said, "This is a 100 year dike with a minimum of maintenance." I pointed out that the dikes wouldn't begin to hold the river at flood stage, even if the water was to the top on both sides, and the dikes would be gone long before that. He said that a state engineer designed the dike, and the "100 year dike" comment was what it said on the plans. I'm told that records of who funded the dike are deep in the dungeons of the Clallam County Courthouse. Hard to get at. We attended a county commissioner meeting and got nowhere. Soon the property behind the east side of the dike was developed. A good portion of the east dike and at least one house was built over what had been river bed, as late as the 1950s. (Not at flood stage either). And as I mentioned, the west dike was also on river bed.

Prior to the dikes, a really high water would pretty much cover most of the river bed, and now they intended to contain it in a narrow channel, between two long piles of bulldozed river rock, which would melt away like sugar. The channel wasn't completely straight, but had been straightened to a point that the velocity of the river, as it emerged at the bottom end of the dikes during high water conditions, would be comparable to a gigantic sluice box.

When I suggest that they had developed river bottom, consider this. I threw a rock, underhanded like you would throw a fast pitch softball, from where I was standing on the west side of the river, across the river and the east dike, and onto the roof of one of the homes built behind the dike, on the east side of the river. I could still throw a rock at that time, but I sure wasn't any Superman.

One of my biggest fears concerning the dike, was that if it washed through at some point, then the river, or possibly a good portion of it, could be coming down behind one of the dikes. In this area of the river, the main flow and certainly any heavy run off, has held to the east side for a long time. The size of the trees and stumps in the woods on both sides, clearly tell this story. A few hundred yards above the upstream end of the dikes, there is a tall clay bank on the east side, and for a good distance above this, the river has stayed in a pretty defined channel for years, due to that property owners bulldozer. Nobody told him what to do! The clay bank diverted the flow slightly to the west side, and then it cut back to the east, towards the Dungeness Meadows development. It's been doing this for a long time before the first white men came on the scene. Now the top end of the west dike extended so far upstream that the river could wash through before its normal "bend" had been accomplished. If the river got behind this side of the dike some beautifully wooded property, including ours, would wind up going downstream. Along with the loss of these woods, there's a potential for tremendous damage downstream, if they are washed out.

During one of the high waters that winter, we were worried about a neighbor who had built on the back property several hundred yards upstream from our place. Our next door neighbor walked back with Trish and me, and after we took Trish over to check with the neighbor lady, Don and I took the flashlights and walked on back to the river to see how the dike was dissolving.

It was raining and blowing and the roar of the river, as it washed these freshly dozed rocks downstream, was deafening. Then it got worse! The only thing I could think of to make that much noise was that some of the river had to be coming down through the woods, taking everything with it. It went through my mind that the dike on our side had washed through, and now the river was on the wrong side of the dike. Just what I'd been yelling about. We both took off running away from the river, falling down in the slick mud and leaves, and then it was on us. And went on by. No wall of water. Nothing!

Some other waterfront property a mile or so upstream, had been developed, and what we'd heard was a mobile home rolling down the river. When the river went down there were pieces of it spread over about a mile and a half. I was told somebody's deck and garage had left, too. Imagine living out on an island on a night that the river is flooding, your only way to safety being a small, narrow bridge, which spanned what was one of the old side stream channels. Another piece of property that never should have been developed, but he finally got his way.

The portion of the dike the county engineer had stood on, when he suggested how long the dike might be there, washed away that first winter, along with other spots on each dike. The Dungeness Meadows side was quickly reinforced with huge rocks, and certainly, huge bucks.

We were invited to a flood control meeting at the Dungeness Meadows clubhouse, and it was suggested that the property owners behind the west side of the dike should repair and maintain that side of the dike themselves. I have to agree that the taxpayers in the county shouldn't have to pay for something like this, but then, none of us on the west side of the river had wanted, or needed, a dike in the first place. They'd only bothered to tell one of us that the dike was going in. When I mentioned that, and the fact that I used to enjoy fishing in what had been one of my favorite portions of the river, within a few feet of where we were sitting in the Dungeness Meadows clubhouse, they didn't want to hear it. You couldn't blame them. People had come into the area in the summer or fall months, loved the area, and that nice stream running down at the edge of the property. They had bought and built. They "really" didn't want to hear it.

Before too long, the reinforced east side did wash through, and several people lost portions of their buildings, driveways, and yards. That time they were able to plug things up fairly soon. With a good piece of the river bed already behind the dike on the east side, it's unrealistic to suggest that any normal system of diking will contain the river when that exceptional shot of water comes through, and if the river got on the wrong side of the dike—?

Will the east side of the dike wash through first? Who knows? What if the Army Engineers are busy repairing some other fiasco and can't come to their aid? With most of the west dike gone, maybe the river will find another path through the woods, because the water will have to go somewhere—but once again, the river would like to hold to the east bank in this area. Another strong Chinook wind, following a lot of snow in the foothills, like the one they had in 58 or 60, and look out! Instead of the nice sunny day, with equipment able to work at one hundred percent, suppose it rains as it's not supposed to in Sequim, the ground becoming soft and unstable and the dike washing through at several points at the same time. I feel sorry for those people who were sold some of this property. Some of the people who should have been most responsible, weren't. Except to themselves.

From river bar, to dike, to river bar, all in a relatively short time. The first mini high water started dissolving the dike, and these freshly dozed rows of rock, sand, and gravel, didn't put up much of a fight. The river bed downstream, almost to the Highway 101 bridge, took on a new look. At a point barely upstream from Ethel's berry patch, the river bar became so high in one area, that you were looking down from it, onto the field that was just north of Ethel's property.

The next high water closed the distance from the riverbed to the bottom of the 101 bridge by well over three feet. Or maybe the bridge was sagging? I used to measure it, reaching up with my steelhead pole. A really good flood about that time would have tested the Highway 101 bridge. The raised river bed just downstream from the bridge, diverted flow again, and considerable property on the east bank was needlessly lost during another high water.

Bar removal, seems to be the only likely long term solution now. Take out the worst, highest spots from the bars outside of the present area of flow, and the river will find low ground before long. Then next summer do it again. And again. Hopefully, this could prevent any further erosion of the extreme edges of the river bank. One way or another, the future cost of this one development will be big, and probably a disaster to some people, there and downstream.

Along with this, over a mile of the Dungeness River's best spawning grounds was pretty much ruined and from what I've been told, they would have needed fisheries approval. I'm beginning to doubt that. Somewhere else, I've mentioned the need for some kind of a river authority. It would have been nice if someone could have held this deal up long enough for it to have been thoroughly looked at, by people who knew the subject beyond immediate profit. Maybe someday we'll learn to watch what some people are doing.

Its hard to tell someone that he can't do what he wants with his property, but in the case of Dungeness Meadows, that's exactly what should have happened. A portion of the Meadows sits back, and is high enough that it would have been all right for development, but the river bed should never have been compromised. As long as river bed reclamation can be disguised as flood control, people will build or develop too close to the river and problems like this will continue to haunt us in the future. If the river does happen to get behind the dike on the east side, or what's left of the dike on the west side, the results will likely be grim.

A couple years ago, I finally went back and looked at this piece of the river from both sides. Now the east dike is so wide in places, it's hard to understand what's taken place since we left. My guess is that the large chunks of rock that had been added to the original dike, washed into the river and were replaced, and now, instead of an abruptly sloping dike edge, they have a wide, gradually sloping bunch of large rock that takes up an even larger portion of the riverbed. Now it has filled to a point that there's no capacity to run off much water. Maybe if they can keep moving the dike far enough to the west they'll be able to sell a few more lots?

I left the pickup out by the dike, and found the top of the channel in short order, although I didn't immediately recognize it. Going back to the east, I came out at the bank edge and some pools of still water, with just a trickle running down through it. I looked at it a bit, the direction the trickle entered the pool and the two pools, separated with a bit of sand and debris from the woods. There it was, the last big hole at the top. At that time, it was only another few hundred feet, over and up, to where the river separated. About 50 yards downstream there had been a log jam, kind of spread out, and the channel had turned almost to the west, then a long deep drift, a slow riffle moving into a deep pool, and then back downstream, to the north. I couldn't believe the change, but it was all right there. The two pools were what remained of that last big hole, one of the spots that had been so full of humpies, that it looked like fish would have to move upstream when others moved up into the bottom of the hole. A steady stream of salmon with a bulge of several thousand each in those first few holes, and many more thousands downstream. Still a grim memory.

I couldn't believe how the stream bed had filled and grown back, but over 45 years of debris out of the woods puts back a lot. For that matter, the meadow between Iverson's house and the riverbank is all homes and trees now. With the exception of that area of meadow, things probably looked about the same now, as they had before the river had branched down through there when I was a kid. I was tired, but happy that I'd made the effort. Being there, it was easy to relive my excitement that first day I'd found the spot, and having a piece of river virtually all to myself for several years. I remembered the exceptional run of dog salmon that had came up that far, and several hours one afternoon, trying to coax a larger than usual summer run steelhead to bite. It didn't. And the humpies, there at the end. Now it was all woods again, and memories. And a glimpse of how short a time we're here.

The west dike, never reinforced, is virtually all gone, and had been for some years before we left. What had been some of the most beautiful woods imaginable, with cedar stumps over seven feet through, and the big cottonwoods that were almost as big, are gone. That piece of ground had held its own for many hundreds of years, and now it's river bed.

What I'm against is the slovenly placement of so many dikes along our rivers. In any case they are an enormous expense to build, but when they are used to make a portion of what should be river bottom, into farmland, developments, or whatever, the cost to most people is going to outweigh the gain to a few. Using the dike that protects Dungeness Meadows as an example, people living across and downstream from the Meadows, along with some responsible "River Authority" should have been notified before putting the bulldozers in the river. Then someone might have looked at the plans, and the developer and county authorities, might have been slowed down enough to at least have been made to do it right. If ever there was an example of irresponsible river management—this is a dandy.

# Chapter 15
# The Columbia

Trolling commercially for salmon has been going on since the late 1800s. It's hard to say where it started; maybe around Seattle or San Francisco, or the mouth of the Columbia. It may have been some kid trying to make a few bucks with his rowboat, or some old guy, trying to grind out enough to get by on. Maybe some young guy with a love of boats and fish, and a family to support. Who knows? There was good availability of the best quality fish and I'm sure the demand for them turned into a fishery in no time.

The use of salmon, beyond personal needs, had gone on long before trolling was ever thought of. Coastal tribes that had good access to salmon used them in trade with tribes living further inland. Later on, salmon would have played a large role in trade with the Spanish, Russian, English and other explorers. It's not likely that any early west coast settlements were without their local fishermen. More likely, most of them were fishermen.

By the mid 1800s they were using horse seines and water wheels to take salmon in the Columbia River, and by the late 1880s, salmon canneries along the river were processing over a million king salmon yearly. Fish wheels, fish traps, seines, and gill-nets, and before the turn of the century the first salmon trollers were working near the mouth of the river. By 1920 this fleet numbered nearly 2000 boats. Well before that time there was a noticeable decline in the amount of salmon available, and with the earlier returning fish being of a higher quality, the majority of the catch was on the spring king salmon runs. "Over-exploitation of spring Chinook eroded the number of seed stock so severely that they collapsed."[1] Restrictions on methods of harvesting, and closed seasons started taking place well before the turn of the century.

There were other problems besides the fishing. Diversion dams on tributaries blocked access to spawning grounds upstream. Unscreened outlets to the irrigation ditches sent downstream migrants out onto farm land, and mining and logging practices began to compromise watersheds and river bottom. Even before the hydroelectric dams, we were coming up short.

By 1941 there were three hydroelectric dams in place across the Columbia River. The first was Rock Island Dam, downstream from Wenatchee, finished in 1933. Bonneville, finished in 1938, and Grand Coulee (1941) were next. This started development of the Columbia River system, for hydroelectric power, flood control, and a massive new potential for irrigation.

Bonneville Dam had three fish ladders, as well as two fish lifting systems. At first the fish passage facilities appeared to be a great success, likely because of a high degree of hope. Considering the volume of salmon going past the dam at that time, over fish ladders and counting stations where they were easy to see, it probably did look good. There were no provisions for the passage of fish over Grand Coulee Dam. The extreme height of the dam (550 feet high, from bedrock) was the reason.

"Over 74,000 square miles of upper Columbia River basin were blocked to anadromous salmon by construction of Grand Coulee dam alone"[2] Over 1000 miles of the finest king salmon spawning grounds in the world were lost. So the large numbers of salmon that once went up the Columbia River into British Columbia are long gone. Some of these kings were huge fish, sometimes over 100 pounds. Undoubtedly their genes are still swimming around somewhere, but diluted many times by now.

"As mitigation for the loss of fish runs from the construction of Grand Coulee, they built three hatcheries located on the Entiat, Methow, and Icicle Rivers. Adult spring kings were taken at Rock Island dam from 1939 to 1943 and transported to the three rivers. The remaining adults were taken to the Leavenworth Hatchery where they were spawned, the eggs incubated to the eyed stage, and then the eggs were divided among the three hatcheries. In eighteen months the smolts were released into each of the three rivers. By 1943 they were getting enough returns to stop collecting fish at Rock Island dam."[3] The Icicle enters the Wenatchee River at Leavenworth. This must have created quite a mixture in the gene pool, considering the mixture of salmon they were collecting, as well as stocks already existing in those rivers.

Twelve years after Grand Coulee was in operation, the flood of dams started. McNary 1953, Chief Joseph 1955, The Dalles 1957, Priest Rapids, 1959, Rocky

Reach 1961, Wanapum 1963, Welles 1967, and John Day 1968, all on the Columbia. The date is for when they were first put in service.

Add to those, these dams on the Snake river. Brownlee in 1958, Oxbow and Ice Harbor both in 1961, Hells canyon in 1967, Lower Monumental in 1969, Little Goose in 1970, and Lower Granite in 1973. Dworshak dam was built on the north fork of the Clearwater River in 1973. Add to these, over 170 more dams on the two rivers and their tributaries, not necessarily for power generation, and definitely not as big as these big (super) dams. Flood control, reservoirs for irrigation, whatever their purpose, they all contributed some way in crippling Columbia and Snake River basins salmon runs. It's hard to say how much more they'll be able to raise the water temperature, and salmon still survive.

I'm not sure why the 12 year gap in dam production between Grand Coulee and McNary dams. The effect on the downstream migrants at the first two dams was already obvious, with no solution in sight. "15% mortality (per dam) was what was originally reported, but with further research that has changed downward. As low as 2 to 3% is given with some estimates. They don't know for sure. Barging is quite successful, with returns much higher than without barging. However, barging can alter the home stream cue and cause delays of adults returning when they get to the smolt release site. That was a problem when they didn't circulate river water through the barge on transit downstream, but when they changed that routine I believe it improved return success. Return success over the last three years has been better than 1%." [4]

"With Grand Coulee, Hells Canyon, and major tributary dams, 60% of the Columbia basin watershed was made inaccessible to salmon, and much of that was the primary habitat of the spring chinook. The remaining Columbia and Snake mainstem river habitat has been reduced 64% by flooded reservoirs." [5]

Recent years show the highest returns of king salmon since pre 1930s, but since these are 90% hatchery fish, the National Marine Fisheries Service continues to beat the Endangered Species Act drum. This may have something to do with their own survival. It wasn't any big secret that there would be problems concerning salmon when the dams were built. They knew that runs of wild salmon would be wiped out, and as mitigation for the loss of wild salmon production, 65 major hatcheries have been built in the Columbia Basin, as well as many other smaller facilities.

Did they work? 2001, 2, and 2003 averaged over 885,000 kings counted at Bonneville Dam. Of this, the average for the three years on adult spring kings was 284,000 fish. For a comparison, the ten year average, 1984 - 1993 was 396, 638 kings, with about 87,000 of them being adult spring kings. So who knows? Maybe in-river or ocean conditions, or maybe some improvement like circulating the water in the transit barges? Or a combination of the above and other—? To even make a good guess, you'd need access to all the information, statistics, and otherwise. Which leaves me out.

If you like to make a living as a fisherman, or like to eat a delicious piece of salmon, whether you've bought it, or caught it, you probably think the hatcheries might be working. The few salmon trollers left off the Washington coast might even dream of enough quota on kings, that they might someday have a chance at making a living again, like fishermen from other states where their fleets are at least ten times as big. Wouldn't that be something? Meanwhile, putting certain Columbia - Snake River stocks of fish on the Endangered Specie List, in light of what's been done to the river, is something I really wonder about.

The dams and locks on the Snake River, made transportation possible for product from a massive area of Snake River watershed. This, along with increased irrigation potential, hydroelectric power, and flood control, helped develop a new economic base for the Pacific Northwest. That was the idea in the first place—to develop the entire region, using the Columbia - Snake River basins water.

Now there's talk about taking out the first four dams on the Snake River side. More accurately, the dams would be breached, which would eliminate their ability to hold back water, allowing free passage past the dam to stocks of fish. The reservoirs behind the dams would be eliminated, and loss of fish moving either upstream or downstream, would be minimized. Downstream migrants would still have to contend with McNary, John Day, The Dalles, and Bonneville dams, after they got downstream to the Columbia. If the four dams in the lower Snake River were breached, at an estimated cost of one billion dollars, it would return 140 miles of Snake River mainstem back to free flowing river conditions. Along with the four dams below the junction on the Columbia, there would still be three major dams in the upper Snake River system, and Dworshak Dam on the North Fork of the Clearwater.

Undoubtedly there would be gains salmon-wise. Would the gains offset the long term costs associated with dam removal? It would depend on which side of the fence you're standing on. Maybe more salmon and steelhead in the lower portion of the Snake and in the Salmon River system. Undoubtedly more, but how many? Who knows?

Removing the four dams would cool down the river water, which is a major plus if you're a salmon, but I wonder here, if there's not some ways of cooling down the water, short of dam removal. How about making cold water trails over fish ladders, maybe even cooler paths along the edges of these lakes. An insulated wall to separate the trail from the lake and some kind of a reflective or insulated cover? Or something? Maybe just a long insulated, refrigerated where needed, cement channel, with an insulated roof. A heat exchanger pipeline underground would at least get the water down close to ground temperature, and running parallel to the side stream, could be metered in as needed. Or something!! Some of this might work for fish going west, as well as east. If they can build a road around a dam, why can't they build a mini-cooled off river around and between them? If you can control the volume of water going down the stream, it sure wouldn't take long to grow some major shade.

Or how about sidetracking water, some refrigeration, and returning it at optimum temp at critical places—fish ladders, hatcheries, spawning channels, or these small engineered streams—? Then again, they might not be allowed the electricity to power them with. That's something they could sell. All my Great ideas always run into reality and those last sentences are Reality.

Lack of Oxygen in the pools behind the dams is another problem, as is nitrogen supersaturation below the dams. Also, there's some pretty significant predation on juveniles in the lakes behind the dams. With all those nice new lakes, somebody just had to introduce a bunch of new species throughout the system.

What about power? The "juice" generated by these four lower Snake River dams, amounts to 5% of the northwest's hydroelectric power. That's a lot of juice. Who's going to volunteer to use less? In case nobody steps up, what will they replace that electricity with? Coal powered plants? Nuclear plants?—That'll be popular.

These dams put water to 37,000 acres of farmland. How many livelihoods would their removal erase? How many lifetimes of effort out the window? On the other hand, they're talking about breaching the dams - not doing away with the water. I don't know a thing about the lay of the land over there, but there ought to be some way to get the water up to them. Or down to them—long term, pipelines from upstream makes good sense. Sometimes there's other options that don't get mentioned till we have to.

So there's lots of points of view and lots at stake. Idaho's in river sport fishery, and the tourism industry, which also affects the whole west coast, Canada included.

And there's a massive agricultural and industrial base, with a more massive supportive network of jobs—small business—big business—small towns and cities.

If transportation of product hadn't been such a big consideration, there wouldn't have been the need for so many dams or locks in the first place, but they needed to get boats and barges from here, up or down, to there. Railroads and highway systems are already in place, but the costs to some, if these dams were breached—I hate to think of it. Then again—

At one point I thought everyone more or less worked together to make things better. You gave a bit and you got a bit, I thought. Maybe some bright young mind would figure out a way to get the smolts downstream, with improved numbers of returning adults. Maybe we could have it both ways to some extent. (tra-la) "Those not wishing to sell into the buyback program should realize a viable fishery, as soon as runs of salmon are rebuilt." You bet. Now they've got to be "wild."—In the Columbia—?

My feelings about this one day, I'm not so sure about the next. I'd sure hate to see people in eastern Washington go through what the fishing fleet has. Now that the state's licensed troll fleet is down to not much over a hundred boats, many of which fish in some other state or two, they'll probably let what's left exist, for awhile. After all, a state like Washington ought to have a fishery, if only on a token basis. I would hate to see those farmers get shoved down that same road.

I still think they're going to figure out some dam - salmon migration solutions. Like I said, some of that lost electrical power could sure make some cooler paths, and money otherwise spent in breaching the dams might be used in establishing streams larger than these fish ladders, around them. But unless they can get adults to habitat where they can reproduce, and downstream migrants past the dams, is there that much gain??????

Otherwise, would an engineered stream, or streams on a larger scale, be part of some answer? Like I said, I don't know a thing about the terrain, and the power authorities probably wouldn't allow them to use the water. How much would a one acre floating island, anchored out, with a reflective roof, cool down a patch of water? Or a few hundred of them? Maybe they could even harness the heat. Somebody ought to be able to think of something, but you can see where this has been a head scratcher, and why people say, the hell with it. After everything else, there's always the big buckeroos at the top, and no matter what, they'll decide what's best. Or what's what.

The loss of salmon as a result of dam placement in the Columbia and Snake

River system, was felt by the Canadian troll fleet, as well as the Americans. Our late release (resident stock) program on silvers was being implemented towards the end of the Snake River dam building, and the combination of the two took a deep bite into the Canadian's troll caught salmon production. They soon realized a massive fleet reduction in all of their commercial salmon fisheries. Along these lines, loosely, is something that I found interesting. In "Grand Coulee—Harnessing A Dream," Paul Pitzer cites comments from an exchange of letters between two Canadian officials, concerning Grand Coulee dam.

(In October 1934, H.H. Wrong, a member of the Canadian Legation in Washington, wrote to the Minister of Fisheries (i.e. Canadian Dept. of Fisheries) advising them that Grand Coulee dam would prevent any salmon migration to the upper Columbia River. On October 27, 1934, the Deputy Minister (i.e. Undersecretary) of Fisheries, W.A. Found, wrote to O.D. Skelton, the Undersecretary of State for External Affairs (Canada). The memo included the following. "The assumption that there is no commercial salmon fishery on the Columbia River in Canada is correct, and hence Canadian interests in that respect will not be affected if the dam at Grand Coulee is not equipped with fishway facilities." [6]

There was some question that the quote actually came from the Minister of Fisheries, but with help from a few librarians in Canada, and Charlotte, here at the Ferndale Library, we found that it came from his Deputy Minister (i.e. Undersecretary of Fisheries). It was suggested that copies of the two letters would likely be found in the National Archives of Canada if someone were interested. Not that it makes much difference at this point, but it shows how something that would have devastating results, to some, can slip through a system virtually unchallenged. It's hard to imagine a fisheries person making that statement, but considering the non fisheries gains to be realized by Canadians, you can only guess at the history behind his comment. These weren't good times in Canada either. The depression was a major fact of life for people from both countries. I'm certain, that for a very thorough history on Grand Coulee Dam, Paul Pitzers book, "Grand Coulee—Harnessing A Dream" would be hard to beat.

In the earlier years of salmon trolling in Alaska, the fishery existed largely on Columbia River salmon. Port Alexander, on the south end of Baranoff Island, was one of the first ports in southeast Alaska to handle large amounts of troll caught king salmon. At first the salmon were filleted and salted in huge wooden drums called tierces, the product still called "mild cure" when I started fishing. When I first came north in 1958, much of the king salmon production was still put up this way. Tommy Thompson, living in Petersburg then, was the best splitter I ever saw, fast and the cuts virtually perfect. He said my fish likely wound up in New York or Germany and were lightly smoked, sliced thin, and sold as a product still known today as "lox." At first the fish were salted ashore. Later they were iced on the packers and taken to town for processing. "Town" at first was probably Ketchikan and Prince Rupert, later spreading to the other towns in southeast Alaska.

This may not have been where hand trolling originated, but each year a good many of them spent their summer there. The small port became a pretty lively little town with stores, a butcher shop and bakery, a hotel, and a few hook shops. A good portion of the boats weren't very big, so in good weather the tenders would go out and the smaller boats could offload on the grounds, saving them from having to come in, and then go back out. This kept the guys fishing, instead of waiting in line to unload. Everyone's purpose in being there was to put king salmon across the deck. Twenty-five cents per king salmon, no whites.

At first a lot of them rowed, but the more progressive ones had a little one banger for power. They pulled cotton lines by hand, with one line going down, and three separate lines off it, each with its own lure and lead. They likely improved on this in short order. In a few years the individual fisherman became more productive, as the skiffs were replaced with a fleet of boats, mostly in the 30 to 40 foot range. Now the individual fisherman could range farther, fish in tougher weather, and have the potential to handle more fish quickly and pack them around himself. These larger boats allowed the fishermen to take ice aboard, and to fish away from port for several days at a time. This spread the effort up and down the coast.

The old timers told me, that once they started building dams in the Columbia, king salmon production dropped each year. Fish camps like the ones at Coronation and Forrester Island would soon be a dim memory, and Port Alexander's population would drop to only a few people for quite a few years.

So now you couldn't go out, using the crudest sort of hand lines, and catch all the kings you could handle day after day. Even so, there was still enough fish around that people made a good living, trolling for salmon. The season was long and the price was good, compared to the 25 cents a fish that had been the going rate, years earlier. Many trollers made a good enough season concentrating mostly on cohos.

When I started fishing in 1957, the average age of the fishermen was getting up there. Many of them had fished most of their lives, and now would go out, fish easy, and make enough to get by on. Scarcity of king salmon wasn't as important to them, as it might have been twenty years earlier. When I started splitting my seasons between Alaska and off the Washington coast, one of the things that stood out was that there had been a big influx of younger people into the fishery. This started taking place in the 60s, and continued on through the 70s. It soon was very obvious in Alaska's fishery too, and in Canada's. It kind of went with the times, but the bottom line was still what you put across the dock. Many of these people would become some of the top fishermen in the fleet. In a short time, the average age in the fleet dropped by at least twenty years. So now, instead of mostly older people fishing their last few seasons, there was a good percentage of younger people with families, in the fleet.

The average boat became more productive. The ones who were just starting fishing were more likely to put out a greater effort than the older people whose boats they were buying. Young families to support, homes to buy, boats to improve or replace; like everyone else, we had our wants and needs. And there was still a lot of fish around. The hatcheries were pouring out silvers and kings, and there was still a decent amount of wild salmon available. Anyone who put out a good effort, could generally grind out a decent season.

Then the dams across the Snake River started taking their toll on what was left of the backbone of king salmon runs. There was enormous opposition to these dams, but it was over-ran by every entity that might have a design on the rivers water, and it's hard to deny that the water is used, or held back, for some pretty worthwhile purposes. Even so, salmon and steelhead runs were diminished more with the addition of each dam.

The fleet took another hit when Washington's Department of Fisheries turned the silver production from many of the hatcheries on the state's inside waters, into near valueless, half sized runts. Most of the juvenile silvers coming out of the Straits Of Juan De Fuca turned north, to later be caught by a massive Canadian troll fleet. Delaying their release at the hatcheries compromised migratory instincts, keeping large numbers of them in the straits and sound to provide the intended sport fishery. But they didn't all stay inside. We started getting them quite a ways below Destruction Island, with much larger numbers closer to the straits, and I'm sure, more yet off Vancouver Island. As well as less poundage and quality, the smaller silvers meant much less value per lb. The bread and butter for a good portion of the Washington State troll fishery was gone.

About that time you started seeing articles in the newspapers—"U.S. 5th in world fish production." The federal government started a program to improve the U.S. fishing fleet, by making a bunch of cheap loans available to fishermen through a program called "The Capital Construction Fund." You didn't need to have fished all that long to qualify, and a bunch of guys got new boats and equipment. The fleets potential increased again. Like one of the fisheries people in Juneau told me, "It's another grand example of one piece of government, having no idea whatsoever, what another agency is doing."

A short time later, state and federal fisheries agencies discovered that the fleet was "overcapitalized." Isn't "that" something? At about this same time, Boldt's "Decision" was just over the horizon. It's hard to imagine what that first troller would have thought, if he could have seen what was happening to his fishery.

# Chapter 16
# Going North

Going north early, and fishing the last month or two of the inside winter king fishery, was something I always enjoyed. Usually I'd go up alone, or if Bill and Nada were ready, we'd run up together. You were always learning things with Bill—boat handling stuff, good harbors, etc. My favorite, was his theory on catching fish. "First, get where there's some fish."

Later on, Sid and I had a couple interesting trips north, and one year, I think in 68 or 69, I went part way up with a couple Canadians. I had stopped at Shoal Bay at the end of the second day out, and was walking up the dock towards the store. The first two days away from home are traumatic, and I might have been out of cookies. When I walked by the only other boat tied at the dock, this guy leans out the window and says to stop by on the way back for a cup of tea. So I did.

Ray and Ken Avery were on their way up to fish shrimp and whatever else they could catch, and would spend a month or more, freezing their catch and then running it down to Vancouver. They'd just installed their refrigeration system, and were pretty enthused about this new venture. Ray was originally from England, and after living in eastern Canada for a bit, decided to move out here. They put their boat on a flat car and had it railed west, and once they got here, decided it wouldn't do for these west coast fisheries. Then they'd bought the "Friendship IV," the old tug boat on which I was having tea and cookies, and hearing about a couple interesting lives. We B.S.ed till late and since we were going up the same trail, they suggested my running along with them the next few days.

"What kind of time do you make?"

"Ohhh, seven, seven and a half."

"Forget it, we make 10."

"She'll make 11."

"Hell, she'll make 12."

"Look, no sense in me slowing you guys down, maybe I'll catch you in the evening and if I don't—no big deal."

"Well, whatever. How far you going tomorrow?"

It was supposed to blow southeast, so we decided to go into Pete's, at Christie Pass. Tied to the floats there, you had to look straight up several hundred feet to see trees at the tops of high bluffs, whipping in the wind, with only some light puffs down on the water. The next morning, Ken threw my bow line aboard, and that was as close as they got to the Camelot till he handed me their bow line in Gods pocket that evening. "————man, did you take off."

I didn't say anything, but while I was putting their line on the dock, it was in the back of my mind, was that a trace of a grin?" They had been on deck most of the day, running on the auto pilot and hammering shrimp pots together, while I spent the day on the wheel, running the beach and the back eddies. We'd bucked the tide a big portion of the day, and I knew that my working the currents had made quite a difference. Still, I wondered when Ray asked, "what kind of power you got in that rig?" Was that a little extra twinkle when he'd said it?"

That evening we got to comparing notes on trolling, and it seemed like they were fishing areas and conditions pretty similar to what I was in Alaska. Apparently a little friendly competition with the guys they fished around, and they had been trying to come up with, at least, an equalizer. So I showed them how to choke herring. Like Ray said, "we all choke the same herring." But we hoped his buddies hadn't heard of such a thing.

We got on across Queen Charlotte Sound the next day, and after a wave goodbye, they took off for one of the inlets. I passed Ray in the Yucultaws a few years later, going different directions, so a wave across the water, and I never ran across them after that. I always wondered, how much did they slow down that first day? And how the choked herring had worked out?

This area where we had separated, reminds me of something else. A few years later I had nicely got across Queen Charlotte and just outside Safety Cove, I looked out the back door, and here's a seagull standing on the stern, as far back as he can get. After that, if I walked back into the galley it spooked him a bit, and he did the side step pretty fast across the stern. I'd stop, and he'd settle down. I'd look back at him from the wheelhouse now and then, and he seemed content to ride along, pretty much running the boat from the stern. I got interested in seeing how far he'd go, so I never did go on the back deck, because he got pretty antsy when I'd get as far back as the galley. That evening when I pulled into Namu, he was still there, and a fellow working on the dock came over when I went to tie up, and it flew away. I'd have scared him off anyway, when I went back to get the stern line. He rode along back there for three or four hours. Lloyd had one aboard for quite awhile, weeks, a month? I forget. It wasn't hurt or anything and probably figured it was eating better than the average duck. They eat a lot of fish on Lloyd's boat, so it was in good company. One other memory from Fitzhugh Sound is several hundred pacific white sided dolphin picking us up, and running along with us for over three hours. They put on quite a show, occasionally jumping as high as the bow. This was in March, three months earlier than I'd ever seen them.

Getting north a little early had its advantages. Like Bill said, "You look the country over, find out where there's a little feed, and if anything will fall apart it's usually during the first trip or so. You can deal with it before the fishing gets going. And, you get a few fish." Sometimes quite a few.

Except for the occasional tug boat going up or down country, you might fish the whole trip without seeing another boat. I got along with that pretty well. I remember thinking of the machine, fathometer, and radio, all as crew members. Or the fire in the galley stove. That erratic flame in the fire pot in the Neptune II was great company. Fresh coffee and cookies, so you can see I wasn't completely bats.

Occasionally the weather was just too much to fish in, even in inside waters. Those were days to wash clothes and make up a batch of bread, and I always had a lot of reading material aboard. I listened to standard broadcast on the radio, and most of the time you could get either Juneau, Ketchikan, or Sitka. Coming out of one harbor early in the morning, I could always pick up some station in Hawaii like I was right there. Then, when I turned the boat to put out the gear, it was gone. Some of the time I listened to the marine bands and the occasional tugboat giving their position, speed, weather conditions, E.T.A., and the like.

The Arthur Foss was my favorite tug boat, and I guess just about my favorite boat, period. I got to go aboard once and the engineer gave me a tour of the boat. After seeing their engine room, mine was always in better condition. My first three boats didn't have all that much space around the machine, but the Elusive did, and the engine room always got that extra bit of T.L.C. After "Arthur Foss,"

*Summer Place—Built by Jess Richmond as the "Family Affair"*
*I made most of the bolts and hammered on a lot of the nails*

my favorites were the old halibut schooners, and then any wooden workboat, especially the older ones. Lou Scott, who used to have Tokeen Cold Storage, and later, put in the one at Craig, summed it up when talking about his "Genador." "A wood boat's been alive, and I feel like they still are." That's the way I feel too, even though we'd been through enough with the "Elusive," that we still felt of it as a family member. But imagine having a wooden boat that you'd built, or helped build, yourself.

I'll go you one further. Across the river from where the Elusive was built, was a small yard owned by the Makela Brothers. Boat lumber had become hard to get in California, too, so each morning they were going out with their truck and chain saw mill, and coming back in the evening with the days efforts. They'd stack and strip the material to air dry in their shop, and were well along towards the material for their last boat. They were getting along in years, and this had already been quite a project. Their boats were some of the finest.

Back then, there was only the odd fishing boat on the air till about the first of April. After that it got pretty noisy. Years later everyone had a V.H.F. radio and that made the radio department a lot better. I decided after the first few years, that I would be a lot happier by minimizing my use of the radio, listening and otherwise. Except for standard broadcast.

They started paring down the season for salmon, more and more each year. Before too long, it got to where I enjoyed the summer fishing less and less. When it got to where there were openings instead of seasons, the effort on the traditional hot spots just got more intense. Being someone who had always avoided crowds of boats, I found myself spending quite a bit of time looking around the edges in hopes of still finding enough fish, and maybe not hating being there. There were others who had the same attitude, and these were usually easy people to fish around. I always felt that no matter who you were, where you were from, or if you were out there in the Queen Mary or a bath tub,—if you had the license you had the right to an equal pass at whatever you might have been fishing around. My only exception in this feeling was that I thought that fishing should be some reasonable percentage of a persons livelihood, as eligibility to buy the license. Some years of deckhand work could have qualified a starter.

When the boys were 10 and 12 they started coming up, and would fish the summer season with me. Trish had brought them and Deann up for short trips, and they had also fished trips with me in Washington, so they weren't exactly strangers to the boat. This made things a little better, as there was always something going on, and it made the days a lot shorter.

When the tide wasn't right for some spot, we'd go in to some harbor early and put the skiff down. Quite a few streams got investigated and beaches combed.

*The boys first joint effort king salmon*

182

No one knew the shorelines of the harbors we used, better than they did. If we were going through Chatham Straits it was always great to stop and see Wally, and soak out in a hot tub after some trout fishing in the river. Wally was always a big deal, and would have some good stories for the kids.

The river at Warm Springs is a mini, length wise. It comes out of the lake, and about a hundred yards downstream, goes over the falls and into the bay. When I first started fishing, the Short family lived there, and I fished around Pap and the boys quite a lot, as we all liked the same areas. It was just their families there then. They ran the bath house and the store, and you could use their laundry house. They sold to Wally and it didn't change for years, but now he's left there, and the ugly hand of civilization is starting to squeeze.

The first time I stopped there with the boys there was only one trout pole aboard, so they flipped a coin and whoever won would use the pole that afternoon, and the other would get it the next morning. Chris won, so Keith was using a hand line he'd rigged up, and was fishing around this rock he was standing on. I don't know why he hadn't cut a limb for a pole, but that's what he wanted to do. Probably too used to jigging with a hand line in the harbors. So, as luck would have it he was the one to hook into a bigger than usual cutthroat trout, and after playing him around the rock for a bit we'd all got into a position on the edge of the river where we might grab it. Before we got the chance, the hook pulled out, and Keith was slightly down in the lips.

The next morning he was back on the rock, armed with the trout pole. After getting a few eaters, he had another nice cutthroat on, and this time it didn't get away. A nineteen incher and it looked like it might have been the one he lost yesterday, although I couldn't see where it had been hooked before. So if it wasn't trout fishing, there would be fishing in the harbor from the boat or skiff, or beachcombing, or clamming, or rowing over to some other boat to hear some fish stories. Most of the time Sid would be around, and they figured he and Granny were the neatest thing going.

I had met Sid in Pelican in 79 and fished around him some that year, and we started fishing together the next season. He liked the crowds even less than I did, so the only big difference in our operations was that the Miss Everett was a small 39 foot boat, and the Elusive was a relatively big, 54 footer. There are small boats and big ones, and some are much larger than other boats of the same length. The Miss Everett was one of the older boats around, not too deep, and a double ender. (Sharp on both ends.) She couldn't help it, she just wasn't a big rig. Sid didn't

*Sid Ward*

look at it that way though. A lot of the time if it was miserable going he would follow along behind me, and the Elusive would break it down for him. The only time I ever had to slow down much, was if we were running before it, and then the Elusive thought she was quite a grand lady. I had to slow way, way, back or I'd walk away from him.

On one of our trips north in February, we had decided to go behind the Melvilles and Dundas Island, to save the drubbing that would have been if we had gone the usual route up behind Green Island. On the trip up through Chatham Sound the previous year, I had plenty of reason to figure it out. Either wait it out, or find a better trail! This was one of those days, with southeast gale warnings forecast. There was no doubt in our minds that this forecast meant even stronger northeast winds, out of Portland Canal. By the time we were a few miles past Lawyer Island, there was a pretty decent southeast breeze on our sterns, and a good surge coming towards us from the north. We started adjusting to go over behind Lucy Island. We'd get some real estate between us and Chatham Sound.

Before getting in the lee of the Melvilles, it got breezier yet from the southeast, mixed with occasional blasts from the northeast, and the surge from the northeast was running stronger. It was obvious we'd made a good move, and soon we were running easy before it, the wind and surge behind the Melvilles both going the right way. Pretty soon Sid was dropping back, and I was slowing down. We went past the bottom end of Dundas Island, and were rewarded with a really big surge coming from around the Chatham Sound side, so we felt pretty clever because we would soon be above it, with all our feathers intact. Gradually the surge from the northeast gave way to a nice steady sea from the southeast, and we had an easy ride running before it. The slop would probably get bigger, but we should have a nice ride on across Dixon Entrance.

When we had gone out from Dundas a few miles, I started running through logs and smaller stuff, and where you can normally pick your way through, it wasn't long before we could see we wouldn't get through this without a bulldozer. I could see up ahead for quite aways, and in front of us there was a lot more wood showing, than water. In the 34 years I fished, this was the only time I had to turn around and go back for a few minutes, and then way to the side to get around some spot. There must have been kind of a catch basin area, where the currents from both sides of Melville, Dundas, and Zayas Islands, got together, and this stuff accumulated. While we're at it, currents out of Clarence and Hecate Straits, as well as Revillagigedo Channel, feed this area, too. Anyway, now that we're past that, it's good going. For the Elusive.

Sid only had one good arm. He'd crushed one elbow while working in the woods in Oregon, and although the hand and wrist worked fine, the elbow didn't bend. He was one of quite a bunch of people with a mini handicap, who had turned to fishing for their living, and he was good at it. His auto pilot wasn't keeping up, so it was steer by hand for the last five hours across Dixon Entrance. It was dark when we got behind Mary Island, and after we'd each anchored, he said, "the only time this—was on course all afternoon was when it happened to cross it. I think my arms a foot longer than it was this morning." So I did a little thinking that evening. Sid was 67 at that time, going on 14, and he didn't feel like slowing anyone down. Especially himself. It wouldn't be necessary very often, but I might need to start backing off now and then.

We couldn't get ice in Ketchikan or Wrangell. We could in Petersburg, but didn't feel like going that way, so we decided to shovel off a few docks as we moved up country, and put enough snow in the Elusive to fish on up to Sitka. We got some in Myerschuck, and took the top foot or so off a section of the dock in Wrangell. Incidentally, the snow up there generally stays white. The weather was clear and cold now, so when you'd go across some spot that was open to the north, the northeast would pick up. We got a good taste of this, with it blowing down out of the Stikine River, after we had left Wrangell. Sid mentioned that we might want to watch this, as we would soon be running through some areas where the northeast would be funneling out of. When we were back towards the river, some of the spray was freezing, but the wind velocity dropped as we moved along, and for a ways, there was no problem. When we got down by Point Baker it was another story. With northeast wind coming hard out of Rocky Pass, (Keku Strait) Sid moved around to the lee side of me, hoping to cut down on how much spray he took. He couldn't stay there, because he was getting quite a bit of my spray, as well as his. Everything that came aboard froze instantly. The Elusive would be fine for awhile, but the Miss Everett needed out of it right away.

Port Protection looked pretty good. Lots of snow on the dock too. We were able to tie down on the far end of the dock, and stayed there for five days while the wind blew up to 60 MPH, and the temperatures were between 5 and 15 degrees. It was interesting, listening to the weather. Instead of hearing that you could expect to get your lips blown off from the southeast, you heard warnings of icing conditions, and that all boats were urged to use extreme caution. They were out of stove oil in Hoonah, but the tug and fuel barge weren't moving. Colder yet up there, and a lot more wind coming down out of Lynn Canal. We were happy to be where we were. We ran the machines every three hours when it was at its coldest, and with the stoves going steady and lots of clothes on, it wasn't too bad. The guys from Port Protection would come down to check their boats and come over for coffee, so we heard lots of good fish stories.

On the way north we had stopped early one evening, at a spot where I had picked out some good north-south, east-west lineups. I had adjusted Sid's compass

*"Miss Everett" on the grid in Sitka after Ted bought her.*
*Photo courtesy of Gail Stromme.*

186

for his auto pilot, hoping to get him some better steering. It hadn't helped, and I was going bats trying to figure out what could be wrong. Everything I thought I knew, said it was the compass. Looking at his book, I read a paragraph I'd sort of skipped over, that mentioned to be sure the right end of the compass was looking towards the bow. Why wouldn't it be? I went down and looked and sure enough, it wasn't. I asked him how long it had been that way, and he didn't know. "But I did take it out of there when I painted the focsle this winter." So at least, now he would have good steering again. Finally the forecast changed, and was for southeast gale warnings. Southeast meant warmer, which was fine with us. We thought, if we could, we would try to get across Chatham Straits to Port Alexander. If it was blowing too hard when we got down around Cape Decision, we'd just ease up the Kuiu Island shore, and hide out somewhere. We knew some good hideouts.

Lots of possibilities in Port Alexander. It's a small fishing village on the southeast end of Baranoff Island, full of friendly faces, a mini library, and a basketball court. If it was too rough to fish, there was always someone coming aboard to B.S. or we were up at their places. One year they had a pie baking contest, and Sid and I came along just in time for me to be asked to be a judge. They didn't ask Sid, which made it even better. Someone might have offered him a small slice. On the other hand when you've got 25 perfect pies, and you have to say which is best with 25 of the local ladies glaring at you??? I should've fainted after I was full, and let Sid take my place.

Jim and Nita Hendricks would be the King and Queen of Lower Chatham, except that would make Jimmy a prince, so they're just commoners. Jimmy does have some good points. He made mediocre coffee in the mornings, and had a decent view through the trees and rocks out to the straits. We could sit at his table and watch the whitecaps in Chatham, and decide if we wanted to cringe and cower, or go out and brave the elements. Also, he let us use his smokehouse. That's about it. Big Jim was the winter watchman at several of the herring reduction plants in Lower Chatham, and they retired at P.A. Now Nita is Gramma to all the kids in town.

During the summer P. A. has a troll closure—open. Everyone's allowed one club, and when the tide's out enough they tee off from the airplane float, and golf their way down the beach, onto a mini Island which is mostly very uneven rock, back to the beach, and on around the inner lagoon. The kids ferry you across from beach to rock to beach.

The next bay down the straits from Port Alexander, is Port Conclusion. This was where Vancouver stayed at the last of his expedition, prior to starting the trip back to England. It was always neat, going into the different bays in British Columbia and Alaska, knowing they'd been there. They and a few others. A look at charts along the west coast shows that Spanish, Russian, French, and American, as well as the English, had been there quite a while before Captains Ward and Cameron came stumbling along.

But we wouldn't make it up that way this trip. Not much wind at all going down Sumner Straits, and on around Cape Decision. No one at the lighthouse anymore unless they had a maintenance crew out there, and that wasn't likely, right now. When the station was still manned it used to be good for a wave, and when Herb Johnstone used to go around, they'd give him a blast on the horn. With over 50 years of trolling under his belt, I think he deserved it.

After you go through the pass and get into Chatham Straits, you're in kind of a lee of Coronation and Spanish Islands, from any southeast surge, and although there was only a light southeast breeze blowing, there was a lift coming out of the straits that I wondered about. Maybe it was sort of a leftover surge from the northeast of the last few days? I asked Sid what he thought, and he was all for getting across Chatham and on up the Baranoff shore. Lower Chatham wasn't the place to be if there was a lot of northeast wind, which, minus any lows, was what you could expect a lot of, this time of year. Now we hoped to get up above Cape Ommaney, before the southeast forecast became reality.

We had ten miles of nice going, and then you could look out ahead and see quite a breeze coming out of the straits. Sid found his spot behind me and to the left, and in another twenty minutes we were taking quite a ride. Its hard to say whether this northeast had just came back up, or if it never had gone down. It seems to me that it should have been blowing back down the Kuiu Isl. shore, but we had to come out to about the middle of the straits to get into this. The tide was flooding, and we had thought that would have been fine in southeast weather, because they wouldn't be opposing, but now the northeast wind into the tide made it like a large ocean size swell coming out of the straits. And not too far apart.

I always regretted not having a camera aboard, and getting a few pictures of the Miss Everett that day. You could see why it had been around for so long, plus Sid was a bit of a boatman. The next fifteen miles were pretty hard for him, though, even though it was big enough that we could ride around on top. We had the big stuff for another hour and a half and then the tide changed, and the wind picked up more, still from the northeast. We gave up on trying to hit in on the shore, and just put the boats in the trough so we could run freer. When we got over towards Cape Ommaney, the wind had gone from 30 to around 50, but happily, this was one of those times when the wind blew it flatter. Usually, it takes more wind than that.

We wouldn't realize the quick lee that the Baranoff shore would have given, but as we moved further up the beach from Cape Ommaney, the wind kept easing off. We started angling in, with Snipe Bay in mind. In a few miles there was only a light northeast breeze.

It took Sid a couple days to recoup. This was quite a ride for an old boat and a guy who was 67, no longer going on 14. I was pretty disappointed in myself, but I guess if everything were the same today we would probably make the same choices. We'd sure had enough of Port Protection, and lower Chatham didn't seem like the place to be, but we still shouldn't have jumped the gun on Chatham Straits. I doubt that when the wind finally did change direction, there was more than a short period of slack between the northeast and the southeast winds. Probably the low was responsible for the lack of wind on the Kuiu Island side, as well as the raise in temperature.

Tammy was an old German Shorthair and she was his deckhand. He called her Tammy if he was mad at her, and Granny or Granny Grump when they were on speaking terms. She snored in her sleep and moaned and groaned in her dreams, and sometimes Sid didn't come up with too good a nights sleep. When all else failed, she'd get up and get a drink at night, and he said it sounded like he was taking water over the bow. But her water bowl was always full when he went to bed.

He had bought a new pickup truck when Tammy was a pup and had parked at a turnout on this logging road, leaving her in the cab while he was hunting. A few hours later, he was walking back up the road and looking down in this ravine. He could see where someone had lost their rig sometime back, and it had went all the way to the bottom. A little further up the road he could see the color, and picked up his pace a bit. Sure enough. But Tammy had survived. He said "she was a lot happier to see me, than I was her." A year or so later he got married, and before long his bride said, "either that dog goes, or I go." Sid told her, "Well, she was here first."

We were in town and Sid came aboard, and says he had to go to court and bail Tammy out. The ticket said something about doggie vagrancy, and also that

*Tammy*

she didn't have a license. She was in jail up at the vets, so was only in danger of putting on a few pounds. I went with him when they held court, and when Sid's turn came, he asked, "she has a license for home in Oregon. Do I have to get a license for every port we go into?" She said she didn't know but it was a good point. Meanwhile he owed the city of Sitka ten bucks.

A car got up on the curb in Sitka and missed Sid, but hit Tammy. The worlds greatest Vet lives in Sitka and he saved one leg, took off another, and Tammy became one of 5 or 6 tripods hopping around town. She lived to go on the beach, or if we were in Sitka, to go up to the restaurants. She'd sit patiently inside the door if the weather wasn't good; kind of a mournful, long

*Tammy and Deann*

190

eared, hostess. Otherwise she'd be right outside, and when we came back out, that's where she would be. The waitresses would send out a doggy bag fit for a queen, and she wouldn't stop until she was aboard with her bag, waiting for Sid to hurry up and open the door for her. Then she could eat.

Before we went out in the morning there was always time for coffee and cookies, and lots of stories. Because the days were so short, this time was expanded when we were winter fishing. I always sat on the steps going down into the focsle, and Tammy's bed was at the back of the wheelhouse. She'd sleep through one or two cookies, and then she'd be hanging over one shoulder or the other, looking for her share. I used to put some cookie in my shirt pocket, and she'd put her good leg over the other shoulder and try to get her nose in the pocket. When people ask me if I miss fishing, these mornings are some of the things I think about.

Most of the troll fleet was broken up in groups of boats that worked together. The first consideration would be the safety aspect, and it was always good, knowing that even if you weren't fishing the same area, there was someone who would be concerned when you didn't call in on schedule. Generally there would be two to five boats, but off Washington and Oregon, a few of the larger groups numbered ten boats or more. In Alaska, generally two or three boats would be plenty, mostly because of the pothole nature of much of the fishing.

Working with a few boats allowed coverage of more area, and information within a group was passed along over the airwaves. It was an interesting thing to watch over the years. Bill Wilcox summed up many years of a successful fishing partnership, and it couldn't have been any simpler. "If you want it to work, each party has to put out 110%. This was apparently hard to do, because you'd see some guys change groups every year. Some would work together from now on. Others tried to have a code with everyone in the fleet who had ever brought in a decent trip.

Some of the guys had every radio and scanner their wheelhouse space would allow. Others spent their time in the trolling pit working gear, comparing notes on schedule, or talking back and forth on the little radio when they were close enough. I was one of these, and for me and the people I fished with, it worked well and made for a more enjoyable fishing operation. Of course we missed out on a lot of "radio" fish, but frequently we'd compare notes with friends from other groups, while in town, and we'd know about major hot areas before too long. There was a lot of inter-group info changes, and we made sure it went both ways when a good area of fish warranted it.

Pothole fishing, human nature, too many king sized egos, openings instead of shorter seasons, and a fishery, ever more, becoming a rat race. I guess I saw pretty much every range of behavior on the grounds, over the years. I count my blessings to have fished with Steve, and then with him and Lloyd in the group we were in off the Washington coast. Later on, Sid, Lloyd, and I fished together in Alaska.

Sid and I both enjoyed the winter fishing. It was closed inside a line up of the ocean capes, so you could fish anywhere on the inside waters, and in any of the bays on the ocean coast. The days were shorter and not many boats out anywhere, so it made for pretty enjoyable fishing. You had to put up with some weather, but we knew the country enough to do pretty well in that category. Most of the time. The moves we made were pretty well thought out in those early mornings before fishing. You needed to make maximum use of the daylight hours for fishing, and the tides for moving around, and also for fishing.

Some of the winter fishing was pretty deep, and some of it you went along, almost with one hand on the beach, and this was what I enjoyed the most. Sometimes you could be a hundred feet or less from shore, fishing twenty fathoms of gear. I used to fish one spot where I turned out for a cedar that was leaning over the water, this fishing 15 fathoms (90 feet) deep. It was almost like being ashore, because you were right there.

I was always amazed at the volume of deer on some of the beaches, during a really severe winter. In some areas there would be an awful lot of snow, and later in the winter, in their weaker condition, many of the deer would never leave the beaches. They were probably warmer, and many of them wouldn't have had the strength, anyway. One year in February, we fished one spot during most of two trips, and every day you would see 50 or so deer on this one stretch. Most of them were almost gone. Some couldn't get up, others were already dead, and you would see others tearing apart the same kelp islands, day after day, looking for something to eat. The vegetation along the beach was eaten down to nothing. They'd eaten from limbs as high as they could reach, bark off the trees, and the coarse beach grass down as far as they could go. The snow was so deep at the tree line, that I don't think they could have moved far in it, considering the condition they were in.

Wolves would have done well for awhile but there were none on this Island, and on a winter like this, the bear were still well dug in. I've been told that with most of the heat loss being from the head, nature has given the bear a smaller brain to keep warm, and this stretches out the energy department during hibernation.

Anyway, when you see what we saw year after year, you might look at hunting through different eyes. Many of the families look at the deer and other game as their winters meat, and a quick bullet in the fall would have been a blessing, compared to what they were going through now.

And you saw other stuff. There would be bear out in the early spring months, and some of the guys who trapped said they'd see them off and on all winter, if the winter was especially mild. I guess I saw a Lynx one time when I was fishing along a mainland beach. It seemed like it had longer back legs and wasn't as big as a cougar.

I only saw two moose in all the years I fished Alaska. There weren't that many where I fished. One was over by Beacon Point, on the Kupreanof shore. Apparently she had tried to swim across from the mainland to Sukoi Island to have her calf, and the tide carried her on past the Island. I was fishing, and watched a big halibut boat coming from Petersburg, pass me, and then turn around and go back. They stopped up ahead and I could see something in the water in front of them, and I thought they'd lost a man overboard. Then I saw the flash from a camera. After running inside and grabbing the binocs, I could see what it was. They herded her into the beach with the boat, and I got a good look at her when I fished on up to where she was at. This was about a five mile swim, and she was a tired lady.

The other one I saw was in Lituya Bay, and it was standing out off the beach with its head under the water. Every once in a while he'd raise up and look around for a bit, and then back under. I didn't know they would eat out of the salt water, but I'm not sure how salty the water right along there is, with the glaciers further up in the bay.

Chuck Barker saw another cross-sound swimmer, this one almost all the way out to Turnabout Island. Quite a story there, and I hope he's somewhere in that perfect harbor, telling it right now. This last one, the one up towards Petersburg, and one that finally made it all the way over towards the middle of Kuiu Island were the only moose I heard of that went across to the Kupreanoff side. You know there were lots more. They have hollow hair, so they'll float from now on, and they're so strong they can swim forever. I think they're a bit long on determination, too.

Years ago I was fishing near this same area Chuck was in; in very heavy fog and no wind. Another of those days where you can't separate the sky and water. After the fog set down, there wasn't much to do but stay at the wheel and look for that boat that isn't there, till it is. I was wishing I'd pulled the gear aboard and went in and anchored, but I hadn't. You couldn't really leave the wheel now, but if the fog lifts even a bit, I'll pull the gear and go anchor against the beach somewhere and wait till it clears up. All of a sudden there's something there, and I stare hard for a second and about die. There's a plane coming right at me, and it'll hit me in a couple seconds. It doesn't, because it's not in the air. It's one of Ellis Airlines gooses, and as we pass, the pilot opens the window and leans out and waves. I can see people inside waving too, so I step out on deck, and hold my hands apart in the classic (how many ya got?) sign. He did the smart thing, and set down on the water, where the hillsides weren't going by as fast. I never see a "goose" again without thinking of this.

Another thing Sid and I both enjoyed about fishing early, was fishing in the snow. In a good snowfall, the sound from the boat would be absorbed, and all you heard was a low thrum from the exhaust. Absolutely peaceful. Fishing in the sea foam was the same way. There was one place especially, where this would occasionally be about 10 or 12 inches thick, and would cover acres. I loved to put the boat through it and eliminate the boat noise. I never did get many fish, while fishing under one of the really thick sea foam blankets. You'd think they'd have stayed under it.

But it wasn't all a sight seeing cruise. Being out there in the winter was a constant challenge, and you didn't take too much for granted. I only remember a time or two when I drug anchor with the Camelot, and this was with another boat tied alongside, or once when I'd anchored in the ocean. It was a different story with the Elusive, it being so much heavier. There aren't that many good anchorages, or what you'd call a winter harbor. Bill Small had told me early on, that there wasn't a good all weather harbor on the Kuiu Isl. side in lower Chatham. He was right. There were a few for one wind direction or the other, but when the wind turned around, or the temperature nose dived, you might be pretty unhappy.

Moving around at night had its own set of problems, made worse by bigger than usual tides, or occasionally, around times of heavy rainfall. There's been plenty of logging over the years, in Canada as well as Alaska, and an awful lot of the product has wound up on the shorelines of both countries. If there's going to be a good southeaster, it'll likely be over the big tides, and the combination of the two put plenty of what had been on the beach, back in the water.

Southeast Alaska is basically a bunch of rock, sticking out of the water here and there. What you'd think of as topsoil might be skinnier than you think.

With enough rain, a patch of trees, along with whatever top soil they grew in, might slide down the hillside a hundred yards. Or many times that. What's left is a stretch of bare rock, usually no more than a few hundred feet across. The trees, topsoil, and rock, slide downhill till the slide either stops against some hill or ravine, or keeps on going into the water. Then the process of rebuilding starts again, and the soil that's left between the rocks soon turns green with something, maybe moss, or fern, or if it's a tree it'll likely be alder. Before too long, the whole hillside is covered in alder, and eventually you'll notice the odd spruce, hemlock, or cedar, sticking out above it all. If you live that long. This doesn't happen overnight, but the slides you notice when you're young, recoup quite aways in thirty or forty years.

So if there was a lot of drift around, I either wouldn't run at night or I'd get the boat nicely offshore before it got dark, and then move up or down the beach, half speed if we'd been seeing much drift. If the bay you were in wasn't fishy, or if the harbor wasn't up to the current weather, you were pretty much inclined to move to the next bay, and this made for a few pretty wet rides. Chris was with me, fishing down towards Ommaney, and Sid was still up at Snipe. It blew all night and after quite a bit of anchor drill, I had decided to get around to Port Alexander in the morning, and see what Mr. Hendricks was up to. Pretty sloppy at the corner.

We had a super dinner at Nita's house, and mentioned this when we checked in with Sid that evening. Then we told him she had suggested fresh cinnamon rolls the next morning. Jimmy was with us on the boat when we called him the next day, and mentioned she was baking bread that afternoon. "I'll bet he's here this evening." He was. The weather had gone down a bit, and when Nita was baking, Snipe was the wrong address.

We tried to be ready for the harder blows, and be in town, or maybe Port Alexander before they set in. When our position made this out of the question, we had a few really good anchorages around the country, and would move towards them if it looked like there would be a screamer. There aren't a lot of really good storm anchorages around, and between the two of us we'd pretty much used them all.

Sid spent one Thanksgiving back in the mud hole in Malmesbury, and for awhile at high tide he actually had to throw out the stabilizers. No day to have been going across Chatham. That same storm did a major amount of damage further up the straits at Tenakee. I heard there were 150 MPH winds out of the southwest, which is pegged on most wind gauges.

195

Sometimes you could go into some harbor with the best of intentions, and find sheet ice clear across the harbor in the morning. This doesn't do a wooden boat any favors, so if Sid was with me we'd warm up the machines for half an hour, and after breaking the ice all around the boats, I'd go out of the harbor in the fast mode and he'd be close and directly behind me. Once I'd created a good bow wave it was fine.

I was alone on the boat, running north one year, and tied up the second night out in a little spot just above Stuart Island, at the Yucultaws. There was a cruiser tied there, and this old fellow came out to grab a line. We wound up visiting for quite awhile that evening. He and his wife had been living on their boat, somewhere up in Lake Union in Seattle, and when they raised their moorage rates, again, they could see that they would have to move. One of the fishermen had told them that they might do all right in Alaska, and told them of a spot or two where they might tie up without being bled so bad. They took off with the hopes of stretching their dollars, by trying to put a lot of fish on the table and cutting other expenses.

He was completely unfamiliar with sheet ice, and when they left some harbor just above Vancouver they soon discovered they were taking water. The Canadian Coast Guard got a pump to them, and they made it back to some yard in the area. They wound up with a substantial bill for a bunch of planks that had to be replaced. It was one of these old boats where the planks angled up more sharply at the bow stem, rather than gradually tapering on the bow end of each plank. Built this way, they wound up cutting through more individual planks than you might have thought. All they had to do was move slow speed and the thin ice would cut almost like a saw, and once down into the corking the water started coming in. With this in mind, quite a few of the Alaska boats have iron bark over the planking, all around the waterline.

These were old people, with an old boat, and their going up at that time of the year had me worried. I offered to spend whatever time it would take to see them across Queen Charlotte Sound. They said they didn't intend leaving this spot where we were for several more days, and would only move in the best of weather, and then, only when the tide was with them. I spent some hours that evening, and before the tide changed in the morning, going over their charts, showing them some good anchorages, and anything I could think of to make the trip better. I was glad to see they had a good chart collection they'd bought from someone who had quit fishing. I always wondered how they'd made out.

Lawrence made the trip north with me in 1961, and his company made for one of the most enjoyable trips in that direction. He was made for Alaska, or vice versa, but got there 50 years too late. He, Sid, and Burt, another guy we met later on, were all peas of a pod. They all became 14 again, when the boat left and they were on it.

Burt and Tim, a buddy of his from California, had flown into Sitka one fall to make the trip south on the Elusive. Tim would ride down as far as Ketchikan and fly home, and Burt and I would run the Elusive home. The ride down to Ketchikan was near perfect, with only a few hours of strong winds in the Sergius Narrows to Rodman Bay stretch. Tim said he really enjoyed it as it was completely different from anything he got to see around La Jolla, California. I told them it would get better in a few hours and where that would be. When it did, they were impressed. It's great to have a little local knowledge, so you can be a hero,—not that I'd milk something like that. So they had salmon and clam feeds and pictures of a bear and an iceberg, and Tim flew home with a wetlock full of salmon. A great start on the trip.

Beautiful fall days, timed well on the tides, and Burt thought he was in heaven. He had been a commercial airline pilot, plus some other stuff, and now he would calculate our time to the next point, or light, which there is one after another on the way down the inside passage. Always something going on.

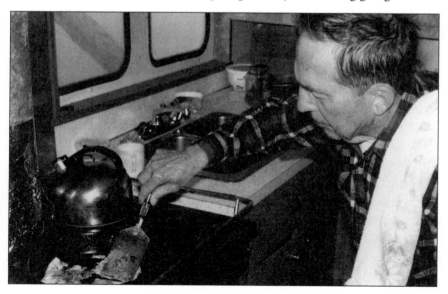

*Burt Orchard*

Towards the end of the second day below Ketchikan, we got a call from another troller on his way home from Alaska. His machine was surging now and then, and he wasn't sure exactly what was wrong. He thought maybe the governor, but it had only happened a few times, so was hard to pinpoint. We cut the day short and anchored in Horsefly Cove, and a little after dark they tied alongside. Two lazy days later we crossed Queen Charlotte Sound and anchored in front of Alert Bay, in the evening.

When I'm pulling the anchor the next morning I hear a little grumbling in the anchor gear, after the nylon is on the winch and I get into the chain. The hydraulics are straining a bit, not bad, but you can tell something's going on. More commotion at the bow roller, and in the anchor chain, reinforces this opinion. I stop the winch and look over the bow, but can't see anything yet. Up a bit more and there it is—an old car body, which we stare at for a few minutes. This is the first one of these I've ever got. Up a bit further—stop, and we study it some more.

My first plan is to idle in to the dock and get someone to torch me free, but as I look at it I can see several hang-ups that could come free if the chain got some quick slack. The first thought, was just drop it to the bottom and see what happened, but then I got to thinking, why lose what I thought would be at least a partial sure thing if I could just give it a good yank? After tying the chain off, I eased about a fathom of it from the spool, and then reset the dog on the winch. When I cut the line holding the chain it sounded like the bow was coming off the boat, and Burt and I are standing there, big eyed. I pull the anchor aboard and away we go. Those hang ups I'd seen didn't look like they'd carry the whole thing, but whatever was going on down the gear, it came free.

The other boat isn't too far ahead, and I assume he had slowed down till we got underway. As I go by him, he looks out the window at us, kind of surprised, and then down at the water. He calls in a few seconds and tells us his clutch is apparently slipping, because according to his tachometer, he was up to cruising speed when we went by. What he had thought was some kind of problem with his machine, was in his clutch or reduction gear. We turn around and talk it over, bow to bow. Alert Bay is close by, but it's in-season for the Canadian net fleet, and it's possible they might not get to him soon. They want to get on south, so we put a line on him and away we go again, this time a little slower. I make a yoke from our stern cleats, and a line from it goes to his anchor gear, minus the anchor, so we have a dandy surge line once he's let out fifteen fathoms of chain. In anything short of good weather we'd have tied off on his anchor, but as nice as it was, we pulled from the chain the rest of the way south.

It was an enjoyable trip. I turned the machine a few hundred more turns, and we went along nicely at six knots, or almost. Perfect weather, the best scenery in the world, and a little change of pace during the last part of the trip. We dropped off our hitch hikers in good shape, and anchored in a little anchorage outside Deception Pass. Trish always sent me north with cases of home canned meats and fruits, and always several cases of spaghetti sauce, the last of which went to make a perfect dinner to celebrate an equally perfect trip home to Washington. He loved it, and during the off season, whether it was down to haul out in Port Townsend, or just running around out in front of Port Angeles to test something out, he was usually along. Burt would make his final trip on the boat.

Another memorable trip south was running with Bud and Jo Taggart on the "Apollo." Bud told me before we left that his machine was a little ill and he'd have to baby it home. We stretched out the hours, fine tuned on the tides, and had beautiful weather all the way down. In all the years of running the boat at night, I never saw a northern lights show like the one put on for us going down Clarence Straits. Hours of it, with the best colors and more motion than I would ever have thought possible. In a lifetime of fishing you go through some grim times, but things like that night even things up a bit.

Sid lived down by Coos Bay and would usually get the urge to head north along in January. He'd run up the beach, come in at the straits and sometimes stop in Port Angeles, sometimes not. Sometimes the first you'd hear was when he got to Ketchikan or Sitka. The two trips we'd ran up together were two of the worst, weather wise and otherwise. There was this one I just mentioned, and the other one was pretty nice traveling, aside from heavy snow most of the way, after the second day out. We had anchored at Lewis Island the evening before we would go across, or around, Chatham Sound. When I was putting the machine to bed, I noticed a bit of a lube oil leak in the line that went between the block and the oil filter. A little moving it while I was looking it over, just made it worse. No spare, and one inch fittings, which I had none of, so it was band aid time. I always carried some strips of inner tube, so while Sid steadied it, I wrapped it with a bunch of passes with this tube, pulled really tight. We tried it and I could maintain 800 turns with no problem. Gale warnings from the southeast was the forecast, so we decided to leave early in the morning and try to get into Prince Rupert before the wind came up. Sid would put a line on my anchor, and after he was out aways I would kick out the anchor and some chain, and we'd have a nice trip into Rupert.

Which we did, with me idling along behind him. I called ahead and their Coast Guard said to tie up wherever we could, and when we were settled, call them, and they'd send the customs our way. We tied up at an out of the way corner of the cold storage, and Sid handed Granny across. Pretty quick we were getting caught up in the coffee, sandwiches, cookie department. From where I was sitting I could see someone getting from a skiff onto the Miss Everett's stern, so we all went out on deck.

"Who owns this boat?"

Sid said he did.

"You aren't allowed to leave your boat without going through customs. Why are you on that boat?"

He told her that we hadn't eaten this morning, and were just having a sandwich. When I went to lift Granny across, "Is that your dog? She's not allowed to leave the boat either. Have you got a table I can write on? There's already two violations. I'm sure there will be many more."

There was. The only one that amounted to more than the first two, was the fact that he had his handgun in a locker, but the locker wasn't sealed. She documented a few other sins committed by this Yank and his deckhand, and then came aboard the Elusive. I hadn't found a good spot to hide. Before long she left, armed with both of our handguns. Mine wasn't in a sealed locker either. The reason each of them were aboard, was for stopping the occasional big halibut. A pop from my 32, while still in the water, would prevent unimaginable commotion once you got a halibut in the 80 lb. plus range on deck. Some of them are three or more times that, and among other reasons, safety was a big consideration. I had seen a ruptured 2 by 12 checkerboard, and a handle on a Kolstrand gurdie, pounded flat by untamed halibut. Joe Cash might still be alive if a large halibut he had caught, had behaved. It wound up breaking his leg, and a bone severed an artery. Most any halibut boat will have a stopper aboard and I know Joe did. Maybe his shot wasn't quite on.—Who knows?

She said that it would be possible to have the guns shipped into Alaska, and I forget the cost, but somewhere in the fifty to seventy dollar range. Sid and I had each agreed to this. Before she left she said, "If either of you are ever caught in Canadian waters again without having entered Canadian Customs, all of this," as she waved the handfull of our sins at us, "shall be brought to bear, and there will be very dire consequences." I hate to put something like that in the book, but that's what she said. Sid and I started quite a few radio conversations with

200

it, over the next few years.

We waited till she was out of sight and went up the ladder to the nearest phone, and called the Customs office there in Prince Rupert, asking for the head of the office. We were pretty sure she was wrong in her parting statement unless there had been some drastic changes, and if there were, we wanted to know about them. Prior to this, you didn't have to enter customs, as long as you didn't tie to their docks, go ashore, or tie to a Canadian boat. You could anchor in their harbors, or just run on through, and you wouldn't be bothered. We thought any change would have had some publicity, and it wouldn't be likely that we hadn't heard.

We told the man of the handgun thing and what she'd said before she left the boat, and his reply was " Oh—, you got——." He said that nothing had changed regarding passage through Canada, and asked if we had a locker or stack of drawers with handles, that he could seal together to put the guns in. Then he would call over to Ketchikan, and one of the customs officers there would come down and unseal them when we got in. I did, and he said he would bring the hand guns down after lunch and take care of this. After lunch here comes —— with our artillery and she was maaad! Who knows what happened to the man we talked to.

I had cleared some room in a gear drawer, which could be sealed closed and both of our cannons could be put there. You build boat drawers notched at the bottom, so they can't slide out during sloppy weather. Seizing the drawer handle to something solid below it prevents you from opening the drawer. She asked when we would be leaving, and we told her probably in the morning, depending on the weather. I still needed to get uptown and get some new hoses made, and there wouldn't be a lot of traveling time when I got things back together. With gale force wind conditions still existing, it would be nice to approach Chatham Sound with some visibility.

"I'm not going to leave these guns aboard if you're going to stay over night. God only knows what might happen."

I was ready to lose it. Sid too. He told her "Look, what would it take for us to just give you these guns?"

"Sign right here." Which we did. What a wonderful place to leave. I was lucky Sid was there for a buffer. When I was short circuiting, he was still thinking. On the halibut guns, I replaced the old faithful with a 22. In comparison, the 32 caliber is way better for halibut, because of the extra shock value.

When we got to Sitka one of the guys listened to the story, and said he'd write to a friend of his who worked at the Nanaimo Customs Office, including a note from us, telling what we'd run into. The reply back reaffirmed what everyone thought to be the situation regarding travel through B.C., and said he would send the letter on to the head office in Vancouver, asking them to send us a more official letter from that office. These are the three pertinent paragraphs from that letter.

"This will confirm the advice you received by telephone from our Prince Rupert office. It is not necessary to report to Canada customs when entering Canadian waters if you are in transit only and do not dock or contact any Canadian vessel. You may anchor, but only for purposes of rest and / or making emergency repairs to your vessel."

"In the event you decide to dock at a Canadian port or are forced to do so because of crew illness, vessel damage, or severe weather conditions, you must report immediately to Canada Customs. If you are forced to dock or tie up at a location which has no Canada Customs Office you must report to the nearest detachment of the Royal Canadian Mounted Police."

"It is helpful when traveling in Canadian Waters to have a locker on your vessel which is suitable for sealing. In the event you are carrying restricted items such as handguns, excess liquor or tobacco, these goods should be placed under seal by Canada Customs."

Another Customs person expanded on this later, in response to our "what if" question.—"If there are no police in the area, report to any Canadian authority. You could even call one of the lighthouses and leave word."

The Seafood Producers Cooperative Office in Sitka copied off a bunch of these letters, and most of the boats carried a copy with their papers in case they ran into ———. That's been a few years back and in light of what's taken place in recent years, what's specified in that letter may not be the situation now.

A few years later I was flying south, and was visiting with one of the people from a fish company in Alaska. The subject got around to tuna fishing and an occasion that had taken place at Winter Harbor, years earlier. On the ocean side of Vancouver Island, towards the north end, Winter Harbor was a handy spot for the tuna fleet to hide in poor weather. Most of the fleet was in, and some of the American fishermen got drunk and made a spectacle of themselves, including some shots being fired. Canadian authorities were called in, the outcome being closure of Canadian Ports to the American tuna fleet. Maybe ——— was from Winter Harbor? Who knows?

The ban was lifted a year or two before I quit fishing. Port Hardy, Vancouver, and I think Coal Harbour, and Prince Rupert?, were designated ports for Americans to sell tuna in, and Seattle, Astoria, and San Francisco were opened to the Canadians. I never saw an official notice on which ports were involved, and there may have been more. Eddie Grotting and I used Port Hardy several times, coming and going while fishing tuna, and sold one trip there. Couldn't have been treated better.

Anyway, it was great fishing with Sid. He started fishing a few years after I did, and with different backgrounds and different ways of doing things, it made for having a good partner boat. He would rather fish cohos than kings and the Miss Everett was a coho catching machine. The Elusive wasn't too fussy, as long as they were "nice sized fish." Sid was always a big deal with the kids, and—he had Granny Grump.

For both of us, fishing in the summers got to be pretty hard to take. As the seasons (openings) got shorter it was less feasible to fish our little out of the way spots, and eventually the summer part of the seasons found us somewhere on Fairweather Grounds, or up at Yakutat. Which was probably where we should have been all along. Lloyd Gowdy had started fishing Alaska, so he made the third partner. I had fished with him and his brother for years, whenever I was fishing Washington, and we enjoyed his company these last years we fished Alaska.

Eventually the effort and what you had to give up in time, increased costs, and other considerations, didn't justify my trolling in Alaska, at least not if we weren't living there. We decided to buy Oregon and California permits and try fishing to the south.

# Chapter 17
# Some Poems

THE EARLY DAWN
Every day is a new day and we have to hold it close to our hearts
It is just for a brief moment, then it will close to darkness
only to refresh itself in the dawn

Life itself is like day, it holds darkness and a dawn
and refreshes itself with a kind word, a look of approval
knowing that you are loved, and that you love.

*Trish*

THE GATEKEEPER
On a windswept reef in the land of the midnight sun
There stands a staunch old dwarf, with memories of
The bitter harshness of winter storms, where wind and wave
Made sweet the spring morning, where the crisp freshness
Of dawn brought the wind whispering through his bows
And out to sea again, only to return at dusk

With the pride and dignity of a thousand warships
Is the tree that in it's time has seen what few ever have
Or ever will, for it has looked upon the great whales
Searching the blue depths for food and sometimes even having
To beach themselves lest their tongues become food for the Orcas

The tree has heard the lonely cry of the wolf as the moon
Slowly rolls across the sky, and it has heard the futile
Beller of a hamstrung moose. The tree has seen the Northern
Lights streak across the night and then disappear again

Like so many men the tree has seen come and go
Their presence brings no joy nor does their passing
Bring any grief, for it is all the same for
The gatekeeper of Malmesbury Bay

*Keith—8th grade school assignment*

## THE TREE ON THE BEACH
The sea's gone down and the swell rolls on, the winds come around
    to southwest
My throat's in a knot and my eyes are damp, there's a lump like a fist
    in my chest
Who knows what happened sometime in the night, Andy's horn
    yanking me from my rest
"Mark heard a mayday, just the one word, and he thought that it came
    from "MY NEST"

He'd started for town at the end of that day,
and would run through the night, well offshore,
Southeast wind at his back, through the pass at first light,
he'd be in fore it came up much more
Better men you'd not find, and the same for the boat,
and it goes through my mind, what went wrong?
It just shouldn't be, but then, this is the sea,
and it takes both the weak and the strong

The coasties ran right to his E.P.I.R.B. at first,
then they said that they'd found a float bag,
They'll search up and in, case he got in his skiff,
but our hopes have now started to sag,
We'll stay in this grid, two more hours at least,
cause the skiff could take off like a kite,
And now Pete's up above, coming hard down our way,
which he's done since he heard at first light,

206

The swell, close and high, seemed to mock me at first,
as it rolled to the beach from the west,
And we search all day long, and the next, and the next,
and it seems like the end of "MY NEST"

Andy and Mark, Pete and I in a sweep, and I know now they're here
    just for me,
The chopper just called, say they'll give up at dusk,
and they're sorry as sorry can be,

They've searched long and hard, as have I and my friends,
and a better group you'd never find,
And if "Mornin cap"

What the hell?—Jesus Christ, he's all right
Or is there something wrong with my mind?
"Yeah there is, always was, but then I've been there too,
now I'm here in the woods east of you,
And I'm there in your mind, so when you get on in,
there's a walk on the beach, overdue,
On the way down, I figured it out, cause I sure didn't like where I'd headed,
Poor location, location, location for sure, the location that I've always dreaded,
So I'm not going down, and I'm not going up,
cause a cloud up in heaven won't be,
I'll do better yet, and you'll like this my friend, cause the next time we meet,
I'm a tree! I'm the tree on the beach, and if which one you ask,
Any tree that you want me to be,
So I'm glad that I'm here, and I'm glad you've been there,
and I'll wave as I see you go by,
And when you come ashore, then I'll see you once more,
and we'll each be a tree in the sky,
Mark, and Andy, and Pete head for town, and I'm heading on in to
    the bay,
And the swell coming down, tries to comfort me now,
It's okay,—it's okay,—it's okay.
        *VFC*

## TIME AGAIN

Comes again that joyful ( ? ) season
When you rise before the dawn,
To tune up the engine
While the coffee pot is on.

Hair trigger is your temper
And your eyes still full of gravel
As you eat a hurried breakfast,
And for the "grounds" you travel.

Scarcely has the dawn broke through
But your busy dropping gear
As you think "I'll quit this damn business"
But you're back there every year.

Your nerves get frayed and frazzled,
Long and tiring is the day;
Sometimes the catch a poor one
And expenses it won't pay.

But always a lure to the fishing game,
With it's "Maybe today I'll hit em";
So its rise again after four hours sleep
And on your way to "git em."

*Nada E. Small*

# Chapter 18
# Wild Stocks

"We've got to protect the wild stocks!" If things aren't flowing your way during a fisheries hearing or meeting, those few words can change the flow of thought. But to save wild stocks of salmon—in numbers that would be worthwhile—considering todays circumstances—I really wonder if we're going to do that. Right now we have too much trouble figuring out what a wild salmon really is.

A few years ago a friend called and said, "quick, channel 5," or maybe it was 7 or 4—it doesn't matter. It was a salmon related bit about the Dungeness, and the taking of a few "wild" king salmon. He knew anything about the Dungeness River would interest me. These fish, or rather, their eggs, would be ran through the Dungeness hatchery, with the intentions of preserving these last few wild king salmon in the river. So what would the results of this effort be called? Wild or hatchery fish? How many cycles through some hatchery would a strain of fish have to go through, before they were looked down on as "hatchery" fish? Where did the first hatchery fish come from? What would you call the offspring of second or third or sixth generation hatchery fish that happened to spawn in some river? Hatchery fish, or sort of wild salmon?

The term "wild salmon" doesn't always create the same image in the minds of those who hear it. Those who have participated in the various net fisheries, remember when they made a good living fishing runs of sockeye, pink and chum salmon in Washington State and Alaska. For years, virtually all the production of these three species was from wild stocks. That's no longer the case, with hatcheries in Alaska putting out some pretty huge numbers of these species, as well as kings and silvers.

The salmon trollers and most salt water sportsmen, will generally identify with the kings and silvers, with the addition of sockeye in British Columbia. Not all that many trollers targeted humpies, and trolling for chum was something I'd never heard of until later years, when large numbers of hatchery chum started returning to the Sitka area. The freshwater sportsmen in both countries target whatever's going on at the time, wild or not, and some Washington State Fisheries personnel might consider a half sized delayed release, hatchery raised coho, bearing an adipose fin, "a wild one."

"Really worthwhile numbers" will depend on who's doing the defining. King salmon are only one species of the salmon resource. Management has the lovely job of trying to meet escapement needs of all five species, while balancing an ever growing demand by consumers, commercial fishermen, and an ever growing sport fishery, some of which is restricted to catch and release of wild kings.

Some suggest that catch and release in the rivers is like throwing a dead short on a battery that is no longer being charged. Others say it doesn't harm them. Others say it's better than everybody taking a fish home. If they can get that figured out, there's the Indian treaties. The various catches have to be managed so that tribes located way up some river system get their share of the Indians 50%, or so, of the harvestable salmon. By the time massive numbers of salmon arrive upstream to some reservation, or not at all, it's too late to do any adjusting for that year.

Back when conditions were as good as they ever got, salmon runs maintained themselves quite nicely. With no fisheries other than for sustenance by the various Indian tribes, without development of any kind—intact forests, no dams, mines, farms, cities, industry or cement, you could say the Indians were realizing worthwhile production. Salmon runs more than maintained themselves year after year, beyond those fish taken, and with no help from something like a fish hatchery. Things aren't so simple now.

When I suggest that "really worthwhile numbers" of wild king salmon will be nearly impossible to rebuild, a lot of things enter the picture, some of which don't necessarily apply to the other species, where regeneration would be a lot simpler. If worthwhile production means extreme measures of restriction to any particular user group, chances are that group of people will question how worthwhile these numbers really are. That's about where we are today. People like to eat king salmon, make a living catching them, and go out on the water or their favorite river and catch them on a sport pole. A beautiful fish, the kings are exciting to catch and delicious to eat. They are so popular that even with every northwest river turned back to pristine conditions, I doubt they could supply todays demand for king salmon, through wild production. Salmon hatcheries have helped fill the gap, but now there's people who wonder how worthwhile "they" really are.

Coho, chum, and pinks can do well in short, smaller streams, and generally aren't inclined to move as far upstream as some kings in the larger rivers. The productivity of our smaller salmon producing streams has gone downhill, especially in the last 50 years. In some cases, the path back to production wouldn't take much. In others—it's not likely to happen. Because of the dams in the Columbia and Snake River systems, a much greater percentage of the king salmons habitat has been lost, than in the streams and rivers the other species would favor.

Grand Coulee Dam was one of the first hydroelectric dams across the Columbia River. It was too tall for fish ladders, so well over a thousand miles of the best spawning grounds, for some of the finest strains of king salmon in the world, were lost to salmon production. The Hell's Canyon dam on the Snake River was about equally disastrous to runs of salmon and steelhead. All the other dams on the Columbia - Snake river system, each took it's toll on what was left. (See chapter 15.)

Dams have also blocked the upper portions of the Skagit and Elwha Rivers to salmon migration. Two on the Elwha and three across the Skagit, with two more on its Baker River tributary. There's talk about removing the lower dam (or both dams??) on the Elwha, and it would be interesting to see how that would work out. It's hard to imagine all the accumulated silt not having quite an effect on the lower river, and you have to wonder if this silt wouldn't affect the lower rivers production for some time. On the other hand, it would open up a nice stretch of productive river to salmon again. Long term, king salmon wise, the upper river would be much more productive than the relatively short stretch below the lower dam.

Otherwise, some of the rivers on the coast north of Willapa Bay haven't been compromised by the effects of civilization to the extent that rivers on the inside waters of the state have. Most of them still have some amount of wild kings, so they wouldn't be starting at ground zero, but almost all of them above the Willapa, including the rivers inside the straits and Puget Sound, are subject to Indian gillnetting. You can't line up a lot of plusses.

Our inside waters have their own set of problems. There's been a fortune spent by pulp mills and other industry in the Puget Sound - Straits of Juan De Fuca area, some to clean up the past, but far more has gone towards cleaner air and water in the future. Some operations closed rather than commit more expense in the face of dwindling timber supply and ever increasing restrictions. I've still got doubts about deep water diffusion. It may have been the easiest answer in many cases, but I'm afraid the bill we'll pay would gag us if we could ever know it's true cost.

Many of the state's streams, both large and small, have been virtually strangled by urbanization and everything that comes with it. Properties that never should have been allowed for home sites are developed, either by multi - home site developers, or individuals building that dream home close to the river. What they wouldn't allow for years, suddenly, somehow, gets done and you don't hear about it till the river gets high and someone's cherished property is getting washed away. Lots of blame and public bucks spent and, chances are, it will have to be dealt with again and again in the future.

Farms are still supersaturating fields with fertilizer next to our rivers. Put ten to forty times too many cows on a piece of ground too small to absorb this much manure, and that's what happens. Where there might have been buffer zones, field goes right up to the dike, and in too many cases, the dike was built on the river-bed. There's a fit all pesticide, chemical, or fertilizer for every crop, lawn or flower bed, and the run off goes into our streams and rivers. This benefits the user, but in too many cases, isn't doing our fish and other sea-life any favors. Major cities are dumping their sewage into our waterways, with lots being said about it, but no change. Too often we don't hear about "the new thing on the block" till it's there, and then we look the other way till it's grandfathered in.

Everyone wants runs of wild salmon, but the conditions that are eliminating them keep expanding. These wild salmon will need to live in the rivers, and then in the inside waters and the ocean, before returning back to the rivers to spawn. We're not making it too easy for them. People whose employment deals with these things aren't anxious to compromise jobs or stifle careers, by saying what they really think. They are very careful as to what they say, and who they say it to. Politicians look at votes through the same eyes. "How can I look good to the biggest blocks of voters?" "Who contributed the most to my election fund?"

All of this makes me wonder about something else. What if we didn't have to protect what's left of our wild stocks anymore? Suppose, for whatever reason, that they lumped wild stocks, semi wild stocks, and hatchery fish into one group. What worries me, is that we would have lowered the bar enough, that the habitat safeguards the "wild salmon" movement have helped establish, would dissolve like a cup of sugar thrown in the river.

What I've hoped for is a more fine tuned approach in the harvest of some of the northwest's natural resources, with less waste and an eventual goal towards much improved production. I think this would be impossible under some of todays methods of management. Considering what's been done to salmon habitat in the Columbia - Snake River basins, it's hard to justify putting any of those salmon stocks on the endangered species lists. What else could they have expected? Applying major management policies around something like this isn't a very realistic foundation for dealing with the Columbia-Snake River basins salmon runs.

Years back, the timber industry finally decided that their image was drooping, and according to advertising and documentaries on TV, have been cleaning up their act. I've seen some of what was done in Alaska and the west end of the Olympic Peninsula in Washington, and you have to wonder how a lot of it was allowed. A lot of it wasn't, but happened anyway. There's been a major effort in re-forestation, and you can only hope that logging practices will be a bit more refined the next times around. I can understand the economics of clear cutting, in areas where immediate runoff into some river system isn't an issue, but when there's a river or small stream involved, a little restraint would have been nice.

I can't see a thing wrong with careful selective logging along the rivers, especially if the band of trees alongside the river were widened a bit. (If there even were such a band.) Why not take out trees that have reached that point of maturity where growth virtually stops? Soon they'll barely hold their own before some happy woodpecker finds a great bug source, and before too long they've fell the wrong way, taking a few vital younger trees down with them. There's eventually some nutrient value to the forest floor from the dead tree but much of that would be left there anyway, prior to removal of the logs. A little work with the chain saw, and the limbs and tops become floor in a hurry. Remove the occasional mature tree, and the younger trees that have been stifled under their canopy can grow, unrestricted. Like you can't imagine. Long term, I think both the woods and river will be healthier. Long term, the woods would provide more and better product and jobs, because of less waste through disease, fire, and rot. Again, if there is such a band. Too often they've logged to one river bank and started again at the other.

I know this won't satisfy people that like to stand among large dying trees. I don't think anything will. And I'm definitely not suggesting that we cut down all our old trees. I'm a greater tree hugger than most. But I can show you second growth trees that are getting of a size that would hold their own in a lot of old growth stands. The big difference is that they are still a vital, growing tree. In terms of "viewing," or "feeling serene," does that older tree that has virtually stopped growing, and is stifling the growth of trees around it, reeeallly make you feel that much better? You say, yes? Well—me too, in certain conditions. There's definitely stands of old growth timber that should be out of bounds, but I still think there's better use for a lot of our mature trees, than bug wood. It all depends on location, location, location. Anyway, I think that vital, healthy forests are a lot better than a bunch of older trees, surrounded by a criss-cross of fallen dead trees, waiting to fuel a fire that takes everything.

It seems like just about every part of a salmons life is determined by water temperature. How long it takes to hatch, time of emergence from the gravel, and then the affect on food sources and other in- river conditions, prior to and during downstream migration. Same thing during its life at sea, and all over again as a migrating adult, moving back to and up the river. When it moves up and where and how long it might spend in some hole, or stretch of some river, waiting for that change. Logging practices affect water temperature. They also affect the contents of runoff, following rains. The nature of the river and the general climate in its watershed makes this a river by river consideration, but certain rivers have suffered from too aggressive logging practices. I'm told this is a topic that is getting some pretty thorough attention by the young people in our forestry classes.

I spent most of my life living near the Dungeness River. Everyone always said that to do anything on the river you had to get Department of Fisheries approval, and that they would allow almost nothing done on the stream bed. I've often wondered if this was actually the case. If not, it would have been a good idea, along with having some local river authority, (whose only interest regarding the river would be it's overall well being.)

Using the Dungeness as an example, this person could have worked with the agencies overseeing development, the Department of Fisheries, ditch companies, and the property owners and possibly have made a big difference to a few people who built in, the wrong spot, and maybe to a lot of salmon that went up the wrong side of the river. Anyway, we definitely need more responsibility in managing all of our streams and watersheds than what there has been. Along those lines, this "river watcher" would have to be tall enough to see over dollars, through developers, and around certain officials, elected and otherwise.

To have "wild salmon" you have to have "wild rivers and streams." The rivers that I'm aware of inside the mouth of the Straits of Juan De Fuca won't fit the title of "wild river" very well. That doesn't mean that they can't produce a few wild salmon, but its hard to get serious production from streams that have been dammed, sucked dry for irrigation, their watersheds logged to death, or turned into narrow, diked ditches, or septic systems for our farms, towns, industries and developments. Salmon are going to have a hard enough time as is, in just dealing with the stuff nature throws at them.

Dikes are a necessary thing. You can't imagine existing in western Washington without them, but I think it's a shame that many of them weren't built a little further apart. That extra width would be right down the middle, maximum capacity. Sure, there would have been loss of land, but generally, the dikes should never have been installed on existing river bed in the first place. On so many of the western Washington rivers, the dikes were put so close together that every real flood goes through or over them. So certain people might have lost, or wouldn't have gained some land. But how much does dealing with floods year after year cost? Also, when you crowd any stream with a dike, you are probably raising water temperature from that point, on downstream. Stands of short term deciduous trees are either too far back, if they even exist, or destined to short life within any "close" stream bed.

When you make a ditch out of a river by placing dikes too close together, you eliminate most of the side streams where the adults would successfully spawn, as well as pretty much cancelling out any in-river spawning. Then the dikes virtually eliminate in- river habitation for the fry. They'll have to make it there for about a year, so what percentage of these fish are lost because of washout, siltation over the eggs, no shade or other protection, increased water temperatures, and darned little to eat? The dikes should have been put far enough apart in the first place to allow room for some vegetation and for a wild river to flow normally. When you put a dam across a river you strangle it, but it can be choked off just as well from the sides.

Just above Ethel's place was the biggest log jam I've seen on the Dungeness. It was there when Rich and I were first allowed to go to the river, and was there for almost another three years. If you aren't familar with log jams, think life. You wouldn't think there could be so much going on. You could get out on it and look down in, at maybe a dozen or more locations, and there was an abundance of every kind of life the river contained. It probably was a rearing area for more salmon and trout than you'd find in the next mile of river, or the next five miles of todays river. During late August and September, when the river used to get so low, this spot still offered food and protection to whatever fish were in the river at that time. Big fish or small, this was where they were.

Pull a piece of wood out of some log jam that's been there for awhile and look it over. All kinds of life will be hanging on it, and this is one of the conditions that exists in what might be called a wild river. In a real river, the area out of the main current will be teaming with life under the sand or gravel, and on, or under, the debris that accumulates at the edges of the holes. This is another thing the dikes have pretty much eliminated. These forms of life depend on the others and when you start monkeying with river beds, log jams, or vegetation along the streams edge, you're assuring that some portion of that stream will start to die, and it will start a chain reaction. However—there's such a thing as letting a log jam get out of hand. I never saw it on the Dungeness, but I can think of one on the Skagit that needs pruned, and has for several years. It all gets down to common sense. Sometimes common sense gets trumped from some surprising directions.

Part of this food chain is the salmon themselves. If they don't return to the river, and then spawn and die, their bodies won't be there as a vital, natural part of the food chain in that particular stream. Since the pink and chum fry spend almost no time in the stream after emerging from the gravel, the carcasses of their parent salmon could almost be looked at as a free food source to any given river system. Declining runs of either of these two species is going to have a definite impact on small wild king and silver salmon that may be in the same stream, and would affect their survival.

When we were kids, the stretch of river from the 101 bridge, up the mile and a half or so to the power line, was remarkable in that there was lots of log jams, trees, clumps of willows, stumps—something in the river or on the river bank every 150 feet or so. None of them were what you might really think of as a "jam," crossing and blocking the river, but there was lots of stuff in the river. Some were pretty good sized, most were not, but nearly all of them contributed to the lives of fish stocks in the river. Then one year they sent crews in to burn the debris on the river bed. Log jams, whatever, it all went up in smoke. Who authorized that? I always thought that the log jams did more to prevent flood damage than to cause it. At least on a river like the Dungeness.

Wild fish wise, this stretch was the most productive portion of the river, simply because year after year it had this better habitat—shade from trees, small jams and other debris, and the side streams. Lots of them. Above the power lines the owner kept the river, as well as the river bank, pretty much bulldozed where he wanted it. The debris was stacked and burned. What should have been a productive stretch of river, I always thought of as sterile.

An interesting stretch of riverbank maintenance was on the next piece of property, which is just below the powerlines. Here, the owner fell good sized sacrificial trees with cables going back to large stumps, or other trees in the woods, anchoring them against the bank. The tree protected existing bank and when the river happened to be against that bank, the limbs provided excellent shelter for both large and small fish. This bank held its own for at least 20 years that I'm aware of, prior to installation of the dikes behind Dungeness Meadows. Those "dikes" alone, are reason enough for the residents of Clallam County to push for more responsible river management.

Because of the velocity of the Dungeness, the "big" jams never got all that big because the river sort of pruned them. They slowed the river, possibly caused a slight change in direction for a short ways, but definitely lessened the cutting torch characteristics of a stream this fast. The damage I witnessed over the years was to homes that shouldn't have been there in the first place, or to property that was compromised by some very irresponsible things that were done to and around the river.

Some of the older neighbors told me that this stretch of river had held good sidestreams for as long as they could remember. The lay of the land was part of this, along with four large springs, a creek, and channels leading to, and the overflows from, the irrigation ditch screens. The occasional bulldozer encouraged water to feed the ditch outlets, even if they sometimes overdid it. Several of these provided good spawning areas for years. One of them probably still does. Then there were the streams that separated from the river, and rejoined it downstream. Some were small and others were major streams in themselves, a few of them remaining virtually unchanged for two or three years at a time. Salmon would stack up in the holes and log jams in the main river, but once they had ripened to the point of spawning, these sidestreams would be alive with fish. You saw very few coho spawning in the main river. There's no doubt in my mind that, at that time, this short stretch produced more wild cohos and kings, than all the rest of the river.

The kings would spawn in either the larger sidestreams or the main river and this made their survival more dependant on the conditions in the river on any given year. Humpies and dogs (pinks and chum) aren't too fussy, but large numbers of them certainly used the side streams for spawning. There's only so much actual spawning area alongside and at the bottom of each hole in the main river, and the side streams certainly expand the spawning capacity and add to the productivity of the river.

The thousands of small streams in the state, or the small river spurs that I've just mentioned, barely exist now, compared to what there was and how they were, a few short years ago. So many of the free flowing streams have been channelized, with the only goal being getting the water from the foothills to the bay, or main river, with minimal disruption to anything along the way. Shade, protection, and anything else involving decent habitat for the fish populations has generally been eliminated. Pasture right up to the creek bank, takes over the creek.

River-bed reclammation, irrigation, or just keeping that nice pond extra full, has had a grim price. I've seen too many years when there was as much water going down one of the main irrigation ditches, as what the Dungeness held when it got below the last ditch outlet. How much water is lost under the ditch bed in all of these ditches? Can a relatively small river like the Dungeness be used to maintain a water supply that largely didn't use to exist, with ditches extending for miles to the east and west of the river, and all over the valley? People keep moving to the area, and I guess I can't blame them, because we moved there once, ourselves. What I wonder about is, at what point do they address water use from the river to accomodate the people that live in the area, and at the same time provide adequate water for whatever stocks of fish live in the river? No one wants to talk about it, but when what's left of the river starts arriving at the bay, underground, someone is going to have to think about some pipe lines. I hate to think of the other alternative, but I can't say that someday it won't get to that. There's still a lot of houseless farmland and hillsides.

The Sequim-Dungeness valley is being populated at a much faster rate than most other areas in the state where the life of a river is in question. I chose it as an example, because I'm more familiar with it. There aren't many salmon producing streams in the state that won't have some of the conditions I've mentioned, and I think that in most cases, salmon hatcheries, are a big part of the answer. One of the biggest reasons, is the survival rate of hatchery reared fish compared to wild fish spawning in the same river. With so much of the king and silver salmons survival depending on in- river habitat for the offspring, hatcheries are making more sense all the time. Especially in a place like Washington State, where habitat keeps taking a back seat to anything else. There's a lot of hatchery people who think they could have the state overflowing with salmon, if given the chance.

For some reason, hatchery fish have picked up a bad reputation. Part of the problem is that too many people think farmed salmon and hatchery raised salmon are the same thing. There's a world of difference. Salmon that begin their lives in the river, or at a hatchery, eat the same stuff in the ocean, so both mature into a very nutritious, healthful, food product. At a fish hatchery, the eggs and milt are taken from adult salmon returning from the sea, incubated, hatched, and the offspring raised to a point that they can be released to migrate out to sea and spend the next portion of their lives in the ocean. Anywhere from less than a year (jack salmon) to four years, or more, depending on which species, when they were released, what river they're from, and what their ancestors have been doing the last few thousand years. They live off the lush food chain in the ocean till nature calls them back to the river, and the process is repeated.

I caught several hatchery kings (Washington origin) in Alaska that dressed over 50 pounds, and the largest average weight per fish, of any coho trip I ever sold, was from down in Clarence Straits, just north of Ketchikan. Their average weight was 10.4 lbs. head on, dressed out, and I was told most of them were from the Neets Bay hatchery. This is another run of salmon that didn't use to exist. That trip was a welcome shot to the end of one summer season for me and quite a few others. In contrast, it's a shame that so many people are looking at the runty cohos produced in Washington State's late release program, as the best example of what a hatchery fish can be. Or like I said, thinking that farmed salmon are comparable to fish that have spent the salt water portion of their lives, feeding in the ocean.

Along with those fish from Neets Bay, there's quite a few new runs of salmon in Southeast Alaska, funded by an aquaculture tax that each fisherman is assessed, each time salmon are sold. In Southeast Alaska it started at three % and now I'm told it's been raised to four % of the gross sales on salmon. That's a lot of money to raise salmon with. Applied correctly, it can't go wrong.

Milo Moore, Director of Fisheries under two separate Governors in Washington State, went to Japan and helped their government do what he'd wanted to do here. Take lots of eggs and hatch and then raise them to the point that they could be turned out to sea. The ocean, our most overlooked and under appreciated feedlot, would raise them to maturity. The ocean would have raised the pink and chum and provided most of what the king, silver, and sockeye salmon consumed during their lifetimes.

Due to Milo's efforts in Japan, the Hokkaido area realized a return of 49 million adult chum salmon in one peak year. Since chum can go to sea almost immediately after emergence from the gravel, or at the same stage of development in a hatchery, the cost in getting them out to sea was only 5% of the value of the catch. It's hard to argue with success. It's a shame that his ability had to be used overseas, rather than here at home. Milo had wanted to do projects in Washington State, enhancing runs of all five salmon species. The state has many times the potential for hatchery production that Japan has. It makes you wonder, what's been running our state?

When you were unloading your catch in any of the Alaskan ports, they had a person on the dock whose job was recording data on any hatchery salmon that were landed. A good percentage of the king salmon landed were from hatcheries in British Columbia, as well as from Washington and Oregon. Print-outs were sent back to the cold storages, making it possible to track certain fish you might be interested in.

At that point, Southeast Alaska's hatchery efforts on king salmon were just starting to chip in. King salmon entering Southeast Alaska's rivers and moving upstream to spawn in Alaskan, or further upstream in Canadian waters, has been a bucket of worms in the past and a strong hatchery effort on kings and cohos, separate from these international river systems, sure couldn't hurt a thing. Imagine what could have been if we'd had the brains to work together, long term, concerning our salmon runs.

People tend to forget about the troll catch on British Columbia's outside coast, from the fifties to the mid eighties. It seems like the guy up the beach from you gets a lot of the fish that were spawned or raised in your waters. Without the salmon produced in Washington and Oregon, the Canadian troll fleet could never have developed to the point that it did. Include British Columbia, along with Washington and Oregon raised salmon, and the same thing could be said for Alaska's troll fishery. It seems to me, that instead of eliminating most of this fishery, we could have done a lot better. An international aquaculture tax, with a goal of developing both countries fisheries, instead of stifling the fishiest place in the world in favor of the farmed salmon interests, would have been a good start. With some of our major corporations eyeing the salmon industry as fill for their coffers, it's not surprising that many local politicians sat on their fence. Salvaging a strong commercial fishery wasn't a goal of a surprisingly large group of people, and a sharp turn to port or starboard would have broken the necks of a good many civic leaders, who had been following that new dollar on the block. At the front end of a couple paragraphs back is a good excuse for me to tell a fish story. Time for a brief change of topic.

When the kids started fishing in Alaska with me, one of our first trips was in June, out of Sitka. I'll leave the area vague as some of this is about a few special, or maybe just unique, fish that we ran across. A nice percentage of the kings we were getting, were near the surface, and the feed being good sized needle fish, it wasn't too hard to find a lure that would enthuse them. There were also some dolly varden in the area, and every few days one would take one of these lures. They were an exceptionally beautiful fish.

Most of the dollys you get in Alaska would be a drab fish, more of a ho hum dolly body, some reddish orange spots on grayish silver sides, and a dull green color on the back. These that we were getting were bigger than you'd normally see, most of them at least 18 inches long and built more like a small salmon. Chunkier than you usually see in a dolly. The pattern of coloration was more like I've seen in Eastern Brook trout, and the coloration of the spots and rings, and on the fins, was very vivid, with the color on the back being the deepest emerald green I've ever seen on a fish. Some of this was because they would soon be headed towards some stream to spawn and were starting to show a little extra color, but then I've seen lots of dollys showing the coloration that goes with spawning, and never anything that came close to this.

So one day here comes a dandy, and the kids took one look and wanted to keep it and show it to Sid. It was over two feet long and would have weighed between four and five pounds. When we cleaned it the meat was a much deeper color than a normal dolly. More like a fresh steelhead. Exceptional for a dolly.

We ended the trip and weren't able to find Sid anywhere in town that evening, so the next morning found us at the Sitka Sound dock. The coop plant didn't exist yet. While waiting to unload, I was visiting with the fellow that did the tagged fish operation I just mentioned, and somehow or other, the topic got turned towards chumpies. Chumpies are a chum- humpie cross and wind up with humpies scales, chum head and tail, and also, the body shape and size will be more of a small chums. Like mulies, they won't reproduce, and aren't real common. I've only seen them in the ocean so I don't know if the males would get a hump like the humpies get in the river, or not. We got two down in lower Chatham on the same day once, and I don't think I ever did get much over thirty of them, all told. It's interesting that they are the only two species of salmon that will occasionally cross, and other than certain fall kings, are the only two species that spend almost no time in freshwater, after coming out of the gravel. Kings and silvers have crossed, but it's so seldom that you may as well say, never.

So anyway, we gabbed while he worked with a few tagged fish and before long boats started moving, and I went back down to move the boat under the hoist. When unloading they drop a big aluminum tub down into your hold, and after you fill it with salmon, they lift it up to the grading table on the dock, where the fish are separated according to specie, size, and grade. This goes on hopefully for a long time, until you've unloaded. Then they repeat the process with the tub while you shovel all the used ice out of the hold. After that, a major washdown, scrub with soap and water, and another washdown. The cleaned bin boards go back in place, and you're ready to take ice for next trip.

When I came to the dolly I hesitated, thought—why not, and threw it in with the salmon. They don't buy dollys. A few buckets later the tag man looks down over the dock and says "hey, you did get a chumpie." When we'd finished unloading I went up to get my slip and noticed they had put my "chumpie" down as a humpie. I thought I might as well run this into the ground, so I asked the girl that graded the trip, if it was half humpie and half chum, how come I was getting paid for the least valuable kind? I wanted the big chum price. Maybe another nickel a pound. Her mom, Mary, was the floor boss, and had looked at it when they first saw it so she came back over, talked to her daughter, a long stare at me, and our dolly varden was now a chum on the ticket, worth another quarter.

When you keep fish in ice the coloration may change in some cases. Especially in fish that might be starting to show a bit of maturity as they get close to their river. When the dolly had come out of the ice it looked like a nice bright fish, but after being out of the ice for a few minutes, its true colors had started to show. While I was starting down the ladder, Mary was looking in the tote with the dolly in it. "Damn you, Vince."

The hats the cold storage workers wore were color coded to show who was a dock or floor worker—red, or superviser—blue. I liked to kid Mary that they were trying to find her a green hat. Any kidding aside, Mary was one of the best, and Sitka Sound Seafoods was lucky to have her.

Here's another area where people get a twisted view of hatchery fish. Off the Washington coast, regulations call for the release of wild silvers (cohos) in both the ocean sport fishery and the commercial troll fishery. Any coho with a clipped adipose fin will be a hatchery fish (definitely) and any wild ones will still have their adipose fin. And then there's the grey area. A good percentage of the "wild" cohos released by sport and commercial fishermen, mainly off Washington's north coast and inside waters, are of a size and condition that suggests that they

222

are really unclipped, late release (resident stock) hatchery reared salmon. Chafing on their tails and fins indicate they've spent considerable time in a hatchery pond, and their size, which is about half of a normal wild or hatchery fish, suggests that they haven't spent much time feeding from the ocean's rich table.

Some fisheries people will tell you that "all" of the hatchery cohos are adipose clipped. Others will tell you otherwise. It varies and I know it varies from hatchery to hatchery and within each hatchery, depending on who you talk to. Comparing the ratio of "wild" - hatchery cohos on the north coast, it ran about 6 so called wild fish to one hatchery fish. This is if you go by the clipped - not clipped adipose ratio. Talking with quite a few sport fishermen on the docks in Neah Bay, they thought it was somewhat more; anywhere from 7 to 20 "wild" cohos to one hatchery fish. Twenty was probably a stretch. What they told me was still close enough to what I had seen (outside of that 20 to 1 ratio) that it seemed like we were looking at about the same thing. I don't think the ratio this shows, is accurate. I'd rather accept numbers I didn't like, and we all deal with them accordingly, than have to accept numbers I think are skewed.

The ratio of clipped to not clipped adipose fins on the south coast, during the three seasons prior to this, was about even. You saw very few late release cohos below Cape Elizabeth, less as you went south, and the size of any clipped fish was more of a normal coho's. With the percentage of clipped - unclipped, adipose fins, and the resultant management policies, it's no wonder a lot of people are gritting their teeth.

Why have late release stock hatchery fish? I'm probably a poor person to carry that ball because I hate the idea from every angle I approach it from. Lets give it a try anyway. Prior to the late release program, a very large number of both Washington State's wild, and hatchery reared salmon, would go out of the Straits of Juan De Fuca, or through the Georgia, Johnstone, Queen Charlotte Straits route, and spend most of the ocean portion of their lives in Canadian waters. This was also the case for large volumes of salmon spawned in coastal Washington and Oregon rivers. A massive Canadian troll fleet caught them in huge numbers.

The state started holding young coho longer at hatcheries inside the mouth of the straits, with the intention of compromising their migratory instincts to a point that they would stay in the state's inside waters, rather than going out the straits to the ocean, turning right, and later, finding their way over a Canadian grading table. It worked on a large number of these fish. This stifled their natural instinct to move to the ocean's rich feeding grounds.

Prior to this, as adults, they simply weren't around all that long, from the time they entered the straits, until they went up some river. On some dryer years, probably a little longer in the outer straits, but even then, six weeks would generally be stretching it. Also, cohos at that point in their lives are feeding less, so less likely to get on a hook.

So now there were cohos around for extended fishing time, in that many of them now spent little or no time in the ocean, adding months of availability to the inside sport fishery. And the state started looking good—on paper. I wonder how much the months of extra feed cost, with the fish already past their normal pre-release size. When they leave the hatchery as smolts they're larger than normal and they return as runts, but after virtually eliminating the state's commercial salmon fisheries, the difference between a coho returning at normal size, 7 to 10 pounds, and an adult coho that returned to the river at half of normal size, is sort of a moot point. To some.

Even so, you ask, what's wrong with that? To start with, I get nervous anytime they start interrupting migration patterns to this extent. The straits and both the north and south sound waters are compromised by colder water temperatures and more pollution, so there's much less feed when compared to the ocean, for whatever fish stocks might be there at any given time. Granted, there's always been a certain percentage of blackmouth that seem to stay inside for some portion of their lives, but expecting inside waters to support these new volumes of resident fish—something's going to go without. If they get hungry, go to the ocean even later yet—how much juggling can they take? Will they find their parent stream, any old stream, or will they get to one or the other completely off schedule? It worries me how much of this manipulation they can survive. And now this late release program applies to king salmon, as well as the coho.

Some people will tell you that salmon don't eat salmon. That's not the case. It gets down to conditions. On quite a few occasions, I've been cleaning fish and noticed a small salmon come out of a belly. This has often been when they were feeding on herring, and these smolts being about the same size, got picked up during the feeding frenzy. No great cause for concern, because I don't think the numbers are that huge. Generally, nature has shuffled things, so at that size, they aren't as likely to be served up on that particular plate. But—salmon do eat salmon. You don't look at the contents of every belly when you already know what they're eating, and there's no doubt that I missed this, much more than I saw it.

Then there's this. Years ago a bunch of us fishing out of Petersburg had went in to complain about the herring seiners coming into Frederick Sound and mopping up local herring populations. The ADFG guy we were talking to informed us that salmon didn't eat herring anyway. So sometimes people see things others don't, and sometimes they just see things differently.

Back to salmon, say that we're in Puget Sound, where there's not the abundance of feed that's in the ocean. We've juggled nature once more, and have programmed a large volume of coho salmon to be out of place when far greater volumes of pink and chum fry are in the same area. These very small chum and pink fry are at the estuary a short time after emergence from the gravel, and both species are likely to spend more time near the estuary, or in sheltered water along the shoreline, than king or coho smolts would. There's no doubt in my mind what takes place here, and even if I had pictures of a cupfull of inch long fry spilling out of a cohos belly, the state will still look good on paper. "Look at our statistics." But they've pretty much done away with the state's commercial salmon fishery to provide these great numbers. As long as there's enough chums for the Indian's salmon egg fishery, there's no real problem. Is there?

There was an old guy that used to come down to the boat a lot during the winter in Port Angeles and sometimes BS the afternoon away. His main area of interest seemed to be salmon, rearing them at the hatcheries, the problems and challenges involved, and the returns back on any given year. Sometimes the subject was not much of a hatchery, outside of a few beaver ponds. This could turn into quite a topic, so I'll end it by saying that there are all kinds of poachers and we need more like Bill and his Buddies. We should all be that way, or if not, at least share the same goal. He was also very familiar with the Dungeness hatchery, and he thought that Ernie Brannon was at least 12 feet tall, which we agreed on.

He stopped at the house a few times on his way back down from the hatchery, and one of these times, said that I ought to go up and look in the stream behind the hatchery. That afternoon I took the boys up, and in one of the long pools in the stream behind the hatchery we saw around 400 very small cohos, probably less than a 4 ½ pound (round weight) average. They had made it the nine miles up to the hatchery over a month before the earliest cohos normally showed at the mouth of the river. There had been no freshet to raise the river, so it was about as low as you ever saw it. Normally these fish would have gone no further than the first few "estuary" holes at the mouth, and then waited for that first rise in the river to move on upstream. I went back up the next morning, before going back out to the coast, and Bill was up there again. We both wondered what was going on with this particular bunch of fish, and neither of us had any idea. The late release thing was still new stuff to us, and that's what these must have been. We both wished Ernie was still there, to ask about this.

In a few days I was home and this time I talked to a guy that worked at the hatchery who told me they were thinking of trying to start a bunch of early returning cohos, using the eggs from these fish. Several weeks later I started seeing the first dead ones, only a couple at first. After that, each day that I happened to be in from fishing I'd head up, usually first thing in the morning and each time—more dead ones. The most we ever saw was 5 or 6. They were all in poor shape, considering that they were still bright, or a sort of drab bright. I never did see any, alive or dead, that had started to show any color, and that's something I wonder about. (Same sort of thing in the next chapter, on the blackmouth) The few females I opened up, still looked to be a long way off from spawning.

I got to wondering, and spent a few hours behind our place, and on downstream, checking out several of the best holes, thinking that maybe there were others that hadn't made it all the way up to the hatchery. Nothing till I went down below the railroad bridge, and then about 25 in a log jam and quite a bit more in one of the slower, deep holes. At least a hundred or so. I didn't take the time to look at the lower river and now wish I had, especially in the holes just up from the mouth of the river. It's hard to be on the ocean and on the river at the same time.

The next time we went up to the hatchery they were all gone, truck tire tracks next to the creek and a pretty disgusted hatchery worker. "If I didn't need the job so bad, I'd quit." He wouldn't say much more. So, I never did quite get all the dots connected there, but between the two of us, Bill and I figured out to our own satisfaction that the late release program compromised migrating instincts a lot more than just during the early salt water portion of their lives.

Since then I've wondered how much not realizing normal ocean feeding, both in volume, and duration, cost them in the end. I had the impression that their batteries ran down, and they couldn't bridge an extended time between this earlier river entry, and spawning. You still run across the occasional half sized, dead, coho that pretty much mirrors what we saw that September, but this has been in other rivers. It's been years now, since we moved from the Sequim area.

Anyway, "We gotta save the wild stocks," sounds good, but I can't think of anything that gives me much hope that we will do it. Aside from the things I've mentioned, we still have to consider reality at some point. Things like a burgeoning population from Queen Charlotte Sound to Los Angeles and its effect on the fisheries, habitat wise and other wise. Reality is Governors appointing some very unqualified buddies as Directors of Fisheries, here today, and gone tomorrow, and some of our fisheries bureaucrats, the latter seemingly entrenched in the system for life. And there's always the Boldt Decision. It hangs there like a wet blanket and if the price for salmon (or salmon roe) is right, the pressure from in-river gillnets is severe, and the gillnets don't care about wild salmon versus hatchery fish. They, or their eggs, all sell about the same.

The king salmon are a fascinating fish. They are the largest pacific salmon, and have adapted to conditions along more than 3000 miles of coastline. At one time, some Columbia and Yukon River kings, migrated well over 1000 miles upstream to spawn. Yukon fish still do.

The Snake River fish that migrated to its upper reaches were unique, round and heavy, and with sides so thick that there was barely any belly cavity. They were the darkest, bright salmon that you ever handled, with a very small, bullet head which was also much darker than any other strain of king that I ever saw. They looked like they had been heavily sprinkled with a finely ground black pepper. The meat would be a deep, reddish orange and would carry so much fat that it would amaze you. The flavor was fantastic! Lee Harbaugh told me they were Columbia River springs and later, when I talked to guys that had spent lifetimes fishing off the Washington coast, most of them said the same thing. A fish grader in Port Angeles, who had spent much of his life on the lower Columbia, expanded it a bit more, saying they were from the Snake River side. When the big push on dam building on the Snake River started, they gradually became another memory. In a lifetime of eating king salmon, I've never tasted any that were better.

We used to get some very large, heavily bodied kings off the Baranof shore that would have a grayish tinge to the scales, and almost all of these would be a white. They were fall spawners, so maybe fish from some Fraser River tributary? Who knows? Its safe to say that they were from some Canadian system, though. There's rivers in the lower states that have some whites, but I've never heard of any that were noted for it. I remember getting one in the Dungeness when I was a kid and wondered what was wrong with it.

The difference in the appearance on the outside and the color of the meat is only part of the picture. There can be reds and whites and some that are red and white (blotchy), as well as spring, summer, fall, and early winter returning adult king salmon, all in the same river system. The strains of salmon that have been going up this same river for the last thousands of years have adapted over time to where they survive as well as possible in that system. The amount of time spent in the gravel prior to emergence, is tuned to them and their river. Migrating patterns, either upstream by returning adults or downstream by the smolts, have evolved over time to fit conditions in their parent stream, or maybe in some portion, or tributary of a larger river system. They may be more resistant to certain disease or water conditions, and may have developed the ability to load so much fuel on their bodies that they can move way over a thousand miles up some river, prior to spawning. Another king salmon going into some smaller system might look poor in comparison. One way or another, these "conditions" will have something, or everything, to do with water temperature.

Salmon are quite a wonderful thing, and I'm not saying we should give up on stimulating wild salmon production. There's lots we can do, even if we can't put the rivers in perfect condition. They never were. But I do think it's time we stopped using "wild salmon" as the point that west coast salmon management spins around. And I think that those who run down the salmon hatcheries program, ought to support perfecting it. Especially if they hope to make a living catching them, or catching and releasing them with a sport pole for hours at a time. Or just like to eat them.

The big hydro-electric dams in the Columbia and Snake Rivers took a huge toll on the worlds largest source of king salmon. "With Grand Coulee, Hells Canyon, and major tributary dams, 60% of the Columbia Basin watershed was made inaccessible to salmon and much of that was the primary habitat of the spring chinook. The remaining accessible Columbia and Snake mainstem river habitat has been reduced 64% by flooded reservoirs. The production potential of the remaining natural habitat in the tributary systems is also much reduced." [7]

So they built salmon hatcheries. Lots of them. Salmon from rivers many hundreds of miles apart, probably having very different conditions from a river way upstream or maybe in another state or Canada, were thrown together to try to maintain king salmon stocks in the river. They went with the knowledge available at the time, so mistakes were made, but you learn from mistakes. They're still learning. Numbers of kings up the Columbia in recent years tells me someone's doing something right, even if certain fisheries bureaucrats don't count the 90% of these returns (hatchery fish) as real king salmon. Where do they think they're going to get all these "wild" kings? Most of the habitat in the system has either been closed off to salmon runs by dams, or buried under a bunch of lakes. If salmon runs are going to stand up to the demands of the future, salmon hatcheries will have to be smack dab in the middle of the picture. Lets support perfecting them.

Now they've got a new idea—going behind the dikes (or not?) from scratch, or possibly just rebuilding existing conditions. (engineered streams) The Dungeness happens to have a piece of this concept, and I've walked it several times now. It compares to several of the side streams that used to be a few miles downstream, only with even more perfect conditions. It was designed with natural type coho production in mind and is pictured on page 123, "Population Structure of Columbia River Basin Chinook Salmon And Steelhead."[8] With careful site selection, I think this will be one of the big things in the future of salmon. Ideal conditions can be built or grown if they aren't already there—shade, cover (debris), deep pools and gravelly shallows and riffles. Even the possibility of cooling what might be a relatively small amount of water to obtain optimum water temp—almost everything a salmon needs short of a good source of water. If a food source is lacking it can be added to, and the success rate is many times what might be hoped for in normal wild conditions because there would, or should, be some protection from the main blast of flood water.

In comparison (from Ernie Brannon) 0.001 to 0.04 wild smolts /m2 of natural stream habitat compared to 5 to 10 wild like smolts /m2 of engineeered stream area. (/m2 would be about 40 inches square) The cost of development per river mile is relatively low, and would vary, depending on the project, but it seems that a minimal amount of money could provide a nice stretch of very productive side stream.

Two years ago I went back and walked the upper hundred yards of what was my favorite piece of my favorite river. Now it's gone back to old stream bed, heavily grown over, and I'm not going to say that they haven't allowed development along it's banks further downstream. I didn't go all the way through. There are a few homes next to it, right at the top end. If they haven't done too much development downstream, or maybe even if they have, this stretch just might be a dandy for this engineered stream concept. Before it was bulldozed closed, it amounted to about half of the river, but if it were to be used now, I suppose they could meter any desired amount of water down that branch.

I'm hoping to get back and walk all the way through. I wonder if these fish, once established, would be even sort of acceptable to the "wild salmon" advocates? Maybe not, but I think that this concept, along with ever improving hatchery technology, will be the future of west coast salmon fisheries.

# Chapter 19
# My Fishy River

When I was a kid my favorite place in the world was anywhere along the Dungeness River. In describing it as we go along, you've likely seen a comparison here and there to your favorite stream, which may not even be in the northwest. It's quite a bit faster than most, and for a stream of its size I think it has a bit more going on.

The Dungeness salmon hatchery has been roughly in the same place, now, for nearly a hundred years. From where the river runs into Dungeness Bay, up to the hatchery, is about nine miles. Half a mile below the hatchery the river comes out of the foothills and onto the valley. Except for the occasional bluff or clay bank on one side or the other, this lower portion of the river runs down over much flatter country than that upstream. It would still be considered fast water in this lower portion of the river.

For years the river above the hatchery was lost to king salmon, since the racks at the hatchery prevented almost all of them from getting on upstream. Sometimes during some high water in the spring a few might get over the racks, or go through when they were open during humpie runs. Last summer I was at the hatchery, and the racks are gone. I don't know when they took them out, but somewhere in the last fifteen years or so.

Some years, portions of the lower river would re-route itself, and of course this left salmon eggs, silted over, high and dry, or washed away. The various side streams, some of which weren't quite as likely to be washed out, could make an enormous difference in the rivers production of wild salmon. In this I'm thinking of streams separating and re-entering the river downstream. A tributary (it's own system) wouldn't likely be as affected by conditions in the main river. The lower Dungeness didn't have too many tributaries, and for that matter, the upper river doesn't, either.

From "the narrows," just upstream from the hatchery on the Dungeness, two hillsides met at the river and from there, on upstream, there are very few spots where it is wide enough for there even to be a side stream. On the other hand, the river channel is definite, lots of big rock that is there year after year, and for much of it there was seldom any real change. A lot of the holes you fish today were pretty much the same twenty, or even fifty years ago.

I've mentioned the dolly varden that are in the Dungeness, and I'll tell you a bit more about them because they are a big part of the fish picture in the river. As you move upstream on the Dungeness branch, or in the upper stretches of each of the Graywolf tributaries, you'll find a point where you suddenly catch no more rainbows, and what dolly varden you get will be very small, usually 4 to 7 inch fish. It's been 48 years since I've been back into Three Forks, and one thing that still picks at my mind is that I always thought there was something a little different about these small "dollys." They weren't as colorful as the eastern brook that are in most of the higher Olympic Mountain lakes, but they definitely didn't look like the dolly varden that lived downstream. They didn't look like the eastern brook you got in the upper Sol Duc, either. These upstream dollys? were called glacier trout by a lot of the old timers and for now "glacier trout" is good enough for me, but I wouldn't bet that they weren't malnourished eastern brook. Once you get up into this area of the river, rainbows are an almost never thing and the (glacier trout) make up the entire fish population from there, on upstream. Generally the break will take place within a very short area of river, and it seemed to be the same location each year.

It's interesting that the big dollys that you got in the Graywolf branch, below Three Forks, would never be up in this area where the glacier trout were. Probably not enough to eat. We used to get them down in the main river using a little piece of belly, or salmon eggs and when we got one they flew back into the woods. We had caught too many with a lump in its belly that would turn out to be a small rainbow. I even caught one that grabbed a rainbow I had on my line and wound up on the hook itself. We would open some of them up to take a look, and nearly every time they would be wormy and in very poor condition. If their bodies had been proportionate to their heads they'd have weighed twice as much.

It's about four miles from the hatchery to Two Forks and another eight miles up the Graywolf to the Three Forks area. They don't all junction at exactly the same spot. When you got downstream, more towards Two Forks, the dollys you caught were usually in nicer condition but not as big as the scuzzier ones upstream. Something to wonder about. Dollys are scavengers. I guess most fish are, but the dolly doesn't rate too high in my book. They used to pay a bounty on them in Alaska.

The dollys even further downstream are usually a better looking fish. There's quite a few sea run dollys that will follow the salmon in, and they will usually be a fairly firm fish in the 12 to 16 inch range. I got one 24 incher and heard of a couple that were bigger. Nice and firm or not, if you catch a dolly that you can't get in your wheelbarrow, it still won't be much of a fish to eat. Any rainbows you caught in the same portion of the upper river that these big dollys came out of would always be in exceptionally nice condition and excellent eating.

Not all the dollys in the lower river were sea run. You'd get them at any month of the year, and the best spots were the deep holes or the log jams. Unless the salmon were spawning. Then you fished the water at the head of the hole or right at the bottom end, even on some riffles. We'd catch a lot of them using light gear, a split shot and a single egg. It always amazed me that a fish so small could hold so many salmon eggs.

Now lets go back upstream, past Two Forks, up the Graywolf some miles above Duncan Flats, and we're up not too far below the canyon. There's a big hole that you can fish best from the west side and its the best spot I know of in any of the upper portions of the Dungeness system. There's an enormous rock across the river and the current runs under it, who knows how far, and there's a big area of the pool that's deep enough that you can't see bottom. Actually, I think the rock's probably connected. You can't fish it from the east side except at the very bottom or just at the top of the hole, and I've done very well on nice rainbows there. Across the river you can get up on another big rock, and its almost like fishing in a mini-lake with a river running into it. This is the only spot in the Dungeness system that I ever caught an eastern brook trout in. Two of them, and several years apart. Many of the lakes in the Olympics have eastern brook, and I always wondered if there was some way that they could have made it out of Moose Lake. Now I wonder how they made it to Moose Lake. Ernie Brannon said that he thought the few sockeye in the Dungeness may have had some history with the lake at some time, and that a landslide or something had closed it off to any salmon migration. I've never went all the way up the Grand or talked to anyone who had, so I don't know. Lawrence told me that Moose

Lake wasn't named for a moose. He said there was a guy named Frank Moose that it was named after.

These dolly varden, the eastern brook, brook trout, and arctic char and there are some others, are all supposed to be in the char family. So there's all kinds of things going on in the dolly (char) department in this one stream. Maybe different strains of fish adapting over time, water temperatures, availability and types of feed and all the other stuff that goes with habitat. And just like the rainbows, some of them go to sea.

On one of our Three Forks expeditions we found an elk antler jammed into the crotch of a tree, and over the years the tree had grown around it. I was describing it to one of the old timers, (Bob Priest) and he said he'd put it there over thirty years earlier, which would be over eighty years ago, now. Then he got to telling about the small elk herd that was often in that flat then, and I told him about fresh droppings and spots where they had bedded down there, probably within hours of when we came through. He said you couldn't imagine the fishing there, then, and described this one spot, where I had caught the two eastern brook trout. It was implanted in his mind just as it is mine, now. I was glad to be able to tell him that it hadn't changed.

The rainbows have their own separation, and I can't explain it but I'll tell you a bit about it. Many of the river's rainbow trout population never leave the river. They live in the upper stretches of the river and will move further upstream, usually in the late part of August or September, to spawn. A lot of this spawning will take place in the three Graywolf tributaries, or the East Dungeness, and you get quite a few trout that are as small as seven inches, ready to spawn.. Then they apparently drop back downstream into the main river again. Some of them grew to be exceptional for the Dungeness, because what most people think of as Dungeness rainbows were the 5 to 7 inch guys that lived in the lower river. A few of these upper river rainbows would go nicely over 3 pounds. I remember that many of the small males milt would already be running in September, and some of the females would also be exceptionally ripe. This makes me think they'd have been more of a fall spawner.

The smaller rainbow in the lower river would migrate to sea and would return in a year or so as steelhead. Some would spawn, move back downriver to the straits and on out to the ocean, re-charge their batteries, and a year or so later, do it again. Others likely spent more time in the ocean before their initial return and who knows where their time at sea took them? Unlike salmon, some of them go well offshore, into the warmer blue waters in the ocean. I never did get one, but over my years of fishing tuna, heard of several that had taken a tuna jig.

Some steelhead, especially summer runs, move farther upstream than the areas that the native trout spent most of their lives in, so there's quite a bit of overlapping within the river. Who knows what sends some one way, and some another? We'd start getting returns—steelhead that had spawned and were heading back downstream in early February, and this makes me wonder how many summer runs wait till spring to spawn. The early winter Dungeness steelhead were awfully green fish in late November and December, and I'm fairly certain the summer runs were better represented in these earlier returns heading back out.

So where most steelhead spawn in late winter - thru spring, the resident rainbows in the upper river spawn in the fall—September or later. Or at least, some of them do. Maybe some of them are spring spawners like the steelhead. I don't know, because we never got up there till June, and they were all fat and bright by then. The few times we went to Three Forks in September most of the fish were up in the three branches, with very few fish down in the main river.

The cutthroats in the Dungeness are all sea run and mostly it's a September through November show, with a few in the spring and only a sprinkle, otherwise. They come in, eat a lot of salmon eggs, and apparently go back out after spawning. The cutthroat are a gorgeous fish, beautifully marked and very good eating, but unless they start planting them, don't hope for too many out of the Dungeness. I remember there being quite a few one fall, but aside from that, four or five in an outing was a pretty good gather. It always seemed that they fell in two size ranges, either around a foot long, or about sixteen to twenty inches, which would be about a years separation in salt water. A twenty incher was a very seldom thing.

Some of the smaller western Washington rivers like the Dungeness have runs of king salmon that are spring run fish, entering the river mostly in May and June and spawning in July and August. Others will have summer and fall run fish with most of the movement from late August—through November, the spawning pretty much spanning mid September, through December. The Dungeness had both, although not many coming in as late as November. Like so many rivers with king salmon runs, there were stragglers. Most of these stragglers wouldn't get in the river until along in July, and they were usually bigger than the average Dungeness fish. In the years from 69 to 73 there were quite a few more fall run kings in the river than what was usual, their location in the river making you think they were from the Hurd Creek part of the Dungeness hatchery, which is located only a few miles above the river mouth. Then again, maybe that's the area where they were released. These were generally a smaller fish—12 to 20 or so, pounds.

I think I mentioned them earlier, but these two kings are worthy of another go-around. One made it up the middle branch of the Graywolf a few hundred yards, and several years later we saw one down in the canyon below Three Forks. Both were by themselves and we never saw another king salmon on either of these two, or any other trips up there, so their efforts meant nothing except to themselves and me, and now maybe you. This is a short river compared to most, and I've fished it all, up to Three Forks and then some. I can tell you that those two fish went through a "lot" to get up there. I went through a lot going through the canyon, and I was going downstream.

Blackmouth is one of the names that immature kings go by and refers more to their gum line, which is black. The term is the one most often used in Washington State to separate the king salmon that aren't that years spawners. They could be less than 3 pounds or over 50 because they could be spanning two or more years fish.

Along in the mid to late 50s we started getting the occasional blackmouth while we were fishing steelhead in the Dungeness. Not very many, because no one spent more time on the river than I did, and the most I ever got was four in one winter. I heard of a few others, and since it would have been illegal to keep them, I'm sure there were others I didn't hear about. You would also see the occasional bright fish laying dead on the edge, or out in the river, and when you fished them out they'd be one of these blackmouth. I caught them between 5 and 20 lbs. and heard of a couple that were bigger. Now and then I'd take one up to the hatchery, knowing that Ernie was interested, and he'd open them up and look them over and never saw anything that he thought stood out.

"Who knows, Cameron?" In some of the smaller fish, the skeins of eggs were only three or four inches long, with eggs so small that you could barely tell what they were. Some of the larger fish might have a skein that would have put them in that next seasons category but they would be in the river four to six months too early. Even though they were all still bright, or what you might call dull bright, the ones you found dead were in very poor shape. This went on for about six years that I'm aware of, and maybe longer. I helped build a boat one winter and then got married, so didn't put in the time steelhead fishing that I had before, but still heard of some of these fish being caught. It sounds like more of what we saw with the late release cohos, only with king salmon, but then Ernie would have known (unless maybe they'd been part of some program outside the Dungeness.) When I get to thinking about it, the first one of these that I caught was years before they started the late release program on silvers. Ernie's only thought on this that I can remember, was that maybe they'd just got in with a bunch of steelhead and followed them in. Then he immediately shrugged that off, saying, "why would they just start doing that now?" But I still think it smacks of some "late release" thing.

The only Dungeness kings I haven't mentioned are the jack salmon. You hardly ever got a "jack" with the early fish. You'd start seeing them along towards late June and then on through the summer, and there were lots of them. They are a little male that has matured a year or so early, and occur in both kings and silvers. The kings would range from barely over a foot long, up to over two feet. A silver jack usually runs from about a foot to sixteen inches. They are fully developed and will spawn with adult females. Some say they reproduce mostly jacks and others said it didn't make any difference in the ratio of offspring that were jacks. I don't know. No Jacks in chums and pinks and I haven't been around sockeyes enough to know.

There are a few "jills" but darned few. I've caught four or five and heard of a couple others from guys that would know the difference. These were all fully developed female kings that would spawn that fall, all of them in the three to six pound range. Looking back, it seems like they were all in a two or three year span and were caught trolling in the ocean, more on the south end, like from Destruction Island - south. Maybe another experiment? Never having caught or heard of any, outside of these few, makes me think so.

Another interesting thing about the king jacks (males) is that if you happen to catch them in the ocean at prime time, they always carry so much more weight than a feeder king of the same length. The minimum legal size for kings was 28 inches and most feeders that size would dress out at eight or nine pounds. I've seen jack kings that would dress out from eleven to over twelve pounds that weren't long enough to keep. The time span to see this is short, and although they probably look really good in the rivers, this mid July- mid September fish, out of the ocean, will look like a football for all the weight they're packing.

The few sockeyes in the river was just another of Ernie's on- going projects. Each year he'd take what collected in the pond, put them through the hatchery, and each year he'd get a few back. I don't know how he managed the pond, or lake, part of their lives, but he did. He said they were there when he first came to the hatchery and he always made the effort to keep them going.

236

The Dungeness is a really good humpie (pink) stream, especially considering its size. The humpies down here only ran on the odd numbered years, and being only a two year fish, most of them weighed 4 to 6 lbs.—maybe slightly heavier on fish entering the river towards the end of the summer. They would let them through the racks at the hatchery, giving them access to the upper river. The first part of the run, with a few starting to show even before the first of July, would move upstream at a pretty good clip since the river usually carried a good amount of water at that earlier part of the summer. You could find a comfortable place with good visibility to sit and watch, and a steady parade of salmon would move by, ten, fifty, maybe quite a few hundred in a minute. Day after day. After the first few weeks it slowed down but there would still be humpies moving into the river in late August and September. The river would be full of humpies from well above Two Forks to the mouth of the river, with these later fish generally spawning in the lower river.

Since there would occasionally be a few late summer chum in this river and others, this is likely how the occasional chumpie comes along. It's interesting that neither chum or humpy fry spend much time in the river after emergence, and that they are the only two species that frequently interbreed. Probably not all that frequently either, because you see many southeast Alaska streams with good runs of pink and chum occurring at the same time. I mentioned that the humpies were mainly an odd year fish in Washington State, but seiners have told me the "square" years provide the better runs of pinks in southeast Alaska, although every year can see good numbers of them.

Chum, (dog salmon), usually favored the lower portions of the Dungeness and as well as the occasional good shot of late summer run fish, there would be thousands of them, almost every fall. Other rivers like the Skagit and Nooksack have good runs of upstream chum, as well as lower river spawners.

I forget the year, but one fall quite a few went up the branch I mentioned earlier, that got bulldozed closed. At least several thousand up there and I imagine lots more in the lower river. That's the only year I remember any volume that far upstream. The chum might return as small five pound fish, or some would weigh well over twenty pounds, and I remember that those fish were on the small side. Their average weight in most streams will run from 10 to about 14 pounds, depending on which river. The fry spend virtually no time in the river after emerging from the gravel and their time in the ocean could vary from three to five years. They picked up the nick name (dog salmon) because they were the main food source for the sled dogs in Northern Alaska. The Eskimos would dry them during the summer and have them stacked like cordwood for use during the winter. I've heard them called "calicos" too.

I've talked enough about the cohos in the Dungeness, so no use going over it again. Except, if I haven't mentioned it, at one time the Dungeness was a really great coho stream. There really needs to be someone watching what takes place along our rivers. Each stream seems to have an area that is especially productive in terms of good spawning grounds and the area from Highway 101 up to the power lines was that area in the Dungeness. It should never have been compromised like it was. So that's a bit more about the Dungeness. To me it was a magical stream.

Now there's a move to get the dams, or at least the lower dam on the Elwha River, removed. This was Ernie Brannon's favorite river and I think he would have been very pleased if it were to happen. Then again, considering todays circumstances, who knows what he'd have thought? I know if he were around today, he'd be working with his kid on the engineered stream projects.

More likely than not, this dam removal thing is just some tummy rubbing to get some politicians some northwest votes, as well as an (instead of Snake river dams) project. It is one area though, where not too great a pile of money could be spent to regain some perfect habitat for wild king salmon. I don't know where there's a better river to improve because most of it is in the National Forest or the National Park. Also, the strain of king salmon in the river is some of the best, a fall run king, some of them getting to be quite large.

If the lower dam were taken out, it would open up seven miles of river up to the dam at Lake Mills. Over two miles of this seven would be what is covered by Lake Aldwell and I don't know what the situation would be there. After all these years there must be a tremendous amount of silt at the bottom of the lake. Imagine the salmon and steelhead stream the Elwha could be if both dams were taken out. This would throw another twenty five miles of river into the system, not to mention some major tributaries.

If the money was spent for dam removal and to address whatever silt problems or other conditions that might arise, what would the Elwha Indians do? It's hard for me to forget what I saw on the Dungeness, after the Boldt Decision. I sure never saw anything that looked like restraint. As long as the Boldt Decision is in effect, the salmon picture in Washington State will be stifled.

Now I hear on the radio that they're going to take out both dams on the Elwha in 2008. How about that?

# Chapter 20
# The Waves

There were eighteen of us, making half hour circles in front of Snipe Bay, on the outer Baranoff Island coast. Eighteen being about ten too many for comfortable fishing, I had been wondering about a change of address. Then, after considering who else was here, there might not be much else around, short of a half days run somewhere. There had been a few fish off and on all spring, here at Snipe, and I'd keep going back and stay a day or so, until boredom got the best of me, and then move up or down the beach to some other hot spot. Then after a day or so of darned little, back to Snipe. Most of us were probably wondering about this better address, but it was going to blow, and the harbor in Snipe is a dandy in a real hard southeaster. Most of the time.

A light breeze turned into a stiff, gusty wind and broken clouds had become a deep gray, approaching a sort of bluish color to the south. Some of the guys started pulling gear aboard, and before long the channel up to the harbor had a stream of boats going in to anchor for the night. A few of us stayed out, thinking of maybe a few more kings after the gear had thinned out. I definitely wasn't going to be able to anchor in my favorite spot in the corner, where a waterfall would lull me to sleep. That would be one of the first spots to go. By the time we got in to drop the hook there wasn't any room along the little shelf that you normally anchored on. Worse yet, the wind wasn't doing it right. It's pretty hard to tell what you'd do in storm force, or more, wind conditions on the south end of Baranoff Island, because the wind doesn't always do the same thing. Especially out of the southeast. This is the case in a lot of other spots in Southeast Alaska. Usually it stays southeast in Snipe, and being anchored against the steep hillsides and cliffs, the wind blows by way above you. However, in a hard southeast blow I've seen it scream out of the bay from the northeast several times, and on one occasion it maintained steady strong winds from the west. When this happens, the wind velocity is usually quite a bit stronger than the southeaster that is the true storm in the area. You can look up and see the cloud cover tearing by from the southeast, and down on the surface you're getting your lips blown off from some other direction. The trouble is, you can't really bank on it doing any one particular thing, and this makes picking a harbor really tough. I've always thought the summer storms were more likely to maintain their true direction than those occurring at other times of the year. This, not just with velocity in mind, because I've seen a few dandy storms in July and it can blow your hair off in August. Anyway, that has gradually become my opinion.

So here we were, eighteen of us in Snipe, with the wind funneling out of the bay from the northeast, and eighteen being about ten too many for comfortable anchoring, especially in this kind of wind conditions, I and a few others had dropped the hook out in the deeper part of the bay. The boats on the shelf were pulling against the slope of the beach, so they were fine, but further out the bottom was flatter, with no good edge to pull against, and not very good holding ground. We dragged anchor, re-anchored, dragged again, and decided to go up to Sandy Bay where there might be a little better conditions. The New Day and Triad were going up there too, so I fell in behind them and we ran up the beach with the wind now blowing offshore, 70 plus mph all the way up, not just funneling out of the bays as I'd expected. Running in close to shore, it still made for a comfortable ride.

We met the folks on the Sailfisher II? III?, just as we were entering the bay. He was just coming down out of the bigger arm and called on the phone telling Denny and Bruce not to go up in there. "It's picking up water and blowing it higher than my mast." He was going back over to the small arm where he said it was a lot better, and when we got there and anchored, that seemed to be the case. We were all in a dandy little spot, not too far down the channel. I'd used it as a summer anchorage, although never in bad weather, but it looked fine. We hit the sack, thinking how smart we were, and about twenty minutes later the wind is screaming out of the west, and everyone's dragging the hook again. One thing most of the south Baranoff harbors have in common is a soft mud bottom. The holding ground in most of them is about equally poor, so what it takes is to find a spot where the wind doesn't blow as much, with fairly good holding ground.

240

There's a spot back in a little bay south of Snipe, but it's kind of small. The best is behind the Island in Little Branch, but I'm not about to go all the way down to either of these spots now.

The Triad was the inside boat, and he had pulled in to where his anchor was pulling against the hillside, so he was in good shape. The Sailfisher and New Day picked up and started moving further up into the small arm, so that gave us lots of room and I decided to stay put. I had used the same drill that Bruce was using many times with the Camelot, with the anchor pulling into the slope at the edge of a hillside. A little scope on the gear and you were in fine shape. There wasn't a lot of room against the beach here though, and with the Elusive being so much heavier I felt better about keeping further off the shoreline. We spent the night running up into the wind, almost to the other side, drop the hook, and leave the machine running so I could jog on anchor into the stronger gusts.

It would smoke, (blow water off the water) and with the moon lighting up the clouds you could usually see the gusts coming at you. Even with jogging on the anchor to take the strain off the gear, we had to pick up and reset a few times. I stayed on watch, BS'd on the radio with Bruce now and then, and would get Ken up when we'd plowed our way across the bay. Then we'd pull up, re-anchor and try it again. The wind finally died down, and the next morning it was 20 or so southwest but the ocean was still too sloppy to fish. We went over and looked around the big arm and just took the day off. It had been a long night, and we were thinking tomorrow we'd go up and try Whale Bay.

It was better the next morning, but still a strong southwest surge coming in, and the wind seemed to be holding at about twenty, southwest. There was a lot of commotion right in front of Sandy, as the big southwest swell echoed back into itself, and it made for a confused, miserable slop. Once we got out of the bay we headed straight out for a few minutes, and it was obvious that the program would be a slow speed ride up to Whale Bay. I'd start angling up and out, after we got outside all this craziness in close, and gradually work our way up to where we could almost slide before it, into the bay.

Outside of us, about as far out as I could see, I noticed what seemed like an awful lot of white water in one spot. There was lots of uneven ground out there, but you could get over most of it with 18 fathoms of gear out, and this looked like it was much further offshore than that. I kept watching out that way and pretty soon I saw it again, breaking over quite a wide area. Trouble was on its way, and with the southwest swell coming straight at the beach, we would have it to deal with before long. I wondered if we turned right then, if we could get back inside before it got in. We would have had to make a 90 degree turn to port just as we went in, and I was afraid it was too close and might catch us quarter stern or in the trough just as we were almost in. It was already bad enough in there without that. I yelled at Ken to close the back door, square away quick, and come up and take a look. We were ready for a sloppy ride when we came out, so in seconds he was in the wheelhouse, watching this thing come at us. You'd still see the top come crashing down pretty often, and it was close enough now that you could see that it was really a dandy.

I slowed the boat down to barely steerage speed, which was still more than I wanted to hit it with. We didn't have long to wait now, and my mind was racing through every possibility that might happen. We had plexiglass over all the windows and had tested it considerably over the years, so I doubted that we'd punch out any windows. On the other hand, this wasn't going to be just another green one over the bow. I already knew I'd never seen anything like it. There's always a big hole in front of the really big waves but this was something else, to a point that we were going uncomfortably downhill when we went into it, and at the moment of impact it was like hitting a wall, green against the windows, lots darker in the wheelhouse, and tons of water over the bridge. I thought I was pretty well braced, but between falling off, and the impact, and then getting slammed against the console, I wound up on the wheelhouse floor. Admiral Singhose, being a real hero, stayed on his feet. Even after the wave has gone through, you have a sluggish feeling boat as it pushes its way up to clear itself. There was a waterfall where the ladder comes down from the bridge. The back of the boat has been completely under water and it takes a bit before it clears, but before too long the Elusive was moving free again.

No window casualties, except that later I could tell that the plexiglass that covered the ones across the front of the house were distorted. Plexiglass over the windows is strong medicine. Half inch lexan is even better. Ken had closed the back door, so we didn't get any more water inside than what had squirted through around the doors. At first glance everything seemed okay. Ken went out on the back deck and saw that the pole on the port side was hanging back, quite a bit. When rigging the poles, most guys use a metal collar that bolts around the pole, and the tight wire, fore and aft stays, and stabilizer gear, all attach to this collar. We used to drill through the pole just under the collar and put a $\frac{5}{8}$ bolt through, double nutted, so the collar couldn't slide down in heavy weather when a lot of strain would be put on the rigging attached to it. This time, the strain put on my stabilizers was enough to bend the ⅝ bolt down on each side, enough that the collar could slide down over the nut and bolt head. It had ruptured the wood in fairly new poles to do this, and the 48 foot poles that I use are nearly 6 inches thick at the point that the collar attaches to the pole. That's power! These were the big metal and wood stabilizers with a 50 pound lead sawed in half and bolted together at the front to make them dive.

When I put them on, a year or two earlier, I started using the collar to attach the rigging to. It's a two piece circle with flanges on each side, so you can bolt it together around the pole. Each side has a tab welded on in the center, and you hang the stabilizer from the bottom tab. A cable that floats in the rigging on a block, that rides on a forestay when the poles are up, goes in the top. When the poles go down, these cables, tied into the mast on each side, makes things absolutely rigid, which is what you have to have, towing these large stabilizers around. The flanges on the collar don't quite close on the pole, so there's room enough for the main fore and aft stays to attach around the bolt on either side. The two haul ups attach separately on the pole, the bottom one double blocked just under the cross tree.

I used one inch nylon as a shock absorber, from the pole to a large swivel that ran about four feet above the water when the poles were down, and then ⁵⁄₁₆ chain down to the stabilizer. To take the back strain off the poles, I ran a poly line from the top of the swivel to the front of the boat and when you were running this would pull tight as the stabie line pulled back and would take a lot of strain off the pole. Our main concern now, was to go slow speed up the beach to keep the strain down on the haul up lines. When the collar was pulled down the pole, the cable backing up the stabies was no longer tight and with this size of a stabilizer in the water, in these conditions, it didn't make sense to see how much the poles and rigging could stand. We would have had to go slower anyway, with the sea conditions, but now it was real slow. We felt that we had got off easy.

A few hours later we were at the back end of Rakovoi Bay, one of the arms in Whale Bay. There would be no surge back here and we could lay the pole down flat to the water to work on the rigging. Water had come down the housing for the exhaust stack so a few buckets full of hot fresh water over the alternator had everything happy in the engine room. Our troll gear in the stern had taken quite a stirring up too, so we spent the afternoon there, getting ready for the next day. When we got to town we would bore through the poles and collar and put the bolts through the collar instead of under it. We would never slide another collar but it would be new pole time, next winter.

So by that time, 1979, I had fished for over twenty years before running into one of these troublemakers. You take lots of water over the bow, and everywhere else, but in terms of force or volume, these waves aren't in the same department with the stuff encountered in normal sloppy weather. If a boat has a weak point they'll point it out and even if you're pretty squared away, they can still tear you up.

A few years later my youngest son Chris, and I were fishing winter kings up in Whale Bay. The winter season was almost over and the day before had been a better day than we'd been getting. We tried the same area the next morning without much success and had moved up further into the bay. Teddy on the "Ginger" was the only other troller in the bay, but there was a big cruiser from Sitka that had been running around, apparently running a few shrimp pots and sight seeing over the weekend. We had all anchored in Kritoi Basin the night before, and it blew southeast, so we were up and down, checking our position all night. Poor holding ground in the basin, too. Now the wind had gone down to 15 or 20 southeast and we were feeling pretty good about the situation. We only had a couple fish for the morning, but they wouldn't bite much till the afternoon tide anyway. With the weather coming down and an occasional spot of sun, it looked like a nice day.

I heard the guy on the cruiser call the Sitka Air Station on channel 16, the VHF emergency channel. He was about half a mile from North Cape and was taking on water. There were two on board and they intended to get in their skiff and "get out of here."

North Cape is at the ocean entrance on the northwest side of the bay and can really be a rotten place. I yelled at Chris to start getting the gear aboard. I'd stay at the phone for a minute and try to get a more definite position from them, as the cape sticks out into the ocean in such a way, as to make half a mile from it cover quite a bit of water. The ocean had to be sloppy after last night, and I didn't know how a skiff would make out. It would be nice to be able to run right to them instead of a lot of looking around. He had told the Coast Guard that they were leaving, so I figured it must be filling up fast. I called and asked for a direction from the cape and got " we're about half a mile from the cape and we're getting out of here, now!"

I went back to help Chris pull the rest of the gear, and we pulled the stabilizers to make better time going out. You didn't need them fishing back in the bay except

244

that they helped slow the boat down when fishing only a small amount of gear. We were back in the Great Arm, so it would take us a while to get out of the bay. Teddy had heard the call too, and I saw him come steaming out of Rakovoi, through the slot into Kritoi Basin, and then pop out of the Kritoi Basin entrance.

There didn't seem to be as much slop as I'd expected, but its hard to tell in southeast weather till you get further outside, especially on the flood. We went out more on the north side of the outer bay and Ted cut across towards the middle, from the other side. It was good enough weather that I decided to cut between the breakers and the cape and at least have it checked out in close, on the first pass. Maybe they had cut the corner and were half a mile up the beach from the cape. There was no way of knowing.

We had company now too, as a Coast Guard helicopter had come down from Sitka. I called him and told him we had seen nothing in the bay coming out, and he told us that the boat was just around the Cape from us, apparently no one aboard, and that they were going to go up into Necker Bay and check out both sides. I told them that we had seen them in Whale Bay over the weekend, and that they had been towing what looked to be about a 14 footer behind them, as well as having a smaller skiff aboard. They asked about possible protection in Necker Bay, and I suggested Yamani Cove as it was more in line with the wind direction and wasn't too far up in the bay. They could have slid before it and gone in there, but it didn't seem likely to me that they would go into the bay beyond that. Then again, you never know how familar someone might be with the area. I didn't know anything about these people. I asked the chopper how they'd come down from Sitka and they said, "pretty much down the outside beach." The beach, if you can call it that, is dozens of Islands, sprinkled with hundreds of rocks, all the way from Sitka Sound to Walker Channel.

I told them that we'd run to the boat and run a course from there to the entrance to Walker Channel. They had what looked like a good enough boat that they could have run before it in no more sea conditions than there were, and once inside the channel they could run up through the islands, all the way to Sitka Sound. Coming down the outside, it would have been nearly impossible to have seen a small boat going up the inside channels. Also, they may have missed them in the ocean, as there had been snow flurries going through all morning, none of them lasting long, but it wouldn't take long for the chopper to get by something.

Ted called and said that one boat should be enough, now that the helicopter was here. Being alone on the boat he wouldn't be very effective anyway, and there was only a small area to cover on the ocean. He'd be in Still Harbor, which is at the south entrance to Whale Bay. He'd leave the phone on.

When we got to the boat we pulled in close, but couldn't see anyone. The runabout was gone, and they had obviously "got out of there," so we headed for the entrance to Walker Channel. We had to stop a few times for snow flurries, as they cut your visibility to almost nothing, but once they passed, you could move along and see pretty well. We didn't want to chance going by anything in a squall.

The wind was down to around 15 southeast, with a big southwest swell running, but if they had ran for Walker Channel they should have had easy going. This was still the first thing to check out, on the chance that they hadn't made it up into the channel. This whole area can be hairy on the ebb, but it was flooding now, so once inside they should be fine.

We spent most of the time on the bridge, and by the time we got down to the entrance to the channel the only thing we'd seen was another coast Guard helicopter. Then another snow squall, so we hugged the stove and coffee pot for 20 minutes. As soon as it cleared, we would go back up, outside the rocks to Necker Bay, and then make a course that would split the area between the beach and our original course.

Now the tide was starting to ebb, and the wind was picking up from the southeast again, so with the current from the two bays pouring into the ocean, the southwest swell had picked up considerably. We didn't see either helicopter, so I gave them a call. No answer.

When we got up a little further off Necker Bay we started running through a lot of debris that was washing off the sinking boat. We decided to take the skiff aboard and found it awkward, with the swell and an ever building wind. It was held down on one end by a bunch of stuff wrapped around its line. When we finally got up off Guibert Rocks we came up on the boat which was sinking stern first, and not too far from going down.

I called Teddy and asked if he'd heard anything, and no, he hadn't. Red Raleigh, on the Stamsund, called and told us they'd found those guys, running along in their skiff, up by Goddard Hot Springs. Apparently one of the helicopters had made a pass down the inside channel and spotted them. They must have called the other chopper on another frequency and we hadn't heard, or maybe while we were on the bridge? Red and I talked for a few minutes, and I remember saying that I couldn't believe the ocean was no worse than it was for all the wind that had gone on the night before. That's the sort of thing an Irishman shouldn't say.

We watched the Winterhawk go down and then started back up towards Whale Bay. We still had tomorrow to fish, and I figured we could get up there in time this evening to make a couple passes at prime time on the tide. The further we got up towards North Cape the more the wind came up, and I had slowed down, and then some more. We'd have to go well outside the breakers instead of hugging the cape as we'd done on the way out. I've had enough grim rides around this place that I'm sort of paranoid about it. When it wasn't good weather I'd give the cape at least a mile of clearance to stay more out of the echo and shallow grounds in close. Right now the conditions weren't too fancy, at least 30 southeast, with the tide ebbing into a big southwest swell.

When we were nicely past the cape I called Ted and told him where we were, and what we had in mind. We'd started angling over to the south side, and as soon as we got a little lee we'd throw out the gear and fish on into the bay. There would be time for a couple passes, and that would be the day. I told him we'd go into the basin to anchor up. He said to call him when we got further into the bay. "Then I won't worry about you and I can shut this thing off." The further I moved down in front of the bay, the worse it got.

We were taking quite a little water over the bow, but you could still look ahead for a moment, in between. When I first saw it, it was well ahead of the boat, about 200 feet away, and the ocean was going crazy. There was an enormous sea coming from the southwest, across this southeast slop I'd been bucking into. It was falling off, like it will when you're walking along a beach with a big surf running, and it made the slop that we'd slowed down for, seem like a ripple in comparison. Looking through the front windows I could see that it was way, way, higher than the wheelhouse, and seconds later, looking up at it out the side doors window, I could see that it would be above the top of the mast. Now the tip of the trolling pole was in the wave, so that it looked like there was a fire hose aimed down at the boat. Even If I had reacted immediately, I still don't know what would have been the thing to do. All of this took place in a few seconds.

When it hit the boat it sounded like we were inside a cannon. The noise of the wave, combined with everything that was being torn loose or was airborne in the focsle, engine room, cabin, and wheelhouse was deafening. I had dropped down behind the door just as it hit and was slammed against it, and then I was sort of weightless as I went across the wheelhouse floor and was slammed into the wall on the other side. Chris had been laying down in the stateroom and wound up on the wall. When I got on my feet I was standing on the wheelhouse wall and could lean against the floor but couldn't get footing on it, and we had to get out of there. Water was still spraying in from around the wheelhouse side door and made getting on my feet all the harder.

For the first few seconds it was gloomy, as I'd had no lights on, and I was sure we were sinking. I reached up and grabbed the wheel and tried to pull myself up by it, but the hunting, back and forth motion of the auto-pilot wouldn't allow that. I finally got a handhold on the corner of the alley way leading back to the galley and had just started pulling myself up towards it when I realized I was on the floor. The boat had suddenly sort of righted itself. We still had a horrible list, and when I looked out the back door, the stern was down so far that it looked like we still might go down. While the boat was on its side and still on the auto-pilot, we had turned over a hundred degrees to port from our original course, putting us more or less in the trough from the southeast sea, and on the stern from the swell, and heading more towards the small arm of the bay. I punched it (full power) and in 20 seconds or so, the boat started feeling freer, and soon we could see the stern. When it cleared, I slowed down and turned back into the east.

In case there was ever the need, I'd told the kids what to do if they had to make a "Mayday" call. What frequency, Mayday, Mayday, Mayday, This is the Elusive, position, what's wrong, how many aboard. Then if somebody answered, they could get into any details, or what they intended to do if it looked like they might have to leave in a hurry. We even had a card taped to the wall to tell them how, in case they might be excited during a bad time. While doing some work in the wheelhouse, I'd taken the card down and hadn't put it back. Now I called Ted on the frequency we'd been using and said, "Mayday here, Teddy." So, when the pressures on, a card on the wall might help. You'll have plenty on your mind anyway. I told Ted we'd just taken a wave over the boat, where we were and that we were pretty tore up, and I still wasn't sure how bad off we were, or that we could still make it. I said we would head right at the entrance to Still Harbor which was where he was at. He said, "I'll be right there."

Chris took the wheel while I went into the engine room. I had switched the pump on, and now I opened and closed a combination of valves that would pump the engine room. Then I got the hydraulic system going so we could use the 3 inch tyee deck pump for the hold. We stopped the boat long enough to pull the stabilizer and other rigging and pieces from the broken pole, aboard. Some of the pole had come aboard with the wave and some of it was still dragging. It had broken in five pieces, but the port pole was still intact. You could hear something was in the wheel, but it didn't matter right now, just as long as we kept going. Now I took a bit off the course, still heading for the south shore but angling more into the bay. Past experience said that the wind would drop by about half before we got into Kritoi Basin, and right now that sounded good. We saw Ted come out of Still Harbor and he followed along behind us and tied alongside after we'd anchored, just inside the Basin. He'd been thinking ahead and brought over hot fish chowder and a pot of fresh coffee. We got warm inside while the pumps ran, and we surveyed the damage.

When the wave hit, it had taken out the two windows above the sink in the galley. When the boat had been slammed down on the other side, the two windows at the galley table were taken out when the port side of the boat hit the water. Water had gushed in hard enough on the side the wave hit that it had tore out a cabinet on the back wall by the sink. It had also tore the table loose, on the other side of the galley, and had broken the light on the ceiling, above the table.

We needed to go down to check out the fish hold and also to bring up a shovel for scooping out the back of the house. A piece of the broken pole had jammed into the halibut checker at the side of the hatch, and up under the overhang at the back of the bridge. It was jammed in tight enough that it took considerable bashing to drive it out. This was across the front corner of the hatch cover to the fish hold, on the side that the wave hit, and was the reason the boat didn't go down like a rock. I hadn't had the hatch cover tied down. Apparently the piece of pole kept the hatch in place long enough for water pressure to take over, and the force of water secured the pole and hatch. Or like I told Chris, "God is saving us for something much worse."

By now, the fish hold was pretty well pumped out, and aside from having to re-ice all our fish and re-stack a bunch of bin boards, it was in good shape. Not much to go wrong there. We still had a big list, so I moved leads to the starboard side to level up the boat, while Chris started bucketing water out the back door. When the water level finally got down, he took to the shovel.

On the Elusive, the doorway from the back deck into the back of the house was 14 inches above deck level. The lake Chris was working on was in the back of the cabin, and the raised floor at the back of the house only allowed an eight inch deep lake, above the floor. A nipple at deck level, through the back wall, with a valve on it would have been a nice thing, or better yet, just a nipple on through, into the fish hold or engine room. The water was under this floor and behind the walls, clear up to the wheelhouse. He would be shoveling off and on, for hours. Ted had started a project of closing the back windows up with some visqueen, and I got the oil stove sponged out and started again, so there would be some heat. After going through something like that you have a hard time getting warm, even with a dry change of clothes. With the stern down so far, the bow had stayed high, so we had taken practically no water into the focsle. Likewise, most of the clothing drawers in the stateroom had stayed high and dry.

Ted finally talked us into getting some rest. He said he'd go fishing in the morning but would be back in to see how we were making out. So—we went to bed, glad to be alive, but so numbed and tired that we resembled a couple zombies.

Our plan the next morning was to get the boat ready to run to Sitka the following day. We spent the morning getting stuff back in place and secured till we could work on it in town. While I was in the engine room, I came across the one thing I still can't believe in this whole incident. (other than the wave) We have a 400 gallon fuel tank on each side of the engine. They are identical, about three and a half feet high, and each has three angle irons welded to the top, running fore and aft. These are for securing machinery and equipment to, and they also make a dandy spot for securing boxes for storage. On the starboard side, next to the back bulkhead, I had two square plastic dishpans that fit perfectly between two of these angle irons, and I kept some spare hydraulic motors and valves in them. One of these motors was lying among the stuff on the port tank. It had been thrown across the engine room, behind the engine, to land on top of the opposite tank and those motors and valves are heavy. It's over six feet between the two tanks. There was a big gouge in the lagging on the engine exhaust system, that was above the level of the top of the tanks by three or four inches. The valve that did that was in the bilge along with most of the rest of the stuff that had been on that tank. I know how hard the boat was hit, and the "weightless" feeling I'd had as I went across the wheelhouse floor makes me think that the boat was thrown, or carried, pretty far on the side of the wave before it was dropped on its side. I still can't imagine the oomph it took to get the motor from one tank to the other, but then the further the boat went over—the less actual distance horizontal-wise between the tanks. At some point, things fell off to the port awfully fast.

Later that day while working on the bridge, I noticed that the brow of the bridge was caved in along the side the wave had hit, and the side door to the wheelhouse wouldn't budge. When we got to town we turned the boat so that the door was to the sun most of the day and about ten days later we used oil, wedges, and pry bars, and gradually got it open so that we could remodel it. Apparently the house had done a little flexing, too.

The only thing we lost in the way of electronics was in the stern. We had a plywood box bolted to the hay rack that the gurdies and the trolling blocks were attached to. It was bolted to two supports running up from the deck, two feet apart, and the ¾ inch plywood side was still bolted to the supports, but was broken in two in the middle by the force of the wave. The rest of the box, holding a fathometer, deck speakers and gear, was gone. Two plastic spoon buckets, each with an aluminum bucket inside them, had been shoved across behind the trolling pit and were crumpled together between the side of the boat and the trolling pit, as if some giant press had jammed them in there. It took some more bashing to drive them free. The small skiff that belonged to the cruiser had been tied on deck and would have been a lot happier if we'd left it in the ocean.

If anyone had been on deck, they'd either have been crushed against something, or been washed overboard. Luckily, Chris had laid down in the state room, because I'm not sure he would have survived if he'd been at the galley table. The flow of water that came through the windows was directed more towards the back of the galley which would have been where he sat at the galley table to do his schoolwork. A lot of stuff that had been in the galley, even under the galley table, we never saw again.

That afternoon we put the skiff in the water and went ashore to look for another trolling pole. We used thick 48 foot poles, but any tree we found was too big at the butt to be useable. Your best bet is to find a place where they've logged and the little trees have come in thick, or occasionally there will be a slide or blow-down area where they've come back thick and tall. Also, hillsides where they have to reach up for light can produce a long, straight pole. Anyway, we couldn't find a good enough pole, but the time in the woods had worked its wonders again, and by the time we headed back out to the boat our frame of mind was very much improved. Nature is always the best tranquilizer.

We headed for town the next morning in pretty nice weather, still a big southwest swell running, with a 15 mile southwest breeze and a comfortable ride. Of our six fuel tanks, the only one that hadn't guzzled some water through the vents, was the big middle one in the stern. It vented into the starboard side tank. They all ran into a big settler, prior to hitting the first filter, and I'd drained

251

fuel off the bottoms of each before we left the basin. Even so, when we started moving with the swell, we noticed some fluctuation in the fuel pressure gauge, so I left Chris at the wheel and went down and drained more water off the settler. For now, our fuel problems were over, and we could wait till we got to town to change filters, one of the nice things about an extra adequate fuel system. By the time we ran up the beach and into town, any doubts I had about the Elusive being okay, were gone. It would be fine.

So the odd wave is liable to find you anywhere on the ocean, but this particular neighborhood has treated me to the only two of them I've ever seen. The first was huge. I still have trouble understanding how the last one could happen, or that we survived it. It was more than two of the first one. Whale Bay, especially around North Cape, is a spot people should really be aware of, in anything beyond moderate weather. The tide is almost never on your side in southeast weather, because on some stages of the flood it runs south from Necker. While we're at it, the tide runs pretty strong on the flood all the way down to Ommaney, from Whale Bay and you can get a good ebb most of the way back up, as long as you stay reasonably close. If it's running against you, move out a bit and you'll notice a difference. It's pretty useable. I'm thinking of tidal flow, not ocean current. I don't understand it either, but it's there to use.

I've already mentioned the echo or bounce back at North Cape. It's twelve to fourteen fathoms right up to the beach, so a pretty decent sea or swell can hit the beach before it gets turned around. This can really turn the area around North Cape into a washing machine, and its worth remembering that on the ebb this condition will exist quite a ways further out from the cape, than on the flood. In good weather you can go between the cape and the breakers, but in any slop at all this shouldn't even be a consideration. Stay on the south side or in the deeper water in the middle of the bay if you're going in with really poor weather. Make sure you are far enough to the south, if you are going in the bay, that you clear the spot where we got hit. It's more towards the center of the entrance, slightly outside, and shows three soundings on the chart of 19-26-29 fathoms, moving inshore, and if you run back and forth around it with your recorder, you'll run over several walls or bluffs, as you move in. A big swell, or one of these odd waves comes in and has nowhere to go but up. Chris and I just happened by at the wrong time, when one of these devils was going through.

You don't think of twenty some fathoms as something that is a shallow ground breaker, but then I guess shallow ground is relative to how deep the water is around it, and in this case you can practically spit into 68 fathoms from the end of the reef, and to the south it's half a mile into 180 fathoms. When it's blowing out of the south, with a really big lump running up and in, you might not like to get between the reef and the deep water. I guess I'm running this subject into the ground but it would be time well spent if it makes a difference to someone.—Maybe you—Especially if you have gotten used to the nice gradual slopes that are the shoreline off so much of the Oregon and Washington coast. The nature of the ocean floor off Southeast Alaska needs to be one more thing to consider during poor weather. In poor conditions this is a haywire spot! Alaska's coast has many of these spots.

I'm still intrigued by the floating, or weightless, feeling I'd experienced between the first impact and when the port side was slammed into the water. The port pole didn't break, and the only hold down being a buckling stiff arm against the side of the wheelhouse, I think the pole had to be speared into the water rather than slapped down on it. Otherwise it should have broke. Then the boat turned around the pole, while on the auto pilot, before the pole finally got out of the water. I think the Elusive was thrown quite a bit sideways and I'd liked to have seen it—from a helicopter.

When we first went out, I didn't think of it as poor conditions. If I had, I wouldn't have considered taking Chris out there. Remember, it was nice enough

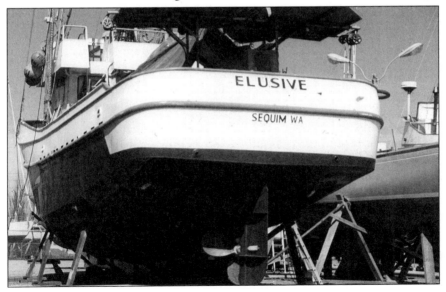

*High and dry in Port Townsend*

that the guys on the cruiser got into a fourteen foot skiff and ran before it, up to Walker Channel. The conditions changed. Prior to getting hit by that "odd" southwest wave, the conditions we had with the south-east slop were something we moved around in quite often while winter fishing.

There's no reason not to have the hatches tied down in ''Any'' weather. I didn't. Ted heard my mayday call, but he was close. No one else did that I know of. I talked to a few guys in Sitka about it, and they all agreed that the antennas, being solid to the boat, would have been at such an angle with the list we had, as to have put out only a poor signal at best. One antenna broke off, but not the one for the phone we had used to call Ted.

The best help you can get is the things you've done yourself, before it happens. E.P.I.R.B.s (Emergency position indicator rescue beacons) weren't mandatory yet, then, and there seemed to be a lot of bugs. They're built to float free if a boat sinks from under them and one of those might have been nice, bugs or not.

If the boat happens to be sinking, up in the wheelhouse might be a nervous place to get out a distress call from. Undoubtedly, a lot of distress calls don't even get sent, because for one reason or another, someone can't get to the phone. I think a VHF phone just inside the cabin, that you could reach from the back deck, and kept on Channel 16, the emergency channel, could make a big difference when the chips get down. The cabin, or just inside it, might offer a little protection and even if it didn't, at least you'd be a lot freer than up in the wheelhouse. Along those lines, it would be nice to see the loran or its repeater from the back door or, window. Survival suits should be accessible from the back deck. Ours were in a locker just inside the back door, reachable from the deck. The self inflating life rafts weren't mandatory then either. We didn't get ours until they were, some years later. We kept a twelve foot aluminum skiff on top of the bridge or on the trolling pit cover.

Two of the guys from Petersburg had separate experiences with fire, so there can be more than one reason for a phone on the other end of the boat. One of them had talked to me about where I fished in the spring, with so little help available if anything went wrong. I spent the next five seasons fishing off Washington, and sure enough, the first spring he found himself in the area we had talked about. Our conversation was one of the things that flew through his mind while he was putting a fire out. I don't know if he did or not, but it seems like a fire extinguisher you could grab before running inside might be a good idea. Or drink a lot of water.

One of the really nice things about the Elusive was that the engine sat way higher than on most boats. You could put a five gallon bucket under from the front to change oil and this big bilge made it nice, because you could take a few hundred gallons of water into the engine room without compromising the ability of the engine, or the bilge and hydraulic pump, to function. Even so, when I went down to throw on the bilge and hydraulic pump, it was getting close. We had taken an awful lot of water down the exhaust stack and through the air ducts on each side of the wheelhouse. Another thing that helped, was that our bilge was always clean. A lot of people have got into trouble when they couldn't pump because their bilge pump got plugged with crud.

To get the 3 inch Tyee deck pump going with the hydraulics, I had to go down into the engine room and throw the belt on the hydraulic pump. This was awfully primitive. An electric clutch with the switch in the wheelhouse or better yet, behind the house, or both, would be the way to go. I always kidded myself that it was a reason to go into the engine room and look around, but in the worst of conditions you might not want to go into the engine room. But you do need to go into the engine room and take a peek around on a three hour schedule. It only takes a minute and could be some of your best spent time.

The one thing I might harp a little more about is moving up or down the beach, from Cape Ommaney to Sitka Sound. When it is really rotten, (hard winter type weather), you're better off going in on the flood, at Whale Bay, Necker Bay and Walker Channel. Not even considering Snipe, Sandy, or Cameron Pass, makes good sense to me. Going into Little Branch on the flood is good, and you'll have a good southeast anchorage. The echo in each of these other three spots can make unbelievable sea conditions and by the time you find this out, you'll wish you were somewhere else. If someone is just moving up the beach, with no intention of going in somewhere till they get up towards Sitka Sound, it just makes good sense to stay in the deep.

When we got to town, there was weeks of work getting the boat patched up for the rest of the season. When we went up on the grid we would see what the noise in the propeller was about. Each fluke looked like someone had pounded across the tip with a heavy hammer, a couple hundred times. We looked at the stabilizer chain, and a couple feet of it was pretty much the worse for wear. What had apparently happened was, minus the pole, the stabilizer line hung from the stiff wire from the mast, to the collar, nylon, swivel, and the 5/16 chain down to the stabilizer. With the boat on its side, the stabie chain wrapped around the boat to a point that the tip of the prop flukes found it. These are heavy wood and metal stabilizers, with a 50 lb lead bolted to the front, to make them dive. I've always wondered since, if one of the lighter, all metal ones, would have allowed the chain to loop on a fluke.

So, the Elusive started healing up. Before too long it would be ready to tackle the season, and after the season ended, most of the winter was spent tearing everything out of the cabin and wheelhouse, down to the metal deck and the urethane foam that was sprayed over the metal on the walls. When I'd originally finished the house I'd used styrofoam under the floor as a sound barrier. I'd never do that again! The styrofoam soaked up water over a period of time, and the wet foam, framing, plywood flooring, and siding, started smelling like a winery. We had a mess.

When we put it back we used sheet lead for a sound barrier between the framing and flooring in the cabin and wheelhouse. The engine room is right underneath the house and the lead proved to be an excellent sound deadener. We didn't put any other kind of insulation around the framing this time.

I wasn't done with the wave, either. I started dreaming about it at night, sometimes two or three times a night, and it made for mighty poor sleep. I was fine during the day, no obvious signs that I was any more bats than pre-wave times, but it must have been bothering me to have shown up in my sleep like it did. The dreams weren't always of the wave, but they did always deal with the Elusive sinking. I usually had a gallery seat, about a hundred feet out, but not always. Then I would be aboard, with nothing ever going right, and never able to move beyond slow motion. And the Elusive wasn't the fine 54 footer that I rode around on all day. It would invariably be an old hulk, or some "Little Toot" type, but tougher than nails, and always put up a real battle before they finally gave up and went down. One night a "Little Toot" type refused to go under and it's ordeal went on for what seemed like forever. I'd finally had enough and jumped up on the rail, using the trolling pole as a lever, and with my feet against the side of the wheelhouse, pried her on over, and down. I woke up laughing, and after that I seemed to get a better nights sleep.

# Chapter 21
# There's a Bear

Seeing the occasional bear was always a highlight while fishing in Alaska, and with so much of the trolling taking place close to shore, sometimes you'd see them on a daily basis. It depends where you're at as to which kind you might see and if I were to say there were all black bear in some certain spot, I could very well be wrong. I can say that I've never seen a black bear on Baranoff, Admiralty, Kruzof, or Chichagoff Islands, and that I've never seen a brown bear on any Island south of Chatham Straits.

So generally you don't see brown and black bears in the same spot, but then there's Murphy Cove. Situated on the mainland beach, just above Cape Spencer, the bear population there seems to be about evenly split. I've always seen bear when we were there, but I never did see a black bear on the beach when a brown bear was in sight.

There's been lots of inter island swimming over the last thousands of years, and I've even seen quite a bit of it in my little blink of time. It would be quite a swim from any black bear Island to any of the brown bear Islands, but from the mainland to either one or the other? Could be. Will one type cross with the other? I don't know, but I can't see why not. I've heard of bears that were rust colored but these weren't in Alaska. They were in areas common to black bears and of the same size, so apparently there's such a thing as brown black bears. There are throwbacks in a few other species too.

We had stopped in Elfin Cove, on the way up to Yakutat for a halibut opener, and were visiting with some guys that had flown in on a helicopter. They were excited about pictures they'd got of a glacier bear over on the Spencer side. They were working for one of the big magazines and were using the cove as a base and hadn't been successful at first, but this time they'd connected. They said the bear appeared to be a black bear, but was lighter colored, with a sort of bluish tinge. I don't know what attraction they have for the glaciers, but for some reason they live around them. As for their color, it's possible that like a lot of other instances in nature, their color adjusts to their surroundings.

The only other quirk I've seen color-wise, can do without an address. Cal Olds and I were trout fishing when Cal caught my attention and pointed downstream. A sow and her cubs were walking upstream towards us and apparently didn't realize we were there. It seemed like they were going to just keep coming, so Cal yelled at them and they stopped, whirled around, and took off full speed downstream. While they were coming up towards us, we noticed that the sow had a white patch on her brisket and one front leg. When they whirled around, one of the cubs had a patch on it's side and rear end. The other cub seemed to be completely black.

On another outing, Cal was one of those lucky people who found a handy tree when rights to the stream he was fishing trout in was questioned. In this case, a black bear, and the stream was full of salmon.

Usually when you see a bear, it's kind of a slow speed operation. They'll poke along, tipping rocks or logs over, getting whatever's to eat under them. They have a reputation for being real fishermen, but the stuff you see on TV has all the non catching parts edited out. Kind of like last nights basketball game on the news. I've seen them in wall to wall fish and they'll miss one, whirl around to get one going behind them, miss it, and chase another upstream till it gets in too deep a spot to catch. There's lots of fish though, and the bears make a good living.

I don't know much about hibernation. Apparently a smaller brain makes for less heat loss while snoozing, so nature has accomplished that over the years. Sometimes you'd see them in the early spring and they'd be working some rock on the beach, and stop and roll and squall like a baby in pain. I don't know what it was all about, but saw it several times. Maybe the empty belly didn't like whatever went down, or maybe they were just playing, but it didn't look or sound, like play. You could hear them over the boat noise at trolling speed. I've been told by people who lived right in the middle of the bear department, that they wouldn't see them for months during a cold spell, and then it would turn mild and they would see them out and about, during the middle of winter.

Some of the guys that were trapping on Kuiu Island in the sixties and seventies talked about the wolves killing bears in hibernation, and I don't doubt it. I can remember there being wall to wall deer on the Island a few years either side of 1960 and by 65 or 66 there was a wolf behind every other tree. That's how it works in nature, abundance of one thing will support an increase of something else until scarcity starts taking it's toll and the cycle will swing around to the other extreme. Severe winters probably have a larger effect on deer and wolf populations than anything else, and there's no doubt in my mind that when the deer count is down and the winter is harsh, certain older and younger bear make easy picking for the wolves.

This reminds me of another story which I wouldn't mention except for its source. Cal was pretty fussy about what he repeated. I met him in 58 so this was sometime prior to that. There was quite a deer over-population out on Coronation Island, to a point that they were semi starved and very small. Probably, in-breeding accounted for some of their condition. Alaska fish and game, or whatever they called it at that time, took some wolves out to the Island, as a test, to provide a little balance. I forget the exact amount, but it seemed like 3 or 4 pair. One of the team that went out to survey the results a few years later, told Cal about it. They only saw deer sign in a few spots on the Island and they shot (or trapped) several wolves to examine them. They were in very poor condition and an examination of the stomachs showed some mussels, and in one of them, some wolf hair.

So that's given me a few hours of something to think about. Would wolves resort to cannibalism? Had this one, or could it have got hair in its belly by maybe licking a wound or chasing a flea or something? Sometimes that hair might come off pretty easy, maybe due to the health of the critter, which the guy said wasn't too fancy.

Another possibility is that the males of quite a few species will kill the young male offspring. Who knows? Decision Passage, which runs between the end of Kuiu Island (Cape Decision) and Spanish Islands, which extend inshore from Coronation, is a spot where I've seen a lot of swimming over the years. Mostly it was deer, but I've seen wolves going for the Kuiu side too. I never saw deer, or wolves, trying to get out to Coronation. Its got a certain reputation. You don't see them getting across anywhere near the Cape because the current carries them on past, which ever way it's running. There's generally enough surge on the Chatham side that they wouldn't make it, but I've seen them well out into Sumner Straits, still angling towards the Kuiu Island shoreline.

The best part of bear watching is a sow with cubs. Your first thought might be to liken it to a dog with pups. The only similarity I can think of is that the pups and cubs are playful. Where the dogs have known many generations of life with mankind and the security that provides, the bears instincts are intact. The dog knows it has been sheltered, fed, and otherwise looked after, but the bear draws from a completely different background while raising her cubs. Their survival will depend on it.

I've only seen cubs fishing a few times and never did see one catch a fish, but I do remember plenty of running and splashing. Their short legs puts their face pretty close to the water, and when they start chasing a salmon up or down some riffle there's a lot of water flying, both from the fish and themselves. Mom always used a little more finesse, but at some point she'd had to learn too.

When they aren't fighting with each other they'll pester mom, but from what I've seen she usually won't put up with much nonsense. We were in the mud hole in Malmesbury one year, and hours of heavy downpour had turned what was normally a trickle into a pretty fair stream. We had put the skiff in and Keith was rowing around the bay, doing a little sport fishing and just watching the shoreline. He had stopped rowing and was watching a sow and her cubs that had just come out on the beach. After a little beach inspection and creek watching, they decided to cross this stream. She went first, with one of the cubs right behind her, but the other cub stayed on the bank. She went up the beach a ways and looked back, but he still hadn't budged, so she moved back to the edge of the stream kind of fast. He could tell she was mad. The stream wasn't very wide but it was pretty swift and held enough water that the cub was nervous about jumping in at the point where she had crossed. She was on one side and the cub was on the other and he'd get down, poised, ready to jump in, and then he'd back off. Keith could tell there was a lot of encouragement going on, but the little guy couldn't gather up that last bit of nerve it took to make the big plunge until mom jumped in and headed for his side. In he went, and although the current moved him downstream a few feet, he made it across fine, and quick.

Our only fairly close incident with a bear was up in Rodman Bay in Peril Straits. There was a closure for salmon trolling, and Keith had a chance to go with his buddy, Knut, and his parents on the Lillian S. They'd be packing halibut for the co-op. Chris and I decided to go up in Peril Straits, fish a few crab and shrimp, and maybe some trout fishing. The first afternoon up there, we anchored in Appleton Cove and threw out a crab pot, before rowing up to where a stream entered into the head of the small bay. The spot was typical of so many other estuaries in Southeast Alaska, in that there was quite a bit of open meadow or grassland that the stream would run through, before entering salt water. The size of these areas would vary, sometimes an acre or two, or sometimes fifty acres or more. Some, you would find fairly smooth going and others would be very uneven, with washes and occasional small Islands of trees. Each was a spot where you would see Canadian geese in the spring, and deer or bear almost anytime.

This place was wooded within a hundred feet of the creek on one side, and there was quite a little grass flats on the other side. We had the trout pole and the twelve gauge, some hot dogs, marshmallows, and had built a fire for a mini-cookout before hitting the trout department. A noise caught our attention upstream, and we looked up in time to see a big brown bear splash once in the middle of the stream and then nearly out on the other side. His speed and size were enough for us. In not too many seconds we were rowing back out to the boat, wondering about going over into Rodman Bay the next morning. We had been told it was a good trout stream, but at this time of year it would likely be full of dogs (chum) and humpies just as the stream in Appleton Cove was. We hadn't made it past the estuary holes, but there had been hundreds of salmon and that meant bears.

Rodman Bay is a long channel with a sort of bulge at the head of the bay where two streams dump in. We had seen three bears on the way into the bay, and there was a good sized bear on the beach when we got up to where we would anchor. We wondered about going in at all, but the tide was out, leaving quite a little room between any cover and the water, and the bear we had seen on the beach had disappeared. We decided to go in and fish the estuary holes that would cover at high water, leaving the skiff within a few feet of where we were fishing. No cooking hot dogs today. That bear over in Appleton Cove was probably still drooling. I'd watch while Chris fished, and we would have plenty of time to get in the skiff and out into the current if a bear headed our way.

We spent a few minutes fishing along the edges of the salmon schools, but in the estuary holes they're always moving around a lot and it doesn't make for very good trout fishing. I decided to move up to the first hole at the grass line, which seemed to be a more likely spot to catch a few cutthroat. There was a little knoll next to the stream, so I left the thermos close to where Chris was fishing and climbed up for a little more visibility. There was a dry wash that left the stream about a hundred yards above us and came down through the grass at about a forty-five degree angle to our left, before running out into the bay. What looked to be the same bear we'd seen earlier, was walking up the wash, just above the beach. I hadn't seen him when we started in, so he must have been laying in the grass. I told Chris there was a bear, and where it was.

We were about sixty yards from him and I said it quietly, but he either heard it over the noise of his walking through the gravel, or he got a whiff of us, or maybe he already knew we were there. He came up on his hind feet, looking right at me and moving his head from side to side to pick up our scent. Then he dropped down on all fours and ran hard, up the wash. He wasn't coming right at us, but almost. The wash angled just above the little knoll I'd started up, and in seconds he'd gone out of sight, behind it.

I had climbed about halfway up before stopping to look around, and I stayed there now. He could easily have caught me before I got to the skiff, if he'd wanted, and I had it in my mind, that if he came at us at all it would be at one side or over the top of this small hill. Sid had told me a good many times over the years, " if it ever happens, wait till he gets close. Ten or twelve feet. You'll only get the one chance anyway. Make it good. Break em down in front." So with both sides of the twelve gauge full of double 00 buckshot, I thought I had a good chance to stop him if he came over the hill. He didn't.

I glanced back to see that Chris had moved back to the skiff, pushed it out, and was standing there ready to leave in a hurry. No bear. I backed off the hill carefully, and out to where Chris was. When I got there I realized that I'd gone right by the thermos, so I told him I'd go back and grab it, and we'd get out of there. I don't know what kind of a value I thought this thermos had but I went back and retrieved it and backed up to where Chris was, one more time. From here we had lots of room, and still no bear, so we decided to wait a bit and see what happened. In a minute or so the bear raised out of the grass, just above the point on the hilltop where I'd been. If he had headed right for that spot, I'd been within twenty-five feet of him the first time, and not much more than that when I'd gone back.

That was enough. We got in the skiff and moved out into the bay and the bear came down on the beach and for about twenty minutes put on the craziest show we ever saw. He'd get up on his hind feet and look out at us and, just as he had earlier, he'd swing his head from side to side trying to get our scent. Then he'd take off and run across the beach, maybe fifty or a hundred yards, no rhyme or reason as to how far or which direction he would go. Each time he stopped he'd stand up and look out at us, even after we'd got back out to the boat. He crossed the stream several times, and while he was doing all this, he never did get more than a few hundred feet from it. Obviously, this whole thing had to do with territory, and we had stepped into his. Especially, when it was full of salmon. We gave up on the trout fishing for that outing, and headed back to Sitka. We still had some time on the closure and maybe there would be a softball game or something.

While we were still living out by the river, Trish took Chris and Deann for a walk, back behind our property. Deann wasn't quite two years old, which would have put Chris at about eight. They had just put some fresh gravel down and Deann spent a lot of time falling down and getting up, but she didn't have far to fall and the unpacked gravel was soft. The road went back about two hundred yards and then made a turn to the right. They had gone another hundred yards past this when Trish noticed some bushes shaking, down in this little wash. They moved ahead a little so that they could see what it was and a bear poked his head out to see what they were. Trish picked Deann up and started running back towards the house, and in the soft gravel managed to fall down a few times, on top of her. Chris was running along, just ahead of her and he'd look back and say "he's right behind you, mom!" She couldn't run any faster in that kind of footing and was completely exhausted when they made it into our garage. The bear could have caught them any time it wanted to, but seemed to be satisfied ambling along behind them. Within a week or so, someone saw her at the edge of the woods with two cubs. Maybe she had decided to take it easy with another mom and her cubs.

So if you surprise a bear or happen into its back yard like we did, or come up on a sow and her cubs like Trish and the kids did, its hard to tell what might happen. Usually they'll run away. With very few exceptions a black bear will run. A brown bear might not. Sometimes they are crazy, and when that happens, you either need to be a good tree climber if there is one, a good shot with a pretty worthwhile weapon, or awfully lucky. Running might be an option if you've got something to run to, but remember, they can outrun a race horse for a short distance. A shot that might easily drop a bear when he's calm, might not kill him for twenty minutes when his adrenalin is up, and he could be killing you while he's dying.

If you're in their territory a little planning ahead might save a lot of sorrow later. I made one mistake after another when we went into Rodman Bay, starting with going ashore in the first place. Going back after the thermos, even if it was a Christmas gift, was dumb. Forget all the family friendly stuff you've seen on TV, when you're planning an outing in a brown bear neighborhood. If you get an opportunity to wrestle with one of these soft, friendly fellers, there are three probable results.

He'll hit you with a front paw, probably hard enough to kill you. He might bite you, usually in the head or neck, and if you're still on your feet, one swipe with a foot can tear your guts out. Then there's possibility 4, an in depth version of probability 2.

So, like I said, do a little thinking before you go into an area where you know there will be bear. Especially when there are salmon in his stream. You will be the intruder.

# Chapter 22
# Longlining

In 1984 we finally became longliners. Part time, because that's what fishing was becoming. Trolling, our bread and butter, had long since become a part time fishery. Very few people made their living in just one fishery anymore, or in just one area. State and Federal Fisheries people played with the term (overcapitalized) like a new toy, suggesting that there was more money invested in individual boats and in certain portions of the fleet than was warranted. They kept coming up with regulations that maximized the cost of harvesting the fish, minimized the quality of the product, and decreased it's value. The ratio of waste in fish handled, was extreme. When you have to equip your boat to participate in three to five fisheries to make a living, you become overcapitalized.

Letters sent to our elected officials concerning fisheries matters would be passed back to state or federal fisheries personnel, and you'd receive a nicely written letter, generally suggesting that the conditions you'd described weren't really the case at all, and that "our statistics show"—. There were a few though, that seemed very aware of the situation, and had some well thought out ideas and solutions to what we both thought of as solvable problem areas. These people never seemed to advance very far in the departments. You'd also get a letter from the senator or representative you originally wrote to, dripping with concern and promises, "to continue to do all I can to ensure that our fisheries remain strong into the future."

It seemed that the best bet was another fishery—maybe longlining, or tuna or crabbing? Or the same old fishery—but in another state. Or two. So, like hundreds of others, we became longliners. Equipping boats for some of the fisheries can be expensive, and the big winners at that time were the gear stores and their suppliers. I'm still glad I did the longlining bit and I wish I'd gotten into it years earlier, but I guess that then, I hadn't seen the need to. As well as being fascinating, it can be exciting, is always hard work, and there's always that anticipation of the next set. And I liked the fish you caught, on a plate and otherwise. Many of the rockfish might be described as ugly, especially head on, but most of them are absolutely beautiful fish to look at.

Our efforts in longlining were for rockfish, halibut, and black cod. Each fishery is different in the depth fished, type of bottom set over, and different ways of setting up the gear. I liked handling all the species, and was impressed with the quality potential of the product that could come out of the bottom fish hook and line fishery. I especially liked the fact that, properly managed, wastage would be minimal. Except for the derby atmosphere in the halibut and black cod fisheries, I really enjoyed it, but I liked fishing rock fish best, probably because there was no derby involved. At any time that we fished rock fish, we were the only boat working that immediate area. Probably in the wrong spot again.

Longlining is labor intensive. There's quite an investment in time and dollars setting the boat up, and whether you're snapping on, or using the conventional system, there's an enormous amount of time spent, setting up and maintaining the gear. We did both, so I'll tell you a bit about each. Keep in mind that I'm not any kind of an expert, and that there are lots of different, probably better, ways of doing things.

*Hi! Come on aboard*

We're going to make a halibut set using snap on gear. You pre-select the spots where you want to set, looking for certain types of terrain and other conditions that you want to set gear over. You have your loran readings lined up the night before, with alternatives in case you've got some competition on the spot. The first thing you do is throw out a long aluminum or bamboo pole, weighted at one end, with a flag on the other and a short line leading from the pole to another line tied into a large, red, air filled buoy bag. You tie a buoy line to these, long enough to reach bottom plus enough extra scope, so as not to pull the buoy under in strong currents. In very strong currents in deep water it sometimes requires an extra float or two, tied on in tandem.

A small midline float is attached part way down to take any belly out of the bottom part of the buoy line, and keep the buoy line off the bottom. Then the buoy line and the ground line are tied together, and coupled into a short line attached to the anchor. You put out a good anchor. Something you could anchor a 30 foot boat with. You want it to stay put. As you drop the anchor someone takes a loran reading and writes it down. If something goes wrong, you might have to haul from the top end of the set and knowing the exact spot the anchor went down could make a big difference when you're looking for the flag with a big slop running and poor visibility.

So—Top of Set # 1 buoy # 7, your depth and position. Then you start out, hopefully going with the current. It's better to make a three mile set than three miles of gear, set in a three hundred yard stretch. We kept our ground line on a large spool that held around 14 miles of gear and the buoy line was in tubs or garbage cans. Using sprockets and chains and a 47 to 1 gear box,

*Chris and friends*

267

we had built a level wind system that worked well and this ground line, usually ⅜ or 9/32 nylon or one of those new synthetic lines, started leaving the boat in a hurry as soon as the anchor hit the water. The gear involved a 42 inch long, heavy cord, called a gangeon, and a strong hook and snap tied into loops at each end. Hundreds of these were baited in washtubs, coiled for fast removal, and these were snapped on at intervals as the gear went out over the stern. It varied, but for halibut, lets say at 4 fathoms apart. Occasionally mid- weights were snapped on to get a better lay to the gear and if we noticed a change in the bottom we put extra weights on to keep the gear from clothes-lining across some deeper area. The line was fed out through blocks and a heavy metal ring, and went across the middle of the trolling pit and over the stern. One of us would stand on either side and we took turns snapping on. The third crew member would keep the tubs of baited gear coming and have the anchor and buoy line ready at the end of the set.

After awhile you get to the end, tie on the buoy line, anchor, midline float, buoy, flag, Set #1 Bottom, Buoy #4, depth and position. With the position written down you should be able to find the buoy and flag later with no problem. Having the buoys numbered helps avoid some miserable confusion. You want to pull the gear back in the right sequence. A brightly colored flag helps in poor weather and radar reflectors on the flag pole are nice if the visibility is poor. Mini strobe lites are nice for finding a set at night.

When you start hauling,—flagpole, buoy #4 because you want to pick up into the current,—this, in the ocean and assuming the current stayed constant. If you're in inside waters the tide may have changed since you set)—buoy line, anchor, and then hopefully you catch a halibut. It seemed like we always got a few nice fish right after the anchor. The line comes up through a block hanging over the side and then over to the hauler which is a pair of big metal discs, hydraulically powered, with a heavy, tapered, wedge between them to peel the line out. The hauler is usually positioned towards the middle of the boat, and the person at the rail has controls to run the hauler, steer the boat down the ground line as it comes up, and for forward and reverse and throttle on the machine. Once the line is through the hauler it either is fed through blocks onto a drum or falls from the hauler into tubs.

The person running the block unsnaps the gear as it comes up, hanging the gear on racks and gaffing any reasonable sized fish aboard. A two, or more, man fish gets a pop from the pistol and whatever manpower is needed brings the fish aboard, into the halibut checker. For awhile we used the manpower department, but later rigged a boom winch to help coax the big ones aboard. Some of them get over three hundred pounds round weight, and considering how tired you get anyway, the winch made good sense. Nice for putting a bunch of big fish into the hold, too. We had one man "in the checker", unhooking and moving fish and gear racks, and helping with the bigger fish. The rest of the crew was cleaning fish on the hatch, putting them into the hold, and icing.

Running the block was fascinating. You had to stay on the gear, steering the boat down the ground line, keeping it just ahead and barely outside, as you moved down the line. Generally you saw movement on the line to indicate the

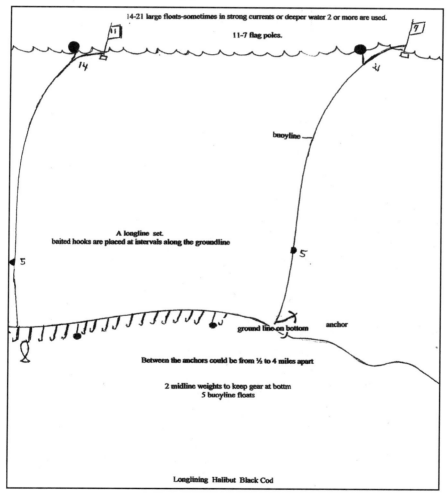

14-21 large floats-sometimes in strong currents or deeper water 2 or more are used.

11-7 flag poles.

buoyline

A longline set.
baited hooks are placed at intervals along the groundline

ground line on bottom    anchor

Between the anchors could be from ½ to 4 miles apart

2 midline weights to keep gear at bottm
5 buoyline floats

Longlining Halibut Black Cod

arrival of a nice fish. Sometimes enough so that you were saying, "get ready," before the fish came into sight. Sometimes while fishing rockfish you couldn't seem to "get over" the line, way off to one side, and then another. Soon a bunch of orange would come in sight and your problem would be a bunch of bloated yellow eye that had floated the line. Nice to get back on the gear, but you hoped it would happen right away again. And again. All this, along with adjusting speed, unsnapping and racking snaps, gaffing fish aboard, and untangling snarls in the gear. Sometimes you got some dandys. (snarls)

Using conventional gear, the big difference in hauling is that the line feeds over a roller mounted on the rail instead of through a block from a davit, and then over to the hauler where the line is peeled off and falls into a tub. The person at the rail doesn't have to unsnap each gangeon to run the line, because the gangeons are tied into the ground line. Also, the gear goes over the stern much faster when you're making the set, using the conventional system. When using conventional gear you use a soft lay line so it will fall like spaghetti from the hauler into the tub. The gear is carefully placed in tubs when it is baited, so that when it goes out it goes out smoothly and in order. As the tubs of gear go out, the ends of the "skates," (lengths of gear, about three to a mile), are tied together, and a large amount of gear can be set in a much shorter amount of time compared to moving the boat ahead slowly and snapping each gangeon onto the mainline.

*All but the big ones go up in the net*

The depth might vary. I never intentionally set on halibut much over 200 fathoms, but caught them while fishing black cod in well over 300 fathoms. Then again, we caught them in harbors in four fathoms of water. Then again, once more, we caught two fifty pounders in over three hundred fathoms off Biorka Island, while fishing for cohos. Each was on a coho spoon and both were caught at about 15 to 20 feet deep. So halibut aren't always on the bottom. Some of the better halibut trolling I've ever seen was in a couple areas in Frederick Sound, and they were

*Camelot—Easter Sunday 1965—Bella Bella B.C.*

from 10 to 35 fathoms in water that was between 45 and 50 fathoms deep. I was telling one of the old Petersburg fishermen about it, and he said that they were likely fish that were moving.

On the trip I just mentioned, fishing cohos off Biorka, we were at the outside of a small fleet of boats and had good weather, not much wind, and good visibility. I happened to look outside of us and saw a wisp of steam or vapor and naturally, I thought a whale had just blown. Nothing unusual there, but in a few minutes I happened to be looking that way and noticed it again, but nothing that looked like any whale. Now it had us interested, and at least one of us was watching all the time and we never did see a whale blow. Just steam coming out of the water. This went on for ten or fifteen minutes and we never did see any mountain tops come bubbling up, or any periscopes either. Sid said maybe it was a halibut spouting? Who knows?

271

Most of the black cod fishing is done with conventional gear and generally in deeper water. Three to five hundred fathoms, give or take either way, and the rockfish that we worked on were generally in the 10 to 60 fathom range, but when fishing halibut a few times, I got the impression deeper might be better, next time we tried for rockfish. You always got a variety of rockfish while trolling but until we started longlining I never dreamed there were so many species. For bait, small pieces of herring were the usual for black cod and rockfish. Herring, octopus or chunks of larger fish worked well on the halibut. The hooks were much closer together for black cod and rockfish, than for halibut.

An I.F.Q. (individual fisherman's quota) system is now in place for the halibut and black cod fisheries, allowing fisherman a portion of the allowable catch determined by past catch records. The idea was to try to reduce the chaos that existed in these two fisheries when the fleet was turned loose for pre-scheduled, short openings. One goal was to reduce the wastage of fish, which were often a by product of the rules in effect prior to this new system. Breakdowns, injury, and weather that can change in minutes, left too much fish on the gear after the allowed fishing time ran out. Now fishermen can combine their quotas while fishing other longline fisheries, or perhaps bring in the incidental fish caught in

*The Elusive in Lituya Bay. Sid is anchored over against the beach. New growth at the base of the hill is where the wave went out of the bay in 1958.*
*Photo courtesy of Gail Stromme.*

the troll fishery, and whatever else, at least they can pick their weather. It should make for a better product, allowing the availability of fresh fish for an extended time each season, and less cost in producing the pound of fish, so of course, more profitability.

On the other hand I'm certain that some deckhands are having trouble finding work because some boats now choose to hire less help, fish slower, less expense, and more profit out of the trip. It should provide safer conditions to fish in, but boats and lives continue to be lost, and I guess I might as well get this over with.

It seems like only yesterday, but over twenty years ago the Camelot went down with the loss of two young lives. Then, a few years back, we were told the Elusive had been lost, again with the loss of another young man. I've heard a few versions or theories on what happened, but at this point—I don't really know. Trish and I felt a deep loss when hearing of each of "our" boats sinking, and our hearts break for the families of these young fishermen.

As hard as it was leaving home to head north, and I can tell you that several times I wondered about going back, into the second day out, I know it was worse for Trish and the other wives and mothers left at home. We had the luxury of knowing what was going on. If there happened to be a storm at home they worried, no matter that they knew we might be a thousand or more miles away. They are the ones who go from window to window, wondering, hoping for, and dreading each phone call when you're a day or so late getting in. With so much wrapped up in some of the longline openings, they knew at least as well as we did how important a successful opening was.

These loved ones at home don't deserve that one phone call, or the knock on the door from a close friend. I don't know any answer, other than training and training and training and preparedness. Your best help when the chips are down is still the preparation you've done yourself, before you leave the dock.

# Chapter 23
# The Rules We Fish By

Each year you would take quite a few king salmon that had been released at some earlier point in their lives. Generally just a small hole, or occasionally the corner of their mouth would be torn. All but a very few are in good condition, many of a size that indicates they've had a good year or two in the ocean after being released earlier.

Since the people regulating the fisheries seemed to have you releasing one species or the other most of the time, it came on the fisherman to develop his own system for releasing them and avoiding the species you didn't want to catch. Sensible management would have gone a long way towards solving this problem. A combination of types and amounts of gear allowed, barbless hooks, smart area openings and closures instead of senseless ones, and to every extent possible, elimination of one species only, or ratio fisheries, would have been a good start. This could have put better numbers of larger salmon, in better condition, through the various fisheries or back to the rivers. It doesn't make sense to turn a fleet loose (sport or commercial) in an area that is saturated with immature fish, or another species of salmon they must release. At least, not without specifying gear restrictions that would help avoid them. Like the people managing the various fisheries, not all the people doing the fishing have the experience to know what's going on. Most of it doesn't come out of a book.

At certain times of the year, some areas are full of small, immature salmon. During those times, any salmon fishery in these areas, sport or commercial, would be unjustified. I asked for short, temporary closures in some of these areas but we never got them. Moving outside of these areas a few miles usually worked wonders. If they aren't going to have temporary closures, sensible gear restrictions would sure clean up this situation by increasing the size of the fish handled, while handling much less of tomorrows catch.

After I'd gained enough experience that I could figure on catching a few fish, I started comparing anything I could think of, from one season to another. Things like when fish showed where, and on which stages of tides. I was always looking for anything that might show a pattern. A note in the log, on a chart, or in your mind, might make a big difference in what you did a few years down the line. Steve even kept graphs.

One thing that showed up was that every four years would be a cycle year, with good returns of king salmon during those years.—66—70—74—78 and so on. Bear in mind, that this reflects my own thoughts and has nothing to do with whatever the fleet might have been doing. I doubt that on some of those years, my catch would have impressed anyone but myself, and I can also remember some of the odd numbered years as being what I thought were good seasons.

In 1982 the Alaska troll fleet was stopped from taking king salmon in a silver only fishery, that most trollers consider should have been one of the best king salmon seasons in many, many, years. The Washington troll fleet was shut down completely at that same time, with exceptional numbers of king salmon available, coast wide. Alaska fisheries personnel said that the fleet could have taken another 500,000 king salmon without it making a difference. That would have put twenty million more dollars into the catch for Alaska's troll fleet and at least several times that, through all the processing and related industries, on the way to the consumer. Most of this would then have trickled or washed through the rest of our coastal states communities.

It's sickening when conditions finally get where everyone would have a chance at a really good season and then to have to release them. The Canadians took 2.2 million of these same kings that year and used the figure as part of a historical catch average in negotiations soon after that. Alaska fishermen were stopped at 363,000 kings. Much less than that for Washington State.

It seems to me, that in management of a resource there ought to be some consideration to take advantage of that rare bumper crop. To the fishermen, these are the seasons that allowed the more expensive boat repairs, or for the upgrades of equipment, those that meant profitability and safety in future seasons. Now, for too many, overhauls were put off for another year. Or so. Stretching this, and another year out of that.

Meanwhile, the people managing our fisheries kept getting their paychecks and benefits, and moved on closer to retirement. I've met darned few of them that gave much thought as to what it took to allow profitability in any of our fisheries, let alone, that cared. You'd think it should have been an important part of their education. Establishing seasons that maximize the cost of harvesting the product doesn't make sense when they don't accomplish other goals, like allowing for a good flow of product, and minimizing wastage within the various fisheries. When they miss these goals completely, you get the idea that management of our fisheries is in too many of the wrong hands.

We were accused of wanting to catch every last fish, but how could we want that? No commercial fisherman in his right mind would want the catch to jeopardize future runs of fish. One thing we wanted, and asked for, was a slowdown in the amount of new gear coming into the fisheries. A cap on the number of commercial fishing licenses was long overdue, but those holding the reins wouldn't hear it. In most fisheries, the cost of producing the pound of fish was becoming unreal. Under the regulations we fished by, senseless wastage of one species or another seemed to increase each season, and each wasted fish meant one that didn't go through the various fisheries, or live to reproduce.

Milo Moore was appointed Director Of Fisheries in Washington State under Governor Wahlgren—1945 to 1949, and again by Governor Rosselini—1957 to 1961. In 1988 he made this comment in a ten year resource enhancement plan, recommended to the Washington State Legislature to improve sagging salmon runs. "First—get rid of all the biologists." I think that might have been a bit severe, but maybe a little selective pruning would have been appropriate. I don't know if the term "overcapitalized" applies here, but for quite a while now, I've thought that fisheries management has looked like a boat with all the heavy equipment on top of the wheelhouse.

Trolling and trawling are two completely different types of fisheries. The salmon troller pulls various types of fishing spoons, plugs, and other lures through the water at a slow speed and catches each fish individually—hook and line fishing, using multiple lures on each of one to eight lines. The number of lines varies, depending on the state he's fishing in. The fish are bled, cleaned, washed and re-washed, and then iced down, or frozen for delivery.

The trawler tows a long sock like net, held open in front by two large doors that each sheer to opposite sides. Heavy chain holds the bottom of the net down in front, and without getting too detailed, rollers, chafing gear, winches full of cable that attach to each door, enabling them to fish at extreme depth——or not, all enter into the picture. High tech electronics show them where the fish are at, and large volumes of fish can find their way aboard in a short amount of time. Dropped on an untargeted species, the trawl can do a lot of damage in a hurry.

During the late 60s and 70s there was a fleet of large Russian trawlers working off our coast, in as far as the 12 mile offshore limit. Closer at night if the location and volume of fish warranted it. The target specie was supposed to be hake (whiting) but whenever a good bite on cohos was taking place it seemed like they found you. First, one or two Russian boats outside you, and before dark you would see the plumes of smoke as the rest of them moved your way.

Generally, most of our fleet would move into the 20 to 25 fathom depth to anchor. By that time these Russian trawlers would be outside us and would work the area all night and although I'm not saying they were targeting on cohos, there's no doubt in my mind that a "Lot" of cohos took boat rides to Russia. Salmon and hake eat the same feed and there's no way that large amounts of cohos and king salmon, as well as the other three salmon species, and steelhead, avoided being scooped up, as these large and very powerful trawlers targeted on hake. Or whatever. If our own smaller and much less powerful boats caught salmon in their trawls, how could these larger boats with larger nets, towed at a faster speed, not get them?

This was during the detente era, and for some reason we couldn't seem to get a thing done about it. It went on for a few more years, and then the 200 mile limit was established. We thought we were finally rid of the Russian whiting (hake) trawl fleet. We replaced it with our own boats, generally larger boats of a size used in the Bering Sea crab fisheries. From these, the tow was transferred to the Russian mother ship, brought aboard and processed for delivery to Russia.

It's been years now, since any significant numbers of troll caught cohos have been allowed off the Oregon and Washington coasts. Washington's troll fleet has been all but eliminated and Oregon trollers fish kings only, four leaders to a line, to avoid handling cohos. The Canadian troll fleet has been reduced to a small fraction of their peak numbers.

So who's catching the cohos? According to the U.S. Observer database—Appendix A—Source NMFS, NWR—the six year average of cohos taken in the whiting trawl fishery from Cape Blanco—north, 1991 thru 1996, was 366 cohos PER YEAR.—FOR THE COMBINED FLEET. Of these 2196 fish, 1697 were taken in 1995. The process mode was separated on the readout—1 = catcher-processor,

2 = mother ship.[9] I'm told the number of U.S. trawlers fishing for the mother ship varied, and generally ran in the low teens. This number of boats pretty much compares with what I saw during the late 70s and 80s and what others have told me in more recent years.

I know of another hake (whiting) west coast trawl fishery that more than doubled that number, (2196 fish) of incidentally caught salmon in a day and a half fishing time. I have no way of knowing the ratio of individual species, but fishing in that general area, what came up on our gear was kings and cohos. Their fleet was one catcher processor and a couple smaller boats.

The data from NMFS was from Cape Blanco - north, and the other fishery I mentioned is at the north end of the Washington coast, but cohos and king salmon are in either area. Large volumes of cohos are still pumped out by our hatcheries and in either area, hake and silvers (cohos) still feed on the same stuff.

I know what I saw while fishing salmon around the Russian hake trawl fleet, and what I and other boats witnessed in years after that, around the U.S. Joint Venture trawl fleet, when it was working off the Washington coast. When trawlers who have spent years fishing off our west coast, and have owned boats that participated in the joint venture fishery, look at these numbers and say,— "that wouldn't be possible," I get nervous. Sometimes these guys who've spent their lives on the ocean have a harder time understanding statistics like these, than someone who's never been on the ocean. No wonder they don't want us out there.

The high seas gillnet and trawl fisheries, our own trawl fisheries included, are decimating ocean fish stocks and in the trawlers case, habitat. Much of the worlds trawl catch goes into pellets, as feed to supply fish farms. The anchovy, mackerel, and other species targeted are a major part of the ocean's food chain. I think that the millions of tons of fish taken annually for this purpose, would be better left in the oceans, alive. Fish stocks in the ocean live from these same sources of feed.

The kill of untargeted sea life is enormous. A good portion of this is tomorrows catch, but the governments of the world, ours included, don't want to hear about it. Our fisheries apparently make good trading stock. Unless the worlds trawl fisheries are confronted there's going to be some "huge" holes in tomorrows fisheries—if there are fisheries. Sometimes you wonder if those holding the keys have something else in mind. Once the trawl is set—it's set. It can be raised or lowered, but the only way they know what's in the net is when they bring it up, or in some cases, when the net fills to the point that it floats to the surface.

Whatever is in the path that the trawl goes through, comes up in the net—dead. Too much has been wasted by the, "make it now—I'll deplete something else, somewhere else tomorrow," attitude. It's not the job of fisheries management to look the other way.

Years back, a resolution was submitted to PMFC (Pacific Marine Fisheries Commission) that said, "To maximize the poundage yield to the commercial troll fishery by minimizing the taking in that fishery of chinook and coho salmon having significant remaining growth potential, however recognize that the desired yield to the sport fishery is primarily in the recreational value of the fish caught, not in pounds produced, and therefore, that optimum value does not necessarily require harvesting only mature fish. (These resolutions weren't law—just recommendations)

The first time through (1972) it didn't pass, but the next year, when it was reconsidered, it did. The spokesman for the three advisors from Alaska voted for, after two of the three had agreed beforehand to vote against passage. A fisheries person from Juneau was spokesman for the Alaskan delegation. Tommy Thompson told me that he and Dick Elliason looked at each other wondering, what the hell goes on here? When they approached the chairman he wouldn't change the vote, so it passed. Lots of complaints and letters, but it still stood.

It sounded good, and in the right atmosphere the conditions within the resolution would have been an acceptable approach, but there were already indications that survival of the ocean troll fishery wasn't any big goal of fisheries management. What did they really have in mind here? I know there was a lot of concern in Alaska, regarding the big federal thumb, which was already locking up some pretty massive chunks of the state. The big buckeroo shouted yes, yes, YES!!—"We'll show you what's good for you" and whatever was left screamed "no, no, Noooo!" Alaskans were beginning to feel like yallerditters without a swamp.

Early in the season a few years later, some of the boats make really nice troll catches on the northern Washington coast. Nice sized fish and good numbers. The next spring that area is closed and the whole fleet is bottled up on the south end. The size of the salmon on the south end was what they usually get at that time of the year, about two thirds as big as salmon from the north end. Less weight per fish, less value per pound, and a greatly increased cost of producing the pound of fish, so of course, far less profit per fish to the fisherman.

The waters of the state known to provide better sized fish during the spring fishery were closed, and the fleet was jammed into an area noted as being more of a nursery area that time of the year. For a troll fleet to make sense, the boats need to be able to move away from smaller fish, while looking for more mature stocks, but now the only option the fleet had to move away from these immature fish, was going in and tying to the dock. It was hard to understand them promoting maximum poundage or profitability, and then setting up this kind of a fishery. Likewise, although this wasn't targeted in the resolution, embracing the terminal area harvesting concept on such a big portion of the state's salmon net fisheries. As hard as they'd pushed to get certain resolutions passed, you'd think they'd have tried to make them work.

It's your vacation, you've been looking forward to going salmon fishing for months, and the first day out, you and your wife have limited on rather small fish within several hours of having put your gear in the water. While getting your limits you released quite a few even smaller salmon. You had heard there were some really nice fish being caught in this area, so you go in and spend the day ashore, thinking of trying it again tomorrow. Next day the same thing happens.

*Chris with his second steelhead.*
*Photo courtesy of Stan Goerz.*

At certain times of the year, certain areas are saturated with immature salmon that will hungrily grab everything that goes by. Some fishermen, probably locals but not necessarily, will be able to get the odd bigger fish while handling much less of these "shakers," but the majority of the gear out there is held by people like yourself who have been lured to the area by advertisements like,—Whopper Point Hot! Limits to 30 pounds.

"Hot," to some resort owners, is lots of people going out in his boats, using his motors and gear, and staying in his cabins at night. Meanwhile, how many thousands of small salmon are sifted through by this fleet of people who are unaware of what's really been going on in the area, and too many who really don't care, as long as they keep biting and they can catch and release all day, or until that big one comes over the side. Who's managing this fishery? The sports fishing magazines or the resort owners?

Since this type of fishery will likely continue to be promoted, remember that the 3 pound salmon you've just killed while releasing it (getting it off your hook), had a potential to grow to full size. By handling less of them, you'll kill less of them! Larger lures, NO flashers, and timing your fishing time to the tides that

*Keith and an Alaskan steelhead*

fish in that area, especially the slack tides, will take less of the immature salmon and really boost the size of the fish you take home. If you're going to fish these shaker patches you'd ought to leave the herring and treble hooks at home, too.

Another phase of this sport fishery has been gaining popularity. At considerable expense, people can fly to areas in Alaska and British Columbia, to enjoy fishing where world class salmon and halibut can be had on a pretty regular basis. It's cost a lot to get there and apparently human nature takes over. When sport fishing newsletters out of British Columbia openly brag about seeing how many large salmon can be brought to the boat in a day, it once again points out how a natural resource can be exploited. I'm sure these guides and their customers will say they've never released a fish that didn't live to spawn, but people who have handled enough salmon on hook and line will know the truth. I don't know how they would deal with this, even if they were inclined to. Joe Bucks has spent a lot to get there and he's going to keep trying for that even bigger one. His guide's wallet likely feels the same way.

*VFC, "a nice fish" and Keith*

When we were kids on the Dungeness the limit was 15 trout over six inches long. The fifteen trout would make a nice meal for three people. On the other hand, the majority of them were small rainbow, and in this portion of the river, would soon be migrating out of the river to salt water. Next year they would return as steelhead.

On the other hand once more, there seemed to be a nice amount of steelhead around at that time, and I liked to eat trout. That was then and this is now and conditions have changed. We kept the dollys, but not for the pan and only an occasional cutthroat made it up to where we fished, so generally the fifteen fish would be in the 6 or 7 inch department. Along towards the late fifties they changed the possession limit to less fish, with a minimum size of ten inches. Depending on the year, I think the number was six fish a day, maybe more. I forget and it doesn't really matter now. If you came into the area from out of state you were likely to read the regs. and think the river was full of 10 inch plus, trout. It wasn't. People would catch and release all day long and maybe not get one of these prize dolly vardens the cats liked so well.

Now it was against the law to go down and catch a nice meal of trout, the only trout worth eating in the lower river unless you happened to get a few cutthroat, but it was legal to stand there and catch and release these small rainbows all day. I fished down behind a guy one day and much of the time I was within sight of a dead or dying rainbow. I wished he could have kept 15 and went home.

I see now that the lower river is closed during the time period that would allow the heaviest catch-release on these small rainbows (future steelhead). Having moved from the area, I'm not sure how long this has been in place, but I'm glad to see it. Maybe not popular, but it's sensible management, especially considering the amount of people who've retired into the area. It's no great benefit to the fish to be hooked, played out, and then released. To make sense out of various hook and line fisheries there's a definite need for careful releasing of some untargeted fish, but I have a hard time understanding these people who can stand there by the hour, releasing one after another. Some people would be happy to take a few to eat and go home grinnin. Too many just keep on catching.

So what do you do? Depending on which direction you might be approaching these things from, you might possibly have other viewpoints on the subject. That's as it should be. If you're pissed off,—Good. You'll be thinking about what I've said and somewhere down the line, the shoe might fit. Maybe a bit snug. When our thoughts balance out, we'll be doing a little better.

If you're thinking I hate sportsmen, don't. I sure do hate what a lot of them are doing, though. If there was ever going to be a turn around everyone is going to have to clean up their act. I used to be quite a sport fisherman, myself. I always thought there was a little extra sport if the season was closed. Outraged? You should look at what is called "sport" fishing through my eyes. It ought to be about enjoying time out on the water, or river, targeting the best available fish for the table, as long as it's not on some extinction list, and taking it home and enjoying a fine meal of fish that you've caught. This, with minimal or no damage to anything else.

Some of those in fisheries management have talked of making the salmon resource, or at least several of the species, game fish. This allows the people who live next to the resource, or those with enough money to get out here, to be the only ones to enjoy them. I've asked a few folks what they thought consumers around the country should do if they wanted a nice piece of wild salmon for the table? "Well hell, let em come out here and catch one." No use arguing with someone like that. I hope the guys on the east coast don't lock up the lobster.

Meanwhile, bit by bit, to where you hardly see it happening, the commercial fishermen, what's left of them, have been slowly pushed to a point where profitability, or hope for such a thing, has pretty much disappeared. But they didn't really put you out of business. You had to quit on your own.

# Chapter 24
# **Whales**

Fishing down in Chatham Straits one spring, I'd gone in to anchor for the night, moving past the outside anchorage to a good harbor at the back end of the bay. Pretty good holding ground here, and much less surge, so this would make for a better nights sleep. When I went on the bow to kick the anchor over, the stench was so bad I could have thrown up. In record time I was back inside with the door and windows closed.

There was a dead whale in the rocks up on the beach and from the smell of things, he'd been there awhile. He was only about 200 feet from the spot where I'd anchored, so with the glasses I could get a really good look at him. He was still pretty much in one piece, but was opened up here and there, and several eagles were taking advantage of this.

At first I wondered if the surge that came back in here might have chafed him on the rocks, but the open spots that I could see were all pretty much on top. To eat as much whale as looked to be gone seemed beyond these eagles capacity, although they were really going at it. Before long the answer came ambling down the beach. I'd never seen many bear in this particular spot before, but right now there was a good reason for this ones presence. You'd see a bear or two on the beaches in the outer bay almost every day and this might have been one of those. He'd probably got a whiff of whale and came on across. He climbed up on the whale and chased the eagles away, and then he spent a little while looking out at the boat. You could see he was trying to get my scent but the wind was wrong. Really! He finally started to eat, but every few minutes he'd stop and that nose would be up, trying to get my scent. He probably figured I was going to come in and eat some of his whale.

After that, if the weather was even halfway decent, I'd lay in the outside anchorage, but some nights, if you wanted to get any rest at all, you'd have to go on up inside. On those nights I wouldn't go all the way to the back of the harbor and the smell wouldn't be quite so bad. I'd anchor up and within five minutes the bear would come down out of the woods and climb up on his whale. When you're lucky enough to get something like that, you need to guard it.

Years later Sid and I were fishing the bays outside Baranoff Island for winter kings, and I had stopped at one of the bays on my way out from Sitka. It was March and the herring would be spawning soon and large schools of them would move into the bays prior to spawning. They were here now. I threw the gear in and in two short swipes at the beach, caught several nice salmon. Sid was in the next bay down and not doing much, so he came up and tied alongside after I'd anchored. The next morning started out pretty good for winter fishing. I had seven nice fish for one short pass, up and back, and was down in front of the harbor again. I had a fish on the gear and was on the way back to the trolling pit to rescue him. There were a few birds outside me so I thought I'd make a long turn back into the bay while the fish was coming up.

There was hardly any wind, so a bunch of splashes in the ocean, outside of the bay, caught my eye. A bunch of killer whales were coming into the bay and were really moving. Normally you didn't see that many in this area but this time would be a memorable exception. I had kind of a bad feeling about things, so jumped into the pit and started the fish up, a little faster than usual, but before long there was a hard lunge on the line and he was gone. That's the only time that I can definitely say that a killer whale took a salmon off my gear.

They were crazy, charging around like a bunch of porpoise will, and where minutes before, my fathometer and recorder had shown constant patches of herring, there wasn't even a blip now. There had been twenty to thirty of them where I was, and at that same time there were pods of them in the middle of the bay and Sid had them across the bay, too. I had never seen them so crazy.

He called and asked me what I had in mind now. We both knew this spot was history but there had been something and we couldn't think of anywhere else we wanted to go. We decided to go clamming and we'd try the salmon department again in the morning. I remember while we were clamming Tammy started growling and the hair on her back was standing straight up. She'd apparently picked up the scent of a brown bear. We moved the clam digging closer to the skiff and the skiff closer to the water, for a quick leave. We kept a close eye on her but she seemed to settle down after the one time.

The next morning we got nothing. Sid called and said he was going to pull his gear and move back down the beach. I told him I'd be right behind him. He called about half an hour later and said to watch, just as you get around the corner. "There's a whale on the beach, way back in the slot, and you can see her back when the surge goes out." Before I got to the first one he called again and said "there's another one in here, same thing, head into the beach and she's up as far as she can get." They both were, and each had got into a spot where it would have been nearly impossible to get at their heads. I couldn't find the first one till it happened to blow, and if it had been anything but very nice weather, they could never have been where they were. Likewise, we probably wouldn't have been in close enough to see them. They must have been against the beach, because when each surge would go out you could see considerable whale. I'm sure there was enough water to carry their weight pretty well but what if the surge got bigger? If the killer whales had attacked them from the tail end would these whales have got on the beach to a point that they couldn't get off? Had they already?

Like most areas on the outer coast of Southeast Alaska, at least below Icy Point, these beaches aren't the nice, sloping sand beaches common to Washington, Oregon, and California. Generally it's solid rock, harsh and very uneven, and that's what it is here. A very irregular shoreline with lots of points and niches and each of these whales had found, or been driven to a spot where they had escaped these killer whales. Sid told me that evening that the killer whale would go after the mouth or tongue on the bigger whales and that was the reason for their position in the rocks.

It's hard to imagine the panic that took place underwater when that mob of killer whales hit the spot where I'd first stopped. They were on the other side of the bay at the same time, too. It's hard to say how many, but at least forty and probably more. There had been one big patch of herring after another, some of them showing solid on the recorder paper for thirty fathoms deep and this over a stretch of beach over two miles long. After the frenzy of those whales took place we never saw one blip on the recorder or sounder and not even a scrap fish on the gear. To see where the two whales were, pretty much tells it all.

The fishing in the next spot wasn't very fancy either, and for the next few days you had to get way back in the potholes to get anything at all. We looked for the two whales when we went out of the bay and they'd apparently got back into deep water. After the commotion when they'd stormed into the bay, we didn't see any more of the killer whales.

We saw killer whales in action again, this time forty-some miles off Yakutat. We were getting in position for a halibut opening and this was one of the few times I remember when the derby and good weather happened at the same time, especially up there. We were almost to where we would set gear and were just poking along slow speed, getting all the last minute stuff ready for our first set. We noticed quite a few dolphin going by the boat, coming from offshore. Lot's of times they'll follow the boat, riding the bow wave, and charging around within a few hundred feet of the boat for sometimes an hour or more.

Unlike the Dall Porpoise, these will frequently jump clear of the water, and when they feel like it's party time they seem to be a lot more flamboyant than the porpoise. But today it was strictly business and they seemed to be going pretty much one direction, meeting us almost head on and putting the Elusive about in the middle of their path. They were in little groups of three to a dozen or so, and there were hundreds of these groups, extending out on each side at least eighty yards. It's hard to say how many there were, but quite a few hundred, maybe over a thousand. They went by for quite awhile. Sure enough, a couple minutes after they'd gone by, here came the killer whales.

Where we had seemed to be right in the middle of the dolphin parade, from its beginning till they had gone by, we were well to the side of the killer whales. They were right on course with the dolphins and were moving very fast. We didn't see that many, probably five or six groups, totaling thirty at the most. Chris got up on the bridge with the glasses and a few minutes later, yelled at us to come up and take a look. No more than a quarter mile from us, five acres of calm water was churned literally to a froth as the dolphins tried to escape these killer whales. Once again, the words that come to mind are terror and panic.

Did the dolphins just happen to aim right at us? They sure could have gone a lot of other directions. Maybe they were trying to scrape the killer whales off on us? We could only see one other boat, and he was almost out of sight. Were the killer whales we saw the only ones, or did the dolphins get hit from another direction, too? Things came to a head mighty soon after they went by us and in an area many times smaller than they were spread over when they were moving.

I've always wondered where all the killer whales went. They used to call them "blackfish" but you never hear the term used anymore. When I was a kid I got to go fishing in the Straits off Sekiu or Pillar Point a few times, and I remember the fishing was always over after they came through. The volume I remember on a few occasions seemed like quite a few hundred and you'd see them from the beach, out as far as you could see. They'd go by for what seemed like forever, on a fast, one way pass down the Straits. Well over a hundred pods was probably a closer amount, and it seemed like most of the pods had 5 or more whales.

I only saw this kind of volume once after I started in the commercial fishery and it was in the Umatilla reef area, south from Cape Flattery, and it was in the late 60s. There were less whales in this group, but still several hundred at least. I know that over time there's a tendency to exaggerate things in your mind, especially with my being so young when I first saw them. This was in my mind at Umatilla, and I gave complete attention in trying to come up with a reasonably close number. If anything, I'd say there were more.

I talked to people who had fished all their lives up in the sound or San Juan Islands, and they had never seen anything approaching those kind of numbers. They talked of 15 to 30 maximum, usually less. Other people who spent a lot of time fishing more towards the outer straits, remember seeing them in numbers closer to what I had seen.

I'm told they are very susceptible to problems caused by pollution, but this difference in numbers seems pretty severe to me. If something like pollution killed that many, why didn't it get them all? I'm not even sure how we know pollution is what's killing them, but fat is supposed to readily absorb poisons and toxins and I suppose there was plenty of each, and more, in the inside waters of Washington State and southern British Columbia.

Why hasn't it had a similar effect on other species of whales? The only thing that I can think of is that the other species don't seem to spend that much time in these inside waters. They sure seem to like the inside waters of Southeast Alaska but those waters are clean, compared to down here. Can the salmon ranching sites be affecting them? Too many boats? Submarines from Bangor? Electrical stuff from subs—sonar—etc ? What else? Who knows? I don't.

How about not taking any more and putting them in some petting zoo! If they are as sharp as I suspect they are, this might have had a far more devastating effect than we like to let ourselves think. Maybe pods of them have simply moved from this area? Killer whales eat salmon if they are around. If they (farmed salmon) are being lost, turned loose,—whatever, in the numbers I've been hearing about, an autopsy of the next dead whale might have some interesting results. These escaped, turned loose,? fish pen salmon might make easy pickings for a pod of these whales.

At any rate, the number of these killer whales isn't what it used to be, and accordingly, the numbers of the California sea lions has exploded along the west coast. Killer whales eat sea lions. Many people in the northwest are familiar with what happened at Ballard locks and a sea lion they named Herschel. That situation compares to a straw in a haystack with what's taking place coast wide. At river mouths and rookeries, where you used to see fifty to several hundred, there are many times those numbers now. Once again, we've lost a balance in nature.

Where the whale in that bay in Chatham Straits was, in behind those rocks, makes it almost impossible that it got washed in there by wind and current. How many times when you hear of whales, porpoise, or dolphin stranded on a beach somewhere, did they hit that beach in a state of panic? Did killer whales or maybe shark put them there?

Trish and Deann came up to join Chris and I for a short winter king trip in Chatham Straits. We hoped what we'd been seeing during the last trip would still be there for them, and it was. First, a few seagulls flying over a spot, a little noise, gradually more of each, and over the next three or four minutes, lots more of both to the point of several hundred seagulls going absolutely crazy, hovering over this small spot. Then the water would erupt as seven or eight humpback whales came straight up together, nearly out of the water, and "Crash" in this near perfect circle. In a few minutes there was no indication it had happened, but it was obviously some part of feeding and I'm sure it was interesting under the surface. Two or three hours later it would happen again. And again.

There's another critter I'll mention here that you don't see all that often, and although they aren't whales, they still get pretty good sized. We saw only one of these in the ocean, off the Straits of Juan De Fuca, and pretty well off the beach as he was along the blue water edge when I was fishing tuna. In the inside waters I've seen elephant seals from Lund B.C., to well up into Chatham Straits. Most of them were in British Columbia, but I've seen three in Alaska and heard of a few others. Two of these were three days and thirty some miles apart, and we wondered if it could have been the same one, since I fished this area off and on for years without seeing another.

Some people thought they were sea cows, as the head of a female elephant seal and a sea cow are sort of similar. The males will get a snout that gets pretty prominent and without knowing this, for years I thought I was seeing two different types of critters. I told one of the deckhands about them, and on a trip north he had his camera laying on a towel on the galley table, ready to go. We are both up in the wheelhouse gabbing and all of a sudden there it is, closer than you ever get a chance for a picture. Both of us run to the window at the side of the wheelhouse to get a better look and then when our brains finally switched on, ran for the camera. By the time he got out on deck it was too far behind the boat and the pictures he got, turned out blurred.

I never did see more than one elephant seal at a time, and that makes you wonder. They seem like they might be on the timid side because I've stopped and drifted on several occasions, and only twice saw one resurface, quite a ways out. As pokey as they are they'd be easy pickings for the killer whale, so maybe they don't taste good to them. You have to think that, for there to be any at all, there must be some reason why the killer whales haven't picked them up.

# Chapter 25
# Getting Worried About My Country

When I was a kid the old guys used to go on and on, "It can't go on like this, it's all gonna come tumbling down." You can just hear the "I told you sos," if they could see where we're at now. But even if it seems like we're testing it a bit, it still hasn't come tumbling down.

Well, maybe a bit, but there's been a few gains, too. I wasn't exposed to much then, except some barn and a herd of cows, or the river. When I was around grown ups, one of the expressions I remember most clearly was—"A guy could get ahead"—doing whatever was the topic of the moment. These people had lived through the depression and two World Wars, and they saw life through different eyes than most of us use now. Remembering that far off look in their eyes makes me wonder if they were really looking ahead or backwards. Compared to what had been, "getting ahead" wouldn't have taken much for some satisfaction and happiness. By today's standards, their hopes were pretty basic. A job or small farm, food on the table, a little something put away, and the families health. Only fifty some years ago. How did we change so much? And sometimes I wonder why?

Some of these people had ground out enough money to get a piece of property, twenty to forty acres or so, and then enough cows to start building a small herd. At that time, for many of them, things were a bit tight and they wondered about the future. There at Sequim, there had been over 300 dairies, mostly 20 to 60 cow herds. Now there's only a few. Somebody told me six or seven. At some point it got to where the smaller herd couldn't provide the profit to justify staying on, and the last few years I was in high school saw an auction or two nearly every week. Some of the younger farmers bought complete herds from those going out of business, and generally this went along with the expense of satisfying upcoming requirements, new milking parlors, pipeline milking systems, bigger milk tanks, liquid manure holding tanks, and so on. Before long, many of the farms were being split up and sold as home sites. Using a couple milking machines and working your way down a line of cows in stanchions, packing the milk into the milk house, and then washing up by hand and shoveling out the gutters afterwards, was soon just another memory.

Now the land was more valuable, and as the cost of holding the land became more expensive, farmers started keeping more cows in a relatively small area, hauling feed to them, and milking many more cows than had been on the farm in years past. This was survival, but at some point many of the farms went over the point of balance. The land can only absorb so much. This gets obvious when you wade in some stream that flows through a farm or get close to a field that has just been plowed and it smells like you're walking through a manure pile.

The nature of farming was changing, too. Not necessarily in dairying, but probably there also, is a situation where farms, ranches, and orchards are owned by some jillionaire who needs a place to shelve some money, not necessarily for immediate profit. Now these farms product is there in competition with the guy who is trying to grind out a profit to keep his place. Where one guy is trying to make it any way he can, the other guy might be aiming at a loss that year or the next. Then his personal situation might call for balls to the walls profit the year after that.

Frequent surplus caused by erratic volume of product, more federal subsidy sucked up, increased strain on the land and water reserves, more fertilizers and pesticides applied, and worst of all, once again we've upset a point of balance. How can an actual farmer, rancher, or fruit grower survive in this kind of an atmosphere? Too often, by becoming so big that he becomes part of the problem. We've gotten to the point that most small farmers have a near impossible time surviving in todays economy, too often, because of things beyond their control.

Say that you have a business in some small town, maybe the bakery or the grocery, or hardware store. The town builds up and some big outfit comes in and is all three of these businesses, and more. Now you can't make it, so you close and get a job working for the big store.

A bigger outfit comes in and in addition to offering any conceivable food or household item, offers a pharmacy, deli-cafe , nursery, lawyers offices, a drive thru psychiatric clinic, cosmetic surgery, banking, and a wedding chapel. Soon you are working at store C, store B having become a bowling alley, bingo hall, and feed store,—all three of which are businesses which had already existed in town.

The shareholders in the corporation that owns 500 store C's are growsing that too much has gone into expansion, and they are dissatisfied with profits and the less than skyrocketing state of their stocks. The board of directors meet and decide to hire this hot CEO who has just turned around a company suffering the same symptoms theirs now is. He comes aboard, flies around the country taking notes in his laptop, and at the next board meeting, informs the directors that what it's gonna take is closing 50 stores, which happens to include the almost new store you are currently working at. In addition, he wants another 2000 employees around the country laid off. Streamline the operation, trim fat, and funnel that percentage of the payroll, along with the revenues from the sales, or rent - lease, of the 50 soon to be closed business sites, into whatever winds the shareholders clocks.

The CEO and a thousand others like himself, who have increased profits, and accordingly, share value, receive "huge" salary increases and bonuses. A lot of directors are doing all right, too, especially considering the effort expended.

Rooms full of people with computers buy the company stock and hold it for minutes, rarely hours, and when their timing is right, their profit per minute is "huge." Their contribution to anything other than themselves is pretty obscure.

The quality of the product, or services, from these 1001 mega corpses start to sag. Soon production and sales have the sags too. Time to get out the scissors, again. The people that worked for these businesses may be someone you know. Some find other work locally or move to an area where work may be more available. Maybe Indonesia. The one big thing they all had in common is that they were all consumers. Soon they are only buying necessities, and the products from a good portion of these 1001 companies are things or services that you don't consider necessary when the going gets tough. Chances are, what will follow is the great chain reaction. So it all gets back to balance.

Don't worry about the CEO's. They've all been hired to lead other companies that are now experiencing runaway sags, into bright new futures. But I do worry about some young family trying to hang onto a third or fourth generation farm. They can't weather many mistakes—their own—or the ones that get handed to them. Likewise, the guy now unemployed, that ground it out in some job for the young part of his life. Working hard and doing a good job might not have as much to do with success as it once did. This tears at the guts of our country.

A monopoly game is a dandy example of balance. Once a couple guys get all the good stuff, going out and playing in the rain sounds like fun. Maybe they should have called it "Capitalism." And don't get me wrong, I'm not against capitalism, but I'm getting worried about what it's turning into. Things like responsibility, restraint, and conscience don't seem to matter in this environment. They are right and their position, or holdings prove it. Getting to the top, no matter how, and no matter what, have become the guidelines to success. And once "THERE"—"I don't wanta quit now, to me this is play, Let the bodies fall where they may."

So often you see a really good idea, with hopeful, dedicated people looking for a long lasting change. They organize, gain momentum, and eventually become a force to be reckoned with. Then, too often, they're taken over from the inside out by people who use them to further their own agenda. They lose credibility because their ranks have been swelled with people who are mad at everything, ones that have forgot the good things they had intended to do, and others that feel the need for revolution.——Or something.

That wouldn't be so bad if they were people willing to take an honest, thoughtful look at the other side of the picture, wanted to make things better, and had some well thought out ideas. Some of the ideas out of the past would be the political parties, the various green—bunny hugger movements, and The United States Of America. Sometimes people lose track of why they're there, or they become so extreme they ruin their cause. Sometimes voting for the best candidate might be better than re-electing someone who's done nothing but run down "that other party," but we re-elect him anyway. The waste involved with partisan politics, one way or another, is one of our countries biggest expenses and it keeps getting worse.

With professional politicians who spend millions of dollars to get elected and re-elected, the money pours in from every imaginable special interest and not many politicians get there without some bills to pay. They vote down term and age limits, limits or conditions on funding elections, determine who will be our Federal Judges, and vote in such a way as to keep the pork rolling, towards their voters or towards the big interests backing their campaigns, because all too often, what somebody stuffed in their pockets enables them to see what's best. We like to think we've gotten rid of the protection rackets that flourished in the 20s and 30s, but now I think it's just changed faces.

Our courts and politicians aren't something we ought to make jokes about. Our country has some serious problems and too many of the people elected, or appointed to address them are coming up short. In the absence of responsible, dedicated politicians, our bureaucracies have free reign to do whatever their personal wants and agendas dictate. They bury their actions, or lack of them, in a mountain of paper that will intimidate or impress our politicians to the point that not many questions get asked. Our bureaucrats are likely there till they retire and the politicians spread enough pork around to keep getting voted in.

Too many potential voters say the hell with it, or vote straight party line, and too many people who might make good qualified candidates for some position, wouldn't consider running for office because they don't want their families and themselves to be subjected to the press. A smooth ride for the large special interests to select and promote their boy from the leftovers.

I'm getting really worried about our country! As I get older, I'm beginning to wonder if maybe those old guys weren't right.

# Chapter 26
# The Boldt Decision

We were in Olympia, at a hearing concerning regulations and other actions that would be a part of implementation of the Boldt Decision. Fishermen from the net fleet were there too, and the crowd had overflowed the room the hearing was in, leaving hundreds more outside. We were standing outside with some of the trollers from the Port Angeles fleet, and I remember Bud Carlson saying—"you probably couldn't get a group from any other industry in the country and have as docile a bunch of people as there is here."

He was probably right. "Docile," or something along those lines. Maybe gullible,—or naive. At any rate, we were sure wondering if we hadn't put too much faith in our system. So many of the fishermen had gone into the profession because they were sick and tired of whatever else they'd been doing. Now we were our own bosses, and up to this point the fishing industry had provided most of us a better way of life. We were paid by the pound and for the quality of whatever we put across the dock and there's a basic honesty to that. Something that many of us had been looking for, or trying to get back to. Others had been born into it and had been in a trolling pit when boats going by could only see the top of their heads. In many families their dads could say the same thing. Three generations fishing at the same time wasn't uncommon.

The boats they owned were like family members, each with its own personality, and the care you gave them was reflected on a daily basis. Those who thought you made it big in a couple months, and then took half a year off, had a poor impression of fishermen. One way or another, you paid for not keeping your boat up, and a well maintained boat meant spending a lot of time and money, both while you were fishing and during the off season.

At this meeting in Olympia there was a variety of interests in the crowd, besides the fishing boat owners. Deckhands, family members, and people whose livelihoods depended on the fishing fleet were all well represented. To the fishermen, fishing meant long hours of work, often in uncomfortable and even miserable conditions. The lure of the good season had gradually become a hope for the occasional good day. If the good day did happen, it seemed like adjustments were built into the next seasons agenda to where time or area closures would adjust the likelihood of very many good days.

Now, after the Boldt Decision, seasons that had ran from mid April to the end of October were being pared from both ends and in the middle. Most of us were fishing in weather we wouldn't have dreamed of operating in a few years earlier. The guy who had some breakdowns or had just been on the wrong piece of ocean early in the season, didn't have the time to make it up as he might have in the past. Past records showed the most productive times and these times were generally straddled by any mid season closures. Now the effort was spread over periods of slack fishing, and accordingly, the cost in producing the pound of fish grew out of proportion each year. Loss of life was becoming more of a reality each season.

Good seasons meant profitability to a lot of people besides the fishermen, and paid for the repairs and overhauls that were such a safety factor in future seasons. If you worked in, or perhaps owned one of the thousands of businesses that supported the fleet, from supplies, gear and equipment, to fish processing, boat building, engines, or repair, your livelihood depended on how well the fleet did in any given season. The repairs, old equipment replaced, and the new boats ordered, allowed you and your employees another years work—if the season was there. Like I've said, fishing was becoming more of an any weather grind, increasingly regulated, and with a rapidly diminishing margin of profit.

Regulations that would have improved our fisheries would have been something we all could have supported, especially if these regulations had addressed less wastage of the resource. Now the fisheries would be regulated to satisfy conditions of the Boldt Decision, which, along with a few other new policies, would pretty much stifle most of the west coast's fisheries. Soon the only healthy portion of the west coast's salmon fisheries would be the agencies that regulate them.

We were listening to outside speakers they had set up, but I had been inside the hearing room on other occasions. It was fascinating, listening to people from different departments and agencies list all their credentials and the committee members hanging on every word they said. Then when someone from one of the fishermen's groups got up to speak, the committee seemed to lose interest unless they recognized the speaker as one of their constituents. Then they would sit tight and look interested. I had seen two of these people in a conservation with some other guy while a fisherman was at the microphone, trying to get his point of view across to them.

I remember once, when quite a few boats had anchored behind Destruction Island during some stiffer than usual northwest weather. Some of us had decided to go ashore for a walk on the Island and a salmon bake. On the south side of the Island you could look up and see bushes at the top of the bank whipping in the wind and the cloud cover sailing by. Down on the beach there was hardly a breeze. A bunch of us were sitting around the fire and one of the lady deckhands made the comment—"At first I thought it would be kind of romantic, with the rolling swells and the sunsets and all, but after awhile it's just gutting fish." Now she could have added "occasionally" to that comment.

The fishermen from the various salmon fisheries threw off quite a few reflections. Where the seine, gillnet, and reef net fisheries were made up of people looking at the fishery to make a living, trolling might be another story. Some really nice yachts and even a few fancy sailboats were being written off on taxes, as trollers. Hundreds of cruisers would be on the ocean during vacations or weekends—helping to get that salmon to the consumer. For some it meant that they didn't have to quit when they got their limit sport fishing. Their boat and expenses could be written off as tax deductions, and what a way to spend your vacation, maybe not completely paid for, but definitely written off at tax time. And Ohhh—those sea stories that next winter. What really ground your teeth, was that all too often these people promoted seasons, or openings, that didn't take place till they finally got out there.

If they didn't have the facilities to handle their fish, or hadn't gotten around to taking care of them, it didn't seem to matter to them. Too many of the buyers on the coast only saw poundage and dollars and these fish went together with fish that had been well taken care of, so their lack of quality was subsidized by others who had made a good effort towards a quality product. Where the quality of the product had a bearing on todays and tomorrows price for fish, it didn't mean as much to too many of this segment of the troll fishery.

On the other hand, there were hundreds of others who came out yearly and fished small boats to make an important part of their living, or to bolster poor or non existent retirement income. The Department of Fisheries said that at one point there were about 650 out of 3300 troll license holders that made most of their income from trolling salmon in Washington State. Many other fishermen split seasons, fishing salmon in at least one other state, as well as in Washington. Others combined trolling with other fisheries, usually crabbing, longlining, gill-netting, or chasing tuna.

In 1963 the State Legislature commissioned a report on fisheries related problems and were told that about half the existing number of boats could catch the fish that were caught at that time, something along the lines of what the fishermen had been trying to tell them right along. Then the Non Indian fleet doubled between 1965 and 1974. Who's in charge here?

It's hard to look like much when you are averaged out with one or two "gravy train" boats. Fisheries personnel happily used these figures in pointing out that the troll fishery wasn't a viable fishery. Even a 25% of income dependence on fishing, as eligibility for a license, would have cut the license total by over half, but the Department didn't want to do this. Once again, you don't improve something that you're trying to eliminate.

Another condition in Washington's troll fishery at that time, was a massive Canadian troll fleet, which at times had more gear in the water off the Washington coast than the American fleet had. Where a big portion of our coastal fleet was made up of boats more comparable to the Canadians "inside" boats, their coastal fleet were generally very good boats and well equipped. As their fleet built up during the 60's and 70's, many of their boats turned south, rather than north, as they came out of the straits. This was reciprocal, but during this time period, Canadian trollers fishing south, far out numbered the Americans fishing north out of Juan De Fuca, or south from Dixon Entrance. Also at that time, there were Canadians fishing north, off the Southeast Alaska coast. Before long, this would end for both country's fishermen.

George Boldt was the U.S. District Court Judge who interpreted the treaty that read that the Indian shall have the right to fish in common with all citizens of the territory, to mean that the Indian shall have the right to harvest 50% of the harvestable salmon and steelhead in Washington State. His ruling goes well beyond that, but that one segment of the ruling would have devastating results for Washington State's commercial fisheries, as well as those in Oregon, Alaska, and California. And as much as we cherish the word citizen, or citizenship, people all across the country now had something else to consider. How much would terms like "equality" or "citizenship" be diluted to provide special rights for any group of our citizens? Or how far off center could some judge's ruling go, before something like the 9th Circuit Court didn't uphold it?

Now the fisheries would have to be managed in such a way that the Treaty Indian Tribes, representing a small percentage of the citizens in Washington State, could harvest half the harvestable salmon and steelhead. In addition, their 50% didn't include a very substantial grey area of uncounted fish, including those caught on the reservations, those used for ceremonial purposes or subsistence needs, and of course, those left for escapement. (The Supreme Court later ruled that fish caught on reservation had to be counted in the treaty share.) On paper, the Indians got a lot more than they'd bargained for. Off paper, some of them told me as early as that first summer that "it isn't going to be worth it." Quite a few of the coastal tribes members didn't support, or weren't exactly for, what resulted from Boldt's decision. The non Indian fleet had meant jobs for many of them and I know that others were thinking how their lives might be affected aside from fishing, in the future.

Prior to the Boldt Decision there was an in-river set net fishery in the larger coastal streams north of Grays Harbor, with a lesser effort in the rivers going into the Straits of Juan De Fuca. There had been no Indian fishery in the Dungeness River. The Jamestown Indians live on land they purchased themselves, so it was never considered a reservation. Indian fisheries on salmon and steelhead also existed in the Puget Sound, Hood Canal, and the north and south inner-sound areas.

The main tribal effort on the outer coast was by the Makah Tribe. They had a small fleet of gillnet - troller combination boats, plus a few others, and there was one tribal member out of La Push who put out a good effort in the troll, and later on, the crab fishery. After the Boldt Decision, Danny's "Irish eyes were smiling." For that matter, they were before. Danny was a good, tough fisherman. The Quileute Tribe (La Push) also had an in-river net fishery.

I never really understood why those Indians that wanted more fish hadn't made the effort to come out and "fish in common" with the rest of us. Some did, and generally, those were the ones that worked at it and were considered to be pretty good fishermen. Others had boats but you rarely saw them on the ocean. For that matter, there were quite a few non Indians that had managed to get a boat, but kept it pretty close to the dock.

The Treaty Indian had more access to the resource than anybody, but it wasn't enough. The various tribes at the end of the line felt that by the time runs of fish had gotten up some canal, inlet, or river to them, their numbers had been thinned down out of proportion, regarding their share. I'm sure, that in some cases, they were right, but the option of "fishing in common" had been available to them, to use any time they wanted. All they had to do was get a boat and equipment and buy a license like the rest of us citizens. Then they could have fished the same seasons and areas that any non Indian citizens fished. This would have been in addition to their on reservation fishing rights, as well as off the reservations, in usual and accustomed grounds. They could also have fished other Tribal grounds, by invitation.

Statistics from the Northwest Indian Fisheries Commission show that in 1977 the combined Washington Treaty Indian fleet had 39 trollers, 245 gillnetters (power reel), and 10 seiners. I have to assume that prior to the Boldt Decision (1974) they had considerably less boats than that. Why was this? Did they believe that each tribe should support itself from whatever salmon went up "their" river, or rivers. Considering that such large percentages of salmon went through when the rivers are virtually un-fishable, wasn't this expecting an awful lot from those river fisheries? And what about those at the bottom of the pecking order within the tribes? There certainly was nothing like "in common with," here. Where certain members of the tribe fished the choice spots in the river, according to whatever "tribal hierarchy" existed, others would be upstream, not necessarily out of it, but definitely not fishing "in common with" members of their own tribe. Boldt's ruling didn't mention this, but you sure heard a lot about it on the reservations. I think they'd have had to wait till hell froze solid, even without any non Indian catch, to have satisfied every tribal member who thought he or she should be able to make a living fishing in the rivers.

How do you manage this under the Boldt Decision? When do you cut off the catch in the ocean to assure that Indians inside the straits and up the various rivers, have a chance to catch their 50%, months later? They didn't have the boats and equipment, or in too many cases, the inclination to catch 50% of the harvestable salmon and steelhead. Once the salmon passed the non Indian fleets, it was over for the season, regardless of how many fish had gone through. What might have been very good seasons, would now be guaranteed poor ones for the non Indian, and we weren't backed up by any Bureau Of Fisherman's Affairs. If anything, it was very much the opposite.

Non Indian trollers, seiners, gillnetters, and reef netters seasons were annihilated so that the Indian would have this opportunity to get their share. Accordingly, a whole dockside supportive industry collapsed. The once prosperous salmon charter boat fleets out of Westport and Ilwaco suffered the same fate as the commercial boats.

Why was there ever a Boldt Decision in the first place? It seems to me, that one responsibility of an agency like the Bureau Of Indian Affairs would have been to inform the Indians that it might take some effort to "fish in common" with the rest of the citizens. They should have been told that if you don't pay your moorage, or other bills, your boat might be part of some auction. Or that every once in awhile you need to change the oil.

Any bureaucracy should be responsible to the well being of the country as well as whatever program they are overseeing. In this instance, I think the Bureau Of Indian Affairs came up short. The treaties didn't guarantee the Indian a free ride; only the opportunity to "fish in common with—." At the very least, absolute, equal opportunity had been available to any of them, at the time of the Boldt Decision. This was beyond their reservation fishing rights, and those of fishing in usual and accustomed grounds. Instead, they went to the courts.

Governor Isaac Stevens negotiated treaties with the Northwest Indian Tribes, which stated—"The right of taking fish at usual and accustomed grounds and stations is further secured to said Indians in common with all citizens of the United States and of erecting temporary houses for the purpose of curing, together with the privilege of hunting and gathering roots and berries on open and unclaimed lands; provided, however, that they shall not take shell fish from any beds staked or cultivated by citizens. So it all gets down to "In Common With."

I'm not sure how Judge Boldt's decision will affect the Indian cause, long term. Apparently forever, considering that our courts aren't likely to go against the Treaty Indian, or the vast majority of guilt laden Americans who couldn't care less about Washington State or any fishery connected with it. It makes a poor atmosphere for Indian kids to be born into. Many non Indians living in the Pacific Northwest cherish the salmon resource as much as any "Native American." They consider the salmon resource, as part of their heritage too. Or do we get a heritage?—How long will we have to wait? In what order?—It should have been handled differently.

Should the west coasts fisheries be stifled because some group of citizens felt they could only operate in the rivers near their homes? It would take some effort to take 50% of the allowable catch and "some effort" seemed to be kind of a vague concept to a lot of Washington State's Treaty Indians. What was the difference? I never could understand it. The natives in Alaska were some of the tougher operators in the fleet. Some of the best fishermen, too. Like the rest of us, they got paid for what went across the dock, and I always felt they held their own.

Now you never knew what to expect. In June that year, we were in the middle of a trip and had just pulled the gear aboard and were running for the Spike Rock- Umatilla Reef area, where we'd been told there was a decent bite taking place. We ran for hours and were almost there when one of the partner boats called, and said there would be an announcement on the radio in a few minutes. The announcement said that all boats would be off the ocean and unloaded by midnight, or be subject to arrest. Compliments of some Judge. This would begin a seven day troll closure.

I got to thinking about it, and time wise, it would be impossible to get into Port Angeles and unload by midnight. This was where we'd been selling all our trips and where we would tie up the boat for the seven day closure. Selling what we had in Neah Bay and then running for Port Angeles only made sense in that I might arrive in Port Angeles legally, but the difference in price between the two ports was more than I wanted to drop, since we already had a good start on the trip. It didn't take any imagination to see that Neah Bay would be a madhouse. Every port on the coast would be, with the Quilleute and Neah Bay the worst, because the majority of the fleet was on the upper end of the coast. They'd never get everyone unloaded by midnight in Neah Bay. I doubted they'd be done by midnight tomorrow.

What would the fish buyers do? A whole sequence of product demand would be torpedoed, and it seemed that the future would be questionable availability, too much, or too little flow of product to the market, and a greatly increased cost per pound in getting the fish from the boat, on through to the consumer. All managed by some Judge, or whoever. What a way to manage a natural resource. How could something this haywire and far reaching come from people who are supposed to have gotten "there" because of intelligence and responsibility?

When we got to Umatilla we threw the gear in, figuring on sampling the fishing for an hour and heading for Port Angeles. Fish on the lines immediately and it was tempting to fish till dark. We wouldn't be illegal till midnight, and that was a given anyway, but we sampled it for 50 minutes and, just as I'd heard, it was exceptionally good fishing. The word must have gotten out, because boats were pouring into the area as we were leaving, mostly bloody Canadians, cheering on a bunch of bloody Yanks, on their way to some bloody dock. They had to love it. Before long we were going down the straits, and I was wishing I was a bloody Canadian.

I decided to call the Coast Guard Station at Ediz Hook in Port Angeles and double check on the unloading part of this closure. The O.D. said he sympathized with our situation, but if they were ordered out they would have to go by the judges order. Then I called John Rhodes at Star Products and told him I would be in at 3:30 in the morning. He said not to be in any hurry, because there was no way they could unload me then anyway. There were a few boats at the dock and more in the straits ahead of me, and he said there were many more boats behind me that hadn't got off the ocean yet. He couldn't believe this was happening.

I never heard of the Coast Guard boarding any boats and they may not have been called out. The situation could have been covered on the docks anyway. After unloading and the clean-up, we went into the harbor and hit the bunks. A deckhand from another boat woke us up a couple hours later.

He told us that the Judge now said that the boats would have until midnight tomorrow to unload. This would cost quite a few of the boats with good trips aboard, because there was usually 15 cents or more per pound over coastal price in Port Angeles, and possibly double that in Bellingham and Seattle. Many of them, like us, had unloaded or were still waiting in line out on the coast, and had already lost the running time that would have put them further up in the sound to unload at a better price, and have the boat closer to home for the full closure.

This "docile" bunch of people never were able to get their point across. At one time, press releases constantly bragged up the value of the fisheries to the state and also stated that the dollars spent in the salmon hatcheries was one of the few areas where the state realized a positive return on its money. The commercial fisheries was one of the state's three top industries. These weren't press releases put out by the fishermen—they were put out by the state. Now the attitude in the Department Of Fisheries had changed, along with that of the news media. It was impossible to get the whole picture in front of the public.

If they did use a fisherman's viewpoint it would be something like, in the headlines, "Never had it so good." They'd interviewed some guy who had just bought a new gillnetter and had been averaging more than a thousand dollars a night on sockeyes. The boat was one of the smaller, less expensive ones, and at that point they had only fished three nights that summer. He was a bachelor and looked to be well into retirement age, but to read the article, you thought he was flopping in money.

An article about the "piggy commercial fishermen," made you want to throw up. She made it sound like we thought wiping out salmon runs was going to be to our advantage. The industry was older than the State, but now in light of the Boldt Decision, people eating fish caught by non Indian fishermen was supposed to be a horrible thing. A lot of the local journalists and the media poured gas on what was already a one sided fire.

The net fisheries on the inside waters of the state had most of the problems the trollers did, plus quite a few of their own. I've spent a lot of hours listening to the various sides. When I was buying gillnet fish at Dungeness, one of the Neah Bay Indians stopped on the way out the straits to sell me what fish he had caught earlier that night. He had been up past the bridge in Hood Canal and had left, because there was "too much commotion." A group of the local Indians was trying to run off another group of Indians who were infringing on their territory. He said it got too wild for him. I asked him which group he was in and we both had a good laugh. He didn't know how many groups were represented in the area that night, but by the time I'd finished buying in the morning I knew of five, and there may have been more. When the Dungeness River experienced a large, unexpected run of cohos, there were even Indians from Oregon who showed up to help harvest them, and they caught a lot of fish. My little world behind the lighthouse was a pretty small place, but a lot of interesting traffic floated by.

We have a friend who was thrown in jail by Boldt. Along with a few others, he had taken part in some of the protest fishing that followed the decision. He and his dad both told me that the trial was like a worst case court-room scene, out of the old west.

Recently I met another fisherman who was sent to prison by Judge Tanner. Tony's background when he arrived at Tanner's court wasn't quite the same as most people's. He'd escaped Croatia when he was 18 years old, and wound up in an Italian refugee camp. They were treated well, but the days were long, especially for someone that age. A mason by trade, he was able to get permits to work in town, but time still passed slowly. Occasionally a team would come from some country,—Canada, Australia, New Zealand and others. Doctors and various other officials would check papers, bodies, and backgrounds, and a group of people would leave the camp, bound for a new home. Tony wanted to come to the United States. After two years of waiting, it finally happened.

He immediately applied for citizenship, started studying—American History—Government—anything U.S. He loved it and he loved the country. "I knew I was in paradise." His studies went well. His instructor told him, "you could be teaching these classes." When the big day comes and he and the others swear allegiance, he asks the Judge,—"Now I have the same rights as any other citizen?" The Judge told him, "yes, with one exception. You can't be President." He finds work on a fishing boat out of California and spends four years fishing tuna off South America.

He meets his bride, Kata, in California and their three kids are born there. He works ashore for awhile, and then they move to Washington State and he starts a career as a gillnetter, fishing both in Washington State and in Bristol Bay, Alaska. His gillnetting career will span 28 seasons.

He is in Hood Canal, near Bangor, and seeing other boats fishing, finds an open spot and strings out his gillnet. Before long a Coast Guard boat pulls alongside, and he is ticketed for illegal fishing. The other boats he had seen are Indians. Tony and two other fishermen go to Judge Tanner's court at the same time. They are each sentenced to six months in a Federal Prison. Tony had only caught three chum salmon, so in his case it comes out to two months in a Federal Prison, per fish. Tony says that everyone in the courtroom, except the Judge, seemed to be shocked by the sentence. A United States Marshall takes him aside and tells him he would be smart to spend his own money and get to the prison himself. He takes this well meant advise and turns himself in at the prison in Arizona. Apparently it's the closest Federal Prison to Washington State—I don't know. In any case, it was the designated prison. He sits with a man on the plane, who after hearing the story, takes him to the prison gate. Tony says, "It wasn't a pretty feeling."

You can imagine the impact this had on Tony's family. Kata was trying anything she could think of to get Tony released, but nothing worked. She called Senator Henry Jackson and was told he'd look into it. Nothing happened. Finally someone told her to get in touch with the attorney general for the state, Slade Gorton. He had been the one who had represented the state in the Boldt Court, in the case which resulted in the Boldt Decision. Tony worked in the mess hall in prison, and three months to the day he arrived, was told by one of the guards, "you're to be out of here by one o'clock."

Now it was only one month in prison for each salmon caught.

So who knows? Tony says "Kata got me out." Without her efforts, I'm sure he'd have spent the full six months, there, in prison. Tony still thinks he lives in paradise, but like so many of us, he's wondering what's happening to his country. Probably that Judge never thought for a moment that he was lying when he told Tony he would have equal rights with other citizens. But in a few short years it wouldn't be the truth.

Being allowed less and less time to fish soon put Washington States non Indian net fisheries virtually out of business. Those that also fished in Southeast Alaska were reluctant to head south for openings that might not happen, close early, or were targeted on fish, a good portion of which had matured to the level of a cat food product. Also, the late- release silvers were everywhere on the inside waters—small, near valueless fish that the cold storages didn't want, but they still came up in the nets. Many of the net fishermen that normally fished both states would rather fish under more positive management, putting additional pressure on Alaska's net fisheries. Canneries need a flow of product to operate and the few remaining salmon canneries in Washington State soon became a memory, like so many other parts of the industry.

In September one year, Rodney and I floated down the Quilleute River which is a combination of the Bogachiel and Calawah, joining the Sol Duc River, and a ways downstream, the addition of the Dickey River. From the junction of the Bogachiel and Sol Duc, on downstream to the Dickey, we saw 14 Indian gillnets that had been left in the river all summer. Low water made it where they could no longer run their boats up the river to check them, so they left these winter steelhead nets in place, and now there were salmon in all of them. Some were no more than a gray mass of mold, others in a little better condition, but still rotten, and others that were only a week or less, in the net, so even less rotten. Most of these were kings but several nets had a nice shot of early cohos. Undoubtedly they had taken some toll on steelhead moving either up, or going back downstream, but by this time it was hard to distinguish one blob of mold from another.

TV adds showed a tear running down the cheek of some Indian who had rowed ashore and saw the beach littered with garbage. No cameras showed the new multi-purpose building, with kitchen facilities and a basketball court. In less than two years it had aged thirty—windows broken out, doors torn off hinges, garbage cans tipped over and left. These things made us wonder—where was the responsibility? If they managed to get boats would they keep them up? Would some Judge shut down the fisheries till they got going again? Or until they didn't?

Stations from Seattle would send out TV crews to do an Indian - salmon related story and an Indian would row up with a few salmon laying in the bottom of his canoe. They'd walk past skiffs with salmon in them that had been laying there for days, to move on down the dock and get shots of these canoes. This was what the public got to see. The tribe finally did put one of their people on the river to make sure no nets fished, unattended, all summer. At about the same time you stopped seeing boats with rotting salmon that hadn't made it down to the fish dock.

I've worked with, for, and fished around Indians most of my life. One of my better friends in school was an Indian kid from Jamestown. I've spent a lot of hours thinking about what I'm saying here, but when I think it through one more time, I just wish it had been said before someone like George Boldt ever came into the picture. Then again, who would they have said these things to? In my mind, I keep getting back to the Bureau Of Indian Affairs, but it's probably at the top of the untouchable list in our bureaucracies. The courts are too protective of their record and the country's image, to go against the American Indian. I know that the Bureau Of Indian Affairs has been a great help to the Indian on many occasions, but I also know that if you hand some healthy young person a crutch early on, from now on, you'll ruin him.

As I said earlier, the Indian should have been a good part of the "in common" fleets, but generally, they hadn't made the effort. If anyone had said this to Judge Boldt, I'm sure he'd have simply screamed them down, and this makes me wonder about something else. If someone is appointed to some position for life—at what point does age start compromising, or dulling their abilities or decisions? Who oversees our judges? More judges or politicians who may want to see it go on forever for themselves? I think our country would be healthier if we had term and age limits for our judges and politicians.

After the Boldt Decision, rivers along the straits were decimated by Indian nets, within one cycle, three or four years of salmon runs. In some cases they completely fenced the rivers off, nets from both sides, and in the Dungeness there were so many set nets in the bay, that very few salmon made it to overlapping nets fencing off the mouth of the river. For the first time in my life I saw an Indian fishery in the Dungeness River.

They had a guy that looked like some kindly college professor who gave his perspective on some subject a few nights a week. He came on, and said that he couldn't see the reason for an ocean salmon fishery. He said the fish traps used to work quite well, and profitably, and he didn't see why they couldn't do the same thing now. He came on the next evening and said that of all the commentaries he'd given, that was the only one he wished he hadn't made. He said the stations phones hadn't stopped ringing and that he would answer every piece of mail he got.

He did answer my letter. His reply made me wonder who suggested he make that particular commentary. You would hope that when someone holds forth on TV, in front of millions of people, they'd be responsible enough to sort of know the subject. Or did he just read a prepared script? Who knows? He may not have had any choice in his statement, but I didn't hear him rescind, or qualify, a word he'd said. Quite a few people in three states and British Columbia had watched this segment and now had a new, enlightened opinion. People want to believe when they read or listen to the news. Your thoughts and actions on some subject may be largely based on what you read, or see and hear on the radio or television. I'm afraid we've been treated to some major brainwashing by some of our local news media, and along these lines, I don't suppose fisheries has been the only topic.

If an overwhelming majority of the citizens are going to come up with quite a bit less than half of the pie, and the livelihoods and the welfare of families of thousands of people are dependant on a bite of this pie, different user groups start disagreeing. Even people within the same fishery didn't always see eye to eye. I'm not going to say that certain bureaucrats used this situation, but it sure looked like it. They definitely didn't want anything like a united front within the fisheries, and the divide and conquer system generally works. Sportsmen throughout the northwest, as well as many state and NMFS biologists, saw the demise of Washington's commercial fisheries as a boost for their own interests. National Marine Fisheries Service personnel were "excited" about salmon farming, and the timing couldn't have been much better. I've always wondered since then, was it timing, or coincidence? Whichever, a strong commercial salmon fishery in Washington State suddenly didn't fit a whole bunch of agendas.

On November 6th, 1984, 900,000 Washington State voters supported "Initiative 456", which would have outlawed Indian's special rights to public resources. It appears that their voting this mandate in, was a waste of the voters time. Washington's State Supreme Court ruled that the 1974 Judge Boldt Indian Citizen fishing rights decision, was an illegal act. It appears that their time was wasted also. The U.S. Supreme court ruled that the state court could not prohibit the Dept. of Fisheries from doing what the District Court had ordered—dividing the catch down the middle. So both the Initiative and the State's Court ruling bite the dust.

They had a big buyback program and many in the fleet sold their right to fish their license in Washington State for 10 years. This is known as buying silence and it worked. They said that those not wishing to sell to the buyback program should realize a viable fishery as soon as runs were rebuilt, but they never were.

I was dumb and believed them. We were young, had a young family, and we wanted to believe. It had been nice, being able to fish off the Washington coast instead of Alaska while the boys were little. I'd fished 15 seasons prior to

Boldt's ruling in 1974. We had just had the Elusive built and it didn't make sense to sell to the buyback program. There was no way of knowing how severely Washington's fisheries would be cut back. Later on, at considerable expense, we bought permits in Oregon and California. Later yet, we let all three permits dissolve. It's hard now, to describe my state of mind at that point. I won't even try to explain it.

It's pretty much gone straight downhill from there. I've heard talk of record numbers of salmon, but you have to consider that the state's salmon industry has been all but wiped out to provide these numbers. Remember the ocean sport fishery that used to exist? Remember the net fisheries and the ocean troll fishery we had then? After 1976 we fished parts of two seasons in Washington, plus one trip in 1990. We paid for a license every year or would have lost eligibility to purchase one. For most of the years after 1980 the seasons were regulated in such a way as to make even a fair season very unlikely.

"Well, they could have done something else." I've heard that more than a few times, and generally, that's what we did. Each of us had many things to consider while we tried to find a solution to our own individual situation. How long you had fished, and how long you hoped to fish in the future, what other occupations you could go into or had been in before, or which other fisheries you could adapt your boat for, were all considerations. Many had never done anything else and had a lifetimes investment in a boat that wasn't worth much, unless you could fish it.

This started an exodus from Washington State to other state's fisheries. Alaska, Oregon, and California troll fleets absorbed hundreds of these boats. You couldn't blame local fishermen from these other states for feeling put out by the increased gear and new regulations that accompanied it. Alaska also inherited a bunch of new gear in their net fleets. Soon you had to have a permit in order to purchase a license in almost every fishery coast wide, and in no time these permits developed quite a value. People who had retired from fishing still qualified in many cases, and there was plenty of money flying around to buy their permits. A good portion of this money came from the buyback program in Washington State. Others used retirement savings or mortgaged homes or property to buy into some other way to keep fishing. You couldn't blame them. The value had pretty much gone out of their boat, even if they could find a buyer. Trying to stay fishing some way, seemed like the best option for most people.

As the salmon fisheries became more crowded and restricted, other fisheries started feeling the crunch. A few of the fishermen started putting longline gear aboard, and before long, the halibut season that had spanned four months when I started fishing, was down to weeks, then days. Then hours. The black cod and rock fish fisheries would be next. You can imagine how those who had been full time longliners, felt.

Some of the boats started putting a bigger effort into the tuna fishery. Jerry was one of the group I fished with off the Washington coast. The "Blanco" was one of a bunch of boats caught offshore when that worse than usual storm came along. They were 450 miles out when last heard from, which was stretching it for an old boat. His wife and kids move back with her folks. To stretch dollars even further she cuts back on a medication; another disaster in the stories behind the story.

After a poor salmon season, Chris Martin was going to take his boat, the "Adventure," down the beach to Westport for the winter crabbing season. Bill Ryan was going with him to "help out, and maybe make a few bucks." They, and Jerry, had both been in our group of about ten boats when we fished in Washington. Chris fished mostly on the south end and I never got acquainted with him until the last few years, fishing off Oregon.

During the years I fished off Washington, I fished around Bill all the time, especially if there was anything on the "Prairie." He fished alone on the boat and liked to fish big kings. "Less gutting per pound." Then he and I fished a lot together that last season off Oregon and California. He was a character and you always felt good, knowing Bill was in the area. He was going to put another machine in his boat that winter, something with less smoke and more power. Another machine and he wanted to get a pup. He liked to hunt birds.

Darrell was waiting for the crab season to open at Westport and had gone in to Seattle. He went over to see how Chris and Bill were doing, and since they were ready to leave and he had time, he decided to ride out the straits and down the beach with them. They had gone around Flattery and were down towards Umatilla. The weather was bad enough that they had decided to go back to Neah Bay and wait till it got better. Darrell was talking on the radio to his deckhand, who was aboard his boat in Westport. He mentioned that the other boat they were running down with had just turned around, and that they were turning around now, too.

Who knows what happened? Maybe they rolled on the turn, shifted some pots? Who knows? Darrell was raised on a dairy across the river from us and I can still remember him as the little guy getting on the school bus with a fully overcharged battery. He knew every day was going to be a great day, even if he had to help it along. While we still kept the boat in Port Angeles he and Linda kept the "Darlin" a couple boats down the dock from us. Good people, and theirs was a good operation. He lived life 150% till the end. They all did.

When their memorial service was a month or so past, I was on my way to Alaska and had stopped in Bellingham to take aboard a bunch of salt for the cold storage in Sitka. I called home before we left, and Trish said Lou's mother had called and said that he had been out jogging with his son and had died of a massive heart attack. He was hardly middle aged, and appeared to be in perfect condition, but as with so many others that last year, trying to pull a season out of the hat had involved a tremendous amount of guess and stress. The effort he'd put into pre-season repairs and changes would have worn out three of most people. He left a wife and family, including twin daughters that were about five years old.

He was the guy that helped everyone else with their problems and never mentioned his own. We had fished some salmon together and then later that year, two tuna trips, one off the Columbia, and another off the top end of Vancouver Island. One of the nights when we were running north off the Island, we were talking, and he said he was thinking of bunching fishing and going into the ministry. This took me back a notch, because I knew that when he was younger, Lou had raised hell, leveled it, and put it on fresh piling. I wish he could have made this change and lived to become an old man. He was already more than you would hope a minister could be, with or without a Bible.

These people did do something else. They had all fished for years, were good at it, and had considerable investment in boats and equipment. Each of them had made a good living trolling for salmon off the Washington coast, during a time when loss of life was a very seldom thing. They tried to stay afloat by going into other fisheries. They were some of the people I had partnered with over the years, or in Darrell's case, another good friend.

Always the non Indians, until it wasn't. Darrell's wife, Linda, is a La Push girl. Indian or non-Indian, those that knew him lost a wonderful friend and this would be the case with any of the people lost in the fleet. We spent too much time around the tribes on the coast not to form some good friendships and, however you looked at the Boldt Decision, friendship usually survived. Years later, an Indian boat goes down off Westport and some of the family are lost and your heart breaks for them, too. Too many of us have known what they and their families went through.

This did create a new industry, or at least, put fresh blood in an old one. In newspapers, or any of the trade magazines, you started seeing adds like "Injured at sea? We'll help you get what's coming to you." Costs of insuring crews went through the roof, and now that the fisheries were struggling a good deckhand would move on to greener pastures, and you couldn't blame them. They had livings to make and families to feed, too. A lot of people in the troll fishery went back to fishing their boat by themselves, and others had to hire people with little or no experience. There were ever shorter seasons or openings, a poorer price for the catch because of an ever increasing supply of farm raised salmon, and higher costs each season in producing that pound of fish.

Boats were running from Oregon to Alaska to fish a two day halibut opener and, even if you'd been in position, it costs a lot to make a halibut trip. With so much hanging on the results of a trip it was hard not to go out when poor weather coincided with the opening. It seemed like each opening would be marked by loss of at least a boat or two, and all too often, the loss of life.

The E.P.I.R.B, (emergency position indicating rescue beacon) a device that would transmit a signal and position, indicating distress or the sinking of a boat, was soon available to the fleet. Then self inflating life rafts. Now the old A-M radios everyone had, could only be used in case of emergency and would be replaced by the new single sidebands. Halon systems, to put out the fire in an engine room, were installed. Some of these items became requirements by law and some were required in various insurance pools. All of these things cost money, sometimes in the thousands of dollars per item. These things were stacked on top of what would be for many, just too much. Over $300.00 a month for moorage took on a new meaning when you couldn't fish. It broke your heart to see so many of the guys that had fished for years, trying to hang on, or to sell an old boat that had lost its value.

Over the years I was invited to a few of the Alaska Trollers Association meetings and finally did wind up going to two of them. The first one took place during a summer troll closure in Sitka. Attendance was from just about everywhere and not necessarily restricted to ATA membership. One of the topics was the increased volume of hand trollers now fishing in the ocean and what to do about it. The difference between hand trollers and power trollers is that the mainline is wound onto the spools or gurdies with a hand crank on the hand troller, and power trollers use either hydraulic, electric or mechanical systems to power their gurdies. Otherwise, the basic operation is the same, except that hand trollers are generally smaller boats and use less gear. The subject was batted around a bit, but I left the meeting with the feeling that no specific thing had been agreed upon.

The next spring I stopped in at Port Alexander and before too long, had several invites to a housewarming across the channel that evening. Jimmy Hendricks and I found a couple barbecue fish, and when he was ready, I rode over with them in his skiff. I had listened to the news from the Ketchikan radio station earlier in the day, and the same news item that had stopped me cold, was the main topic of conversation at this housewarming. Effective that season, hand trolling would be closed in all outside waters. What had apparently been aimed at one specific group of hand trollers in the Cross Sound area had bitten the Port Alexander community. These people had built a beautiful little house, most of it out of small logs they'd taken off the beach, towed into the harbor, and pulled up to the house with a little winch. Two stories, a winding log mini staircase, a breakfast bar-table, and more, all made from this beach wood. He said if he'd known they were going to do this, they wouldn't have built here.

In the earliest days of trolling, hand trollers had fished out of Port Alexander. A lot of their catch was in Chatham Straits, but much of the time they fished the ocean outside Cape Ommaney and around into Larch Bay. Now a good portion of the town's residents would have their ability to make a living, pretty much stifled. There was no doubt where it had come from. That summer one of the locals went on around the corner where some decent fishing was taking place, and he was arrested. The Governor received quite a few letters, and the next season saw hand trolling allowed up as far as Redfish Cape, which would give them back this area they normally fished in. Without a doubt there were others that fished the ocean north and south of this area, that looked at hand trolling as a serious portion of their livelihood. Now they would be forced to fish other, probably less productive areas.

I never could understand why I was invited to the next meeting I attended. It was in the fall and we had sold a trip of kings in town and Chris and I had an invite to dinner with some old friends. I mentioned to them that one of the guys on the dock had invited us to this meeting and asked if they were going to go. She thought she might like to go and he thought he wouldn't.

"I already know what they're gonna do. First they're gonna bullshit and then they're gonna chickenshit." Apparently he'd attended other meetings. After all the standing around and B.S ing, the meeting got going and one of the first topics that came up was getting the Fairweather Grounds troll fishery closed. This is one of the best troll fisheries for king salmon in the world and trollers from Alaska want it closed? Their reason was they felt that some years the fishermen on the grounds (Fairweather Grounds) absorbed the quota too fast. The fish they catch on the (grounds) are king salmon in their finest condition and at their highest value per fish. Where did they think the fleet that fished the grounds might go? They sure as hell didn't want them in their hot spots. Where did they think they would go when they couldn't chip out livings on the inside? A good portion of these guys would eventually wind up on the grounds and be glad of it. If they got it closed did they think they'd ever get it back? Not likely! Then the subject became the out of state boats and the guy that had invited me and was chairing the meeting, said that he didn't want them here either. I decided some fresh air would be nice. The three of us left. Chris was getting a look at another part of being a fisherman.

This doesn't mean the guys attending these meetings were, or are, ogres. Some of them, though. Their livelihoods were as important to them as the next guy. Or more important to them than the next guy's? But when that guy on the boat next to you isn't making it any longer, how secure is your future? Are the fish raised in his back yard, the ones you catch? Vice Versa? Hold this up to the light and see how thin your walls might be. We saw the same thing in California and Oregon. Hundreds of boats put out of business in Washington State started fishing to the south and before long some of the Alaskan fleet joined them. Too many boats and too much gear. Too much pressure from too many directions and then human nature clicks in.

Fishing had become what so many had started fishing to escape.

# Chapter 27
# Mowing Grass

Finally enough was enough. We decided to bunch it, sold the Elusive, and I wasn't a fisherman anymore. Different people have asked me, "don't you miss it?" You bet I do. But I missed it quite awhile before we quit fishing.

Trish asked me one day, what I thought I wanted to do. I told her it sounded good to just mow grass. All day long. After the last few seasons, I apparently needed a frame of mind adjustment.

A tip from my first stop, on my first day out hunting some tall grass, had me at the Lake Padden Golf Course. After hearing what a hero I was, this guy gave me a job. I would be mowing fairways and roughs. Etc. Like the boss said, after seeing some of my first efforts. "It'll all grow back." The course is a beautiful spot on the south edge of Bellingham. It's set in woods, the fairways separated by a few trees, and more often, by some pretty nice patches of woods. There are no houses around the course like some of them have.

I enjoyed mowing grass, and in a way, found it to be a bit like fishing You can just do it, or you can practice the rest of your life trying to get good at it. Finally I did get to where I was sort of satisfied with my efforts. For a bit. Then another brainstorm, and a month or so of perfecting or discarding it. There was more to cutting grass than I ever would have dreamed. I hadn't thought about keeping reels sharp and the reel to bed knife adjustments, as well as height of cut and what ten separate rollers might be doing, plus a mountain of other stuff that had more to do with the course, or the individual fairway. I used two mowers, a 7 reel 15 foot cut, F15 Jacobsen, for the roughs and a 5 reel 450 Toro which cut an 11 foot swath, for the fairways. The F15 was kind of a relic, still is, and the 450 was a few years short of some major improvements by the Toro company.

As I mentioned earlier, woods are a dandy tranquilizer. Being out there in the mornings, ahead of the golfers, the smell of grass just mowed, the steady noises of the machine and reels—I thought this might be okay. I had been around considerable wildlife earlier in my life, and then again, in Alaska, but most of this in Alaska was like being slightly removed, like you were watching it from a movie or something. It seemed to me that most animals on the beach didn't consider anyone on a boat close to shore, to be of any danger to them.

Now I'd see the same thing, time after time, on a mower. If you were mowing grass or even if you stopped and shut down the machine, no big deal. Get off the machine and away they'd go. Ignore them and occasionally they'd come back. Here's a few little pieces of those nine years that I remember.

I had just started down a fairway and one of the guys in a group that had just teed off stops me and says a little coyote just ran out, grabbed a ball and ran back into the woods with it. Later, I was telling the crew about it and the boss said he'd been setting the course over the weekend and had his dog with him. Zip was a big pup at the time. Jim would throw a golf ball for him and this would go on, a few throws at each green as they went through the course. Jim looked up, and at the edge of the woods is a young coyote sitting there, his tail wagging. It goes out towards Zip and the ball, probably intending to get in on the fun. Jim was able to call Zip back and get him in the truck, thinking he likely wouldn't have done too well if there'd been a scuffle. We heard of another 5 or 6 balls that this guy rescued in the next few weeks, all in roughly the same place. I found two balls, well back in the woods in this same area, that he had done considerable chewing on, so apparently young coyotes like their toys, too.

I'm just starting down the service road that runs between fairways in this area I just mentioned. I see a coyote coming up the road towards me, over a hundred feet away and walking slow. I slow down and stop. After hesitating, he starts my way again, head close to the ground. I shut the machine off. I'm leaning on the steering wheel, not moving except my eyes, and he keeps coming up to about 15 feet of the mower and then raises his head and sort of looks me in the eye as he turns and moves into the brush. Not a sound. Still no sound for about a minute and then I get a feeling and turn around slowly and he's just crossing the road behind the mower, again, at about the fifteen foot distance. The growth between the woods and the road are thick with dead limbs or grass, and there wasn't a breeze, but I still never heard a thing. It looks like he's grinning, but its hard to tell at that angle.

The three coyote expressions that you usually see are a sort of grin, curious, or the smug look, where they're thinking how much smarter they are, than I am.

This particular spot is one of those areas that are everywhere there is any wildlife, and you'd see as much deer and coyotes in this area as on the rest of the course, combined. So back to the same spot. I'm long-striping the bigger of these two fairways and am nicely started back from the green end, when something catches my eye. I glance sideways and here's this coyote trotting along, even with, and about 10 feet from my outside reel, which is putting out a constant stream of grass clippings about three feet high and even further behind the reel than that. This goes on for about a hundred yards and he maintains this position all the way. Occasionally, when I look over, I can see that he's watching me out of the corner of his eye and other times he's just looking straight ahead. When we get to the spot where everything likes to cut through the woods he speeds up and crosses nicely in front of the mower, and then off into the woods.

Same spot on the service road. I see two deer as I come around the turn and start down the service road and they go into the woods as I move past. I stop to eat salmon berries and look for some golf balls and get absorbed in this, forgetting about the deer. And mowing. I hear something different and look around and here's the doe about ten feet away, her neck stretched out like she's trying to catch my scent. I look away and ignore her and before long, hear a couple loud sniffs and when I look around, she's trying to sniff at my hat. The buck is back a bit and you can tell he's really getting upset. I wave my hat at her and when she backs off he runs her into the woods. It was interesting that this happened during the early summer months and not in the fall.

I'm mowing roughs in the afternoon and am on the smaller of these three fairways which is a par three with quite a little rough before you get on the fairway. It's still only about a third, or fourth, as long as the par fives on either side of it. I've come off the service road and mowed down to the tee, turned around and am up outside the mini - fairway. Looking ahead, I see a coyote crossing the green, carrying something by the neck. It looks like it's just caught a rabbit, which would be easy at Lake Padden. It goes out onto the service road and I mow up to the surrounds, turn around, go back down by the tee, and turn around again. When I'm back up to almost the same spot, here comes the coyote back across the green and she's got another one. I get a little closer this time and see she's carrying one of her pups who just hangs there like a dead rabbit. She goes through, out onto the service road and I turn around, back down to the tee and

I see some golfers through the woods, just leaving the green on the last fairway. When I turn around I see her running full bore, back to her den, or whatever a coyote calls home, and in a couple minutes here she comes again, with another pup. I stop the mower, even with about the middle of this short fairway, and shut down the machine, interested in seeing how long this goes on.

The golfers have started to hit by the time she comes tearing back across the green and one of them got it clear up on the green. This is pretty good for these guys. You weren't safe in the woods when they were hitting. I decide to sit it out and see what happens. She doesn't come back across the green, so maybe goes behind it and through the woods? Who knows? When the golfers come by I get some disgusted looks for my efforts. I don't bother trying to explain. Its all golf with some of these guys and a herd of striped buffalo wouldn't have slowed them down. I wonder how many she had to go, or if I just came along at the end of the move.

So this area was pretty popular with the local deer and coyote traffic. Several people said they'd seen a cougar and it isn't unlikely. They had a moose downtown a few years ago so I don't know why cats wouldn't be in the area too. I saw what looked like bear droppings around the salmon berries, a couple times, but I never saw one or heard of any being seen. The Padden course is noted for great salmon berries and one really great golfer, Mrs. Foss.

I only saw grouse twice in all the time I spent at the course and I'm not sure it wasn't the same grouse, a few days apart and in about the same area. Hard to have that many coyotes around and have many grouse. Each spring would see a few pairs of mallards return and before too long they'd be parading around the pond with their chicks and in a short while eight or nine would be down to- one to four. Their nests are usually in the woods and its a wonder the coyotes didn't get them all, adults included.

One memory that stands out on the lower part of the course, was coming off the service road next to the green and looking across at the pond. It was early spring so no cattail growth yet, and lined up for a perfect picture was a shypoke (Norwegian Turkey), two Canadian geese, and three ducks. The shypoke was standing in the dead cat tails at the edge of the pond and everything lined up for a minute or so and would have made a dandy wildlife picture, but no camera. We had a beaver that tried to turn the pond into another lake, but he finally gave it up after we tore apart his efforts a bunch of times. He probably came up from Lake Padden, which at first, I didn't think was likely. Then I got to thinking about where they get to. It was probably just a nice afternoons hike.

I got to work one morning and as soon as I'd stepped out of the pickup I heard a mower shut off and Rick yells at me "Vince, come over here right now!" Rick was a seiner and while I worked at the course I worked with one other seiner and a guy that had worked on a trawler, so you can see I was really slumming it. Being a hook and line fisherman, I got the usual amount of respect. Rick mows greens and gets a barely daylight start each morning, which I do with the fairways, unless I'm mowing with the lights. I shoot over to where he's at, and he tells me about the coyotes going nuts just below the green when he got over there, and there's a dead pup laying over at the edge of the rough.

It starts an interesting morning. It seemed like every time I'd turn around I'd see a coyote going by, way more than the two or three separate times in a morning that would be the exception. Sometimes you wouldn't see one for a week. It was always moving faster than usual and always just the lone coyote. It's likely that most, or all of these, were the same one. When I got up on the hill, in the area I've mentioned earlier, there were two. The female was running back and forth along the edge of a short strip of woods, would dart almost in, back out, back and forth, literally going crazy. She kept this up most of the time I was mowing that fairway, (about half an hour) and where the male might look over my way when I'd go by, she acted like I wasn't there. This entire time, the male stayed out in the rough, either laying down, or moving off to the side when I came by.

These that I'm telling about here, the one that approached and then walked around the mower on the service road, and the one that ran along side the mower are most of the exceptions in thousands of hours of mowing. Usually, they didn't let you get that close. I mentioned that several golfers had reported seeing a cougar and this was right at that time, but I think a cougar probably would have taken the pup if it had made the kill. More likely it was killed by the adult male coyote. I wonder about all the commotion by the female, as it's quite a way through separate patches of woods and across three separate fairways from where she was, and where the dead pup was. Its hard to say if this female was the one I saw so many times while mowing down on the bottom, or if I was actually seeing more than the one coyote. They were both upset. The adult males killing the male pups or cubs is a side of nature people aren't too aware of, but it's there in bears, wolves, and coyotes that I'm aware of. The pup was pretty tore up.

One thing that stood out from the area down around the maintenance shop, is that if you were going to see a nice buck, it would usually be within a fairway of the shop, or else up in that area I first mentioned. The boss saw a 5 point near the shop and I saw seven bucks go single file across the fairway by the pond. They stayed together and quite a few golfers saw them around the course over the next week. This was during the summer when the bucks are more likely to hang out together and it's the most bucks I've seen together in Washington, but I can remember seeing herds of deer in some of the back bays in Alaska when I first started fishing. Probably just before an increase in the wolf department.

The bravest chipmunk I've ever met was at the golf course. I was mowing roughs

*Too much shade on a green.*
*Kevin Ryan standing, VFC, Greg Lloyd.*
*Photo courtesy of Rick Aubert.*

with the 15, the old ford diesel chugging away, seven reels mowing along nicely, and this guy grabs a fir cone and instead of running for the hollow in his tree, decides to get up on his hind feet, still holding the cone, and back me down. He does and I slow down and stop, thinking he's lucky he was off to the side and not directly in front, where the engine end of the mower would have made him hard to see. With the clutch held down, I goose the machine and he drops the cone and gives me hell in chipmunk while he's charging for the tree. We don't meet the next couple passes, but before I'm done I have to make one more pass around a couple clumps of bushes, which takes me back his way. Same thing but this time I'm watching for him and don't goose the machine so he chatters a bit longer before heading for the tree. I don't see him a lot after that and wonder if he knew he could back down a 15 foot wide mower, what he'd do when a measly coyote came along.

After awhile the 450 was replaced with a "Ransomes" mower. It had 5 reels, a slightly narrower cut than the 450, and you had either 2, or 4 wheel drive. You mowed in 4 wheel drive and this, combined with a much lighter weight as compared to the 450, made for a much nicer looking mow. No slipping, less sinking in, etc. and the shorter reels did a nicer job over the rough turf. And it had lights.

I got to where I really enjoyed starting early, no one else around, and I could just go along steady and enjoy the mow. It's harder to see the last pass with lights, when you're mowing a solid pattern, so after a little trial and error, heavy to error, I spent all my time in a crosscut, while mowing with the lights. This, preferably with not too much of an angle, going across. This worked out well because you have to vary the cut a lot, and early was a good time to get in a lot of the nearly flat, crosscutting. I had as many as eight separate patterns I used on some of the fairways.

I was going along one morning, about a third of the way down this fairway, when the lights flashed some eyes in the woods. On the next pass back I see them again, and just before I pick up and turn, I see its a coyote laying down, its back towards me so that it has to twist to look out my way. On the next pass it's moved out on the fairway and I can see it well off to the side of the lights. They really show up, off to the side, their coloration being so light. When you are crosscutting you go back and forth across the fairway, and your turn on each side of the fairway will always be towards the same direction, whether you're moving up, or down the fairway. He figured this out and stayed on the fairway until I had finished crosscutting, always staying to the dark side so as to not have the lights keep sweeping over him when I turned. He'd come up to within three or four stripes of me and maybe sit there while I went by, or just walk around slow, and stayed not too far from the mower until I finished and started the cleanup pass.

Apparently not too much going on that time of morning, for the coyotes. It got to where I'd nicely get started on the first fairway and there he'd be. I didn't always mow the same fairway first thing, either, but he'd come to the engine noise, whether it was down by the pro shop, up on the hill, or wherever. It must not have been as much fun after daylight because he'd usually move on after it got light. Most of the time.

There was one time though, after it got light, when I'd seen a couple golf balls in the creek and was rummaging around looking for some more and looked up and there he sat, about 25 feet away. This time, the curious look. That was by quite a bit, the closest I ever got to one when I was off the mower.

Then one morning I turned back across and there he was, sitting in the middle of my next pass. He took off with what seemed like more than necessary enthusiasm, and after that, he'd more than likely be in the lights when I'd turn. Sometimes he'd run all over like a dog playing, and sometimes he'd wait until I got part way across before he took off. Never close, though. The biggest deal of all was when I'd blink the light switch off and on as fast as I could. He'd wait it out as long as he could stand it and then really take off. Considering that it was about impossible to get one in the lights prior to this guy, this was quite a deal. I hoped he'd never try any of this stuff out on the road.

I mentioned there was darned little birdlife in the way of coyote sized meals, which definitely seemed to be the case. I saw a few owls over the years, and crows; sometimes just crow feathers, so I suppose the occasional one does get nailed by a, luckier than usual, coyote. I saw a crow and a young coyote one day, the coyote jumping as high as it could to get the crow, and the crow like it was a yo-yo, down to about a foot above the reach of the coyote, back up eight or ten feet, and down at the same time the coyote would come up. This went on for a minute or so and ? how long before I got there. One thing I noticed about the crows is that they're just as likely to associate with any other bird on the course as they are with another crow. Or with rabbits and squirrels. You saw it all the time, sometimes several other species of birds and a crow, sometimes more, all strutting around, looking for a worm to pull on. Rabbit-wise, I suppose it was just curiosity on the crows part, but you'd see them within feet of each other quite often. There was no end of small birds and the ones I enjoyed the most were the swallows. They'd show up each year and for some reason, favored the four fairways closest to the clubhouse. They'd fly back and forth around the mower, a lot like porpoise will work the bow of a boat, and I got to thinking of them as golf course porpoise. Who says I don't miss fishing?

I was mowing up on the hill one morning and when I got down towards the green on the last of these higher elevation fairways, I heard an awful commotion. My first thought was an unhappy reel because nothing could out shout the 450. I stopped and slowed the machine down and before I disengaged the reels I could tell they were innocent, because I could hear the noise was coming out of the woods, still at full volume. I stopped the machine and walked back down the fairway a few feet, and the noise is coming out of this snag, fairly close to the woods edge. Pretty quick a woodpecker works its way around so I can see it and while she's picking away at the tree her chick keeps screaming its head off, loud enough to out shout the 450 from about 100 feet away. When she finally gets something good she goes around and sticks her beak clear into the little guys throat, and before she can get back to work he's screaming his head off again. Apparently this is a little grubbier than usual snag and she stays with it for a month or more and the little guys voice holds up well. By little, I mean young. He was about the same size she was. By this time there was quite a little accumulation of rotten wood at the base of the snag, and the next winter it goes down.

The washdown area for mowers and the other equipment is about twenty five feet from the corner of the shop. I'm washing down one of the mowers and notice a chipmunk run from the woods, over towards the end of the shop. It disappears behind a pile of plastic pipe stacked across the end of the shop. In a minute I see it start out of the end of one of the larger pieces of pipe, wanting to go the few feet around the corner and into the shop. I flick the hose that direction, sending a little spurt of water at the end of the pipe. Not much, because there's a lot of pressure. She goes back a few feet and in a few seconds she's ready to go again. Same problem. Now, each time she comes out, I'm receiving a thorough cussing out and she's starting to look a little damp. Finally she goes for it and I keep the water about five feet behind her so she just gets a little of the ricochet. She shoots out of range and into the shop. She, or some of her family, live at the shop for years and several times a chipmunk stands off one of the crew at some intersection in the shop. I always thought it was nice their size didn't match their attitude.

So there was always something going on. I've always felt more comfortable with whatever wildlife was around me, or better said, never felt that I needed to go to Africa or somewhere to feel like I was outdoors. The volume of coyotes and deer at Lake Padden surprised me, but being out there first thing in the morning gave the crew a better chance to see this than after the golfers started their rounds. There are quite a web of service roads on the course and along these were where you frequently saw the critters.

I'm not at the course anymore and now spend some time next to the river during steelhead season, catching darned little but seeing more swans and Canadian Geese than I've ever seen before. At one of my haunts last year I saw eagles, hawks, and owls, and a pheasant, along with the geese and swans and probably every other of the smaller birds that are in the area. And if it sounds like I was slumming it around the crew and hackers up at the course, you ought to see the guys I fish around now.

# Chapter 28
# Hopes and Memories

Now that I'm through fishing, there are many memories to think back on. I loved fishing, the boats, the various fisheries I participated in, and always felt it was a privilege to handle the fish involved. And what a wonderful bunch of people. I count my blessings to have met the ones I did over the years, which included a lot more than the fishermen. With one, to four or more, fish buying operations in each town, there was no shortage of friendly faces anywhere you went. Invites up for a meal were frequent and the memories and friendships are still treasured.

I ran into Andy occasionally, and he was always surprised "you haven't got drowned by now." Not long after the Curlew pulled me behind the Islands at Tebenkoff, Andy moved up to a really fine boat, the "Pacific Sea." For years he'd been one of the top longliners in the fleet. We were in Elfin Cove baiting up for a halibut opening when they came in, and that afternoon he came over and visited for awhile. He said the Doctor told him he had cancer and this would probably be his last season. I stopped in Petersburg on the way through that fall and a friend told me he had passed away. On that particular opening, Andy's had been one of the best trips into Petersburg, as usual.

What a big part of our lives Sid became. He's gone now too, and he and Tammy are together in a spot you go by, coming into Sitka. I can picture them there, watching the boats come and go. There's a Sydney Cameron now too, Keith and Sharla's first. She'll be starting kindergarten next fall and has a brother, Cade, who is two and a half. Chris's son, Vinnie Cameron, is fourteen years old now.

We still laugh about the time in Sitka when they had the opening for the Halibut Producers Cold Storage. Trish and Deann had come up, and after the festivities up at the plant we decided to all go out to the Channel Club that evening for dinner. They have the best steaks and salad bar of any restaurant I've ever been to, so this was always a treat.

Sid said he and the guys were going up to the Pioneer Bar (famous local water hole) and sip a few and he'd be back to the boat in plenty of time to go for dinner. Dinner time came and went and so did what you'd think of as evening. No Sid. "The hell with it, lets go." So we did, and had another really great meal and when we got back, still no Sid.

During a troll closure in Sitka there was no room to tie up, and boats would be rafted out five and six deep from the docks. To relieve some of the pressure the port let boats tie to the breakwater in Thompson Harbor, and this was where we always headed. No footpath from the breakwater to the dock, so you had to use the skiff, and this made a lot less traffic and a more restful stay in town. The breakwater was like a big floating dock anchored out, so you could get off and walk from section to section to visit other boats and the kids could fish, either from the boat or the breakwater. We kept the skiff in the water so it was a big deal for them, ferrying people back and forth from the breakwater to the docks in the harbor.

So here we were, out on the far corner with the Miss Everett tied alongside and Tammy decided to start barking. "Maybe she wants some water." I got up and she had plenty of water so I fed her and almost got back aboard the Elusive—bark, bark, bark. I went back and played with her awhile and got back aboard—same thing. Still no Sid, no sleep, and I was thinking of taking the Miss Everett and running it down to the other end of the breakwater and putting it outside a bunch of bigger boats tied there. He wouldn't have been able to see it from the dock.

Trish says, "Why not just row over and bring his skiff back across to this side." Why hadn't I thought of that? So I did, and if Tammy barked after that, we didn't hear it. Sid finally came down the dock sometime in the early morning hours and saw the skiff tied outside the Miss Everett, but couldn't wake us up. He said he didn't want to yell too loud that time of night, so he walked back up to the parking lot and got a handful of rocks and if any hit the Elusive, we didn't hear that either. He finally gave up and walked back up town to the Sheffield Hotel, and it downpoured on the way, so he got there completely soaked and in a poor frame of mind.

He came back to the breakwater about eleven in the morning and the kids ferried him across to the boats. We were having a late breakfast, early lunch, which he declined. I thought I could see his pulse in his eyes, so he probably wasn't too hungry. He hit the sack and every time the kids asked me something,—"I don't know, ask Sid."

"Rig me up so I can fish off the dock, dad." I'd send them over to get Sid to do it. Pretty soon I heard the Perkins fire up and he said he thought he'd go tie a little closer to the other end of the breakwater. Before we untied him, Trish told him she'd forgive him if he'd take us out to the Channel Club that evening. "Okay—how about six o'clock?"

He loved the country. I remember one beautiful, clear spring day when we came around Cape Decision and Baranoff Island came into view across the straits. "There's no grander sight anywhere, Cap." I had to agree with him. As far up the straits as you could see was this rugged range of mountains, nearly all white at that time of the year. A deep breath of the air brought you to life. We were lucky to be there, and knew it.

We used to speculate about a certain tree in one of the outer Baranoff bays, that had broke off at a height even with the tops of other good sized trees right around it. It looked to be at least four feet through at that height. We were always going to go ashore and measure it at the base but never got around to it, always thinking of next time. We never got back and I'm still wondering how big that tree is.

I never see or think about a bear without thinking about this. He and Tammy had gone ashore and were on their way back to the skiff, as it was getting dark. The wind was apparently behind them as Tammy didn't pick up on anything until they saw a good sized brown bear between them and the skiff. It closed a distance of a hundred feet to about twenty, in seconds, and then was on its hind feet, still coming towards them. Curtain time for the bear. Easier to do when it's up and moving straight at you and when the adrenalin might not be running at full volume yet. I asked him what Tammy did and he said, "Well, she started out after it. But she was awfully easy to call back."

Being around the thousands of guys on their boats, and quite often, their families, you can't help but watch and listen, and eventually you get a feeling that its not going to be easy, to have a family and be a fisherman. I was well aware of this long before Trish and I met and married. You can't be in two places at once and having a family on the boat isn't anything I'd wish long term on any woman. It's a tremendous amount of stress, but then being ashore when the boat is out is no picnic either. On the boat or ashore, the other half puts up with a lot. They are both mom and dad while you're out, take on the entire responsibility of the home front, and at the same time are still a big part of the business, which a fishing boat is.

327

When it happens to be blowing at home they can't help but wonder and worry about what's taking place on the boat, even knowing it's a long ways away, in completely different weather. With a pretty significant amount of time and money invested in that two day halibut opening, the previous evenings weather forecast takes on a meaning most people don't think about. What if he can't get out? What if he goes out anyway? When the good season has become an increasingly seldom, or never thing, the extra money isn't available for that overhaul or renewal of equipment. Now, when the wind blows at home, these things haunt her. And when that unimaginable phone call comes, she carries the world in her mind. What did they do wrong? What did she do wrong?

Recently I read a book that gave a strong impression that if a fisherman wasn't fishing, he was in some bar. That would be a distorted impression. There are likely as many others that have never, or seldom, been in a bar. Like everything else, the average is probably somewhere in the middle. And like any other occupation, success is going to be short lived if the people in it get absorbed in drugs or booze. Probably a lot shorter lived with fishing as an occupation.

One of my memories from fishing the early parts of two seasons in California is talking with one of the fisherman where we sold our fish, up in the Oakland ship canal. He had been a logger until they had become nearly extinct and apparently had tried this and that, and then fishing. He made the comment," now that I'm fishing, my whole family is doing better." I didn't know him well enough to feel like inquiring as to specifically what that meant, but the sincerity behind it left no doubt in my mind that it was exactly how he felt. He didn't have a big boat but worked hard at it, fishing salmon, and then crab in the winter.

We live in homes, have mortgages, kids, illness, and hopes for the future, just like the next guy. Being self employed, the success for our families, crews and their families, and the business, depended on how well each of us did our job.

It also depended on how the various fisheries were managed. Nearly forty years ago I was told of some of the young people not being recognized to speak in the fisheries class they were taking. Their backgrounds and views were different than the professors and he apparently didn't want them suggesting possibilities in class that were contrary to his thoughts. I understand it's still that way in some fisheries classes. Different professors, same attitude. If a class were allowed to hear the thoughts of a young kid from a family that had been fishing 60 some years, they might have heard a few points of view that should have been explored in any fisheries class. You learn (or teach) by looking at a subject from different points of view—discussion—not pussyfooting, or bulldozing your way around some topic to protect your position on it.

Force feeding a lop-sided diet isn't much of a way to teach, but once more, it isn't a new method and not just applied to our fisheries. Something like this throws a shadow over the wonderful thing that a good education should be. I think that a good portion of the woes of the west coasts fishing industry can be laid at the feet of a few of our fisheries professors from the past, and some of their students. It bothers me that some of the kids who were inclined to ask the tougher questions and possibly had a few ideas of their own, were weeded from the classes.

So now Trish and I are out of it. Chris never wanted to do anything else but fish, and straddles crabbing, trolling for salmon, longlining, and fishing tuna to grind out a living. Kory, his deckhand, is one of the best on the coast. When he was younger Kory fished with Chris's wife, Ingrid who operates a charter boat out of Westport.

They've got a fine new boat haven in Neah Bay. A good sprinkling of salmon trollers, most of them former non Indian boats, are in the tribal fleet there now. Some of the younger guys are putting out a really good effort in the troll fishery, which is encouraging. I'm seeing nice trips unloaded, with a big improvement in the product they're bringing in. I was very disappointed in seeing the addition of the hake (trawl) fishery to their fleet. With the associated wastage of every other imaginable species of fish it doesn't serve their image of "conservatores of the resource" very well. It hurts when you see so many of them trying to build a decent fishery and then others turn around and do this.

My big hope in writing this has been to encourage some change in the future. Trish has always said that anger makes change, so my frame of mind a few years back has been a fine foundation in trying to tell about this. If Chris and Kory are going to continue making their living fishing, then what's left of our fishermen, Indian and non Indian, can only have a future if they can work together, and with the fisheries people, to make the best possible use of the resource.

I've tried to tell you about our livelihood from some different perspective, whether it's the fishery, resource, product, or the people involved in the various methods of harvesting or managing the resource. Along the way I may have left the impression that I think there are no good people in our state and national fisheries services. That's not the case. I'm certain that the majority are dedicated, hard working people and are a credit to their profession. For people who live with a natural resource like fisheries, it becomes the most important thing in their lives, outside of their families. When their efforts are compromised, or when the resource is used as political trading stock in some way, it has to be devastating, no matter what level they are working at. I've had to keep reminding myself, level- wise, that there's always someone up the chain from these people. I'm sure there are times when they aren't too thrilled with the path set before them, either. Ernie Brannon Sr. allowed me a glimpse of this when I was 16 and it changed the direction my life would take, although sometimes I wonder if I might have jumped from the pan into the fire.

There aren't many people who love salmon, as a fish, and as a product, more than I do. By the same token, there are darned few that hate seeing where fisheries are, compared to what they might be, more than me. Every pound, or ton of fish that isn't wasted or lost by slovenly regulations and fishing practices, or by loss of habitat, is that much more that could put another fisherman to work, or send more sport fisherman home with a nice fish to eat. It would also mean more fish returning to our streams and rivers. (And salmon hatcheries and engineered streams.) You'd think we could all be working toward the same end. We can't go on as we have in the past and expect anything for tomorrow.

Last summer I hitched a ride on the "Saint Jude" and fished a couple trips with Al Richardson. We had a perfect trip up through British Columbia during the last part of June and were amazed at how little boat traffic we saw for that time of year. We did see some very large cruisers and the smaller cruise ships, something you rarely saw during my time up there. We even passed one paddle wheeler up towards Sitka. I had been warned that things were changing, but being downtown when a couple of the big cruise ships were there, about did me in. I was happy to head out, but I remember that years back, I used to feel the same way. Trish used to hate to go to town at the end of a trip.

We were amazed at the lack of snow up through B.C. and as we moved on up through Southeast Alaska. Generally nothing on the south sides and only a patch here and there in the shade behind some north slope. The ocean water was much warmer than normal and unless you were near the entrance of some place like Cross Sound or Chatham Straits, or where any of the bays or inlets poured into the ocean, you were likely looking at 60 - 61 degree water. There was way more southwest weather than normal, and of course that pushed the warm water right at the beach and kept it warm all summer. We didn't connect at Fairweather Grounds and came back down in the "mink trail" and I was amazed at how far back from the beach the glacier had moved in those few years.

In all my previous summers in Alaska I'd never caught a pomphret, but I did now. There were lots of sardines on the south end, which was something you rarely saw before. Both kings and cohos, generally ran smaller than normal, although we did find a few patches of exceptionally nice cohos and heard of a few king trips that had a good average weight. Still, the fleet realized a very small average for both species, all season. It seemed like there was lots of feed almost anywhere we went, and it made us wonder how long the feed and warm water had been around. Probably next year everything will be back to normal, whatever that is.

I enjoyed some great visits with long time friends, which was one of the best parts of the trip, and Al and his deckhand were always great company. Going back again makes me realize how much I miss it. Sometimes I wish I could have hid Alaska somewhere, or brought it all home with me. Stuff like the starfish in Cameron Pass, or all the honeysuckle in Craig on a warm summer afternoon. Or the bay, or the hundreds of bays and harbors and beaches. There's anchorages where you can leave the Dutch door or a porthole open, and a small stream running down over the rocks, or falls, will put you to sleep in no time, and what dandy spots for that occasional nap on the off tide. Its not that I want to lock it up for myself, or a fishing fleet, but that I'm afraid of the opposite happening. When there gets to be enough sport fishing camps and charter boats spread out around the country it won't be long before many of these areas will be closed to the commercial fishery. Bit by bit, as they have in the past, to where you can hardly notice it happening. We won't exist anymore.

# Endnotes

In chapters fifteen and eighteen I quoted several items from material put out by the **Center for Salmonid and Freshwater Species at Risk**
**Hagerman Fish Culture Experiment Station**
**University of Idaho, Hagerman Idaho.**

They are:
"Technical Bulletin 00-1—An assessment of The ESA Listing Of Columbia River Anadromous Salmonids with Emphasis on Chinook Salmon"—Ernie Brannon
and
"Population Structure of Columbia River Basin Chinook Salmon and Steelhead"—Ernest Brannon, Matt Powell, Tom Quinn, and Andre Talbot

## In Chapter 15
1. Lichatowich 1999 Quoted in technical bulletin 00-1 Brannon—Pg 7 para 2
2. Fish and Hanavan 1948 Quoted in Technical bulletin 00-1 Brannon Pg 8 para 3
3. From a letter from Greg Pratschner 2001—Project Leader - Leavenworth Natl. Fish Hatchery
4. In a letter from Ernie Brannon University of Idaho
5. Brannon 2000 - Technical Bulletin 00-1 Pg 9 para 3—Pg 10 para 1—Pg 11 para 3
6. Quoted in "Grand Coulee Harnessing A Dream" Pitzer Pg 224-25

## In Chapter 18
7. Brannon—Technical Bulletin 00-1 Pg 9 para 3—Pg 11 para 3
8. Pg 123—Population Structure of Columbia River Basin Chinook Salmon and Steelhead—Brannon, Powell, Quinn, and Talbot

## In Chapter 23
9. Appendix A. U.S. Observer Data Base

# Index

This gives the names of people who are in the book, and the chapters they are found in. Some are mentioned throughout the book and there's no doubt that I've missed on a few chapters and I apologize for this.

Jones Frank - 3
Jordan Skip and Marilyn - 6 - 8 -
Kennedy John (President) -8
Kimmel Denny - 20
Knapman Charlie - 2 - 3
Lee Ray - 5
Lewis Merriwether - 26
Lichatowich - Fish and Hanavan—co-authors 15
Loftman Ted - 10
Lotzgesell Leroy - 2 - 3
Makela Brothers - 16
Martin Chris - 26
McAllister Tom - 12
McGilton Fred and Willie - 4 - 8
McWilliams Pete - 4
Meneghini Dave - 10
Moonbeam Todd - 12
Moore Milo - 18 - 23 -
Moose Frank - 19
Murphy Kory
Olds Cal - 4 - 6 - 8 - 21
Olstead Hal - 4 - 8
Orchard Burt - 16
Pavalunas Matt - 2
Payne Danny - 26
Piatt Bill and Tana
Prader Walt and Zelma - 8
Prader Steve - 8 - 10 - 16 - 23
Priest Bob - 19
Quinn Rick, Morrie, and Pauline - 6
Quinn Christie, Rickie, Gary - 3
Raleigh Red - 20
Rhodes John - 26
Richardson Guy and Al - 10
Richardson Al - 28
Roberts Charlie - 2 - 4

*For additional copies:*

Cameron Publishing
PO Box 2125
Ferndale, WA 98248
info@weallchokethesameherring.com

| Title | Quantity | Price | Total |
|---|---|---|---|
| *We All Choke The Same Herring* | | $22.95 each | |
| Washington Resident Sales Tax @ 8.4% | | | |
| Shipping @ $4 each book | | | |
| *or* Shipping @ $6.70 each book for priority mailing | | | |
| Total | | | |

*Please make check or money order payable to Vince Cameron.*